Pat Boone

and

The Gift of Tongues

JAMES D. BALES

SEARCY, ARKANSAS 72143

DEDICATED

TO

PAT, SHIRLEY, AND THE GIRLS
IN LOVE AND HOPE

CONTENTS

INTRODUCTION

When the author's book on *Miracles or Mirages?* was published in 1956 he started accumulating additional material for an entire book on the gift of tongues. In the first part of 1969 he heard rumors that Pat and Shirley Boone were being influenced by the tongues movement; so he sent them some material on the subject. Early in January, 1970, several teachers met to discuss how to help a very small group of tongues speakers on our campus. The author immediately began to concentrate on a manuscript on the subject. In the middle of February he listened for several hours to the experiences of Pat and Shirley Boone. Out of this came a correspondence with Pat. All this has culminated in the present book.

At times the author has expressed his personal feelings in a way in which he usually refrains from doing in a book. The author realizes some will accuse him of protesting too much. On the other hand, if he were unemotional all of the way through, some of the same critics would say that he is cold-blooded and lacks the warmth that a Christian ought to have. There will be two readers, at least, who will not doubt the author's love even though they may doubt his arguments and wisdom. These two are Pat and Shirley Boone. On February 21, 1970, he wrote them that: "The Lord helping me, I shall do what I am convinced is right, even if it bathes my heart in tears." It has. In the phone conversation on February 28, the author said that, unless one of us changed, we were on a collision course. When we hit head-on, the author said, his head would be filled with love. Pat said, that when we hit, we would hug. It is time for hugging, Pat.

Why has the author used the title *Pat Boone and the Gift of Tongues? First,* Pat is the most widely known member of the church who has espoused tongues. His experiences and arguments for tongues will be propagated by writings and personal appearances. When the author told Pat of the title on May 4, 1970, he also said that brethren needed to know that this book dealt with reasons which Pat gives for his present convictions. It was his duty, the author said, to defuse as much as possible the bomb (Pat's book) which Pat was going to drop on us. The motion picture, *The Cross and the Switchblade*, when viewed in the light of Pat's book, will also have some impact.

Second, with or without Pat's consent, the Pentecostals will use Pat's change as an opening wedge to spread Pentecostalism in the church. Editor Thomas R. Nickel, who said God produced the previous issue of *Testimony* which included Pat's testimony, wrote: "Yes, God did do such a thing as this, and to Him belongs the Glory! What He has in Mind for that portion of the Body of Christ which announces, 'The Church of Christ Meets Here,' He alone knows, but be assured that it will be marvelous to behold; and we are grateful that He used *Testimony* for His purpose, so that we may watch Him perform this great work among the men and women who so long have faithfully proclaimed the Name of Christ!" *(Testimony,* No. 31, 2nd Quarter, 1970, p. 15).

There is a startling and striking contradiction in Pat's theory and practice. On the one hand he argues that the gifts are for us today if we ask for them in faith. He thinks that he has some of the gifts and that several operate in his family circle. On the other hand, he denies that anything which he writes is inspired and confirmed by the gifts. *He talks like a man who has gifts and acts like a man who has no gifts.* How long will it be before he will affirm in practice what he advocates in theory? *When will he act the way he argues?* If he has the gifts, anything which comes through a gift, or is confirmed by a gift, is as much the word of the Lord as the word God confirmed in the first century (Heb. 2:3-4). Pat's arguments concerning the gifts are disproved by Pat's denials that the gifts actually work in practice in his life in revealing and confirming God's word. His confusion in this vital matter is also an indication that he has no miraculous guidance of the Spirit.

Although this book deals mainly with the gift of tongues, it involves the entire question of miraculous gifts and a wide variety of arguments.

There are at least three classes of people who give up Christ when they realize they have been deceived by the tongues movement. *First,* those who think that tongues were the only evidence they had of the truth of the gospel. When they lose this ground, they feel there is no foundation for faith. *Second,* those who think that the modern tongues movement does the same type of miracles which were done by the apostles and prophets in the New Testament. When they see that people today cannot do these things which they claim to do, they conclude that the apostles and prophets did not do them either. *Third,* those who become disillusioned and bitter to the extent that they decide everything they have believed is wrong. Instead of reacting in this manner they should be grateful that they have learned the way of the Lord more perfectly. When one ceases to depend on what God has not promised them, but which men have promised them, one should not cease to depend on what God has actually promised in His word. It is the author's prayer that no one will react from tongues to unbelief in the Bible.

As on any subject, some arguments are not as strong as others. However, even these may have a cumulative value. The case should be weighed in the light of the strongest arguments. Of course, there are some who will evaluate the book solely on the basis of some argument which they may consider to be the weakest argument.

In some cases the same point fits under different arguments. To make each argument as complete as possible, at times repetition was deemed important. This may not be helpful to some, but it may be to others.

The author has included a bibliography at the end of the book. Often instead of using footnote references, an author's name is given and at the end of the quotation there is a page reference. When an author is mentioned, and no page reference is given, it is either from a commentary on the verse being considered, or a book to which only one reference is being made, and the page reference will be given in the bibliography.

In an effort to include as much material as possible, the last chapters of the book are composed of questions and answers.

CHAPTER I

IF ANY, ALL

The spiritual gifts were supernatural manifestations of the Spirit of God and not products of human intelligence or character. These gifts were manifested through Christians; some of whom occupied positions of authority in the church (I Cor. 12:28). All the gifts stand or fall together. There is no scriptural argument for the perpetuation of some of them and the cessation of others. If any are available today, all are available. What gifts were given by the Spirit? (I Cor. 12:1, 4, 7, 11).

THE WORD OF WISDOM

Word, as Boise observed, refers to the "ideas of *speaking* and *reasoning* . . . 'the art of speaking to the purpose about things pertaining to wisdom or knowledge'." What is *wisdom?* Gould suggested that it is "knowledge practically applied to the ends of life." Pool's description seems adequate. Wisdom is "a faculty, from a good judgment of the circumstances of actions, to do them at the best time, and in the best manner, wherein they may be serviceable to their ends." Knowledge needs to be used both in love and wisdom (I Cor. 8:1-2; 6:5-6). The gospel, which embodies God's wisdom, is called the wisdom of God, and it was revealed in words which the Holy Spirit, and not the wisdom of man, taught (I Cor. 1:18-2:13). James spoke of a wisdom which is available to all through prayer (Jas. 1:5). This wisdom is not a new revelation, nor does it impart knowledge. It is given to us by God in His providence, just as our daily bread is given in answer to prayer, through God's providence, and not as manna (John 6:31-32). The *word of wisdom* of which Paul spoke was a supernatural gift which was given to some, but not to all (I Cor. 12:8-11, 29-30). Those who had this gift not only *demonstrated* it by their supernatural wisdom, but they would also be approved by those who had the supernatural gift of discernment (I Cor. 12:10). Surely no one in the church could be wiser than were those to whom the Spirit gave the word of wisdom.

THE WORD OF KNOWLEDGE (I Cor. 12:8)

Massie defined knowledge as "teaching which appeals to the rational faculty . . . the intellectual is made the buttress of the moral and spiritual." Man could not of himself know the mind of God, but through *inspired* men the Spirit revealed the necessary knowledge concerning God, Christ, God's will, man, sin, salvation, heaven, hell (I Cor. 2:12-13). Those who repudiate the gospel remain in darkness without "the light of the knowledge of the glory of God in the face of Jesus Christ" (II Cor. 4:3-6). The total truth revealed by the Holy Spirit in the Bible constitutes the total word of knowledge which is available to the church today. Who can claim, and scripturally sustain his claim, to have an inspired word of knowledge which is not found in the Bible?

THE GIFT OF FAITH

No one can be a Christian without having faith which comes by hearing God's word (Rom. 10:14-17). Paul, however, spoke of a supernatural gift of faith which was possessed by only a few Christians. ". . . to *another* faith." (I Cor. 12:9; 13:2). Massie observed that the "Greek word for 'another' in this clause means 'to a man of *another kind*' (see the same word used with 'glory' in 15:40)." Although the Bible does not say much about it, it may be that the individual with the gift of faith knew when God wanted him to perform a supernatural work, and gave him a firm persuasion at certain times when he was to do such a work. This may be what is meant by the prayer of faith in James 5:15. God evidently did not permit Paul to try to heal Trophimus (II Tim. 4:20).

GIFTS OF HEALING

"And to another gifts of healing, in the same spirit" (I Cor. 12:9). "The Greek word for 'another' here means 'another of the same kind' as the man with the wonder-working faith. So also with the next three clauses" (Massie). *Gifts* indicates that more than one kind of sickness was healed.

Christ and the other miracle workers in the first century worked a wide variety of healing miracles. Christ wrought miracles on such as the following: (a) Blind (Matt. 9:27-31; Mark 7:22-26). (b) Dumb (Matt. 9:32-33; Mark 7:31-37).

10

(c) Dropsy (Luke 14:1-6). (d) Leper (Luke 17:11-19). (e) Ear restored (Luke 22:50-51). (f) Fever (Matt. 8:14; John 4:46-54). (g) Palsied (Matt. 8:5-7; 9:2). (h) Withered hand (Matt. 12:10). (i) Bleeding (Matt. 9:20). (j) Every sickness and disease (Matt. 9:35). (k) Halt and *maimed* made whole (Matt. 15:30; Luke 22:50-51). (l) Raised the dead (John 11:39-44).

The apostles worked a wide variety of miracles of healing. (a) The man who was born lame, walked immediately; having become perfectly sound, and it was known to multitudes in Jerusalem (Acts 3:1-10; 4:13-16, 22). (b) All were healed who were brought to them (Acts 5:12-16). (c) Palsied and lame (Acts 8:6-7, 13). (d) Dead raised (Acts 9:37, 40-42). (e) Not hurt by viper (Acts 28:3-6). (f) Fever, dysentery, etc. (Acts 28:8-9).

If there are those with the gifts of healing today they should perform a *wide variety* of healing miracles.

They should also perform miracles which have the *same characteristics* as the miracles of Christ and the apostles. Are they matched by the modern "miracle" workers? (a) Instantaneous (Matt. 8:3, 15; 9:27-30; 12:13, 22; Acts 3:7-8; 9:34; 13:11). Exceptions? No. Study closely (Mark 8:23-25; Luke 17:12-14; John 4:50-52). (b) Faith not always required on part of one on whom the miracles were worked (John 11:39; Acts 13:11-12; 16:18). (c) All, not just a few (Matt. 4:24; 8:16; 9:35; 14:34-36; Luke 4:40; 9:11). (d) Organic diseases, not merely functional disorders (Matt 15:30; Mark 14:47; Luke 17:11-19; Acts 3). (e) Public (Matt. 12:9; 13-14; Acts 3:16; 4:21; 9:35). (f) Complete, whole, perfect (Matt. 12:13; Acts 3:16, 4:9). (g) Acknowledged by enemies of Christ (Matt. 12:13-14, 24; Acts 4:16; 16:18-19). (h) Not used to make money (Matt. 10:8-10; Acts 3:6). (i) God-glorifying (Acts 3:2-13). (j) Used to support truth, not error (Heb. 2:3-4). Not used to establish or perpetuate denominations. (k) Person healed did not have to be present (Matt. 8:5-13). (l) Some miracles wrought over the protest of the individual (Matt. 8:28; Mark 5:6-10; Luke 4:33). (m) Because of faith of others (Matt. 8:8, 10, 13; John 4:50-53). (n) Jesus did not claim that it is God's will to heal all who believe, and then went about with a physical ailment Him-

11

self. (o) No preliminary investigations to weed out hard cases. (p) Jesus did not try and fail, and then insult them by saying that they did not have enough faith. The only case of failure, and this was before the baptism of the Spirit, was blamed on the ones who tried and failed (Matt. 17:19-21). There was no such case after Pentecost (Acts 1:8; 2:1-4). (q) Jesus did not say that He *could not* work miracles because unbelievers were present. (r) Jesus did not try and fail and then blame God by saying, I just pray, but cannot know whether God will work the miracle (Compare Acts 1:8). Miracles proved the power of God (Matt. 9:6; Mark 2:10; Luke 15:24). God did not refuse to work miracles through Christ and the apostles just because unbelievers were present! (s) Christ announced no special healing service. (t) His healings did not require a special "atmosphere." (u) God, when He saw fit, protected them miraculously (Mark 16:17-18; Acts 12:7-11. Contrast Acts 12:2; Acts 28:3-6).

TO ANOTHER, WORKINGS OF MIRACLES

The word translated *miracles* in I Cor. 12:10 is also translated *powers*. This word is used in several other places to refer to *supernatural* works. The casting out of demons in Christ's name, was called "a mighty *(power)* work in my name" (Mk. 9:38-39). Mighty works were done by Jesus in His personal ministry, and Peter presented these as one of the credentials of Christ which showed that God approved Christ (Acts 2:22).

Powers referred to "effects produced by the active exercise of powers, as in Acts 5:1-16; 9:40; 13:11; 16:18" (J. J. Lias, 121). J. Massie suggested that: "The Greek word for 'miracles' here probably implies works mightier and more striking than healings; in this category came expulsion of demons (Luke 10:17, *'Even the demons* are subject unto us')'; perhaps also such punishments as are referred to in . . . Acts 13:11 . . . Healings and these striking works lie in the material region, the two following kinds in the spiritual." Since Paul had just mentioned gifts of healings which involved the supernatural, it is likely that in this context he had reference to other kinds of miraculous demonstrations. However, the word "miracle" also included miracles of healing (Acts 19:11-12).

Deceived people thought that Simon had great power, but he was convinced that Philip actually had miraculous power (Acts 8:9-11, 13). Saul confirmed his preaching with miracles or powers (Acts 19:11-12; Gal. 3:5; Rom. 15:18-19; Heb. 2:3-4).

"Wonders" was used in connection with the miracles (Acts 2:22). This denoted "a work above the ordinary working of nature," which was not designed simply to cause astonishment and fear, but to call the attention of the people to the message (James Hastings, II, 39; Acts 2:1-4, 6, 7, 11-12, 33).

The power which the apostles received when they were baptized in the Holy Spirit enabled them to work a wide variety of miracles including raising the dead (Acts 1:2, 5, 8; 2:4, 43; 3:2-10; 8:14, 18-19; 9:37, 41; 19:1-6, 12; 28:3-6). The power of Jesus enabled Him to multiply loaves and fishes and to walk on water (Matt. 14:17-21, 26-29). Who today matches these miracles?

The context, as well as other passages of scripture, indicates that the gift of powers or miracles involved superhuman and supernatural power (I Cor. 12:10, 28-29; Mk. 9:38-39; Acts 2:22; 8:13; 19:11-12; Heb. 2:4).

The mighty works were signs or prodigies which led the people to be amazed and to wonder (Acts 2:7, 12). They were one of the credentials of the inspired teachers (2:22).

TO ANOTHER, PROPHECY (I COR. 12:10)

When God so willed, prophecy involved a foretelling of the future, but it also included setting forth God's will for man here and now. It included "edification, and exhortation, and consolation" so that men were taught according to the will of God (I Cor. 14:3-4, 31). Although aimed at the edification of the church, it could also reach and convince unbelievers (14:4, 24-25). The prophet received his message by *direct* revelation, and by *inspiration* of the Spirit declared it to others (14:29-30). There may have been an overlapping in the functions of some gifts, since healings were miracles, and a prophet surely had some knowledge revealed to him.

13

DISCERNING OF SPIRITS (I COR. 12:10)

The inspired discerner of spirits could distinguish between those who taught by the human spirit, the devil or evil spirits, and the Holy Spirit. All the people who claim gifts that the author has studied teach some false doctrine. Why don't they have discerners of spirits who point out this false doctrine?

We do not have inspired discerners today, but we have the inspired word of the Spirit in the light of which we test teachers. Examining in the light of this Word, the doctrine and actions of so-called inspired teachers today, the author has been able to show that they do not perform the wide variety of miracles which the apostles performed, their healing miracles do not match all the characteristics of those in the Bible, and their teaching contradicts the Bible in some points. An uninspired student of the Bible can test these so-called "inspired" teachers. If they were miraculously guided by the Spirit they would not teach false doctrine. When pressed with scriptures some of them become angry, or may even oppose in one way or another what the Bible teaches. They are not prophets of God, or they would harmonize with the Bible (I Cor. 14:37).

Pat Boone claimed that he had seen this gift exercised in the accurate exposing of some who claimed to have a message from God. One does not have to have a miraculous gift in order to expose departures from God's word. Has he seen this gift exercised when some, who claim to have miraculous gifts, misinform seekers after salvation as to what they must do to be saved? It does not take a miraculous gift to learn what to do to be saved. If these misinformers are not publicly exposed, as were those mentioned by Pat, at least they should be taken aside and taught. They should accept the correction and teach the truth on this subject (Acts 18:24-28).

TONGUES (I COR. 12:10)

The Spirit inspired one class of individuals to speak languages which they had not learned. Pat Boone wrote: "I immediately yielded my voice and heard myself singing a thrilling new song, the words and the melody composed spontaneously by God's Spirit!" (*Testimony,* First Quarter, 1970,

14

p. 10). If an interpreter had been present, men should have known what inspired words were spoken. They were as much God's word as were Paul's words *if* Boone actually spoke by inspiration of the Spirit.

INTERPRETATION OF TONGUES (I COR. 12:10)

There were others who by inspiration translated or interpreted the foreign languages (14:5, 27-28). If such gifts exist today, the interpreters should give us an inspired translation of the Bible. Any textual problems should be solved by inspired prophets who have the gift of knowledge and prophecy. At least some of them should be able to tell us by direct inspiration all that Jesus taught in His personal ministry, and also be guided into all the truth (John 14:26; 16:12-14).

THE GIFT OF APOSTLESHIP

The word "apostle" means messenger or one sent. Christ is God's apostle who was sent from heaven (Heb. 3:1). Any messenger of a congregation was an apostle of that congregation (Phil. 2:25; II Cor. 8:19, 23). However, there was a unique group, apostles *of Christ,* who were such by gift (I Cor. 12:28, 29; Eph 4:8, 11). Their work continued Christ's work and was a ministry of witness to His resurrection (John 14:26; 15:16, 27; 17:6-8, 15, 20, 21; Acts 1:8, 21-22; 2:32). What were their qualifications? Did these qualifications make it impossible for apostles to be present on earth during the entire gospel age? *First,* they were eye and ear witnesses to the personal ministry, the resurrection, and the ascension of Christ (John 15:27; Acts 1:8, 22; 2:32; 3:15; 4:20, 33; 5:32; 10:39; 41-42; I John 1:1-4). However, not everyone who had this qualification was an apostle (Acts 1:21-22, 26). Eye witnesses finally die and cannot be replaced.

Second, they were chosen by Christ personally, and not by the other disciples or by the church (Lk. 6:13; Acts 1:2, 24; 9:6; 24:16-18; Gal. 1:1).

Third, they were personally taught by Christ. (John 14:26).

Fourth, they were taught by direct inspiration of the Spirit (John 14:26; 16:7-15).

15

Fifth, their word was authoritative in all the congregations (Acts 2:42; I Cor. 4:17; 11:2,23; 14:37; II Cor. 11:28; 13:10; II Thess. 2:15; 3:4, 6, 12-15).

Sixth, they confirmed their teaching with a wide variety of miracles (Acts 2:43; 5:12-16, 19; 9:37-40; II Cor. 12:12).

Seventh, they had the power to confer miraculous gifts on others through the laying on of their hands (Acts 8:14-18; 19:1-6; Rom. 1:11; II Tim. 1:6).

Eighth, along with the inspired prophets, God used some apostles to write inspired scriptures (I Cor. 14:37; II Peter 3:15-16).

Ninth, they are in the foundation, not the superstructure, of God's temple (Eph. 2:20-23; compare Rev. 21:14).

Some individuals had certain of these qualifications without being apostles, but only the apostles of Christ had all of them.

Does Matthias' case show that the other apostles were to have successors? No. (a) His selection was the fulfillment of prophecy (Acts 1:20). It was not predicted that any other vacancy would be filled later. (b) The office was filled before the establishment of the church. (c) It was essential that the successor be one who had been with Christ in the personal ministry (Acts 1:21-22). (d) Selected by Christ (Acts 1:24-25). (e) The twelve were a unique group (Acts 1:26; 6:2; Rev. 21:14).

What about Saul's case? (a) His case was unusual; as a child untimely born (I Cor. 15:8-9). However, he was not behind any of the apostles (II Cor. 11:5). (b) Personally selected by Christ, and not by the church (Gal. 1:1). (c) The apostle to the Gentiles (Gal. 2:8-9). (d) He saw the Lord (Acts 22:14-15; 26:16-17; I Cor. 9:1). (e) Paul was taught the gospel by Christ, not by man (I Cor. 15:1-3; Gal. 1:11-12). (f) Worked a wide variety of miracles (Rom. 15:18-19; II Cor. 12:12). (g) His word, whether spoken or written, was authoritative. He wrote scripture (I Cor. 14:37; II Thess. 2:15; II Peter 3:15-16). (h) Conferred the Spirit in miraculous manifestations through the laying on of hands (Acts 19:1-6; Rom. 1:11; II Tim. 1:6). (i) Christ appeared to Paul last (I Cor. 15:8-9). Who today has the experiences, authority, power, and inspiration of Paul?

ENABLED THE CHURCH

The work which the apostles, and other inspired men, did enabled the church to be equipped for its work. The inspired men were given *"for* the perfecting of the saints, *unto* the work of ministering, *unto* the building up of the body of Christ" (Eph. 4:11-16). The word for "perfecting" means "a fitting or preparing fully." Well over a century ago, James MacKnight pointed out that it signified "to place the parts of any machine or body in their proper order, and to unite them in such a manner as to render the machine or body complete . . . In the metaphorical sense . . . signifies the fitting of a person, by proper instruction, for discharging any office or duty." Young's Analytical Concordance translated it "complete adjustment." James Moffat said it meant "in order to fit his people for the work of service . . . " *International Critical Commentary* translated it: "with a view to the perfecting of the saints *unto* the work of ministering, *unto* the building up of the body of Christ." Through the revelations of the truth the inspired men equipped the church to carry on this work of ministering and the building up of the body of Christ. Having revealed and confirmed the truth in all of its parts, their work ceased. However, it is through the faith which they delivered that the church is equipped for its work.

The church is likened unto a growing temple. The apostles and prophets are in the foundation, not the walls, of this building (Eph. 2:20-23). We have the same apostles and prophets which the church had in the first century, in that we have the truth which they delivered. We no more try to replace them with new apostles, than we try to replace the chief cornerstone, Christ, with a new Christ each generation. We must continue in their doctrine, and hear their word which is the word of the Spirit (Matt. 22:31-32; Lk. 16:29-31; Acts 2:42; 13:27; I Cor. 14:37; II Thess. 2:15; Heb. 10:15-17; Rev. 2:1, 7). Well did Charles Wadsworth ask: "What then will be the condition of those who refuse to hear Moses and the Prophets, Christ and the Apostles, speaking in the Old and New Testaments?"

MORMON APOSTLES

What about apostles of Joseph Smith, Jr.? The Latter-Day Saints, or Mormons, are consistent in their errors; far more so than Pentecostal groups. They claim all the gifts, including apostles, and they write new scriptures. However, as we have documented in our *Apostles or Apostates?* they do not qualify as apostles of Christ. (a) They were selected after, not before, the Church of Jesus Christ of Latter-Day Saints was established. (b) They were selected by men; Joseph Smith, Jr. and the three witnesses to the *Book of Mormon.* (c) They were told to: "Tarry at Kirtland until you are endowed with power from on high." However nothing comparable to Pentecost took place (Acts 2:1-4, 6, 8, 11). (d) None of them saw the Lord before they became apostles. (e) They did not have an inspired recollection of Jesus' teaching during the personal ministry (John 14:26). (f) They were not guided into all the truth (John 16:12-14). (g) They were taught by men, not by Christ through direct inspiration (Gal. 1:11-12). (h) Their teaching contradicts the Bible. (i) Although Judas apostatized before the church's establishment, none of Christ's apostles apostatized after the establishment of the church (Rev. 21:14; II Tim. 4:7-8). Many of Smith's apostles apostatized.

PAT AND MODERN APOSTLES

Pat believes that all of the gifts, including the apostleship, are for us today. He thinks there are apostles of Christ on earth today. When the author requested that he name some of them, Pat failed to do so. However, in an interview in *The Birmingham News* for February 20, 1970, he said, of *The Cross and the Switchblade*, that: "The book is a 20th century addition to the Book of Acts. Wilkerson is like one of those fellows Jesus chose to be an apostle." If this is true, he should bring out an edition of the Bible which includes *The Cross and the Switchblade*. Pat should quote at least some of the writings of Wilkerson as being as authoritative as those of Paul. Of the inspired writings of Wilkerson, Pat should be able to say, "If any man thinketh himself to be a prophet or spiritual, let him acknowledge that these things which Wilkerson writes are the commandment of God." (Compare I Cor.

14:37.) The same should be said of the inspired writings of any of the other modern apostles.

If Pat did not mean that Wilkerson is actually an apostle, it is still true that he believes there are living apostles today. Who are they? What proof do they give that they have the qualifications of apostles of Christ? Do their works match those of the apostles? Does he accept their word, when they are supposedly guided by the Spirit, as authoritative as that of Paul? If not, why not? Will these men themselves claim to be apostles? If not, why does Pat claim it for them? If Pat, his family, and some of his friends have various gifts why would Pat be so confused as to think that there are living apostles of Christ today? Why doesn't he understand what the Bible teaches about apostles of Christ? Why does he fail to see that these men today do not have the necessary qualifications?

PROPHETS AND TEACHERS (I COR. 12:28; EPH. 4:11)

Paul had reference to men who were prophets and teachers not by hard work but by miraculous *gift*. They were inspired. Will Pat tell us who are some of the modern prophets?

HELPS (I COR. 12:28)

To help meant to render support. What all was involved in this gift we are not told. Massie is likely right in thinking that it may refer to helping with "the necessities of those who are weak (Acts 20:35), in health, wealth, or spiritual knowledge." There are individuals who can do these things by natural gift, but these were such by miraculous gift.

GOVERNMENTS (I COR. 12:28)

We are not told what these "wise counsels" were, but they may refer to those who had the "word of wisdom" since they are distinguished from the apostles, prophets, teachers, and helps. The word was used at one time to refer to steering a ship, to guiding, and to presiding. Those who claim miraculous gifts today cannot throw any more light on "helps" and "governments" than can anyone else.

INSPIRED MEN

If men on earth have these gifts today, there are inspired men today who can speak *as authoritatively as the apostles and prophets* in the New Testament. Inspired men were necessary in the first century to reveal and confirm the gospel. Since the New Testament was not all revealed and written at one moment, it was essential that there be inspired teachers in all congregations. They edified the church through revelations, knowledge, prophesying, teaching, and the interpretation of tongues (I Cor. 14:6, 27-28). If there are inspired men today, they should not only confirm the message of 2,000 years ago, but also their new messages today. They, too, should write inspired scriptures. Paul never worked miracles to prove Moses was a prophet of God—although it would prove it in that Paul said Moses was inspired—but to prove that Paul was a prophet (I Cor. 14:37). If there are miraculous confirmers today, there are inspired revealers today who by miracles confirm their own inspired words (Heb. 2:3-4).

E. R. Harper thought some of Pat Boone's remarks in Abilene on February 22, 1970, indicated that Pat thought Shirley was infallible in her interpretations of the King James Version. Pat replied that Shirley was astounded and frightened that anyone should think she was infallible concerning anything. *They are shrinking from the logical conclusion of their own position.* They believe they have some of the gifts some of the time. If any conclusions come through the gifts (of wisdom, of knowledge, of prophecy, of discerning spirits, of tongues, of interpretation) these conclusions are inspired and infallible. These conclusions would be as binding as the apostles' doctrine which came through such gifts and was confirmed by miracles (Acts 2:42; I Cor. 14:37). To deny this is either to deny that one has the gifts, or it is to affirm that the word and work of God are not revealed through the gifts.

Pat believes that the miracles are as necessary to confirm the word today as they were in the first century. If this is true, inspiration is also essential today for the defense of the gospel. "But when they deliver you up, be not anxious *how* or *what* ye shall speak: for it shall be given you *in that hour* what ye shall speak. For it is not ye that speak, but the Spirit of your Father that speaketh in you." (Matt. 10:19-20; Lk. 12:11-12). Are any of Pat's defenses inspired? If men today speak as inspired by the Spirit, they are speaking the word

20

of God and it is infallible. We are not saying that everything they say must be inspired, but when they speak by the Spirit and exercise certain gifts, they are inspired. If they do not think they are inspired in such circumstances, their very confusion in this matter proves they do not have the gifts.

Pat claimed inspiration when he claimed that he sang a new song, "the words and the melody composed spontaneously by God's Spirit!" *(Testimony,* 10). If someone there had the gift of interpretation, we could have known what the "inspired" message meant.

When the author asked Pat if any of his letters, or any part of them, were inspired, Pat hoped they were directed by the Spirit and were true. However, he said he recognized his ignorance and fallibility, so he gave, as best as he knew at the moment, his knowledge and judgment in the matters. His humility is appreciated, but if he has gifts why can he not be more certain than he is? Is he uncertain as to whether he has the gifts? Is he uncertain whether what is revealed through the gifts is true? Does God do such an uncertain work? Pat thinks that at times Paul was uncertain whether he spoke by inspiration. As noticed elsewhere, the author does not agree with this interpretation of I Cor. 7. However, even if Pat is right, this is the only place where Paul expressed uncertainty. Why cannot Pat be as certain as Paul about some of his (Pat's) letters? Which should we acknowledge to be the commandment of the Lord (Compare I Cor. 14:37)? Pat thinks that some in his family have received and spoken messages by inspiration, so why can he not be more certain concerning himself?

If they do not believe, and prove, that the gifts produce in them what they produced in the first century, let them re-examine and renounce their position concerning miraculous gifts.

WHY SO ZEALOUS FOR TONGUES?

If all the gifts are for us today, why are so many zealous to get the gift of tongues and not the other gifts, including those which were better than tongues (I Cor. 14:4-6; 18-19, 39, 12)? The author believes the answer is simple: Of all the gifts, it is easiest to deceive one's self into thinking he has the gift of tongues; because it is interpreted by them to mean ecstatic utterances, and not human languages; as a general rule. Pat thinks all the gifts are available.

REVELATION AND CONFIRMATION

All the gifts involved either the revelation of the truth or the confirmation of the truth (Heb. 2:3-4). If we have any of them today, we should have all of them. They should be for the same purposes and produce the same results today as in the first century. The author is convinced that the Church of Jesus Christ of Latter-Day Saints, and other branches of the Mormon movement, do not have these gifts. However, of all who claim the gifts the Latter-Day Saints are the ones who are *most consistent* in their errors concerning the miraculous gifts. They are right in arguing that if we have one of the gifts, we must have them all. If men are inspired by the Spirit today when they speak and write, they speak and write some modern revelations and not just the revelations in the Bible. This would mean that we would have "more Bible."

CHAPTER II

SILENCE YOUR INTELLECT?

Although Pat Boone recognizes we must use our minds in Christianity, he has been influenced by Pentecostalism so that he minimizes the mind. He sent the author a poem by Florence Sibley which he said spoke to him. It called on one to silence the intellect, and not to bind her with words while she was bringing things from another world. The mind must not be used to deny God and His revelation, but what doth the Spirit say in Scripture concerning the use of the mind by unbelievers and by believers?

SCRIPTURES USED BY PAT

When Pat read Sibley's poem on silencing the intellect, two scriptures came to his mind. *First,* I Cor. 3:18-23. This deals with man's wisdom versus God's wisdom. It concerns man's use of his mind to reject God's gospel and to determine his own way of life. It does not deal with man's use of his mind in hearing, understanding, and obeying the gospel Paul preached (I Cor. 1:21; 15:1-8). In fact, Paul tried to get the Corinthians to learn and to be men in understanding (4:6; 14:20).

Second, Pat cited Rom. 11:33-36. God's judgments are unsearchable and His ways past tracing out. Man of himself has not known the mind of God nor can man be God's counsellor. That men might know God's will, God revealed His will through certain men, inspired by the Spirit, who taught others. They had the mind of Christ and through them we learn His will (I Cor. 2:16, 10-13; Eph. 3:1-21). We are not dictating to God when we maintain that all we can know about God's ways has been recorded in the Bible. The secret things, the unrevealed things, belong unto God (Deut. 29:29). Since man is not God's counsellor, man must confine himself to what God has revealed. Anything which was not revealed in the first century is not a part of the faith, the total truth, delivered to the church (John 16:12-14; Jude 3).

The revealed things, however, belong to us that we may study and do them. Long ago, through Moses, God said: "The secret things belong unto Jehovah our God; but the things that are revealed *belong unto us and to our children* for ever, *that* we may do all the words of this law." (Deut. 29:29.) This same principle is contained in the commands to speak as God's oracles, not to go beyond that which is written, to do what Jesus has commanded, and to continue in the apostles' doctrine (I Peter 4:11; I Cor. 4:6; Matt. 28:20; Acts 2:42). We study His will to understand it (Eph. 3:4). "Wherefore be ye not foolish, but understand what the will of the Lord is." (Eph. 5:17).

Pat wrote that the very strong and wise man was blind and pitiful in his understanding of the ways of God. Although the wisdom of the world could not know God (I Cor. 1:20-21), God revealed His wise ways in salvation through inspired men who taught others (I Cor. 1:21-2:16). Pat thinks that at times he has the gift of wisdom, or can get it, or it is manifested in some with whom he associates. Anything which came through this, or any other gift, would not be a blind insight of man, but the revelation of the Spirit.

Because man without God's word is blind, God has given His word. It does not leave us in the darkness of the world. As David said: "The opening of thy words giveth light; it giveth understanding unto the simple." (Psa. 119:130.) "Thy word have I laid up in my heart, that I might not sin against thee." (119:11). "Oh how love I thy law! It is my meditation all the day. Thy commandments make me wiser than mine enemies; for they are ever with me. I have more understanding than all my teachers; for thy testimonies are my meditation." "Through thy precepts I get understanding: therefore I hate every false way." (Psa. 119:97-99, 104.) To the extent we know and do His will to that extent we are not blind, but wisely walk in the light. One is not trusting in his I.Q. when he loves God with all of his mind, studies His word, and endeavors to furnish good ground on which the seed can grow.

Pat thought man's mind was *capable* of understanding only a *fraction* of the *revealed knowledge* of God. There are hard scriptures, and none of us shall ever exhaust the Scriptures. However, if we under-rate man's capacity to understand the divine revelation, we are under-rating God's capacity—even though we do not design to do so—to reveal His will to man so that man can understand. We are under-rating what it means, intellectually speaking, to be created in the image of God. Of this capacity we do not boast, for it, too, was God's gift. Sin, of course, can lead us to use the mind to avoid truth. The greatness of God, the inability of man to know the mind of God apart from the divine revelation, our sin, and our ignorance, help keep us humble as we continue to search the scriptures daily. We are not relying too much upon our understanding and comprehension, when we study the word with open hearts and diligent minds. We are in trouble when we fail to use our minds, silence the intellect, and wait for some voice or impression. It is not arrogance on our part to accept God's statement that the revealed things belong to us that we may learn to do His will (Deut. 29:29). This principle holds good for the New Covenant as well as the Old.

If man's mind is incapable of understanding more than a fraction of the revealed knowledge of God, only a fraction of the Bible is God's revelation to man since he is incapable of understanding more than a fraction. If we have to be inspired by the Spirit, or have other miraculous gifts, in order to understand the Bible, what follows? *First*, most of the Bible is not a revelation, but is a concealing of the mind of God. No matter how much we search the Scriptures we can understand only a fraction. *Second*, if the Spirit inspires us so that we can understand the rest of the Bible, such an understanding is infallible. *Third*, if we have to be inspired in order to understand most of the Bible, why was most of it given? Without inspiration we cannot understand it, and if we are personally inspired we get the message directly from heaven and not from the Bible.

Instead of minimizing the mind, Pat should have used his mind on these and other scriptures. Surely if he has miraculous gifts, and if gifts operate within his family circle, he should not misunderstand so many scriptures.

After stressing that God's ways are past finding out (Rom. 11:33), and after arguing that God does unpredictable things from man's standpoint, Pat unconsciously contradicted his own argument. He thought he saw some miracles in connection with the work of some people who have not obeyed the gospel as taught in the New Testament. These "miracles" led Pat to reconsider, and to conclude that these men had been baptized in the Spirit and were living the Christian life in living color instead of in black and white as Pat had been doing. Thus Pat traced out what he thought were God's ways. As unusual as was Cornelius' case, he was immediately baptized into Christ (Acts 10:44, 47-48), but these men were not. Since the Bible does not teach that all those men have been baptized into Christ, whom Pat thought received the baptism of the Spirit, how can Pat know that they received the baptism of the Spirit? Since they perpetuate doctrines and organizations which are foreign to the Bible, how can Pat claim they are guided by the Spirit in a miraculous way? How can Pat stay with Rom. 11:33 and make claims concerning God's ways which he cannot sustain from the Scriptures? If God wants to make exceptions on judgment day, it is God's business. However, we must leave unrevealed things to God. We must teach that people must be born of water and the Spirit in order to enter the kingdom (John 3:3-5), and that they should endeavor to keep the unity of the Spirit in the bond of peace in the one body of Christ (John 17:20-21; Eph. 4:1-6).

USE OF MIND UNAVOIDABLE

We cannot avoid using our minds in hearing, understanding, and obeying the Word. God does not understand for us. If He did, we would still have to use our minds to understand that He does understand for us, and to evaluate the evidence which proves that God understands for us. Pat had to use his mind to decide that the gifts are for us today; to understand how they must be sought; to realize that he has received gifts; to evaluate the evidence which proves he has received gifts; to understand whatever knowledge, insights, or guidance which he receives through the gifts; to understand how to apply this knowledge and follow this guidance; and to understand how to share it with others. The individual must use his mind to draw and accept all these conclusions.

It is true that the mind should accept the divine revelation which did not originate in man's mind, but in God's mind. It is true that there are things which transcend our understanding. However, we do not accept a thing as true just because it transcends our understanding. We must use our minds to understand and accept the evidence which justifies our acceptance of something which transcends our understanding. We must use our minds to be sure we do not accept something contrary to the Bible and justify our acceptance of it by saying we cannot comprehend everything. Furthermore, realizing the limitations of the mind, we recognize that almost any subject can be pursued to the place where we say: This is as far as our minds can probe at this time, and here we rest, as it were.

THE UNBELIEVER AND THE MIND

The unbeliever can and should use his mind *to discern God's existence.* Through the things that are made, the everlasting power and divinity of the Creator can be perceived. To fail to perceive that God exists is to become vain in one's reasoning, to refuse to see what God has manifested, and to have a darkened and senseless heart (Rom. 1:20-25; Psa. 14:1).

However, the mind of man cannot of itself penetrate the mind of God; therefore, it was necessary for God to reveal His will through the Spirit to inspired men who taught others the gospel and the new life in Christ (I Cor. 2:10-13). Paul, and other inspired men, *reasoned* and *taught* the word of God, and *persuaded* men to believe in and obey the gospel (Acts 18:4-5, 8, 11). Their word was confirmed by mighty miracles (I Cor. 2:4; Mk. 16:17, 20; Heb. 2:3-4). On Pentecost four lines of evidence were used to establish the conclusion that Jesus is both Lord and Christ. (a) Fulfilment of prophecy (Acts 2:17-21, 25-28, 30, 34-35). (b) The miracles of Jesus, which the people had seen, showed he was approved or accredited of God (2:22). (c) The resurrection, whereof the apostles were witnesses (2:32). (d) The miracles on Pentecost wherein something was heard (sound as of a rushing mighty wind), seen (tongues parting asunder like as of fire), and done (they spoke in other languages. 2:2-4, 6, 8, 11, 33.) These evidences were designed to appeal to the minds of the listeners, and to justify this conclusion: "Let all the house of Israel *therefore know assuredly that* God hath made him both Lord and Christ, this Jesus whom ye crucified." (Acts 2:36.) What was the impact? "Now when they *heard* this, they were pricked in their hearts, and said unto Peter and the rest of the apostles, Brethren, what shall we do?" (Acts 2:37.) The "heart" is often used to refer to the reasoning, the will, and the emotional aspects of man's nature. Men reason in their hearts (Mk. 2:6), the word is sown in the heart (Mk. 4:15; Lk. 8:12), and the word should be written on our hearts and be in our minds (Heb. 8:10). Those who asked what to do were told to repent and to be baptized. They were exhorted to do it, and around three thousand did it (Acts 2:38, 40, 41). They continued in the apostles' doctrine, which constituted what Jesus commanded. (Matt. 28:20; Acts 2:42). They had to use their minds to understand and obey the apostles' doctrine.

Throughout the book of Acts the word was taught, the mind was appealed to, and men were commended when they used their minds to search the scriptures daily to see whether these things were so (Acts 17:11-12).

THE BELIEVER AND THE MIND

Our love for God includes loving God with all of our mind or understanding (Matt. 22:37). If we love Christ we will keep His commandments, but we cannot know His commandments unless our minds are instructed (John 14:15; Matt. 28:20).

If we silence the intellect, how can we do the following? (1) Prove all things in order to hold fast the good (I Thess. 5:21). (2) Try the spirits in order to detect false teachers (I John 4:1). (3) Understand and evaluate the arguments of Pat and others. (4) Understand what God has promised (Rom. 4:20-21). (5) Go to the "law and to the testimony." (Isa. 8:19-20). (6) Contend for the faith (Jude 3). (7) Be stirred up by being put in remembrance (II Peter 1:12-13). (8) Learn not to go beyond what is written (I Cor. 4:6). (9) Understand and imitate Paul's ways (I Cor. 4:16-17). (10) Do what is revealed (Deut. 29:29). (11) "Understand what the will of the Lord is." (Eph. 5:17.) (12) Understand that we are, and how we are, to "prove what is the good and acceptable and perfect will of God." (Rom. 12:1-2.) (13) Learn from Paul's writings how to behave ourselves in the house of God (I Tim. 3:14-15). (14) Continue in what Paul taught, and put brethren in mind of these things (I Tim. 4:6, 16). (15) Give diligence to be approved workmen, handling aright the word of truth (II Tim. 2:15). (16) Distinguish between fables and truth (II Tim. 4:2-4). (17) Know and continue in the hope grounded on the truth of the gospel (Col. 1:4-6, 23). (18) Be admonished and taught that we may be presented perfect in Christ (Col. 1:28-29). (19) Take heed lest we be made spoil of through philosophy and vain deceit (Col. 2:8). (20) Timothy had a gift (II Tim. 1:6), but this did not release him from the obligation to use his mind. Paul said "consider what I say; for the Lord shall give thee understanding in all things." (II Tim. 2:7.) Consider means "to perceive with the mind . . . think about, ponder." Timothy needed to use his mind, and so do we. It may be replied that Paul said "the Lord shall give thee understanding in all things." Yes, but not apart from Timothy's use of his mind. God was giving the Ephesians understanding through the written word (Eph. 3:4). God does that which He does through His agents and instruments. He granted repentance unto life to the Gentiles (Acts 11:18), but God did not repent for them. He made man with the capacity to repent, and, through the word preached by Peter, God gave them reasons for, the opportunity to, and motivation to, repent (Acts 11:14; 10:43; 11:1). God opened the door of faith to the Gentiles, but He did it through His teachers and His word (Acts 14:1-3, 27). (21) Try those who claim to be apostles (Rev. 2:2). (22) Give reason for the hope which is within us. (I Peter 3:15), and be set for the defense of the gospel (Phil. 1:7, 16).

How can we do any of these things if we silence the intellect?

The poet Pat quoted asked not to be bound with words when she brought back "souvenirs of another world." Our reply is that we must all be bound by the law and the testimony (Isa. 8:19-20; Heb. 1:1-2; 2:1-4). All who are truly spiritual must acknowledge, and be bound by, what Paul taught (I Cor. 14:37; II Thess. 2:15; 3:14). If we do not hold fast the word, we shall not know whether we are listening to the voice of God (Matt. 22:31), or the voice of man; the testimony of the Spirit (Heb. 10:15), or the traditions of men (Matt. 15).

The inspired scriptures, and these include Paul's writings (II Peter 3:15-16; I Cor. 14:37), are profitable for (a) teaching, instruction, or doctrine. (b) Reproof or conviction. It enables us to detect error in doctrine and deed. (c) Correction, or making rectification or reformation. Harvey suggested that in reproof, "the Scriptures are perhaps conceived chiefly as the rule of faith, convicting of error and guiding to truth, as Gal. 3:6, 13, 16; but in *correction*, chiefly as the rule of life, rectifying wrong and restoring to right living, as I Cor. 10:1-10." (d) Instruction, or training, in righteousness. "Scripture trains, or educates, by guiding and inspiring the soul in holiness and right living (Titus 2:2). It is the manual of spiritual education; training the man in right moral and spiritual thinking and feeling and action. Compare Psa. 19:8-14; 119."

How are we to use the inspired Scriptures, as described in II Tim. 3:14-17, if we do not use our minds? *To silence our intellect is to keep the Scriptures from speaking to us.*

I COR. 14 STRESSES THE UNDERSTANDING MIND

Paul's discussion of tongues and other miraculous gifts stressed the importance of the mind and the understanding of the word of God. *First,* in order for the word of God to edify men, it must reach their understanding. Untranslated tongues were not, in effect, addressed to men because they did not reach the understanding of men. "For he that speaketh in a tongue speaketh not unto men, but unto God." How do we know this is the case even though men hear the sound? Paul immediately explained in what sense it was not unto men. "For," he explained, *"no man understandeth."* (14:2.) In order for the church to be edified, the understanding must be instructed (14:4-5).

Second, the interpretation of the tongue enabled the audience to know what was being said. Therefore, it was essential that either the tongues speaker, or someone else, interpret in order that the church be edified (14:5, 17, 26-27). The listener can know to say the Amen only if he understand what one is saying (14:16). To be edified the audience must understand. "Else if thou bless with the spirit, how shall he that filleth the place of the *unlearned* say the Amen at thy giving of thanks, seeing *he knoweth not what thou sayest?* For thou verily givest thanks well, but the other is not edified." (14:16-17). Therefore, Paul said that "in the church I had rather speak five words *with my understanding, that I might instruct others also,* than ten thousand words in a tongue." (14:19). One must understand, and use his own understanding in teaching so that others may be instructed and also understand.

Third, if musical instruments make no distinction in the sounds, "how shall it be known what is piped or harped? For if the trumpet give an uncertain voice, who shall prepare himself for war?" (14:7-8). If the church does not understand the sounds uttered by the speaker, it does not know what it is all about and its conduct cannot be influenced so that it does the will of God.

Fourth, "So also ye, unless ye utter by the tongue speech easy *to be understood,* how shall it be known what is spoken? for ye will be speaking into the air." (14:9). To by-pass the understanding is to merely vibrate the air. If my mind is not reached, the speaker is only beating his gums!

Fifth, to by-pass the understanding is to treat one another as barbarians. "If then I know not the meaning of the voice, I shall be to him that speaketh a barbarian, and he that speaketh will be a barbarian unto me." (14:11).

Sixth, to by-pass the understanding of the audience is to leave one's own understanding without fruit in their lives (14:14, 16-17).

Seventh, to by-pass the understanding is to be childish and not mature. In spite of their spiritual gifts, some of them in Corinth were being childish. So Paul said: "Brethren, *be not children in mind:* yet in malice be ye babes, but *in mind be men* (Greek, of full age)" (I Cor. 14:20). They were being childish in exercising the gift of tongues, which made quite a show, when it could not serve the purpose of convicting unbelievers or of edifying saints (14:22-28). When an individual was mature in understanding, he would not be so childish as to use the gift of tongues when no one could understand and be instructed. The mature thing was to "let all things be done unto edifying." (14:26).

Eighth, the mind of the unbeliever must be reached, in order for him to be converted; otherwise tongues which by-passed his mind, because he did not understand them, could leave him thinking you were mad (14:23-25).

Ninth, the entire purpose of the assembly was voided if the mind and understanding were not reached. "For ye all can prophesy one by one, *that all may learn,* and all may be exhorted." (14:31.) He did not mean that every individual was a prophet, for all were not (14:29-30).

Tenth, Paul implied that one should use his mind to understand and to acknowledge what Paul wrote. "If any man thinketh himself to be a prophet, or spiritual, let him *take knowledge of the things* which I write unto you, that they are the commandment of the Lord." (I Cor. 14:37.) Without the mind, one could not take knowledge of what Paul wrote, and could not realize that it was the commandment of the Lord.

A study of the chapter makes it very clear that Paul stresses the importance of the mind and the understanding all the way through the chapter. *Men should teach so that men can understand.* The chapter teaches that it was absolutely essential that the Corinthians use spiritual gifts so as to reach the mind and understanding both of believers and unbelievers (14:22-23). The chapter basically deals with the importance, and the necessity, of understanding. It views miraculous gifts as of importance only if they reach the understanding.

This makes it clear that one is not being miraculously guided by the Spirit when he takes a stand which minimizes the importance of the mind and the understanding. The Holy Spirit through Paul rebuked the childishness of those who exercised the gift of tongues when they by-passed the minds of the audience.

ORGANIZED AND ACCOUNTED FOR

Pat thought that the author faced the potential danger of wanting to account for and neatly organize everything. Therefore, the author might gather arguments to sustain some point which he desired to make. Pat wrote that Saul could have convinced us from the Old Testament that Jesus was not the Christ. However, Christ on the Damascus road showed

Saul that he was wrong. Peter, he thought, could have proved unmistakably to us that the Gentiles had no right to membership in the church, but on the roof-top Christ showed him otherwise.

On this the following observations are presented for the reader's consideration. *First,* we all need to be on our guard lest we twist the scriptures to suit our own ideas and purposes rather than study the Bible to find what it says (II Peter 3:16-18).

Second, all must guard against the pride of intellect. The author uses his mind to study God's word. He recognizes that he is not inspired, and that he can make, and has made, mistakes. It is possible for one to be so conceited that he is unwilling to acknowledge his mistakes. On the other hand, the uninspired man, who recognizes that he has made mistakes, realizes his constant need to measure all things by the Bible. He is helped in this by the fact that his positions are challenged and examined by others, and, therefore, he finds it necessary to continue to study.

Conversely, *is there not a greater temptation to trust in one's conclusions if he has convinced himself that his conclusions have been revealed to him by God in some direct and miraculous way?* Pat used his mind and concluded that he is inspired, at least at times. He said that just as one received a supernatural gift of a prayer language, just so God will provide the other gifts also. He thought he had undeniable evidence of the gifts of knowledge, wisdom, tongues, interpretation, prophecy, and healing operating within his family circle and also in wider circles in which he moves. He thanked God that God was not giving just one gift today, but all of them.

We ask the reader: Will the man who thinks he is inspired have a smaller problem with pride than the man who knows he is uninspired and that his conclusions may need to be revised in the light of additional information? In those things in which he is inspired, the inspired man not only needs no revision *but he cannot even admit the possibility of a need for revision;* for this would be either to raise doubt concerning his inspiration or to doubt the accuracy of God's revelation to him.

We are not suggesting that if a man is inspired he must therefore be proud. Paul was inspired, but it did not mean that he was filled with pride. However, even Paul faced the temptation for he wrote: "And by reason of the exceeding greatness of the revelations, that I should not be exalted overmuch, there was given to me a thorn in the flesh, a messenger of Satan to buffet me, that I should not be exalted overmuch." (II Cor. 12:7.)

An uninspired man today certainly can be far more open to correction of his own ideas by the Bible, than a man today who thinks that he is inspired in at least certain of his positions. The man who thinks he is inspired cannot think that there could be a need for any possibility of correction. As long as he is convinced of his own inspiration, he can only use his mind to marshall evidence, to gather a battery of arguments and convincing proofs to show that he is and must be right.

Third, in proving all things, and holding fast that which is good (I Thess. 5:21), we need to organize and to account for things. We must continue to study, however, to be sure we have not left out something God has put in, or put in something God left out.

Fourth, we do not know how many Paul could have convinced, before his conversion, that Jesus was not the Christ. He could not have done it, however, through the scriptures unless he twisted them, or left out some of them. He did not convince Christians of his day, as far as we know, that Jesus was not the Christ. If he had been able to silence and to convince them by argumentation, it would have been unnecessary for him to have resorted to violence. Although he did not accept it, Christians were even then proving from the scriptures that Jesus was the Christ (Acts 2:36).

When Paul was converted, how did he approach the Jews in order to convert them? He did not tell them that they could prove from scriptures that Jesus was not the Christ, and that Christ would prove them wrong by appearing to them as He had appeared to Paul. *Christ did not convince them in the way that He convinced Paul.* Christ didn't appear to Pat Boone and convince him. He appeared unto Paul last of all, in His literal, post-resurrection appearances (I Cor. 15:8-9). How did Christ convince them? *First,* Paul proved to them

34

from the Scriptures that Jesus is the Christ. "And straight-way in the synagogues he *proclaimed* Jesus, that he is the Son of God . . . But Saul increased the more in strength, and confounded the Jews that dwelt at Damascus, *proving* that this is the Christ." (9:29.) In a synagogue in Iconium he *"so spake* that a great multitude both of Jews and of Greeks believed." (Acts 14:1.) "Paul, *as his custom was,* went in unto them, and for three sabbath days *reasoned with them from the scriptures,* opening and alleging that it behooved the Christ to suffer, and to rise again from the dead; and that this Jesus, whom, said he, I proclaim unto you, is the Christ. And some of them were persuaded . . . " (Acts 17:2-4.) ". . . he reasoned in the synagogue every sabbath." (18:4.) ". . . reasoning daily in the school of Tyrannus." (19:9.) Apollos did the same type of thing, "for he powerfully *confuted* the Jews, and that *publicly, showing by the scriptures that Jesus was the Christ."* (18:28.) Paul told some Jews that: "Having therefore obtained the help that is from God, I stand unto this day testifying both to small and great, saying nothing but what the prophets and Moses did say should come; how that the Christ must suffer, and how that he first by the resurrection of the dead should proclaim light both to the people and to the Gentiles." (Acts 26:22-23.) In Rome Paul spent much time "testifying the kingdom of God, and persuading them concerning Jesus, both from the law of Moses and from the prophets, from morning till evening. And some believed the things which were spoken, and some disbelieved." (Acts 28:23-24.)

Paul did not promise them a Damascus road experience, but he did prove, from the Scriptures, that Jesus is the Christ.

A *second* thing involved in Paul's work in convincing men, was that God confirmed His word, which Paul preached, by miracles. An opponent was struck blind by the Lord after Paul announced it to the sorcerer (Acts 13:8-12). ". . . the Lord, who bare witness unto the word of His grace, granting signs and wonders to be done by their hands." (14:3; see also 14:8-11; 15:12; 19:11-12.) Paul also conferred gifts through laying on of hands (Acts 19:1-6; Rom. 1:11).

Third, Paul also bore testimony that he personally had seen the resurrected Lord (Acts 22:15; 26:16; I Cor. 15:1-9).

35

He did not promise any of them that they would have such an experience. His experience was recounted more than once, but it was never repeated. Paul did not suggest that unbelieving Jews could prove from the scriptures that Jesus was not the Christ, but that Christ would prove them wrong on their Damascus road.

Concerning Saul's experience it is also important to consider the following: (a) He saw the Lord even while on his way to persecute Christians. Do other unbelievers today have such a sight of the Lord? (b) If so, was it done in the presence of others who saw them fall to the earth, and who heard the sound, but did not understand the voice? (Acts 9:7; 22:9). Did the others behold the light? (22:9; 9:3.) (c) Were they blinded? (d) Were they sent into a place to wait for someone to tell them what they were to do? (Acts 9:8, 6.) (e) Did the Lord in a vision inform someone else, and send them to the waiting blind man? In other words, Saul's experience was corroborated by Ananias' experience. Does such a case happen today like that of Saul and Ananias? (f) Did the one who was placed in contact with them tell them to do what Ananias told Saul? "And now why tarriest thou? arise, and be baptized, and wash away thy sins, calling on his name." (Acts 22:16.) Although it was three days since Saul had believed, this was the first time he knew he was to be baptized. He was baptized immediately. Furthermore, he had not eaten between the time that he believed and the time he was baptized. Some people who claim to have seen the Lord have not been baptized yet! (g) Do the modern "Sauls" become apostles as did Saul? Christ appeared unto Saul for the purpose of making an apostle out of him (Acts 9:15; 22:15; 26:16; Gal. 1:1; I Cor. 15:8-9). (h) Do they work the wide variety of miracles which Paul worked? (i) Do they learn the gospel by revelation, by direct inspiration, instead of by study? (Gal. 1:11-12). (j) Do they teach the same doctrine Saul taught? (k) Do they write inspired Scripture such as Paul wrote? (I Cor. 14:37). Can they say that: "If any man thinketh himself to be a prophet, or spiritual, let him take knowledge of the things which I write unto you, that they are the commandment of the Lord." (I Cor. 14:37.)

PETER'S CASE

Could Peter have given unmistakable proof that the Gentiles were not entitled to membership in Christ's church? Although the Lord did not make the full and final revelation on this matter before the time of the household of Cornelius, enough had been said to show that the Gentiles were entitled to the gospel. The church had not understood it, for at least most of them were still viewing the Gentiles in the light of the law. They seemed to think that although the Gentiles could become Christians, they must also accept the law of Moses (Acts 15:1, 5). The great commission, however, had already shown that the gospel was for every nation and every creature. Furthermore, the great commission set forth gospel-terms for salvation and not the terms of the old law (Matt. 28:19-20; Mk. 16:15-16; Lk. 24:44-47). In addition to this, although evidently he did not fully understand it, Peter himself on Pentecost had announced that the promise was also to those who were afar off—the Gentiles (Acts 2:39; Eph. 2:11-13, 18-19).

The experiences of Peter in connection with Cornelius did make it crystal clear that the Gentiles were to be accepted on the same basis as the Jews, i. e. on the grounds of their acceptance of the gospel. Consider what was involved in this case. (a) The vision of Cornelius (Acts 10:4-7). (b) This was corroborated by Peter's vision on the housetop (10:9-16), and the subsequent statement of the Spirit to Peter (10:17-22). (c) The miracles that took place at the household of Cornelius (Acts 10:44-46).

The experience at the household of Cornelius was a once-for-all experience. It never happened again. God has so clearly revealed, through this incident and what had been revealed before, the truth about the entrance of the Gentiles into the church that it was unnecessary for Him to reveal and confirm this truth again through such an experience. This case was used three times to prove that the Gentiles were to be saved through the gospel, but the case itself happened only once. (a) Peter used it to prove to the Jews who were with him that the Gentiles were to be baptized into Christ (Acts 10:47-48). (b) When some in Jerusalem challenged what was done, the series of miraculous events did not take place again to convince them. Instead, Peter told what had taken place, and he had witnesses with him (11:12). The church in Jerusalem was convinced (Acts 11:1-18). (c) Judaizers later attempted to bind the law on Gentile Christians (Acts 15:1, 5). Did the series of events take place again for their benefit? No. Three lines of evidence were presented to prove that the Judaizers were wrong. (1) The case of Cornelius (15:7-11). (2) God's confirmation by miracles of Paul's teaching and work among the Gentiles (15:12.) (3) James' statement that the reception of the Gentiles was the fulfilment of prophecy (15:13-19).

How were the Gentile Christians in Antioch, Syria, and Cilicia informed of this matter? Was a case similar to that of Cornelius re-enacted among them? No. Instead, the church, under the leadership of the apostles and the elders, sent *an epistle* which said the Judaizers were wrong, and they also sent two *prophets* to tell them "the same things *by word of mouth.*" (Acts 15:22-29, 27, 32). These Gentile brethren did not say that they would rather see the miracles themselves, such as had taken place in connection with Cornelius' conversion, than to read about them! Instead, *"when they had read it, they rejoiced for the consolation."* (15:31).

If God is proving things today through such experiences as those of Peter and Cornelius, *what new truths is He thus proving?* In connection with Cornelius, God was not reconfirming an old and established truth, but confirming a new one which, although much of it had been revealed before, was now being revealed in crystal clarity.

LAY ASIDE LOGIC?

Pat told the author that John L. Sherrill's book, *They Speak With other Tongues,* was a milestone in Pat's odyssey and Pat urged the author to read it. Sherrill also made an attack on the mind, and said that Nicodemus' trouble was that he was trying to approach Christ through logic. Nicodemus took the logical position that no man could do the works Jesus did unless God was with Him. Did Jesus attack this logic, and say that Nicodemus needed not logic, but an experience, to know who Jesus is? (Sherrill, p. 10; John 3:2-3).

What shows that Sherrill is wrong? *First,* although a teacher must also be tested by his teaching, Nicodemus' logic was excellent. He was right as far as he had gone in this matter. The next *logical* step was to conclude that since Jesus was sent of God, men should accept His teaching concerning Himself, God, the Spirit, the kingdom, and man.

Second, Nicodemus was rightly responding to Christ's miracles. *God designed that the miracles constitute one of Christ's credentials.* Inspired by the Spirit, Peter said: "Ye men of Israel, hear these words: Jesus of Nazareth, a man *approved of God* unto you by mighty works (powers) and wonders and signs *which God did by him in the midst of you,* even as ye yourselves know." (Acts 2:22.) Approved means "to point out, to exhibit . . . is used once in the sense of proving by demonstration, and so bringing about an approval." (Vine.) The record of His miracles was designed to produce faith in Christ (John 20:30-31). Miracles confirmed the word (Mk. 16:17, 20). From the four lines of evidence which the Spirit presented on Pentecost, through Peter the Spirit drew the logical conclusion that Jesus is both Lord and Christ. The people who accepted this conclusion wanted to know what to do (Acts 2:36-37). Did Peter say, as he would have said if he was guided by the same "spirit" which guided Sherrill, that: "When such logical conclusions are drawn and accepted, one is trying to approach Christ through logic. This can never succeed. What you must do is to have an experience?" If Peter had said this, they would still have had to use their minds to understand it. But Peter made no such response. Instead he told them what to do to be saved, he exhorted them to do it, and those who used their minds and accepted the word were baptized into Christ (Acts 2:38-41).

Third, Jesus told Nicodemus that in order to enter the kingdom he had to be born anew. Faith in Christ is involved in the new birth, and this faith comes by hearing and understanding the word of God (Rom. 10:17).

Fourth, there were a lot of things Nicodemus did not understand, and in this he was not unlike the apostles who did not understand that Christ was to die (Matt. 16:16-17, 21-23; Lk. 24:25-26). However, Jesus did not condemn the logic of Nicodemus concerning the miracles as credentials of Christ.

Fifth, when the individual acts by faith and is baptized into Christ, he undergoes the *experience* of the new birth. Men become servants of righteousness through obeying the gospel from the heart (John 3:2-5; Rom. 6:2-5, 17-18). Living the new life is the experiencing of the new life. These experiences are the results of following God's word.

Sixth, if Sherrill and some of his friends have some of the miraculous gifts, these should have kept him from such a misapprehension of the use of the mind in Christianity. He contradicts the Spirit's word in the New Testament.

INTELLECT AND ACTION

Christianity is more than an intellectual grasp of truth, but it does include intellectual grasp. We must also live by God's word. We must walk in the light, we must do the truth, and the ultimate test of knowledge is whether we keep His commandments (I John 1:5-6; 2:3-6). There is an appreciation of, an increasing knowledge of, and a confirmation of truth which comes *through the application of truth in our lives.* We can understand it is more "blessed to give than to receive" (Acts 20:35), but when we obey this truth we know this truth through the experience of applying the truth. It has a meaning which is far deeper, and more meaningful, than when it was just committed to memory and grasped in the realm of thought only. The mind is involved in understanding the truth, applying the truth, and in the awareness of the confirmation of truth which comes through living the truth.

The author does not deny the necessity of experience, but he affirms that the experience must be based on, guided by, and measured by, the word of God. Therefore we must see with our eyes, hear with our ears, understand with our hearts, and hold fast the word in good and honest hearts (Matt. 13:15-18, 23; Lk. 8:15). Therefore, we reject any approach which endeavors to discredit the mind. If Pat had miraculous gifts of the Spirit he would not minimize the mind as he does. *The distrust of the mind is an essential step into Pentecostalism wherein emotions sweep aside reason and scripture.* Pentecostalism cannot be successful when the individual uses his mind to prove all things by the Scriptures. Pat's hilltop experience, as related in his book, is an example of how people get worked up. Countless examples of emotionalism can be seen in Pentecostal meetings. There are some who are not as emotional as others, but they, too, in some way must blind the mind to certain scriptures in order to get and keep their so-called baptism of the Spirit and gifts.

CHAPTER III

WHY DO PEOPLE SEEK THE GIFT OF TONGUES?

There are a number of reasons why people seek the gift of tongues. Since we do not have the inspired gift of discernment (I Cor. 12:9), we determine the reasons by studying what others say and do. Due to a lack of information and insights we may not know the motivations of a particular individual. However, a knowledge of the reasons why some have sought the gift of tongues can help us to help them, as well as to prevent some from seeking gifts which are not for us. Furthermore, when we know for what lack they are trying to compensate, or what need they are trying to satisfy, we may be able to help them find what they really need.

IGNORANCE OF THE SCRIPTURES

The widespread ignorance of the Bible, or at least concerning the nature and purpose of the miracles, leads some people to think that because some had these gifts in the first century we should have them today. The reason we do not have them—they say—is our lack of faith and our failure to seek the gifts. Therefore, if we seek the gift of tongues in faith we shall receive it. Some do not realize that the tongues were only one of the signs used to confirm the gospel while it was being revealed. They do not understand that the faith has been revealed and confirmed, and that we should contend for the faith instead of looking for the means whereby it was revealed from heaven, and confirmed on the earth, by those whom God chose to make known His will to earth. Furthermore, they may not know the difference between tongues in the Bible, and the utterance of unintelligible sounds today; so they think they have received the gift when all they have done is to utter unintelligible sounds—which even a baby can do.

In some cases, individuals have based their conviction, that the gifts were for the time when the gospel was being revealed and confirmed, on a fallacious argument or on the misinterpretation of a scripture. When their error has been pointed out to them, they have concluded that we should seek the gifts.

EVIDENCE OF

There are those who are convinced they must speak in tongues, or have some other experience, in order to know that their sins are forgiven, or that they are truly devoted to God, or that they are accepted by God, or that they are victorious in the new life in Christ. Since tongues constitute the evidence, they must seek the gift and speak in tongues in order to be assured of their salvation, or that they have attained a high level of devotion and holiness. They are aware of a lack of spiritual depth in their life, and they think that tongues may meet their need. They seek it and find it because they feel they must find it in order to certify that they stand approved of God.

TOO DEMANDING

There may be some who find the Bible too demanding, but they do not want to abandon Christianity. Therefore, they seek a deeper experience and modern revelations which will enable them to redefine or modify Christianity so that the hard doctrine is abandoned or modified.

REACTION AGAINST MATERIALISM

In the face of materialism, there are those who yearn for spiritual realities, but misunderstand their nature and how to avail themselves of these realities. This "creates a tendency to make the great facts and truths of the divine revelation of Christianity subordinate to subjective spiritual manifestations, and to the emotions and experiences which such manifestations are fitted to produce." (Sir Robert Anderson.)

Tongues speaking has appeared in some modernistic churches. They have realized there is nothing in modernism that can satisfy the hungry soul, and in their search for the supernatural some of them have gone from one extreme to another.

EMOTIONAL

There are others who have been starved emotionally, and for whom religion has been a matter of coldly going through meaningless ritual. Seeking and finding the gift stirs them emotionally, and instead of a meaningless ritual they think they are engaged in a truly spiritual experience. Its emotionalism, with many of them, gives their faith a glow which they have not experienced in the past. Being in a religious context they think it is a deeply spiritual experience.

For some it is too mundane, and unexciting, to find their religious experiences in a daily life of service and in worship as set forth in the Bible. They are seeking for something far more mysterious and thrilling. They want to be taken out of this world, as it were. For some this type of experience furnishes an escape from reality.

From his studies, John G. Finch observed that: "Too often, exciting and mystical religious experiences have been used to cover up or to defend against reality. Often one attempts to use such experiences as a substitute for hard work." (p. 2.)

This may be especially the case of some who are very emotional, and highly susceptible to suggestion and the psychology of the crowd. They are touched by the emotionally charged atmosphere, they begin to feel something which they may never have felt before, they are told by the preacher or someone else that it is the work of the Spirit and they should not resist the Spirit. They reason that since they do not know what it is it must be the Spirit, and so they abandon themselves to it. They misinterpret their emotions.

H. A. Ironside, who was once involved in the pentecostal movement, said: "An unhealthy craving for new and thrilling religious sensations, and emotional meetings of a most exciting character, readily account for these things." (Gromacki, p. 44.)

INFLUENCE OF EXISTENTIALISM

The influences of the world are always around us, and to the extent we do not exercise care they will influence us in some degree. With so many channels of communication today we are bound to hear, whether we accept them or not, many winds of doctrine. One of the tremendous influences today in literature, art, the theater, etc., is existentialism. There are many varieties, but at least three things seem to characterize most if not all of the varieties.

44

Existentialism affirms subjectivity in opposition to objectivity. Instead of a standard of authority, or of evidence, existing outside of oneself to which one ought to conform, that which counts is the experience—especially the inner experience—of the individual. Instead of having to deal with facts, logic, arguments, and evidences, one goes within himself and finds the truth for himself in some sort of experience. Each does his own thing, and does not have to give evidence or reason as to why he is justified in accepting or doing his own thing. The tongues speaker does not have to explain or to justify, he simply experiences, participates, and is inwardly confirmed. There does not have to be any rationality about it.

The existentialist stresses the hostility of the environment, which is both alien and incomprehensible; so he retreats within himself. The tongues speaker retreats within himself, and in his experience feels that he has been brought to communion with God, and can be victorious over the hostile world. The world, of course, is hostile, but victory is not through tongues.

William C. Fletcher, who mentioned the above two characteristics of existentialism, but made no application to tongues speakers, also wrote: "The Christian existentialists see another dimension to the hostile environment, for the Christians find themselves confronted by a holy God. God is wholly other, absolutely transcendent and beyond our comprehension . . . Between God and man there is no continuity, as the older theology thought, but radical, infinite discontinuity." (88-89.) Some tongues speakers think that the gap between man and God cannot be bridged through man hearing the word of God, and being convinced by the word and its credentials, but through a direct leap of faith into an experience which brings one into immediate and direct communion with God. However, we may ask why it is that if the mind and the hearing cannot be involved in coming to faith and coming to God by faith, how can the gap between man and God be bridged by any other act or experience of man? Furthermore, one must use the mind to decide to make the leap of faith.

Although many of the tongues speakers have never heard of existentialism as a philosophy, something of its spirit permeates a lot of our society. In fact, existentialism is the outgrowth of influences which have always been present in society, and even the solutions given by various schools of existentialism are found at different times and places in human history. It is true there are limits to reason, and the evidence and reason demonstrate the need for faith in the revelation of God in Christ. It is true there is hostility in the world, and that the world lieth in the evil one. It is true that God is God and man is God's creature, even though he is made in the image of God. It is true the gap between man and God, which has been created by sin and ignorance, needs to be bridged. However, it is not true that the ways advocated by the existentialists, or by the tongue speakers, constitute the way set forth by Him who is the way, the truth, and the life.

It is well to realize that college and high school students today are usually exposed to some form of existentialism in literature, drama, or art, or in all of them. It is even reflected in some of what is called music and songs today.

THE LEAP OF FAITH

The influence of existentialism is seen in the attack on the mind and the emphasis on the leap of faith. John L. Sherrill became convinced that you cannot come to Christianity through intellect, that it must be experienced first, that when you do something you do not understand sometimes understanding follows; and that you must take a leap of faith and confess that Christ is God even without knowing why or understanding. When he decided to do this, something within him died, and with his statement of belief, "there was room in me for something new and altogether mysterious." (p. 11.) Obviously he had an experience, but experiences must be judged by Christ's word (John 12:48; Acts 17:31).

First, the mind cannot be by-passed. It must be used even in deciding that Christianity cannot be approached through the intellect. The mind is used in making the decision to leap by faith, and in the evaluation of one's experience.

Second, as we have shown in the previous chapter, Christianity appeals to the mind of the unbeliever (Rom. 1:20-23; Acts 2:36-41; 17:11-12; 18:4, 5, 11), and of the believer (Matt. 22:37; 28:20; I Thess. 5:21, 27; Col. 4:16; Eph. 3:4; 5:17; Rev. 2:1, 7).

Third, faith is essential to the confession of Christ. "How then shall they call on him *in whom they have not believed?*" (Rom. 10:8-10, 13, 14, 17). Sherrill had enough faith to take a leap of faith. Faith when expressed can increase faith. Mormons strengthen their faith in the prophetship of Joseph Smith, Jr., by affirming that he was a prophet of God, that the Book of Mormon is of divine origin, and this is their testimony to us. Faith unexpressed tends to die. We do some leaping by faith, but there are reasons to leap. Walking by faith is followed by additional confirmation. The proof of the pudding is more and more found in the eating of the pudding. However, there are reasons to start eating.

INSTANT SPIRITUALITY

Others may want a short cut to "instant spirituality" through tongues. Instead of growth in grace and knowledge of the Lord, they want to leap to a new level of existence. Benjamin B. Warfield pointed out that some men "are unable to understand why time should be consumed in divine works . . . God's ways are not their ways, and it is a great trial to them that God will not walk in their ways. They love the storm and the earthquake and the fire. They cannot see the divine in 'a sound of gentle stillness,' and adjust themselves with difficulty to the lengthening perspective of God's gracious working . . . for themselves they cut the knot and boldly declare complete salvation (and spiritual maturity, J.D.B.) to be within their reach at their option, or already grasped and enjoyed. It is true, observation scarcely justifies the assertion. But this difficulty is easily removed by adjusting the nature of complete salvation to fit their present attainments. These impatient souls tolerate more readily the idea of an imperfect perfection than the admission of lagging perfecting. They must at all costs have all that is coming to them at once." (p. 349.) By complete salvation, Warfield had reference not only to forgiveness of sins, but to such a victorious conquest of sin that it is no more a problem in his life.

Some do not want to struggle with the problems of doubt, of arguments for the faith, or weigh the challenges to the faith. They want release from all of this in some mysterious way. Instead of allowing the necessary time for study, growth,

47

and living the principles of Jesus day by day, they want to be transported instantly into a communion with God which raises them above the possibility of any doubt, discouragement and struggle.

They forget that it takes time for the seed not merely to find root in the hearts of men, but to grow after it has been rooted in the soil. And it takes time for it to bear fruit.

COMPENSATION FOR INADEQUACY

Some "attempt to compensate for feelings of inadequacy by taking a leap into the unusual, the extraordinary." (Finch, 3.)

SPIRITUAL ELITE

There are some who want something that almost no one else in their group seems to have. They want an unusual experience of their very own and, if possible, one that will attract attention to them and make them one of the spiritually elite. They are more spiritual than others. In some contexts tongues satisfy these desires.

STATUS SYMBOL

Amongst some Pentecostal groups, "characterized by their marginal socio-economic position in society . . . the ecstatic behavior is both an outlet for repressed conflicts, and means of justifying one's unique position in society as a possessor of truth and righteousness." (E. Mansell Pattison, 75.)

This does not explain all cases. Pattison also spoke of "the function of glossolalia in middle-class Pentecostal groups who do not occupy a marginal social position. In this situation, Gerlach et al suggest that glossolalia functions as a 'rite de passage'—a technique of recruitment, a method of organization, and a means of demonstration of effect of behavioral change. Here, the function of glossolalia is not to serve personal needs, or as a mediating mechanism in relation to the larger society, but as a mechanism for nurturance of the social movement itself." (E. Mansell Pattison, 75.)

PROTEST

Pattison thought that in certain of the dignified and established denominations, which had become ritualistic and intellectual enterprises, speaking in tongues was a form of protest (p. 74). In some cases, children may protest in this manner, and strike back at their parents whom they know to disapprove of such manifestations.

SEARCH FOR INDEPENDENT IDENTITY

There are some who feel they are lost in the crowd and are without any identity of their own. There are others who feel they are overshadowed by someone else, so that they have no identity of their own, but are thought of as being related to so and so. It may be their father in whose shadow they are tired of living. They are determined to show their independence. They are not going to continue to be overshadowed by that person or persons. In certain contexts the gift of tongues provides them with the means of accomplishing their desire. Furthermore, they find additional motivation because speaking in tongues was not the way of the folks back home.

REACTION

Some go from one extreme to another. Pat Boone said that "through all of my Christian life, I had virtually ignored the Holy Spirit." *(Testimony,* p. 8). From this he has reacted to the other extreme, and thinks some things are of the Spirit which we are convinced are not of the Spirit.

RETICENCE IN RELIGION

To speak to others concerning religion is almost taboo in many circles today. In an age in which there is so much stress on science and objectivity, there are those who feel that religion is not intellectually respectable; therefore, they do not speak out concerning their religious convictions. They are afraid of what others will think. Others have sold them on the idea that religion is such a private matter that one ought not infringe on the privacy of others by talking about religion. There are others who are such religious illiterates that they do not know what to say, or they are so afraid of saying the wrong thing that they remain silent. And yet, they must realize at times that one ought to speak concerning his religion if it really has any significance.

Wayne E. Oates pointed out that: "The conspiracy of silence about personal religion prevails even in the theological school as it does in the home and the lower echelon schools—the appearance of being less religious than one really is.

The blasé attempt to be 'secular' bears psychological evidence of a 'protesting-too-much' kind of reaction against the deeper strivings that brought the persons to the theological school in the first place, either as a student or as a professor.

"Seen from a psychoanalytic perspective, this 'unspeakableness' concerning God, Christ, the Holy Spirit, religious decision, and personal commitment has all the earmarks of repression. Repression functions through other mechanisms of denial, isolation, undoing and reaction." In a reaction against this reticence, religious needs and feelings "may erupt into turbulent upheavals and expressions of pent-up feelings, such as we find in speaking in tongues." (Wayne E. Oates, 78, 82-83.)

ADDITIONAL REASONS

In a study based on sixty cases in "staid main-line churches," one psychiatrist concluded that there were six dominant personality patterns. "1) hostility to authority, 2) the wish to compensate for feelings of inadequacy, 3) the wish to rationalize feelings of isolation, 4) the wish to dominate, 5) strong feelings of dependency and suggestibility, and 6) wish for certainty." (E. Mansell Pattison, 76.)

Although this author does not accept any psychologist as the final authority, and although there are all sorts of characters in psychology as well as in religion, he does believe there are reasons why people seek this gift today, and why they think they have found it. Psychologists have not done a lot of first-hand study in the field of glossolalia and, as would be expected, their conclusions do not always agree. After noticing some of the studies, as to the types of personality involved, Pattison said: "To the reports cited above, I shall add my own rather unsystematic, but extensive observations over a 20-year period. In brief, my observations lead me to conclude that rather than being contradictory, the various types of reports and evidence cited above indicate that glossolalia is a psychological phenomenon which bears no necessarily linear relationship with personality variables." (76.)

SEARCH FOR CERTAINTY

In some cases the experience of "tongues" is sought and found because the individual is searching for certainty; a certainty which is based on his own personal experience and which is beyond the reach of the rationalistic criticism of unbelievers. Some seem to live in a sea of uncertainty (Compare George J. Jennings, 14). They have been convinced that there are no rational arguments to justify faith in Christ, that there are rational arguments against the faith, and therefore certainty must be found in some type of experience and, perhaps, the more non-rational the better. Furthermore, they may have been influenced at the same time by an opposing current of thought—the position that no certainty can be found in reason. Reason cannot be trusted in any way; so they seek for some type of inner illumination, feeling, and assurance for which reasons do not need to be given. The more mysterious it is, the more it is grounded in their own immediate experience, the more some think it must be from God.

Of course, the position that there are reasons against the faith and the position that reason cannot be trusted, are contradictory positions. If reason cannot be trusted, we cannot trust the reasons which they bring against the faith. In either case, however, the individual is left without any assurance and he seeks for it in some sort of experience which gives him assurance even though it cannot be communicated to others. But what reason is there for one to trust his experience?

As a Roman Catholic scholar, R. A. Knox pointed out in his discussion of Jansenism of the 17th century, "Those theologies which lay great stress on the corruption of human nature, and the difficulty of salvation, are apt to make up for it by offering to the elect *sensible experiences* of God's favour. It may be the complete inner conviction of the Calvinist that he is bound for heaven; it may be the warm consciousness of the Wesleyan that his sins are, here and now, forgiven: in either case, there is the feeling that things can never be the same again, a threshold has been crossed, nature has been supernaturalized. So it is with the more modern enthusiast who tells you that 'his life has been changed'; with that moment of decision to look back upon, he finds (at least for a time) that virtues or abstinences which hitherto meant laborious effort now 'come easy to him.' Instead of resolving to conquer his temptations, he believes that he will conquer his temptations, and does." (223-224.)

The gift of "tongues" makes the tongues speaker feel they have entered into communion with God, and with those who share this gift or are seeking it. They think that it is an assurance of spiritual security and it furnishes them an experience on which to ground their faith.

Dr. Pattison observed that "The glossolalic knows his 'tongue' well, that it is a familiar object to him. Because of this and his perception that it brings him closer to God, his 'tongue' gives him security when he needs it." (84.)

WHY TONGUES ALONE?

Tongues constituted only one gift, and were inferior to certain other gifts; so why is it that some people today seek only the gift of tongues? Could it be that some seek the gift of tongues, rather than the gift of working other miracles, because it is easier to deceive oneself into thinking he has spoken in tongues, since he can learn how to do it, than it is to deceive oneself into thinking that he can say to a man lame from birth: Rise and walk, and the man rises and walks?

CHAPTER IV

HOW TO SPEAK IN TONGUES

In some cases individuals are taught how to speak in tongues, and in other cases they may learn by the examples which they see around them and which they become confident they can imitate. There is no scriptural justification for *teaching anyone* to speak in tongues. The very effort to teach people how to speak in tongues proves that they do not have what the Bible calls the gift of tongues. Although it is true that there may be conditions attached to a gift, there is no scriptural justification for saying that one of the conditions is that one must learn from men how to speak in tongues. What are some of the instructions given to some of those who seek the gift of tongues?

DO IT

One minister told tongue seekers that: "In order to speak in tongues, you must cease speaking in English, for you cannot speak two languages at the same time. When you have been quiet before the Lord, and your thoughts are focused on Christ, you simply lift up your voice and speak out confidently. You take no thought for what you are saying: to the natural ear it is just a series of sounds. The first syllables may be halting and inarticulate, but as you continue to speak forth in faith, the Spirit will take the sounds of your voice and shape a beautiful language of prayer and praise.

"The Devil will be right at hand to challenge your experience—telling you that you made it all up, or that it sounds foolish and crazy. (Everyone seems to experience this testing.) But if you continue in faith, the Lord will give you freedom and confidence in your new tongues. And as you use it daily in your private devotions, you will learn what a wonderful blessing the Lord has given you." (As quoted in *The Christian News*, Nov. 25, 1968, 11.)

If this were the miraculous work of the Spirit they would not have to start out in a halting fashion, and practice until they did a good job of it. The individual has been told to talk without using English, and he does it. It sounds like non-

53

sense, but to keep him from discerning that he is deceiving himself, the minister said that doubts are temptations from the devil! Instead of listening to the devil you are to listen to God in faith! However, there is no proof this is of God. Furthermore, God has not promised us the gift of tongues today. God has not said that if you will be quiet before Him, if you will refrain from speaking in your own language, and if you launch out and make a series of sounds that He will fashion it into a language and you will be the possessor of the gift of tongues. To believe this is to believe what a man has promised you, and not what God has promised. Biblical faith is not a full persuasion that what some man has promised you, God will perform. Like Abraham, our faith should be a full assurance that what God "had promised, he was able also to perform." (Rom. 4:21.)

God has not promised us, as He did Abraham, that we shall have a child in our old age. We could not have a Biblical faith that our wives will bear children long after their wombs are dead (Rom. 4:19). God has not promised us the gift of apostleship, the gift of miracles, the gift of knowledge, or the gift of tongues; therefore, we cannot seek such with a faith which is grounded on God's word. We must first show that God has promised these things *to us*, and if He has, we should seek and find not one of them, but all of them; that is, someone in the church should have one, some another, until in the church all of them are found. But let us not think we are showing great faith in God when *we* promise ourselves something, or *some man* promises us something, and then we think God will perform what men have promised us.

RESOLVE NOT TO USE ENGLISH

Another author wrote: "You simply lapse into silence and resolve to speak not in a syllable of any language you have ever learned . . . The first sounds will sound strange and unnatural to your ear, and they may be halting and inarticulate (have you ever heard a baby learning to talk?)" (Gromacki, 41.)

On this we observed: *First*, his emphasis was not on the Spirit giving different gifts to different people, according to His will (I Cor. 12:8-11), but that anyone who wants tongues should go ahead and exercise the gift and he will get it.

54

Second, if one gets the gift of tongues by launching out and uttering syllables that are not one's native tongue, why not get the other gifts by just exercising them? Who are they to deny that this is the way you get the other gifts? *Third,* as Gromacki pointed out, Paul said they were to seek to pray with the understanding (I Cor. 14:15). *Fourth,* he also observed that such baby talk, or that which parallels it, does not fit in with Paul's teaching on maturity and putting away childish things (I Cor. 1420; 13:11). *Fifth,* there is no indication in the Bible that people learned how to speak in tongues, and that they improved with practice.

THINK VISUALLY AND MAKE SOUNDS

Another instructed those who sought the gift "(1) to think visually and concretely, rather than abstractedly: for example, to try to visualize Jesus as a person; (2) consciously to yield their voices and organs of speech to the Holy Spirit; (3) to repeat certain elementary sounds which he told them, such as 'bah-bah-bah,' or something similar. He then laid his hands on the head of each seeker, prayed for him, and the seeker did actually speak in tongues." (Gromacki, 42.)

Why not say that if you want to heal the sick, one should think concretely, yield his hands to the Spirit, lay his hands on a person, pray for them, and tell them to get up for they have been healed? The less the sick person has wrong with him, the better this method will work!! If you want the gift of prophecy, think visually, repeat some elementary truths you have heard before, and the first thing you know you will be prophesying by the inspiration of the Spirit.!!

If these are the ways one learns to speak in tongues, there is no reason that anyone should not get the gift, for anyone can think concretely, repeat elementary sounds, and make vocal utterances of some kind or another.

We see how easy it is for them to be deceived. The individual who is told how to speak in tongues, and that he ought to seek this "spiritual experience," follows the instructions and is able to utter sounds. If he tries at all, he cannot fail to do it. Having been able to do it, he thinks he has what the Bible calls the gift of tongues.

YOU PERFECT IT BY PRACTICE

The history of glossolalia, in the few cases which have been closely studied, indicates that they develop from an initiatory stage to a habitual one. "Initially, the individual who pursues glossolalia has attended religious or quasi-religious meetings where the utterances are heard for the first time. There is evidence to suggest that if the individual wishes glossolalia for himself, he sets about to learn how to reproduce it. In some settings, the religious leaders may actually provide a few sample utterances asking the initiate to repeat segments of glossolalia after them. In some instances, the counselor will suggest that the initiate imagine 'foreign words' and try to speak them. In other instances, a charismatic leader speaks in tongues and an impressionistic initiate may attempt to follow the leader whispering or talking to himself.

"Glossolalic utterances which are heard are stored in the memory until the decision is made to speak in tongues. The stored memory fragments may be brought into awareness and may even be practiced, i. e., recited over and over again to oneself until an acceptable form of glossolalia is mastered. With its mastering, 'spontaneous' glossolalic utterances may be externalized for the first time. The glossolalic utterances may first be spoken under a variety of effective and emotional states. When spoken, the glossolalia may be similar to that of the group where it was learned or similar to the glossolalic leader who taught it. As the initiate speaks glossolalia on more and more occasions, the speech becomes more individualized until eventually the utterances are expressive of the personality and behavior of the speaker. With repeated use of 'tongues' the speech becomes automatic and habitual." (Pattison, 80.)

Some of the subjects studied by Dr. Pattison "reported that one of their favorite pastimes was creating new words for their glossolalic vocabulary." (81.) There are cases where the use of it seemed playful and the individuals seemed to enjoy the sounds they produced. On the other hand, some seem to be pleading with the one who is listening. One said that a personal problem occupied her mind at the time she spoke, and with some it is occasionally done without awareness just as one "might blink his eye or tap his fingers without total awareness and volition." (81.) Some did it to reduce tension, some for entertainment or to keep from being bored while "engaged in rote motor tasks used glossolalia to avoid anxiety situations by blocking out the environment through listening to their own utterances, and hereby altering the state of consciousness." (83-84.) This diversion of the attention could lead to peace of mind.

SELF-INDUCED
One Presbyterian missionary who experienced glossolalia, re-examined his position, and concluded it was not from God. At its heart, he wrote, it has "a false mysticism which is contrary to the word of God." It is "auto-suggestion, self-induced —piously, yes, but wrongly and unscripturally." (Quoted by Anthony A. Hoekema, 133.) The instructions which we have mentioned make it clear that such tongues are self-induced. When we add to the instructions, the suggestion conveyed in a meeting in which others are speaking in tongues, we can see how in many cases the examples of others triggers the individual's determination to obey the instructions and to speak in tongues.

SELF-DECEPTION EASY
It is far easier to deceive one's self with reference to tongues, and prophecy, and interpretation, than with reference to the other gifts. If an individual tries to heal a cripple, for example, it is quite easy for him to see that he has failed. However, *failure is impossible* in the realm of tongues, interpretation, and prophecy or teaching. Any individual who can talk at all, can successfully follow the instruction to make sounds in other than his native tongue. Any individual can give an interpretation to what he hears if he just launches out and begins to interpret. Any individual can utter some sort of teaching if he will determine to do it; even if he has to prime himself by reading or remembering some scripture, and then saying something about it; or says the next thing which comes to mind.

Since interpretations and teaching can be delivered if one just launches out and does it, why do so many more seek tongues rather than the gift of prophecy and interpretation? The following explains at least some cases. *First,* tongues seem so much more miraculous than giving an interpretation or a teaching in your own language. *Second,* it is more exciting emotionally and gives one a feeling of confirmation that the others do not furnish as easily. *Third,* some have been taught that they must speak in tongues as a proof that they have received the Spirit, or that God accepts them as His child, or as proof that the gospel is true. Being convinced it is for everyone, and that they should seek it, they seek it and find it.

WHY NOT THE OTHER GIFTS?

As mentioned before, if one can be taught the gift of tongues, why cannot the other gifts be taught so that the seeker will know how to get them? If one can learn the gift of tongues, why can he not learn the gift of miracles? Why not instruct them as follows: If you are going to get the gift of healing you must give up any efforts to utilize doctors and natural means to heal people. With your mind concentrated on Christ, and with faith, launch out and tell the lame to arise and walk in the name of Jesus of Nazareth. At first you may not seem to make progress, and the devil may tell you that you are not accomplishing anything, but only making a fool out of yourself. Do not let your faith be shaken. Keep on healing, and the more you practice the better you will be able to exercise the gift of healing!! If this approach works for tongues, why will it not work for healings and other miraculous gifts? Could it be that it will not be as successful an approach with reference to miracles as it is with reference to tongues, because no one can check on the tongues (since they are unintelligible sounds) but they can check on the miracles? Of course, if they were the tongues which are mentioned in the Bible, we would be able to check and see what foreign language they were speaking and whether they learned the language or got it by inspiration.

If one wants the gift of interpretation, why not tell him: Cease trying to figure out in an uninspired way what the speaker in tongues is saying. Concentrate on Jesus, believe that you can interpret, do not think about what you are going to say, and launch out and interpret by saying whatever comes to mind. The Spirit will see to it that it is the interpretation of the message which was given in tongues. With practice you will improve in your power to interpret! With this type of approach to the gift of interpretation, which is similar to the approach to tongues, there is no reason that any assembly should lack an interpreter.

It is just as unscriptural to speak of learning to speak in tongues as it is to speak of learning to speak by inspiration in a known language; for one is speaking of languages when he speaks of Biblical tongues.

AN ANCIENT ERROR

So many things are new revivals of old errors. The idea of getting the gifts by acting as if one already has them, deceived people in Irenaeus' day (A. D. 120-202). He tells of a heretic named Marcus who taught women to prophesy by telling them to prophesy. "He devotes himself especially to women, and those such as are well-bred, and elegantly attired, and of great wealth, whom he frequently seeks to draw after him, by addressing them in such seductive words as these: 'I am eager to make thee a partaker of Charis, since the Father of all doth continually behold thy angel before His face. Now the place of thy angel is among us: it behooves us to become one. Receive first from me and by me (the gift) of Charis . . . Behold Charis has descended upon thee; open thy mouth and prophesy.' On the woman replying, 'I have never at any time prophesied, nor do I know how to prophecy;' then engaging, for the second time, in certain invocations, so as to astound his deluded victim he says to her, 'Open thy mouth, speak whatsoever occurs to thee, and thou shalt prophesy.' She then, vainly puffed up and elated by these words, and greatly excited in soul by the expectation that it is herself who is to prophesy, her heart beating violently (from emotion), reaches the requisite pitch of audacity, and idly as well as impudently utters some nonsense as it happens to occur to her, such as might be expected from one heated by an empty spirit. (Referring to this, one superior to me has observed, that the soul is both audacious and impudent when heated with empty air.) Henceforth she reckons herself as a prophetess, and expresses her thanks to Marcus for having imparted to her of his own Charis. She then makes the effort to reward him, not only by the gift of her possessions (in which way he has collected a very large fortune), but also by yielding up to him. her person, desiring in every way to be united to him, that she may become altogether one with him." *(Ante-Nicene Fathers,* I, 334-335.)

With such a simple way to get the gift of prophecy, of tongues, and of interpretation, the tongues movement ought not to lack for this type of prophet, prophetess, tongue speaker, and interpreter.

CHAPTER V

TYPES OF TONGUES

What types of vocal activity have been labeled "tongues"? What kinds of sounds have been identified by some people with the tongues spoken in Corinth? Are any of these tongues found in non-Biblical settings?

TONGUES OF MEN

The Scriptures teach that through the miraculous gift of tongues there were some Christians in the first century who spoke in human tongues which they had not learned. The new tongues which the apostle spoke on Pentecost were not new in that they were something unknown to man, but were human languages which they spoke by inspiration of the Spirit (Mk. 16:17, 20; Acts 2:4, 6, 8, 11). In writing to the Corinthians Paul spoke of the *tongues of men* (I Cor. 13:1).

TONGUES OF ANGELS

Angels can communicate with one another and with God. The tongues of angels are languages as surely as the tongues of man are languages. Paul would not have spoken of the *tongues* of men *and* of angels unless both were languages; languages which were known and spoken by men and languages which were spoken by angels.

PAGAN RELIGIONS

Tongues of a sort have been manifested in pagan cults which existed before Christ came to earth, and in others which have not been influenced by Christianity.

Virgil (70-19 B. C.) tells of one who inquired of the Priestess of Phoebus, at the cavern of the oracle of Sibyl.

They had gained
The threshold, when the maid exclaims: "'Tis time
To ask the oracles; lo! the god, the god!"
Before the doors thus speaking, suddenly
Nor countenance, nor hue, nor braided locks
Stayed in one fashion: but her bosom heaves,

Her heart swells wild with frenzy; and more vast
She seems, nor mortal rings her voice, when now
Touched by the nearer breath of deity.

- - -

He made
An end of speaking. But the seer, not yet
Patient of Phoebus, in the cavern storms
Immeasurably, if haply from her breast
She may shake off the mighty god; but he
So much the rather plies her raving mouth,
Tames her wild heart, and moulds her to his might.

- - -

In such
Words from the shrine doth Cumae's Sibyl chant
Her awful riddles, and echo through the cave,
In darkness shrouding truth; so shakes the reins
Apollo in her raving mouth, and plies
Deep in her breast the goad. Soon as had ebbed
Her frenzy, and the frantic lips were still.

- - -

"Oracular possession of the kind above described is also
common among savages and people of lower culture; and
Dr. Tylor, in his *Primitive Culture*, ii. 14, gives examples of
ecstatic utterance interpreted by the sane. Thus in the Sand-
wich Islands the god Oro gave his oracles through a priest
who 'ceased to act or speak as a voluntary agent, but with
his limbs convulsed, his features distorted and terrific, his
eyes wild and strained, he would roll on the ground foaming
at the mouth, and reveal the will of the God in shrill cries
and sounds violent and indistinct, which the attending priests
duly interpreted to the people'" (Encyclopaedia Britannica).
L. C. May wrote: "As a rule, speaking-in-tongues and kindred
phenomena are confined to those areas where there is spirit
possession and where inspirational shamans hold forth. Glossolalia can be and often is the result of spirit-induced ecstacy
making it possible for the inspirational shaman to cure,
exorcise, and prophesy . . . speaking-in-tongues is widespread and very ancient. Indeed, it is probable that as long as
man has had divination, curing sorcery, and propitiation of
spirits, he has had glossolalia." (As quoted by Pattison, 74.)

62

These were manifestations of what these people called "spirit-possession," and these spirits which possessed them were not viewed as the Holy Spirit, for of the Holy Spirit they either knew nothing; or if they had heard anything about the Spirit they had not accepted Him.

Concerning the Shango cult in Trinidad, George J. Jennings pointed out that "The induction of possession is at religious feasts or sacrifices where the combination of crowd excitement, singing, darkness, candles, circular rhythmic dancing, and other ceremonial phases are intensified by incessant drumming. The expected and common result is possession by the spirit or 'Powers' with a dramatic physical transformation including body vibrations, rhythmic bending of the body forward and backward, dilation of the eyes, and a fixed stare . . . The spirit then speaks through the possessed individual in a mixture of genuine language and nonsense syllables—in short, a form of glossolalia." (10.)

This certainly reminds one of some of the meetings in which people get the gift of "tongues." There are others, of course, that are not so visible in their display of emotional involvement, but even in these cases we find the testimonies, prayers, and the repetition of certain words such as the name of Jesus.

Other examples of tongues in pagan religion can be found in the worship of Amon around 1100 B. C., the writings of Plato who died around 347, Pythoness of Delphi, in some of the mystery religions, in Islam, and among Eskimos in Greenland. (Gromacki, 6-9.)

Some students of pagan glossolalia have classified them under six types. *First,* the language of supposed supernatural beings or spirits.

Second, sacerdotal languages which include obsolete words, foreign loanwords, and paraphrases along with the language of the spirits.

Third, the imitation of the sounds of "languages" of animals and birds.

Fourth, phonations frustes which involve groanings, mumblings, gurglings, whistlings and shriekings. In some cases this may take place in a drug induced state.

63

Fifth, they cited some instances where it was claimed that an individual, without having studied the language, spoke in a foreign language. Cases were cited of a shaman—a priest, or soothsayer, or prophet in certain pagan religions—among the Haida Indians in the Pacific Northwest, of an Indian in Northern California, and of some in the Peyote cult under the influence of the peyote drug. Only when under the influence of the drug, or the "spirit," could they do this. The author is convinced that cases of this kind, if they actually occurred, are similar to some other cases where people had heard these languages in times past, or had even spoken them as children, and in times of sickness, emotional frenzy, or a trance have recalled and spoken these languages. One man reported that he had "heard the Tibetan monks, during their ritual dances, speak in English with quotations from Shakespeare, and with profanity like drunken soldiers, or in German or French." This surely was not the work of the Spirit of God, and, unless it was the work of demons (which this author doubts), in frenzy they uttered phrases which they had heard in times past, but had not consciously committed to memory.

Sixth, the interpretation of tongues, or what one author called ermeneglossia. If the "tongue" is not a language of man, and if it is not understood by the audience or by the speaker, who would be able to check on the accuracy of the interpretation? (Jennings, 12-13.) The author once heard a "tongue" when all that was said was: "Angsee, angsigh." This was repeated a few times. Someone in the audience interpreted for around five minutes. The interpretation was a random weaving together of fragments of scriptures interwoven with "Hallelulah," "Praise the Lord," etc.

Tongues in Christendom today, if they were the tongues of the days of the apostles, would be so different from and so superior to the tongues of pagan cults that even the unbeliever could see the vast differences.

ANIMAL SOUNDS

Charles Wesley once shared a bedroom with a member of the Camisards movement, and he said that this man undressing "fell into violent agitations, and gobbled like a turkey-cock." (Knox, 361.)

LOUD NOISES

In the beginning of the Quaker movement, we are told that "many fall into dreadful tremblings in their whole bodies and joints, with risings and swellings in their bowels; shriekings, yellings, howlings and roarings." (Knox, 356.)

TRANCE OR DELIRIUM

The author read of one woman who during an illness recited passages of the Bible in Hebrew. She was an unlearned girl, but in her younger days she had worked in the home of a minister who in his study, and while he walked around the grounds, recited passages from the Old Testament in Hebrew. She had heard these time and time again and they had made an impression on her mind. Although she was not able to recall these passages at will, she did recite them when delirious.

Smith pointed out that: "In certain exceptional states of mind and body the power of memory receives a wonderful and abnormal strength. In the delirium of fever, in the ecstacy of a trance, men speak in their old age languages which they have never heard or spoken since their earliest youth." (1133-1134.)

Alma White wrote that: "I have known persons who were reared in homes where several languages were spoken, and while they were unable to speak in more than one language, through the hypnotic spell of demons in the tongues meetings they have been able to speak, in a measure, in the foreign languages with which they were familiar when they were children. They were enabled to recall things that had been forgotten for years." (86-87.) In the author's judgment this was not a case of "the hypnotic spell of demons" but something psychological which has occurred to other people also.

It would be difficult for a person in our age to keep from hearing at one time or another at least some phrases and sentences of another language. Even if one does not tune in on foreign broadcasts, he will hear languages being spoken, as well as interpreted; in newscasts, for example.

In the Camisard movement, which originated in France and spread to England, some claimed to speak in tongues as well as prophesy. One prophesied that a certain man would be resurrected five months after he was buried, and a John Lacy said he spoke fluently in Latin. Some asked, however, "If the Camisards really spoke with tongues, why did the Frenchmen normally prophesy in French, the Englishmen in English? There was no evidence that Mr. Lacy had forgotten his Latin as thoroughly as he claimed to have forgotten it. Really, nothing miraculous remained, unless it were true that Mr. Lacy could slide along the room with his heels, calves, and knees touching, 'antick gestures' as Mr. Spinckes complains, which 'do by no means suit with the influence of the Holy Spirit'." (Knox, 366, 369-370.)

When the dead man did not rise from the dead, they said that it was because they had been absent from the grave-yard since they were afraid of violence from the people. (p. 370.)

Sayce gives us another illustration where a tongue was long buried in the recesses of the mind, but suddenly returned to consciousness after hearing the language spoken for awhile. In speaking of Greece he wrote, "It was many years since I had last been there, and when I first landed the Greek that I heard sounded in my ears like the twittering of birds. Two or three days later the language seemed suddenly to return to me: I suppose it had been lying buried in the memory under successive layers of later impressions . . . " (*Reminiscences*, p. 324).

LIKE SLEEP TALKERS

Although glossolalia may sound like jargon aphasia, it is not due to a lesion in the brain. Although it may resemble vocalization of schizophasia, it is involuntary with him, but voluntary with the glossolalist—at least in most cases. It may also resemble non-language sounds produced by some who "talk" in their sleep. (Pattison, 78.)

BABBLING LIKE A BABY

Some teachers of tongues have told the seekers to imagine they are babies and then to babble like a baby. Even if they were not given such instructions, some studies indicate that "glossolalic speech tends to resemble the early speech qualities of young children prior to the organization of all the variables associated with adult language."

"Indeed, many of the qualities of glossolalic speech are those found in the speech of young children, which George Devereaux has outlined. A comparison of his outline of children's speech and glossolalic speech is striking. On this scale, one may suggest that glossolalic speech appears to be a regression to an early mode of speech in which vocalization is used for purposes other than just the communication of rational thought. This hypothesis receives further support from other data to be cited."

A higher frequency of vowels is found in glossolalia than in ordinary speech. Infant vocalizations have a high percentage of vowels.

"Study of the morphemic stratum of glossolalia reveals that the phonemes are combined in primarily 'open' syllables, i. e. that they begin and end with vowels. This characteristic is most prevalent in early speech development." Webster defines morpheme as "an element or property of language showing the relations between nouns, verbs, adjectives, and concrete adverbs. It may be a prefix or suffix (John's), a preposition, conjunction, relation adverb, auxiliary or copulative verb, intonation, accentuation, an ablaut variation, or an order of words."

". . . the neologistic stage of speech development in children" resembles glossolalia. Webster defines neology as "the use of a new word or words, or of new meanings . . ." While the child is learning new words and sounds, and experimenting with and practicing them, it resembles the sounds of glossolalists.

One study was made in which the glossolalia was recorded, and the glossolalist was asked, concerning each "word," what thought came to his mind in connection with it. Out of this came a speech "dealing with childhood experiences and unfilled wishes." (Pattison, 77-79.)

From his study of the speech of certain children, Jean Piaget concluded that there were two main divisions; socialized speech and ego-centric speech. Ego-centric speech was directed toward one's self. It involved the following: (a) Repetition of sounds which gave the child pleasure, but did not have to make sense to others. (b) Monologue in which the child talked to himself. (c) Collective monologue which was stimulated by the presence of others, but to which others were not expected either to listen or to understand.

The child also uses speech for the purpose of communicating with and influencing others. (Wayne E. Oates, 85-89.)

Tongue speakers also may repeat sounds which give them pleasure, they may speak to themselves, and they are stimulated in at least some cases by the presence of others to whom they do not speak, but in whose presence they speak. But sooner or later, they try to tell others of the value of speaking in tongues.

RESEMBLANCES TO THEIR NATIVE TONGUES

The sound and structure are related to the language background of the speakers, according to some studies, and not to those of a language foreign to the speaker. Some studies "on the phonemic strata indicate that the phonemes of the glossolalic utterance are closely associated with the language background of the speaker and that one would expect more diversity in the phonemic structure if different language systems were represented." (Pattison, 79.) Webster defines phoneme as: "A group of variants of a speech sound, usually all spelled with the same or equivalent letter and commonly regarded as the same sound, but varying somewhat with the same speaker according to different phonetic conditions (neighboring sounds, stress, length, intonation, etc.). Thus the *l* sound in leave, feel, truly, solely . . . "

Phonemics is defined as "pertaining to or of the nature of, a phoneme; of speech, sounds, constituting members of different phonemes . . . "

Eugene Nida concluded that "On the basis of what I have learned about this type of phenomena of 'tongues' in other parts of the world, apparently there is the same tendency to employ one's own inventory of sounds, in nonsense combinations, but with stimulated 'foreign' features. At least in West Africa and Latin America, the types of glossolalia employed seemed to fit into this description." (Gromacki, 67.)

PRACTICE MAKES PERFECT!

Studies, which included studies of volunteers, indicate that tongues range all the way from grunts to polished forms of utterances. The more they practice the more polished they can become. (Pattison, 77.) If such tongues were the gift of the Holy Spirit, the speakers should do as well the first time as they do after they have had a good deal of experience. When we learn a human language we use it very poorly at first, but as we practice we get better. When these people are *learning*—and we mean learning and not receiving something given to them by inspiration of the Spirit—to speak in tongues at least many of them improve with practice. The author has spoken in unintelligible "tongues" and, if he wanted to take the time to do so, he is confident he could improve with practice. However, his first time was considerably better than the ones he has heard in tongues meetings!

SOME INTERPRETED BY LIARS

The tongues in some cases have been interpreted by lying tongues of men; although in other cases they were by self-deluded men. S. E. Polovina told of going to a tongues meeting where none of the five or six languages which he spoke, nor of others which he had heard, were spoken. The next day he and seven other persons who spoke a number of foreign languages went to the meeting. The interpreter told what languages were spoken, and he told what was said. As it turned out, every one of these languages were known by the men whom Polovina had taken to the meeting, and they knew that none of these languages had been spoken. (A. J. Pollock, 71-73.)

NON-RELIGIOUS EXPERIMENTATION

At least two types of experiments have demonstrated that individuals can duplicate glossolalia just for the fun of it, or just to show that it can be done. *First,* one student group was asked to speak spontaneously in an unknown language. They had never heard of glossolalia. Another group, which believed in tongues, was also tape recorded during the exercise of the "gift" as a spiritual function. Some other people, who practiced glossolalia as a part of their religious faith, were asked to rate the two. They thought that both were genuine tongues, although they rated the one which had been done experimentally as better glossolalia than the one done sincerely.

Second, in another experiment some students were taken to Pentecostal churches. Later they were asked to speak in tongues as a laboratory experiment. They did so. "Their recordings were then played to glossolalists who described the glossolalia as beautiful examples." (Pattison, 78.)

These religious glossolalists should have diligently sought for the gift of interpretation or the discerning of spirits, so that they could have kept from being deceived in this manner!

If this was the work of the Holy Spirit, individuals doing it just for the experiment, and without the influence of the Holy Spirit, should not be able to do as good a job, or even a better job than those supposedly filled by the Spirit.

Dr. Mansell Pattison pointed out that: "Any of us could 'speak in tongues' if we adopted a passive attitude about controlling our body and speech and had an emotional tension pressing for expression. A familiar example is the explosive, contagious laughter of a group which reaches a point where everyone is 'too weak to move' from laughing. Trying to talk while thus laughing results in vocalizations which have all the characteristics of glossolalia." (As quoted by Anthony A. Hoekema, 131.)

CONCLUSIONS

Pattison concluded that: "In sum, the structural linguistic data suggest that glossolalia has specific linguistic structures based on the language tongue of the speaker, that the linguistic organization is limited, and the capacity to speak in this type of semi-organized language can be replicated under experimental conditions. Thus, glossolalia does not appear to be a 'strange language', but rather the aborted formation of familiar language." (p. 78.) In the few cases where actual languages have been spoken, the individual heard these languages earlier in life.

CHAPTER VI

TONGUES WERE LANGUAGES

Were the tongues mentioned in the New Testament languages of men, or were at least some of them ecstatic utterances composed of non-intelligible sounds?

THE WORD "TONGUE" IN THE NEW TESTAMENT

The word "tongue" is used in the Bible in the following ways. It is the physical organ which is involved in speech. Zacharias' tongue was loosed and he spake (Lk. 1:64). The rich man wanted his tongue cooled (Lk. 16:24). Of the person who was deaf "and had an impediment in his speech," we are told: "And his ears were opened, and the bond of his tongue was loosed, and he spake plain." (Mk. 7:32, 35.)

Tongue can refer to the speech which it produces. David said: "Therefore my heart was glad, and my tongue rejoiced; moreover my flesh also shall dwell in hope." (Acts 2:26.) The tongue as the organ of speech is said to speak, therefore Paul spoke of every tongue confessing that Jesus Christ is Lord (Phil. 2:11).

Tongue also means language (Acts 2:4, 11). The book of Revelation refers to a great multitude "out of every nation and of (all) tribes and peoples and *tongues* . . ." (Rev. 7:9; 5:9; 10:11; 11:9; 13:7; 14:6).

Behm maintained that in Corinth "glossolalia is an unintelligible ecstatic utterance. One of its forms of expression is a muttering of words or sounds without interconnection or meaning. Parallels may be found for this phenomenon in various forms and at various periods and places in religious history." He then discussed its appearance in paganism. Furthermore, he said that some glossolalia was made up of the tongues of men, and some of the tongues of angels (Behm in Gerhard Kittel, I, 721-722). He also said that tongues in Acts 2 belongs to the same context, and "bears essentially the same characteristics as the glossolalia depicted by Paul." (724.) He admitted that Luke represents the tongues as being foreign languages, but he claimed that it was "a legendary development of the story of the first and significant occur-

71

ence of glossolalia in Christianity." ". . . the tradition in Acts 2 is confused, and we are not given any very reliable picture of what really happened. The historical kernel is a mass ecstasy on the part of the disciples which includes outbreaks of glossolalia" (725). This illustrates the fact that when the Bible does not agree with their opinions some people repudiate the Bible.

Were the tongues in Corinth ecstatic utterances of unintelligible sounds or were they human languages?

JESUS PROMISED NEW TONGUES

New tongues were one of the signs which Jesus said would follow believers (Mk. 16:17). Did this mean ecstatic utterances? No, reference was made to human languages. *First,* even those who think that I Cor. 14 referred to ecstatic utterances, agree that usually tongues in the New Testament refers to languages. *Second,* the word in Mk. 16:17 for new was *kainos,* not *neos.* Abbott-Smith said it meant "the new primarily in reference to quality, the fresh, unworn," but that *neos* had reference to that which is recent (226). It is likely the word *neos* would have been used if the language was new in the sense of not having been spoken before. *Third,* that new referred to languages new to the speakers, and not to ecstatic utterance, is *proved* by the fact that the very first fulfilment involved human language (Acts 2:4, 8, 6, 11; Gromacki, p. 59).

ACTS IS A COMMENTARY ON MARK 16:20

Jesus said "these signs shall accompany them that believe . . . they shall speak with new tongues." He gave this promise when He gave the great commission to the apostles (Mk. 16:17, 14-15). After His ascension they went forth and these signs followed believers and confirmed the word. "So then the Lord Jesus, after he had spoken unto them, was received up into heaven, and sat down at the right hand of God. And they went forth, and preached everywhere, the Lord working with them, and confirming the word by the *signs* that followed." (Mk. 16:19-20.) Tongues were one of the signs.

The book of Acts records at least some of the things which are briefly mentioned in Mark's summary (Mk. 16:20). It was after Christ ascended, and sat down at the right hand of God, that they went forth and preached and confirmed the word. This is clear from the fact that Christ told them to wait until they received power, that the power would come when the Spirit came, and then they would begin their work of witnessing (Lk. 24:46-49; Acts 1:8). On the first Pentecost after Christ's resurrection, the Spirit came and they proclaimed Christ's reign at God's right hand and pointed out that Christ had sent the Spirit and worked the miracles which took place on Pentecost (Acts 2:1-4, 33, 34-36). Acts, in recording the work of the apostles under the guidance of the Spirit, is a commentary on the statements in Mk. 16:17, 19-20. Acts presents in some detail that which was promised in Mk. 16:17 and summarized in Mk. 16:19-20.

What does Acts, an inspired commentary on the meaning of these gifts, reveal concerning the new tongues? It so clearly reveals what they were, that it is impossible for anyone to read it and misunderstand the fact that the tongues were languages. Luke tells us that "they were all filled with the Holy Spirit, and began to speak with other *tongues*, as the Spirit gave them utterance." (Acts 2:4).

What were the tongues?

They were *utterances*. They *spoke* as the Spirit gave them *utterance*. This equates the *speaking* with the *utterance*, and the utterance with the *tongues*. Literally it meant "as the Spirit gave them to speak." (James Hastings, II, 635.)

The tongues were *languages*. "Now there were dwelling at Jerusalem Jews, devout men, from every nation under heaven. And when this sound (as of a rushing mighty wind, Acts 2:2) was heard, the multitude came together, and were confounded, because that every man heard them *speaking in his own language*." This proves that *"to speak* with other tongues" (2:4), was *speaking in languages* (2:6).

We are again told that the tongues were languages, and the native languages of the Jews who were gathered from many different parts of the Roman empire. "And how hear we, every man in *his own language* wherein we were *born?*" And then it lists many different countries (Acts 2:8-10).

As their own native languages, the tongues were understandable by the audience. They *heard* in their own language,

73

they did not need an interpreter (Acts 2:6, 8), and they knew *these men were speaking of God's mighty works.* ". . . we hear them *speaking in our tongues* the mighty works of God." (Acts 2:11.) The identification of tongues with languages could not be clearer!

Luke gives us an inspired interpretation of the meaning of tongues. They were languages. When the Bible explains what is meant by tongues, we must accept the explanation. When a passage presents some difficulty to us, concerning the nature of tongues, we must not view tongues as something other than languages *unless* the context of the difficult passages makes it clear that something other than languages is meant by tongues.

As Gromacki remarked: "This first instance of the phenomenon of speaking in tongues sets the Biblical pattern and standard for all subsequent tongue-speaking. It must be a foreign language, and it must be the foreign languages of those who are present when the gift of interpretation is not exercised." (Gromacki, 60.)

The household of Cornelius received the like gift as did those on Pentecost, and they spoke in tongues (Acts 11:16-17; 1:5; 2:1-4; 10:46). What they said magnified God (Acts 10:46). In this way, too, it was similar to what took place on Pentecost for then the apostles spoke in tongues of God's mighty works (Acts 2:11).

What took place in Corinth was also embraced in Jesus' promise that tongues, among other signs, would follow believers and confirm the word (Mk. 16:17, 20). The apostle Paul carried the gospel to Corinth (Acts 18:1-11). Through tongues and other signs God revealed and confirmed the word in Corinth. Paul told them that "the testimony of Christ was confirmed in you: so that ye come behind in no gift . . . " (I Cor. 1:6-7.) Paul's preaching in their midst was in "demonstration of the Spirit and of power." (2:4.) Corinth was one of the places which Mark included in "everywhere" when he said: "they went forth, and *preached everywhere,* the Lord working with them, and confirming the word by the signs that followed." (Mk. 16:20.) The confirmation in Corinth, with reference to the signs of Mk. 16:17, was like the confirmation in Jerusalem or any other place. In both places tongues were used and in both places they were a sign, just as Jesus said they would be. (Mk. 16:17; Acts 2:4, 6, 8, 11, 33; I Cor. 14:22). Well did Lenski write: "As the promise (in Mk. 16:17, J. D. B.) is one, so the fulfilment is one regardless of the place where the fulfilment occurs."

Unless there is sufficient reason to interpret the matter otherwise, one should interpret Corinthians in the light of Luke's inspired explanation of the nature of tongues. As Lenski pointed out: "The next step is to recognize the fact that Luke's description as given in the Acts is decisive for what Paul writes in Corinthians. This is reversed by some. They seek to determine what happened in Corinth and then either square Luke's account with what they think occurred at Corinth or posit two different gifts of tongues . . . Luke is the one who fully describes what the tongues are while Paul takes for granted that his readers know what they are and therefore offers no description. Luke writes for a reader (Theophilus) who may never have heard of this gift, at least may never have seen this gift in operation. Paul writes for readers who have often heard members of their own congregation speak in tongues. This is decisive as to the Scriptural starting point." (Lenski, 504-505.)

WHY MOCKED?

If actual languages were spoken why did some mock? "And they were all amazed, and were perplexed, saying one to another, What meaneth this? But others mocking said, They are filled with new wine." (Acts 2:12-13.) If the apostles spoke in other languages, why did these men mock? *First*, there is no doubt that the apostles spoke in other languages. Acts is very clear on this point (Acts 2:4, 6, 8, 11). One must not allow this snap judgment of mockers to offset the clear affirmation that they spoke languages. *Second*, Peter said they were not drunken for it was much too early in the day for people to have drunk to such excess that they were drunken. Of course, this would not apply in our culture where some people stay up all night drinking!! Charles Wordsworth suggested that it was not yet the time of year for new wine to be available, but F. F. Bruce pointed out that they had ways of keeping wine new, or sweet (65.) The main argument of Peter, that they were not drunken, was that this was the fulfilment of prophecy (Acts 2:16-17). *Third*, Charles Wordsworth has suggested what is likely the answer to the question of why they mocked. "The native Jews may have been the mockers because they did not know the foreign languages spoken by the apostles, and those foreign tongues seemed to them like a jargon of unmeaning sounds . . . " This same observation would apply to any others who heard some of the languages which were not their own language. Professor Sayce relates an incident from his own experience which illustrates this. He wrote: "It was many years since I had last been there, and when I first landed the Greek that I heard sounded in my ears like the twittering of birds." He said this even though at one time he had known the language (324.)

HOW MANY LANGUAGES WERE SPOKEN?

We do not have to know how many languages were spoken, in order to know that the apostles spoke in other languages. Were around eighteen languages spoken? (Acts 2:9-11.) The Phrygians and Pamphylians both spoke Greek, but "in different idioms; the Parthians, Medes, and Elamites all spoke Persian, but in different provincial forms." (Vincent, I, 450.) Galileans spoke a dialect which differed from that in Judaea (Acts 2:7; Mk. 14:70).

David Greene suggested that: "As we cannot understand literally, in its full extent, the phrase 'out of every nation under heaven,' so we need not suppose that each one of the sixteen or seventeen different nationalities numerated spake or heard in a language different from all the others. Probably in all the countries mentioned no more than five or six different languages were in common use." (David Greene, 106.)

However, the word for language which is used in Acts 2:6 is the word which is also used for dialect.

Since there were only twelve apostles, some of them must have spoken first in one language and in another if every distinct dialect and language was spoken on that day.

Wordsworth suggested that it may be that "the foreign tongue which each disciple was enabled to speak collected about him a group of those strangers then at Jerusalem who

spoke that particular tongue; and so all were evangelized."
(11.)

A MIRACLE OF HEARING?

It has been thought by some that the miracle was one of
hearing and not of speaking. The apostles spoke in but one
language, but the people heard in their own language. This, of
course, would be a miracle, but we do not believe this is what
took place. First, Christ said *they would speak* in new tongues,
and Luke affirmed that they "began *to speak with other
tongues.*" (Mk. 16:17; Acts 2:4.) If it was a miracle of hearing, the miracle occurred in those—the audience—who did
not have the Spirit in a miraculous way and not in the
apostles who did have the Spirit.

TONGUES OF ANGELS

Paul said: "If I speak with the tongues of men and of
angels, but have not love, I am become sounding brass, or a
clanging cymbal." (I Cor. 13:1.) Some have maintained that
their ecstatic utterances are the language of angels. If one
is not speaking in a human language, it may be an angelic
tongue. On this we make the following observations:

Paul supposed a hypothetical case, and said *"if* I speak
with the tongues of men and of angels." We know he spoke
in human languages, but we do not know that he spoke in
the language of angels (I Cor. 14:18-19).

The reference to tongues of angels may well be a superlative, just as in Paul's statement that though we or an angel
preach any other gospel we are to be anathema (Gal. 1:8).
Paul was not saying that an angel from heaven would preach
another gospel, but emphasizing the fact that the gospel is
the only and the final gospel. Just so, even if one spoke with
the tongues of angels, but had not love, he was nothing. This
superlative underscores the fundamental importance of love.

In his commentary Matthew Pool suggested that just as
manna was called angels' food (Psa. 78:25), without suggesting that angels ate, but that it was a most excellent food, so
Paul may mean that if one expressed himself in the most excellent way it can be described as the tongues of angels.

This would not be the things Paul heard when he was
caught up to the third heaven, for he was forbidden to speak

these; and surely they would not have been authorized for interpretation by an interpreter of tongues (II Cor. 12:4). If this was the language of angels, no one on earth was authorized to use it.

" . . . the very fact that the word 'tongues' is used just once with 'men' and 'angels' shows that human and angelic languages can be grouped together. They have something in common. They are both languages, known and understood by the listeners."

" . . . whenever men and angels conversed together in Biblical times, they were able to carry on an intelligent conversation in known languages without difficulty or interpretation."

"Rather than dividing languages into known and unknown, Paul is affirming that all tongues phenomena were in the form of definite languages, not ecstatic utterances." (Gromacki, p. 63.)

What proof do they have that the sounds which they utter are the sounds spoken by angels? Does someone with the gift of interpretation certify that it is angelic? If the individual has no way of proving that it is angelic, and if no one else can investigate it and identify it, how do they know it is angelic?

How could an angelic language be a sign to an unbeliever, since no unbeliever could know such a language? (I Cor. 14:22.) Even if someone claimed to interpret it, it would still not be a sign. Unless on some other grounds we have faith in the gifts of the speaker and the interpreter, what proof is there to an unbeliever when a series of unearthly sounds are supposedly interpreted by someone whose credentials as an interpreter we cannot confirm? Surely they would have to have some among them to confirm with miracles the existence of such gifts.

Because a series of sounds do not constitute a human language is not proof within itself that it is the language of angels. Do babies speak in the tongue of angels? Because you do not know what a white object in a grave yard is, does it mean it must be a ghost? Because you have never had a certain feeling in a religious service before, is this sufficient proof that it must be from the Holy Spirit? What *proof* do they have, other than their own opinion, that it is the language of the angels?

If the one who interprets the tongue of angels does not give us a message from God which is not already found in the Bible, of what value was it to convey to us through the speaker and the interpreter a message which God has already revealed and confirmed in the Bible?

If it is a new message, what miraculous confirmation do they give that it is indeed from God? What proof do they have that it is in harmony with the Bible?

Even if they have a genuine gift of an angelic tongue, they must not use it when no interpreter is present to inform others of its meaning (I Cor. 14:28).

If these utterances are angelic tongues, some of the tongues speakers are forced to the conclusion that anyone can learn to speak an angelic language by babbling like a baby, and with practice do even a better job.

Even if some in Corinth spoke with the tongues of angels, why is there such an abundance of the tongues of angels today—which we cannot check on and which cannot be a sign to us—and such a dirth of evidence of the gift of the tongues of men? Paul spoke of the tongues of men (I Cor. 13:1), so why do the tongues speakers fail to speak in the tongues of men as the apostles did on Pentecost? We need far more than the unconfirmed word of these speakers in order to believe they speak with the tongues of angels.

If there were such a gift it has ceased because Paul said tongues would cease, and they have ceased (I Cor. 13:8).

KINDS OF TONGUES (I Cor. 12:10)

Paul said that there are kinds of tongues, and there are diversities of tongues (I Cor. 12:10, 28). *Genos* or kinds means a family (Acts 4:6), a nation or race (Mk. 7:26), or "a kind, sort, class"; such as fish (Matt. 13:47), or demons (Matt. 17:2), or tongues (I Cor. 12:10, 28; 14:10). Although different kinds of fish exist, they are still fish. "From this it can be concluded that there are many 'kinds' of languages, but they are all languages . . . they have a definite vocabulary and grammatical construction. Paul could not have possibly combined known, foreign languages with unknown, ecstatic

79

utterances under the same classification. They simply are not related to each other." (Gromacki, 62.)

Paul said there were varieties of tongues, and this suits well the idea of languages. He also spoke of his own use of tongues, and of a tongue (I Cor. 12:10; 14:18-19).

Paul spoke of "kinds (plural) of tongues." (I Cor. 12:10, 28). It was not the gift of tongue as if there were only one, but the gift of different kinds of tongues. If tongues were simply ecstatic utterance which were just a series of sounds unidentifiable with any human language, how could there be different kinds of ecstatic utterance? An ecstatic utterance would be an ecstatic utterance, an unintelligible series of sounds, regardless of whether the individual uttered the sounds slowly, with rapidity, loudly, or softly.

PAUL IS NOT DEALING WITH ECSTATIC UTTERANCES

The tongues had to consist of sounds which convey an intelligible message even though those who heard the speech did not understand what was said. They could not be sounds without sense, because in such a case even a man with the inspired gift of interpretation could not make sense out of them. Unless inspiration put meaning into the sounds, inspiration itself could not get meaning out of the sounds. The tongues contained messages which if interpreted edified the church. How could sounds which embodied no meaning contain material which when interpreted edified the church? (I Cor. 14:5, 26-27.)

Tongues were languages which could be learned naturally, or which were understood by those who had the gift of interpretation (Acts 2:8; I Cor. 12:10, 30; 14, 15, 19, 27). Both these fit in with the position that tongues were human languages, but both do not fit the position that they are ecstatic utterances.

Furthermore, as Charles Hodge pointed out, language—instead of unintelligible sounds—makes good sense even in the passages which have been used by some to show that an intelligible language was not under consideration. Consider the following passages:

The man who gives thanks to God, for example, in a foreign language which no one else understands is speaking to God, but he is not speaking to men (14:14; 16, 17, 2). No man, unless an interpreter is present (14:27), in the audience understands and, therefore, they cannot say Amen "at the giving of thanks, seeing" they "knoweth not what thou sayest." (14:16.) Since they do not understand they are not edified (14:17, 5). It is true that literally no man understands gibberish, but it is just as true that those not acquainted with a language do not understand it any more than they would understand meaningless sounds; for the foreign language is without meaning to them (14:11).

It is thought that the following verses indicate that tongues were unintelligible sounds. "For if I pray in a tongue, my spirit prayeth, but my understanding is unfruitful. What is it then? I will pray with the spirit, and I will pray with the understanding also: I will sing with the spirit, and I will sing with the understanding also. Else if thou bless with the spirit, how shall he that filleth the place of the unlearned say the Amen at thy giving of thanks, seeing he knoweth not what thou sayest? For thou verily givest thanks well, but the other is not edified." (I Cor. 14:15-17.) Hodge commented that: "Although these passages, taken by themselves, might seem to indicate that the speaker himself did not understand what he said, and even that his intellect was in abeyance, yet they may naturally mean only that the understanding of the speaker was unprofitable to others; and speaking with the understanding may mean speaking intelligibly. It is not necessary, therefore, to infer from these passages, that to speak with tongues was to speak in a state of ecstasy, in a manner unintelligible to any human being." We go farther than Hodge and affirm that these very verses indicate that this is what Paul is saying. The main point Paul is making is that one should use the gifts in the assembly so that they will be *profitable to the church*, and not just to the individual using the gift. "But now, brethren, if I come unto you speaking with tongues, *what shall I profit you, unless* I speak to you either by way of revelation, or of knowledge, or of prophesying, or of teaching? . . . unless ye utter by the tongue speech easy to be understood, how shall it be known what is spoken? for ye will be speaking into the air." (14:6,9.) "So also ye, since ye are zealous of spiritual gifts, seek that ye may abound *unto the edifying of the church.*" (14:12.)

How does this apply to the use of tongues in the church? They should be employed so as to edify the church. Therefore, Paul immediately said: "Wherefore let him that speaketh in a tongue pray that he may interpret." (14:13.) Why should he want to interpret—and obviously this means to interpret the tongue to the church so it can be edified? "For if I pray in a tongue, my spirit prayeth, but my understanding is unfruitful." (14:14.) Unfruitful in what sense? What has Paul just been saying? He has been writing of one speaking so that what he says is understood by the church, and therefore his use of the gift has borne fruit insofar as the congregation is concerned. He had just said that one should pray that he may interpret in order that the church might be edified (14:12-13). If he does not interpret, his understanding is unfruitful. In other words, if he does not interpret the message to the church his gift and his understanding have borne no fruit.

That this is Paul's meaning is borne out by what he goes on to say through verse 19. "What is it then?" What will Paul do in order to keep his understanding from being fruitless; from failing to bear fruit in edifying the church? "What is it then? I will pray with the spirit, and I will pray with the understanding also: I will sing with the spirit, and I will sing with the understanding also." (14:15.) If by this he means that he will speak in tongues, that he will himself understand what is said, what good has that done the congregation? Regardless of how clearly one understands a language, if he uses it in the presence of those who do not understand it he is just as unintelligible to them as if he spoke in a series of meaningless sounds which he himself did not understand. Paul is not saying that I will pray and sing so that I understand and am personally edified. He is speaking in the context of the assembly, and the understanding of the audience (14:6-15). If he spoke in a tongue which was understandable to him, but not to them, he would not be authorized to do so in the assembly unless an interpreter was present

(14:27). And Paul had just said that if you speak in tongues, you should also want to interpret (14:13).

That praying with the understanding means uttering words which are understood by the audience is demanded by the thing Paul immediately said. What did it mean to pray with the spirit and the understanding? It means to speak things in an intelligible language so that the unlearned could know what you are saying and endorse it. If spoken only with the spirit, but without understanding—in other words, if your understanding was unfruitful—what would be the impact on the audience? "Else if thou bless with the spirit," and this implies blessing with the spirit only and not with the understanding also, "how shall he that filleth the place of the unlearned say the Amen at thy giving of thanks, seeing he knoweth not what thou sayest? For thou verily givest thanks well, but the other is not edified." (14:16-17.) In other words, to pray with the understanding did not have reference just to personal understanding, without interpreting the meaning to the audience. It meant to pray (either in his own language or followed by an interpretation) so that the audience understood. In this way your understanding was fruitful. If you gave thanks well, but the people did not understand, your understanding was fruitless. If you prayed without the understanding, the people could not understand and say Amen. To pray and to sing with the understanding was to pray and to sing so that the unlearned can say Amen at thy giving of thanks because he knows what you say.

This is made clear by Paul's conclusion that "in the church I had rather *speak five words with my understanding,* that I might instruct others also, than ten thousand words in a tongue." (14:19.) To speak with one's understanding was to speak so that others could be instructed and edified. This shows that it means to pray and sing "with the understanding" so that the audience is instructed and the understanding is therefore fruitful. (14:14-19.)

If one could not interpret what he had said in the tongue, in other words if he could not speak with the understanding so his understanding was fruitful and edified the congregation, someone else was to interpret it or he was to be silent (14:27-28). In this way, through another, his understanding

83

would be fruitful. It would produce fruit in edifying the church.

TONGUES WERE LANGUAGES

It does not take a miraculous gift of the Spirit for an individual to utter non-sensible sounds. Anyone can do it deliberately, or when he is so emotionally stirred that he wants to utter a series of unintelligible sounds. However, it took a miraculous gift of the Spirit to enable someone to speak in a language which he had not learned.

Paul said that his speaking could not profit them unless it conveyed instruction; therefore unless the tongue was understood it could not profit the church (14:6). He illustrated this by instruments. Concerning a pipe or a harp, "if they give not a distinction in the sounds, how shall it be known what is piped or harped? For if the trumpet gives an uncertain voice, who shall prepare himself for war? So also ye, unless ye utter by the tongue *speech easy to understand,* how shall it be known what is spoken? For ye will be speaking into the air." (14:7-9.) Meaningless sounds do not convey meaning. They are just sounds in the air. Even though the speaker in tongues can speak to God (14:2), insofar as the audience is concerned their speech is useless. Instead of instructing the minds of the hearers, it is speaking into the air and not into the hearts of men. It is as vain as merely moving one's lips and vibrating the air. It was not that they were uttering by the tongue sounds which were not speech, but speech which was not understood by the people, and therefore they did not know what was spoken.

Paul pointed out that there are an indeterminate number of voices in the world, but regardless of how many there are each of them has its meaning. "There are, it may be, so many kinds of voices in the world, and no kind is without signification." The margin translates it: "nothing is without voice." (14:11.) In other words, "no tongue is not a tongue" or language (Godet). By voice it is clear he means language, for he continued by saying: "If then I know not *the meaning of the voice,* I shall be to him that speaketh a barbarian, and he that speaketh will be a barbarian unto me." (14:11.) All of the voices of which Paul spoke, in speaking of the use of tongues, were voices which had significance. All languages have signification, therefore he is speaking in the context of tongues. This is further borne out by verse 11. However, unintelligible sounds, sounds of so-called ecstasy, are without signification for they are sounds without meaning. Therefore, they are not the voices of which Paul speaks.

Paul said: "If then I know not the meaning of the voice, I shall be to him that speaketh a barbarian, and he that speaketh will be a barbarian unto me." (I Cor. 14:11.) To know not the meaning of the voice, was to know not the meaning of the tongue.

If one does not understand the voice, language, or tongue, of the speaker it does not mean that the speaker is not uttering a language. It simply means that he is a man of strange speech which is unintelligible to the hearer. It does not mean the individual is without a language, or that he is not speaking a language. The Greeks divided mankind into Greeks and barbarians. A barbarian was a foreigner speaking a foreign language. "The word 'barbarian' is an onomatopoetic word, expressing exactly the apostle's idea of unintelligible speech. It is a man who seems to be saying, ba, ba, *i.e.* utters sounds without distinction. But this is not meant absolutely, but only relatively, to the person of a different speech." (Gould.)

"We at once see how this applies to using the voice when one is speaking with tongues. We also see that what Paul describes here refers to foreign languages. The speaker uses his 'voice' when he is speaking the language that is incomprehensible to Paul. The very term 'barbarian' settles the point regarding the 'voice' that is used in speaking a foreign language and thus also in the analogous case when a member of the church similarly uses his voice in speaking with tongues (foreign human language)." (Lenski.) Unless one wants to be a barbarian to the church, he should interpret and edify the church (14:12-13, 16-18).

As Charles Hodge pointed out, Paul's "complaint is, that a man who speaks in an unknown tongue is to him a foreigner, verse 11. This illustration supposes the sounds uttered to be intelligible in themselves, but not understood by those to whom they were addressed."

"Thus then St. Paul teaches the Corinthian *Greeks,* who gloried in their country and in their intellectual powers, and regarded all other nations as barbarous, that they degraded *themselves into barbarians,* by speaking, in a Greek assembly, strange languages which none could understand."

Tongues must have been languages for they were used in singing, in praying, and in blessing and giving thanks (I Cor. 14:14-17). How could one give thanks well, and sing praises to God, if in both cases one was uttering unintelligible sounds in a state of ecstasy? How could one "verily givest thanks well" unless the sound embodied meaning, and the meaning had to do with thanks?

Although certain men spoke in tongues by inspiration, the tongues were human languages which were also spoken by individuals who had learned them naturally. Those who did not know these tongues were unlearned in these tongues, regardless of what they might know about other things. Therefore, Paul spoke of Christians who did not understand the languages as being unlearned in that they did not know what the tongue speaker was saying. "Else if thou bless with the spirit, how shall he that filleth the place of the *unlearned* say the Amen at thy giving of thanks, *seeing he knoweth not what thou sayest?*" (I Cor. 14:16). Being unlearned was equal to being ignorant of what was said in the tongue. The unlearned did not know what was said. It follows that if one knew what was said, he was not unlearned. The man with the gift of interpretation was learned for he understood what was said (14:5, 9, 27).

The unbeliever who did not understand the language was also unlearned (14:23).

If one did not speak a language the individual understood, the listener did not know what was said, and he would view the speaker as a barbarian; for he was unlearned in the language of the speaker (14:9-11). To be learned was to understand the language. One would be learned in the language if he learned it naturally (Acts 2:4, 8), or if he learned it by inspiration (I Cor. 14:27).

Tongues were languages which employed words. These words were just as much words as were the native tongue. The difference was that the words in the tongues were not understood by the listener. Therefore, Paul said: "I had rather speak five *words* with my understanding, that I might *instruct* others also, than ten thousand *words* in a tongue." (I Cor. 14:19.) Tongues were languages which employed words which were not known by the unlearned. Therefore, the unlearned did not know "what thou sayest." (14:16.)

The fact that a language can be learned does not take away from the miracle of speaking the language by inspiration without having learned it. The knowledge delivered through the gift of knowledge could be learned, after it was delivered, by uninspired individuals. This did not take away from the inspiration of the original recipient of the revelation.

The use of the passage from Isaiah's prophecy, and Paul's comment, shows that Paul identified the tongues with human languages. Paul said: "In the law it is written, by *men* of *strange tongues* and *by the lips of strangers* will *I speak* unto this people; and not even thus will they *hear* me, saith the Lord." (14:21.) This clearly has reference to human languages or tongues of the Assyrians (Isa. 28:11). Paul immediately draws a conclusion concerning the tongues which were given to some believers at that time. He said: "*Wherefore* tongues are for a sign, not to them that believe, but to the unbelieving . . . If therefore the whole church be assembled together and all *speak with tongues* . . . " (14:22-23.)

"Wherefore" conveys the idea here of *and so*, or of *so that*. "The verse contains an inference from the circumstances in which the preceding utterance was made; it being plainly enough implied in the last clause of verse 21, that God speaks to the Jews in the way stated, because they were unbelieving. *Not to them that believe, but to them that believe not*. This follows, as we have seen, from the fact that tongues contain simply the element of proof, and so subserve no useful purpose with those already convinced." (Gould, 120.)

The quotation from Isaiah shows that actual human languages were referred to.

Since the tongues were for a sign to unbelievers, and since the assembly of the saints of which Paul speaks is filled with saints—with possible exceptions at times—tongues as a sign to unbelievers were usually out of place. The assembly is an assembly of the church, of believers. This is clear from several statements in the context. (a) edification of the church (14:4, 5, 12). (b) *"Brethren,* if I come unto *you speaking* with tongues . . . "* (14:6.) (c) "Howbeit *in the church* I had rather speak . . . " (14:19). (d) "If therefore the whole church be assembled together . . . " (14:23). (e) "What is it then, *brethren? When ye come together* . . . " (14:26). "In the church" is contrasted, for example, with the home (14:28, 33-34, 35).

Since tongues are a sign to unbelievers, unless they are understood by those in the church—or by some stranger who comes in and who knows the language, they are entirely out of place in the assembly of believers.

However, a tongue or language would not be a sign to an unbeliever unless he understood the language, any more than a tongue could edify the church unless someone interpreted it. If no one in the assembly of the believers understands it, and if the unbeliever who happens to come in does not understand it, the tongue cannot fulfill any useful function (14:23-25). We shall deal with these verses later.

The tongues of the people of whom Isaiah spoke, were languages (Isaiah 28:11). Why assume that the tongues in Corinth, of which Paul then immediately speaks (14:21-22), were anything but languages?

Ecstatic utterances could not function as a sign to unbelievers (Mk. 16:17, 20; Acts 2:6, 8, 11; I Cor. 14:22). In Corinth and elsewhere pagan worshipers could speak in ecstatic utterances. How, then could ecstatic utterances be a sign that the speaker had a message from God? How could it function as a sign if pagans could do it also? What did they do more than the pagans? On the other hand, it was a miracle and a sign when an individual spoke in a language which he had not learned.

USELESS UNLESS UNDERSTOOD

What conclusion does Paul draw from his illustrations and arguments? That a tongue should not be used unless the speaker or someone else interprets it to the audience, "So also ye, since ye are zealous of spiritual gifts, seek that ye may abound unto the edifying of the church," and to do this one must be understood (14:14-19, 27-28).

If one exercises the gift of tongues, without it being understood by the people present, it is useless to the audience. Paul made this clear more than once. (a) It is not a speaking to men (14:2). (b) It is made up of mysteries so far as the audience is concerned (14:2). (c) It does not edify the church (14:4, 5, 17). (d) It does not profit the church (14:6). (e) It is an uncertain sound the meaning of which they do not know (14:8-9). (g) It is a speaking into the air (14:9). (h) It is to be as a barbarian to the audience (14:11). (i) The individual's understanding is unfruitful (14:14); unless he has the gift of interpretation (14:13), or unless someone else interprets (14:27). (j) It is not known what one says, and so none are in a position to endorse it (14:16.) (k) The outsider who does not understand it will think you are mad (14:23). (l) Paul implies that to use tongues in an assembly where no one understood was a childish display (14:20).

ALL APPLICABLE TO A FOREIGN LANGUAGE

As the *Pulpit Commentary* on Acts pointed out: "All that Paul says to the Corinthians is fully applicable to any language spoken when there were none present who understood it." The reader can test with us this matter by substituting the word language or languages where the word tongues is found.

"To another divers kinds of languages; and to another the interpretation of languages" (I Cor. 12:10).

"Do all speak with languages? Do all interpret?" (12:30).

"If I speak with the languages of men and of angels." (13:1.)

"Languages, they shall cease" (13:8).

"For he that speaketh in a language (unknown to the audience, J. D. B.) speaketh not unto men, but unto God; for no man understandeth; but in the spirit he speaketh mysteries." (14:2.)

"He that speaketh in a language edifieth himself; but he that prophesieth edifieth the church." (14:4.)

"Now I would have you all speak with languages, but rather that ye should prophesy; and greater is he that prophesieth than he that speaketh with languages, except he interpret, that the church may receive edifying." (14:5.)

"But now, brethren, if I come unto you speaking with languages, what shall I profit you, unless I speak to you either by way of revelation . . . " (14:6.)

"So also ye, unless ye utter by the language speech easy to be understood, how shall it be known what is spoken? for ye will be speaking into the air." (14:9.) If tongue in this passage refers to the physical organ of speech, one could say: "Unless ye utter by the tongue speech (language) . . . "

"Wherefore let him that speaketh in a language pray that he may interpret." (14:13.)

"For if I pray in a language, my spirit prayeth, but my understanding is unfruitful." (14:14.) That is, if I pray in the language which is not understood.

"I speak with languages more than you all." (14:18.)

"I had rather speak five words with my understanding, that I might instruct others also, than ten thousand words in a language." (14:19. Which is not understood by the audience.)

"By men of strange languages." (14:21.)

"Wherefore languages are for a sign." (14:22.)

"And all speak with languages (unknown to the audience, J. D. B.), and there come in men unlearned (who do not know the language, J. D. B.) or unbelieving, will they not say ye are mad?" (14:23.)

"Hath a language." (14:26.)

"If any man speaketh in a language." (14:27.)

"But if there be no interpreter (to interpret the language, J. D. B.) let him keep silence in the church." (14:28.)

"Forbid not to speak with languages." (14:39.)

In every case it makes good sense to understand the word tongues as languages which they received by miraculous gifts and which were not known to the audience. In contrast with this, as will be brought out in the next chapter, ecstatic utterances does not make good sense in all these passages.

WHY AN INTERPRETER WAS NEEDED

Why was an interpreter necessary in Corinth, but not on Pentecost? If an individual today speaks a language which is known by the audience, he does not need an interpreter. If he speaks a language which is unknown to the audience, he needs an interpreter. A number of foreign languages were spoken on Pentecost, but these were understood by the various people who assembled. Therefore, there was no need for an interpreter (Acts 2:4, 6, 8, 11). If these languages had not been the languages wherein they were born, or had learned otherwise, they would not have understood and they would have needed an interpreter. A. T. Robertson suggested that: "In Corinth, where no such variety of people existed, it required an interpreter to explain the tongue to those who knew it not . . . In case there was no one present who understood the particular tongue it required a special gift of the Spirit to someone to interpret it if anyone was to receive benefit from it." Paul was regulating the use of the gifts in an assembly of Christians in which unbelievers were evidently the exception (I Cor. 14:22-24). Those who spoke a different native tongue were evidently also an exception in the assembly, although when such were present tongues could then constitute a sign to them (I Cor. 14:22).

IRRATIONAL BABBLING?

There are those who maintain that the tongues which they speak are not irrational babblings, but some type of heavenly language which is unintelligible to man. On the other hand, some of them will admit that some speakers in tongues are babbling. Then, too, some who teach others to speak in tongues tell them to babble. Tongues in the Bible were not irrational babblings regardless of what some mockers might say (Acts 2:8, 11, 13). The following scriptures make this very clear.

Tongues were a gift of the Spirit, but irrational babbling can be done by people who have never heard of the Spirit (I Cor. 12:10). Paul did not teach that the Spirit gave to one the gift of irrational babbling, and to another the gift of making a rational message out of irrational babbling. The tongues of which Paul spoke were not the result of an emotional frenzy in which one lost control of himself and uttered unintelligible sounds. Instead they were the gift of the Spirit, who gave them not to those who got worked up, but to those whom He willed (12:11, 18, 28-30). They were a gift which was as much under the control of the speaker as was the gift of interpretation (14:32). Neither the prophet, nor the speaker in tongues, nor the interpreter, was so carried away that they had to prophesy, speak in tongues, or interpret regardless of everything else.

Paul spoke of speaking with the tongues of *men* (I Cor. 13:1).

Paul mentioned different *kinds* of tongues. (I Cor. 12:10, 28). Surely Paul was not saying they spoke different *kinds* of irrational babblings.

Paul said that he spoke with "tongues more than you all," but surely he did not mean he spoke more irrational babblings than they did (I Cor. 14:18).

Furthermore, in this statement Paul equated the nature of the tongues which he spoke with the tongues which they spoke. Unlike them, however, he refused to exercise this gift when there was no one there who understood the tongue (14:15-19, 28).

Paul surely would have forbidden irrational babblings, but he did not forbid to speak with tongues under the proper conditions (I Cor. 14:39, 15-19, 27-28).

Although prophesying was superior to tongues, Paul would have been glad for all of them to speak with tongues (14:5). However, he knew that not everyone had the gift (12:10, 11), but in this manner he made clear that he was not opposed to tongues as such. His regulations concerning tongues, and his statement that tongues were inferior to prophecy, did not mean that he was prejudiced against tongues or hostile to those who had the gift.

Surely in speaking unto God, and to himself, an individual was not engaged in irrational babbling (I Cor. 14:26, 28).

Although the self-deceived may think that they have in some way been built up by their irrational babblings, surely Paul did not teach that irrational babblings actually edified or built up the tongues speaker (14:4).

Surely irrational babblings could not be said to be a giving of "thanks well" in speaking to God (14:17, 2).

Paul concluded they were to "let all things be done decently and in order." (I Cor. 14:40.) He had just mentioned tongues as well as prophecy (14:39). Surely he was not saying: Let all irrational babbling be done decently and in order (Some of these were mentioned by David Greene, 119-120).

SPEAKETH NOT UNTO MEN

It has been argued that tongues are not human languages because the tongues speaker did not speak unto men, but unto God. "For he that speaketh in a tongue speaketh not unto men, but unto God; for no man understandeth; but in the spirit he speaketh mysteries." (14:2.) This cannot mean that he does not speak to any men at all, for Paul also said that the individual spoke to himself: "But if there be no interpreter, let him keep silence in the church; and *let him speak* to himself, and to God." (14:28.) He is speaking to a man— to himself—as well as to God. Furthermore, when an interpreter was present he was speaking to the interpreter as well as to God. The interpreter then gave the message to the church. As a result the church could Amen what the tongues speaker said. In addition to this there were at least some cases where the tongues speaker had the gift of interpretation (14:5).

"No man understandeth" did not mean that it was not a language of man. The interpreter understood or else he could not interpret it (14:27).

What, then, did it mean that he was not speaking to men and that no man understood? When no one there understood the language, either because it was not his native tongue or because he did not have the gift of interpretation, it was not edifying to the church to speak in tongues. No one there understood what was said, and so far as they were concerned he was speaking mysteries for it was hidden from them because it was uttered in a foreign language which they did not understand. However, those who did not know the language would understand if the speaker or someone else interpreted it (14:5, 27).

No man understood when it was in a language which they did not know. In contrast, prophecy was in the language known to the audience, and the one who prophesied *"speaketh unto men* edification, and exhortation, and consolation." (14:3.) To speak unto men meant to speak to the understanding of those who were present (14:3, 6, 16-19). To speak not unto men meant to speak not unto their understanding.

The one who speaks tongues is saying something, for "in the spirit he speaketh mysteries." (14:2.) They are mysteries, however, only to those who do not understand them (14:3, 5, 6). They are mysteries because they do not know what he is saying; thus they are not instructed (14:16, 19). When interpreted, they were no longer mysteries.

If a speech is not understood, the speaker "will be speaking into the air." (14:9.) He is speaking into the air not because it is not a human language, but because it is not understood by those to whom he speaks. If the audience does not understand, the speaker is a barbarian to them (14:11). However, not all speakers are barbarians to us, for some speak in our own language. Just so, not all speaking in tongues was a speaking unto one's self and to God, not all such speaking was a speaking of mysteries, and it was not always true that no man understandeth it. These things were true only when the audience neither understood the language nor had someone to interpret it to them. He is not speaking to men when no one there understands.

THE MEANING OF "INTERPRET"

What does the word "interpret" mean? Does it fit in with the idea that tongues were human languages which could be translated into another language? The noun herméneia was used when Paul wrote: "To another the *interpretation* of tongues." (Cor. 12:10.)

The verb *hermeneuo* was used in the following places: (a) "Cephas, which is by interpretation, Peter." (John 1:42.) (b) "Go, wash in the pool of Siloam (which is by interpretation, Sent)." (John 9:7.) (c) "Being first, by interpretation, King of righteousness, and then also King of Salem, which is, King of peace." (Heb. 7:2.) (d) "Rabbi (which is to say, being interpreted, Teacher)." (John 1:38.) It is clear that in these contexts "interpret" carries the meaning of "translation."

The intensive form of the verb *hermeneuo* is *diermeneuo*. It was used in the following places: (a) "Tabitha, which by interpretation is called Dorcas." (Acts 9:36.) (b) "Do all interpret?" (I Cor. 12:30.) (c) "And greater is he that prophesieth than he that speaketh with tongues, except he *interpret,* that the church may receive edifying." (I Cor. 14:5.) To interpret was to give the meaning of the tongue so one could know what was said (I Cor. 14:16-17). (d) "Wherefore let

94

him that speaketh in a tongue pray that he may interpret." (I Cor. 14:13.) (e) "Let one interpret." (I Cor. 14:27.) (f) Although interpret does refer to translating a message from one language into another, it can also mean to expound clearly the meaning of a message which the individual has not understood for reasons other than that the message was in a foreign language. To the two on the road to Emmaus Jesus said: "O foolish men, and slow of heart to believe in all that the prophets have spoken! Behooved it not the Christ to suffer these things, and to enter into his glory? And beginning from Moses and from all the prophets, *he interpreted to them in all the scriptures* the things concerning himself." (Lk. 24:25-27). This is the same word which is used for "interpret" in I Cor. 12:30; 14:5, 13, 27. To interpret means to convey to someone *the meaning of a message*. Tongues had to convey a message, for if they had no meaning it would have been impossible for inspiration itself to give the meaning of a message which was not a message, but a series of sounds without meaning. The gift of interpretation involved a knowledge of what was said in the tongue. If nothing was said in the tongue, nothing could be known by an interpreter. What was said had to convey a message in some language.

Diermeneutes was used one time, and it means an interpreter or one who interprets. "And let one interpret: but if there be no *interpreter*, let him keep silence in the church." (I Cor. 14:27-28.)

Methermeneuomenon, a compound word and a present passive participle, was used by John to mean to translate or interpret. (a) "Rabbi (which is to say, being interpreted, Teacher)." (John 1:38.) (b) "We have found the Messiah (which is, being interpreted, Christ)." (John 1:41.)

Matthew used the same word when he wrote: "And they shall call his name Immanual; which is being interpreted, God with us." (Matt. 1:23.)

Interpret means to expound, to explain, to interpret, and to translate. (Kittel, II, 661.) It is to express the meaning of a message which was spoken in another language. It can also mean to explain a message in one's own language of which, for some reason, one did not have the correct understanding. It takes an intelligible message and translates it into another person's language so that he understands the message because it is now in his own tongue. Tabitha in one language meant Dorcas in another language (Acts 9:36). Whether one interpreted by inspiration or by having learned a language, the translation could be checked to determine whether or not it conveyed the same message which it conveyed in the original language.

It is clear, in passages other than those in Corinthians, that interpret does mean to translate or to explain. Unless the context of I Corinthians demanded that one understand the word in some other way, one is not justified in viewing it as having a different meaning. Translation makes good sense in all of the passages in I Corinthians. (a) "The translation of tongues" (12:10). (b) "Do all translate?" (12:30). (c) "Except he translate" (14:5). (d) "Pray that he may translate" (14:13). (e) "Let one translate" (14:27). (f) "If there be no translator" (14:28).

The gift of interpretation or translation was important for at least two reasons. First, to translate the language, or tongue, when it was one which was unfamiliar to the audience. In this way the audience could be edified (14:5, 27-28). Second, it could also serve as a means of detecting anyone who pretended to speak in tongues.

NO TRANSLATION ON PENTECOST

It has been argued that since the tongues of Pentecost did not need to be interpreted, the tongues in Corinth were something entirely different since they needed an interpreter. They could not be translated because they were not human languages. Carl G. Tuland wrote that: "A translator is one who translates from one language into another, while an interpreter is one who explains or expounds either law or religion, not necessarily in connection with a foreign language. Although both the Hebrew and Aramaic as well as the Greek language in the Bible make a clear distinction between these terms, many Bible translators have failed to preserve that distinction." (7.)

"And the verb meaning to interpret is what is used in First Corinthians 12:10; 14:13, 26, and 28, a clear sign that speaking in tongues at Corinth was not the natural talent or the charismatic gift of speaking foreign languages, for which no translation was required. The tongues-speaking in Corinth was ecstatic utterance or babbling. To be understood by others it had to be interpreted, but not translated."

We do not believe he has established his position. *First,* the tongues in Acts 2:4 did not need to be interpreted for the simple reason there were people present whose native languages were being spoken by the apostles (Acts 2:6, 8, 11). In Corinth people were using the gift of tongues when no one was there who knew these tongues. Therefore, what was said was unintelligible.

Second, if the tongues in Corinth were babblings, they were not sounds which embodied a message. If they were sounds without sense, it would be impossible for the interpreter to make any sense out of them.

Third, the sounds were not without meaning, for they included praise and thanks (I Cor. 14:16, 18).

Fourth, when interpret was used in the sense of explaining or expounding either law or religion, there was still a message to expound. Tongues had to be languages or they could not be sounds embodying meaning which another could expound.

MODERN "INTERPRETATION"

"Linguistic comparisons of glossolalia and the 'interpretation' reveal that the interpretation is not a translation. For example, I have often observed a brief glossolalic utterance translated into a whole paragraph of English. Or I have heard the same glossolalic phrases repeated by the same glossolalist in different services, but each time the identical glossolalic utterances are given a different translation. As noted above, the observational data which is available strongly suggests that the testimonials to the fact that the glossolalist has spoken in a foreign language unknown to him, does not represent a linguistic problem, but rather a phenomena of audience social psychology resulting in perceptual distortion." (E. Mansell Pattison, 74.) In other words, it does not involve the identification and translation of an actual language, but is the result of ignorance and reading into the random sounds the sounds of a foreign language.

"There is no direct research on this aspect of glossolalia so far as I am aware. However, the now classical work on perceptual process by men like Solomon Asch and Leon Festinger indicate the crucial influence which social expectation (of that particular group, J. D. B.) and the need for cognitive coherence play in the ordering and interpretation of our perceptions. Thus, we can at least suggest that the reports of audience observers 'verifying' the foreign language of glossolalists is not an indication of either malingering or pretense, but an honest report of *subjective* auditory perception, which of course may be quite different from the objective linguistic patterns spoken." (74-75.) The author is convinced, however, that some cases involve conscious fraud.

E. Mansell Pattison also pointed out that "if the divine message is to be interpreted, the 'interpretation' has been found to actually provide consensual validation for a specific social conflict facing the group. For example, in the cargo cult movement the 'interpreter' tells the 'unconverted' in the audience what the glossolalia of the charismatic leader means. The interpretation validates the 'rightness' of the cargo cult to the unbelieving and also demonstrates that the strange language is something that one can understand after 'initiation.' In another study of an American millenarian cult, Festinger et al found that the 'audience' of cultic believers interpreted spiritual messages according to pre-set expectations of what they needed to hear in order to maintain their 'cognitive coherence' in a setting where reality factors were stretching the credibility of their waiting for the soon-to-appear coming of Christ." In other words, the interpretation told these people that the teachings of their leader, or leaders, were true and they were to rest assured that things would happen as they had been told. Instead of confirming the word of God, the tongues and the interpretation confirmed the doctrines of men. This is the opposite of tongues in the New Testament.

The interpretations of modern tongues which the author has heard have consisted of a random weaving together of fragments, or entire passages of scripture. The observations which were interwoven with these were either very commonplace or in some cases, of course, interpreters let their imagination run away with them. Furthermore, as Pattison observed, a brief statement in tongues may be followed by an extended interpretation.

TESTING INTERPRETATION

When Jesus appeared to His disciples after His resurrection they could test the reality of His appearances. They heard the sounds of the familiar voice, they recognized His personality, they could see His beloved features, they could see the print of the nails in His hands, and they could touch and feel that he was actually there (John 20:24-29). If individuals speak foreign languages by miraculous gift, they should be willing to have this miracle tested. They should furnish proof they have not learned it, nor heard it at some time during their life. They should speak in the presence of those who speak the language as their native tongue, and these individuals should understand them (Acts 2:6, 8, 11). They should be willing to have their speech tape recorded, if no natives are present, so that it can be checked with those who speak the language.

Those who have the gift of interpretation should also submit to similar test. They must not have learned the language naturally, they must give an interpretation or translation that an uninspired interpreter would recognize as valid even though the inspired interpreter should do a better job than the uninspired translator. They should be willing to have both the tongue and their interpretation taped and checked by those learned in the language and in translating this language into our language.

If these are miraculous gifts of the Spirit today, they should be eager for these gifts to be subjected to the tests which would show that they are such. Of course, their doctrinal teaching must also be tested by the word of God.

CHAPTER VII

ECSTATIC UTTERANCES?

Those who deny that the tongues in Corinth were languages are not in agreement as to what they were. Among the interpretations are: (1) Ecstatic utterances which are not languages. (2) The language of angels. (3) Some were ecstatic utterances, some were the language of angels, and some were human languages. (4) Others think that some in Corinth may have been emotionally stimulated as some people today, and uttered a series of sounds which they thought was inspired utterance. These, in addition to those who had the genuine gift of tongues, would utter unintelligible sounds. While there were false prophets in the first century, and while there may have been some who claimed the gift of tongues but did not have it, there is no proof that such was taking place in Corinth. If some were falsely claiming the gift, surely Paul would have dealt with them. Those who had the gift of interpretation, and the gift of discerning the spirits, would have been called on to expose the pretenders.

As we examine the arguments for ecstatic tongues, it should become clear that no other explanation has the weight of evidence for it which can be marshalled for the position that the tongues were languages.

The following scriptures are supposed to refer to ecstatic utterances. "For he that speaketh in a tongue speaketh not unto men, but unto God; for no man understandeth; but in the spirit he speaketh mysteries." (I Cor. 14:2.) The speaker speaks mysteries (14:2). The speaker edifies himself, but not others (14:4). The individual's understanding is unfruitful when he uses ecstatic utterances. "For if I pray in a tongue, my spirit prayeth, but my understanding is unfruitful." (14:14). "But if there be no interpreter, let him keep silence in the church; and let him speak to himself, and to God." (14:28.)

THEIR STRONGEST ARGUMENT

What does the author consider to be the strongest argument that tongues were ecstatic utterances which the speaker

38831

does not himself understand? The argument that if he did understand it he would always be able to interpret it to the audience and, therefore, an interpreter would always be present. Even if we knew of no explanation, this argument cannot refute the many things which show that tongues were human languages. However, it can be shown that it harmonizes with the position that tongues are languages (Acts 2:8).

First, the miracle was obvious to the audience when they themselves understood the language (Acts 2:4, 6, 8, 11), or when someone else interpreted it; especially if they knew this person did not know the language through having studied it. If a man uttered a series of sounds, that no one could check on because they were not a human language, and then told us that it meant thus and so, we would not believe unless we had evidence, on some other grounds, to justify our believing that the speaker had a miraculous gift of tongues. There were some, of course, who had both the gift of tongues and the gift of interpretation (14:5). However, if it was a human language he could be checked on by someone who knew the language, or by a discerner of spirits, or by an interpreter.

Second, unless God gave the tongues speaker the gift of interpretation he did not have *authority from God* to speak in tongues *and* then to give an interpretation. The gift of interpretation was just as miraculous a gift as that of tongues. It enabled one to give an *inspired* interpretation or translation of the message spoken in a foreign language (12:10, 30; 14:5, 28). Even if the tongues speaker understood what he said, and was edified by it, he was not authorized or able to give an *inspired* interpretation. Any interpretation which he gave, without the gift of interpretation, would be an *uninspired* interpretation of the inspired message. He would not have time to study his translation closely before giving it, since in the assembly it would be important that the message be interpreted immediately after it was given. If an individual understood Greek, but God wanted an inspired translation given to the audience when the gift of Greek was utilized, a man without the gift of interpretation could not give an inspired and perfect translation with his uninspired knowledge of Greek. In an assembly when miraculous gifts were being exercised, the interpretation also had to be through a gift. When this was impossible, tongues were not to be used. One was not to use his own learned knowledge of a language as a substitute for an inspired interpretation of the language.

This was also Charles Hodges' explanation of the matter. He pointed out that to identify tongues with human languages, which one spoke by inspiration, "is also consistent with the fact that the gift of interpretation was distinct from that of speaking with tongues. If a man could speak a foreign language, why could he not interpret it? Simply, because it was not his gift. What he said in that foreign language, he said under the guidance of the Spirit; had he attempted to interpret it without the gift of interpretation, he would be speaking of himself, and not 'as the Spirit gave him utterance.' In the one case he was the organ of the Holy Ghost, in the other he was not." Paul, in I Cor. 14 is regulating in the assembly the exercise of miraculous gifts, and although there are principles which would apply to the exercise of natural or cultivated gifts of teaching, Paul was not talking about uninspired utterance. He was speaking of inspired tongues, of inspired interpretations, of inspired prophecy, or inspired knowledge, etc.

The normal thing was that the speaking in tongues be done by one, and the interpreting by another; for the usual thing was that one had the gift of interpretation, and another the gift of tongues (12:10,30). Therefore, Paul said "When ye come together, each one hath a psalm, hath a teaching, hath a revelation, hath a tongue, hath an interpretation . . . If any man speaketh in a tongue, let it be by two, or at the most three, and that in turn; and let one interpret: but if there be no interpreter, let him keep silence in the church." (14:26-27).

Third, the argument for ecstatic utterances is based on the assumption that if the speaker did not understand the tongue it must be because the tongue was an ecstatic utterance. The falsity of this assumption is obvious once it is clearly stated. The gift of a foreign language, which the speaker did not know, would be just as unintelligible to the speaker as it would be to the audience, unless God enabled the speaker to understand it. A tongue does not have to be an ecstatic utterance in order to be unintelligible to one who does not know the tongue, or who does not have the gift of translation. Therefore the entire argument, that the tongues must be ecstatic utterances if the speaker does not understand them, is based on a false assumption. The argument is worthless.

Although the author will give his reasons for believing that the speaker understood what he was saying, the knowledge of the speaker of what he was saying is not really related to the question of whether the tongues were languages. *The case for tongues being languages is neither strengthened nor weakened by whether or not the speaker understood what he was saying.*

SPEAKETH NOT UNTO MEN

When no interpreter was present, Paul said the tongues speaker was not speaking "unto men, but unto God; for no man understandeth." (I Cor. 14:2.) Does this mean it is not a language but ecstatic utterances? Six lines of evidence show he could not mean this. (a) On the day of Pentecost everyone understood (Acts 2:4, 6, 8, 11). (b) Paul expressly said that the man speaks *unto himself as well* as unto God (I Cor. 14:2, 28). He was at least one man unto whom he was speaking. (c) Paul said that in some cases the speaker himself could interpret (I Cor. 14:5). This again made it clear that he was speaking unto at least one man (himself) who did understand. (d) When an interpreter was present, he was speaking unto the interpreter as well as unto God and unto himself (I Cor. 14:27-28). (e) When Paul spoke in tongues he understood what he was saying. (I Cor. 14:15). (f) The men who do not understand it are those who are unlearned in the language which is being used. ". . . how shall he that filleth the place of the *unlearned* say the Amen at thy giving of thanks, *seeing he knoweth not what thou sayest?* (I Cor. 14:16.) The unlearned among the unbelievers does not understand it either, and, therefore, it cannot function as a sign to him (I Cor. 14: 22-23). These things make it clear that "no man understandeth" does not mean that no one anywhere understood, or could understand. Paul is simply saying that when the gift of tongues was used in an audience which did not understand the tongues, the speaker was not communicating with the audience. "Because the language is not the language of those to whom he is speaking, and therefore what he says is hidden from them." (Lias).

It was a vain use of the gift, and out of harmony with love which seeks the good of others, for an individual to use the gift of Hebrew, for example, in a congregation where only Greek was understood. The basic purpose of the gifts was not that just the individual, but that especially the church, might profit by the use of the gifts. (I Cor 12:7; 14:4-6). Therefore, Paul said "Let all things be done unto edifying." (14:26). When no one understood the tongue, no one in the audience could be edified; therefore, the gift was not to be exercised under such conditions (14:27-28).

A speech does not have to be incoherent in order to be unintelligible to the listener. As Hodge well said: "If speaking with tongues was speaking incoherently in ecstasy, it is hard to see how what was said could admit of interpretation. Unless coherent it was irrational, and if irrational, it could not be translated"—or interpreted.

UNFRUITFUL UNDERSTANDING

It is also argued that tongues were ecstatic utterances because the speaker's understanding was unfruitful. "For if I pray in a tongue, my spirit prayeth, but my understanding is unfruitful (I Cor. 14:14). This does not necessarily mean that he does not understand what he is saying. The context indicates that his understanding is unfruitful in the sense that it bears no fruit in the instruction and edification of others. This passage was considered in detail in the previous chapter, so we briefly present the following: *First*, Paul said that "let him that speaketh in a tongue pray that he may interpret." (14:13). He does not say that he is to interpret so that he himself may understand but that others may understand (14:15). To fail to interpret was to fail to have a fruitful understanding. *Second*, that he speaks of fruitfulness in the lives of others is also indicated by the explanation which followed: "What is it then? I will pray with the spirit, and I will pray with the understanding also: I will sing with the spirit, and I will sing with the understanding also. Else (in other words, if I do not do these things with the understanding, what follows?

104

J. D. B.) if you bless with the spirit (and not with the understanding also, J. D. B.), how shall he that filleth the place of
the unlearned say the Amen at thy giving of thanks, *seeing he
knoweth not* what thou sayest? For thou verily givest thanks
well, but the other is not edified." (14: 15-17). *Third,* this is
made clear from the fact that Paul said that to speak with the
understanding meant to speak so others could understand and
be instructed. ". . . I had rather *speak five words with my
understanding, that I might instruct others also,* than ten
thousand words in a tongue." (14:19.) To speak, to sing, and
to pray with the understanding, so that these would be fruitful, meant to speak, to sing, and to pray so the audience understood.

EDIFICATION WITHOUT UNDERSTANDING

If the author is wrong, and the speaker did not understand
what he is saying, the speaker was edified in some way whether or not the author realizes how. It could be that from previous uses of the tongues he knows that he is speaking an
actual language by inspiration. He could find satisfaction and
edification in this knowledge. But, if from previous experience
the church knew he had the gift, could they be edified? However, there would be these differences concerning the church
and the individual. *First,* there might be some unbelievers
present who did not know that the speaker was actually speaking a language which he had not learned. They would find the
speech not only useless, but if the entire meeting was devoted
to speaking in tongues they would think the church was mad
(14:23).

Second, the Holy Spirit wanted the assembly of the church
to be devoted to that which is understandable and, therefore,
reached the intellect and not just the emotions of the audience.
Regardless of how much emotional joy an individual might get
out of speaking in a language which he did not understand, he
was not to waste the time of the church in such an exercise in
the assembly. Massie suggested that: "In public prayer with
a tongue the spirit is devotional, but the thinking faculty is
barren; it shapes nothing that can be conveyed to others. The
ideal in worship is that the devotional and the thinking faculties should work in conjunction, both in prayer and in

praise; otherwise, how can the listener, not understanding your meaning, join himself to your giving of thanks?"

If the individual is edified in some way, even though he does not understand what he is saying, the Spirit surely let him know enough to realize that he was giving thanks. Lias suggested that he "is conscious that he is fervently addressing the Giver of all good in a spirit of supplication. But his consciousness goes no further. He does not know what he is saying." Lenski thought that Paul was saying that: "As far as spiritual benefit is concerned, my spirit alone receives that. And even this benefit is small, for my understanding is inactive. My spirit receives only dim impressions." He receives some edification without understanding because he at least understands that the gift he is exercising is from God. However, he is handicapped even in amening his own prayer seeing he knoweth not what he is saying (14:16).

SPEAKER UNDERSTOOD

There are Scriptures which the author thinks indicate that the tongues speaker could understand what he was saying. We shall list and briefly discuss them.

Tongues speakers will agree that when they speak "not unto men, but unto God" that God understandeth what they say. Man does not understand, but God does (14:2). Since to speak to God means that God understands, why does it not mean that when one speaks to himself that he also understands? It is clear that the speaker is doing the same thing, speaking, to himself as well as to God. For Paul said that when no interpreter was present they were not to speak to the assembly but to themselves and to God. "But if there be no interpreter, let him keep silence in the church; and *let him speak to himself, and to God.*" (14:28.) This regulation is addressed to the same men of whom Paul speaks in 1 Cor. 14:2 when he said that they speak to God. When one does not speak to the understanding of the audience he is not speaking to men. " . . . speaketh not unto men . . . for no man understandeth." (14:2.) In speaking to himself, is he not speaking to his own understanding? (14:28.) If he is speaking unintelligible sounds to himself, how is he speaking to himself in a way which differs from the way he is speaking to the audience?

In order for the church to be edified they must understand what the tongues speaker says. Prophecy edifieth the church because the church understands it (14:3,4). If the tongues speaker interprets, the church understands and receives edification (14:5,16-19). The speaker in tongues cannot profit the church unless he speaks "by way of revelation, or of knowledge, or of prophesying, or of teaching." (14:6.)

"He that speaketh in a tongue edifieth himself." (14:4.) The church cannot be edified unless it understands. How, then, can the speaker be edified unless he understands what he is saying? If understanding is necessary for the edification of the hearers, how can he as a hearer be edified if he does not understand? The other members of the church cannot be profited unless they understand (14:6). How can he be profited if he does not understand? How can he benefit without understanding but other Christians cannot? If non-rational utterances can benefit him why cannot they not benefit them?

"So also ye, unless ye utter by the tongue speech easy to be understood, how shall it be known what is spoken? For ye will be speaking into the air." (14:9.) If the church does not understand it, one is speaking into the air. If the individual does not understand it, he is speaking into the air as far as he himself also is concerned. He no more knows what is being spoken than do the others; if these modern tongues speakers are right.

"If then I know not the meaning of the voice, I shall be to him that speaketh a barbarian, and he that speaketh will be a barbarian unto me." (14:11.) The tongues speaker speaks to himself (14:28). If he does not understand what he is saying, he is a barbarian to himself.

Those who do not know what the tongues speaker is saying, cannot endorse it by saying Amen (14:16). If one cannot understand what he himself is saying, how could he say Amen to his own giving of thanks in a tongue?

"For thou verily givest thanks well." (14:17.) If the speaker does not know what he is saying, how does he know he is giving thanks?

107

"For thou verily givest thanks well, but the other is not edified." (14:17.) If the other is not edified at this giving of thanks, because he does not understand, how can the tongues speaker be edified if he does not understand? To put it another way: In order to be edified one must understand (14:17). The tongues speaker edifies himself, even when others do not understand, therefore the tongues speaker understands what he is saying (14:17,4).

"Howbeit in the church I had rather speak five words with my understanding, that I might instruct others also than ten thousand words in a tongue." (14:19.) Why was it two thousand to one better to speak in a known language than an unknown? Because the known language instructed others. The speaker in tongues, as well as others, is in need of instruction. Why is it not better for him to speak five words in a known tongue so that he may instruct himself than ten thousand words in a tongue which he does not understand? This would be the case if he could not understand himself when he spoke to himself in a tongue (14:28). The tongues speakers, who use tongues in their private devotion, can improve their devotions by two thousand times if they will speak five words in a known tongue rather than ten thousand in an unknown tongue.

Although the author does not have the gift of tongues, five words, such as "Christ died for our sins" (1 Cor. 15:3), are worth more than ten thousand words delivered by someone in the assembly in a tongue *even* if he actually had the gift of tongues.

"Wherefore tongues are for a sign, not to them that believe, but to the unbeliever." (14:22.) The tongues of which Paul spoke were for a sign to the unbelievers. If they were non-human languages, non-human languages were a sign to unbelievers. Therefore, they should have been used when unbelievers were present even though no one understood what was said. However, Paul said that tongues were not to be used when no one understood, for the unbelievers would think the speakers were mad (14:23). Why would not the speaker himself, since he does not understand either, think that he himself was mad? He would have to know, on some other evidence, that he actually had the gift.

These tongues were languages of men, although strange tongues to those who did not understand them (14:21). They were strange only to those who were unlearned in the tongue which was being used. The unlearned unbeliever and the unlearned believer did not understand the tongue concerning which they were unlearned (14:16,23).

OTHERS COULD BE EDIFIED WITHOUT UNDERSTANDING, IF

If the tongues speaker can be edified without his own understanding being involved, why cannot the audience? The audience can hear his ecstatic sounds as surely as can he. If the speaker is awed by these sounds, without his own intellect being instructed, why cannot the audience be awed by these sounds which, although they do not utter them, they hear as certainly as does the speaker? If he benefits from it spiritually because he believes it is of the Spirit, and yet his intellect is not involved, why cannot they benefit from it for they, too, believe it is of the Spirit even though their intellects are not involved? If his speaking in tongues can stir his holy emotions, why cannot his speaking in tongues stir them with holy emotions? We know that others, who believe the individual is speaking in tongues, have been deeply stirred by hearing the sounds which were not spoken to their understanding. The way an individual knows that he is speaking in ecstatic utterance is by hearing himself speak in these utterances. The sounds convince him that he is doing it. Why cannot the sounds convince others?

If soothing sounds, without meaning, can build him up when he hears himself, why cannot they edify the church when they hear the same sounds? If he could be edified by the knowledge that he was speaking in tongues, even though he did not know what he was saying, why could not the congregation be edified just on the basis that they knew from previous experiences, when either interpreters or those learned in the language were present, that the man was actually speaking in tongues? If the fact he is communing with God, without knowing what he is saying, edifies him, why could it not edify others to know he was communing with God even though they did not understand what he was saying? If his understanding does not have to be involved, in the sense that he knows what he is saying, in order for him to profit from the experience, why does the understanding of the congregation have to be involved? If he is spiritually stimulated by hearing himself utter sounds which he does not understand, why cannot others be spiritually stimulated by hearing the same sounds?

In other words, in what way could the individual profit himself from ecstatic, and unintelligible utterances, that the hearers in an assembly of the saints could not profit also? If he can profit by this experience which by-passes his own intellect, why cannot they profit by this experience which they hear and see, but which also by-passes their intellect? If the speaker can have edification without understanding, why cannot the hearer have edification without understanding?

If any of these are means of edification for the individual, the church would no more need an interpreter, in order to be edified by these means, than did the speaker. The author cannot think of any way the individual can be edified, without his understanding being involved, that the congregation could not be edified. If it be said it can be because the individual may feel it better than he can tell it, why cannot the congregation also feel it even though it cannot undersand it?

ECSTATIC UTTERANCES MAKE SENSE IN ALL PASSAGES?

If we substitute "ecstatic utterances" for tongues can we make sense out of *all* the passages? This experiment is not difficult to carry out.

"They shall speak in new ecstatic utterances." (Mk. 16:17.)

"Every man heard them speaking in his own ecstatic utterance." (Acts 2:6.)

"And how hear we, every man in our own ecstatic utterance wherein we were born?" (Acts 2:8.)

"We hear them speaking in our own ecstatic utterances the mighty works of God." (Acts 2:11.)

"Kinds of ecstatic utterances . . . interpretation of ecstatic utterances." (I Cor. 12:10.)

"Do all speak with ecstatic utterances? Do all interpret?" (12:30.)

"If I speak with the ecstatic utterances of men and of angels." (13:1.)

"Ecstatic utterances, they shall cease." (13:8.)

"For he that speaketh in an ecstatic utterance speaketh not unto men, but unto God; for no man understandeth; but in the spirit he speaketh mysteries." (14:2.)

"He that speaketh in an ecstatic utterance edifieth himself." (14:4.)

"Now I would have you all speak with ecstatic utterances, but rather that ye should prophesy: and greater is he that prophesieth than he that speaketh with ecstatic utterances . . . (14:5).

"If I come unto you speaking with ecstatic utterances, what shall I profit you . . . " (14:6.)

"So also ye, unless ye utter by the ecstatic utterance speech easy to be understood . . . " (14:9.) "Unless ye utter by the tongue ecstatic utterances easy to be understood." (14:9.)

"Wherefore let him that speaketh in an ecstatic utterance pray that he may interpret." (14:13.)

"For if I pray in an ecstatic utterance, my spirit prayeth, but my understanding is unfruitful." (14:14.)

"I speak with ecstatic utterances more than you all." (14:18.)

"Than ten thousand words in an ecstatic utterance." (14:19.)

"By men of strange ecstatic utterances." (14:21.)

"Wherefore ecstatic utterances are for a sign." (14:22.)

"All speak with ecstatic utterances, and there come in men unlearned (in ecstatic utterances, J. D. B.) or unbelieving, will they not say ye are mad?" (14:23.)

"Hath an ecstatic utterance." (14:26.)

"If any man speaketh in an ecstatic utterance." (14:27.)

"But if there be no interpreter (to interpret the ecstatic utterances, J. D. B.), let him keep silence in the church." (14:28.)

"Forbid not to speak with ecstatic utterances." (14:39.)

In some cases ecstatic utterance would fit the passage, but not in all of them. Furthermore, the ones where ecstatic utterance would fit are fully explained, and better explained, with the use of the word language instead of ecstatic utterance. For example, (a) The individual who is using a foreign language is speaking to God and not to men, for no men there understand (14:2). (b) The individual is edified even if others are not edified because they do not understand the language (14:4-6, 19). (c) Because no one understands him, he speaks mysteries to them (14:2). (d) His understanding is unfruitful because he does not speak with his understanding—does not speak a familiar language—so that others are instructed (14:15, 16-19).

The author does not believe there is any real justification for maintaining that tongues were ecstatic utterances.

CHAPTER VIII

DEVOTIONAL TONGUES?

There is some overlapping in a discussion of ecstatic utterances and of devotional tongues. However, there are differences also, so this chapter will be devoted to a consideration of the arguments which some Pentecostals make for devotional tongues.

Lewis J. Willis maintained there were two different types of tongues, and these should not be confused. Glossolalia, he said, is not to be identified with the gift of tongues. Tongues in the book of Acts, which were a sign of the reception of the baptism of the Spirit, were evidential or devotional tongues, but the gift of tongues was what he called ecclesiastical tongues. While devotional tongues were not equal to the gift of tongues, there could be "an exercise of glossolalia issuing through the gift of tongues," in which case the gift of interpretation should be exercised. (263-265.) According to Willis, how do devotional tongues differ from the gift of tongues?

Devotional tongues served at least two functions for the individual. *First,* they "function as a means of communion or perhaps intercommunion with God," for therein one spoke to God, and not to man (I Cor. 14:2). In this personal, private communion the individual might pray in a tongue and sing in a tongue (14:15.) *Second,* it was a means of personal edification. "Since this is a personal, private communion, the person speaking in a devotional tongue primarily edifies himself (14:4) whether it be in a private devotion or in congregational worship." (264.)

It could be used in private worship or in congregational worship. When it was used in congregational worship it must be used in an orderly way (14:23). Furthermore, "all spiritual manifestations should be directed toward the common good." (12:7; 264.) Therefore, devotional tongues should not be used, as if one were a public messenger, if no interpreter was present (14:28; 265).

In contrast with this was the gift of tongues which was "for congregational edification," and as such should be accompanied by the gift of interpretation in order that the congregation would be edified. "The gift of tongues is in operation generally during congregational worship, always in conjunction with the gift of interpretation, and definitely regulated in operation (14:27). Properly exercised, these two gifts equate the gift of prophecy." (264-265.)

The gift of tongues was not for everyone, but devotional tongues were a sign that one had received the Spirit; and everyone should receive the Spirit. In speaking of I Cor. 12, Willis wrote: "A careful reading of this chapter should convince any objective reader that Paul is here referring to spiritual gifts and not to devotional tongues as differentiated in chapter 14." (271.) All did not have the gift of tongues (I Cor. 12:30), but this did not refer to devotional tongues. "Not everyone exercises the gift of tongues, just as not everyone had the gift of prophecy or works miracles or has the word of wisdom." (271.)

"Paul's statement, 'I would that ye all spake with tongues' (I Cor. 14:5), is a straightforward, declarative statement. Even when he gave the firm regulations about the exercise of the gifts of tongues and interpretation, he seemed to be careful to make provision for those who would yield to devotional tongues by saying 'let him speak to himself, and to God' (I Cor. 14:28)." (271.)

"Not all persons are exercised by the gift of tongues, but all persons who receive the Holy Spirit speak with evidential and devotional tongues." (271-272.) However, in the assembly it was better for the gift of tongues to be exercised, along with the gift of interpretation, rather than devotional tongues, in order that the service be intelligible to the hearers (272-273.)

WHAT WILLIS WAS TRYING TO PROVE

Some make a distinction between Acts 2 and I Cor. 14 in order to prove that tongues in I Cor. 14 were ecstatic utterances, instead of languages. This was not the purpose of Willis, and some other Pentecostals, in making a distinction between the gift of tongues and devotional tongues. It is his conviction that all Christians should receive the baptism of the Spirit, and that one of the necessary proofs is that one speaks in devotional tongues (272, 283). If it is for everyone,

114

it must be something different from the gift of tongues which Paul clearly said was not for everyone (I Cor. 12:10, 30).

Instead of maintaining that devotional tongues were unintelligible sounds, he identified devotional tongues with Pentecost and said: "From the specific description of tongues speaking in the Acts, glossolalia seemed to be intelligible language." (266.)

ACTS 2 DEVOTIONAL

Willis argued that Acts 2 referred to devotional tongues and not to the gift of tongues. "It would seem apparent that according to the identifying functions as specifically stated by Paul, the exercise of glossolalia in the Acts could not have been a manifestation of the gift of tongues. First, the exercise was clearly one of personal praise and adoration to God (Acts 2:11; 10:46). Second, the gift of interpretation does not seem to have been employed. Third, all those exercised of the Holy Ghost spoke in tongues simultaneously (Acts 2:4; 10:44-46; 19:6, 7) which would have violated perhaps the most stringent rule stated by Paul regarding the regulation of the gift of tongues (I Cor. 14:23, 27, 28). We may conclude, therefore, that the glossolalia of Acts was not only initiatory and evidential, but also devotional and distinctly different in function from the gift of tongues." (265.) Let us consider his arguments.

PERSONAL DEVOTIONS?

Is Willis right in saying: "It is a scene of personal devotion, not a preaching effort." (266.) Or did· it have to do with the revelation and confirmation of the word of God to unbelievers? Was it in connection with a meeting for personal devotion, or did it have to do with the proclamation of the gospel to unbelievers? While waiting for the Spirit to come, the people did bless God (Lk. 24:52). Among other things, someone was selected to take the place of Judas. However, we do not know what the apostles were doing when the Spirit came on them (Acts 2:1). There is no indication they were praying for the Spirit. The fact they were sitting does not fit in with the idea that they were engaged in a prayer service, for standing or kneeling were more likely postures for prayer in those days (Gromacki, 84).

115

When the Spirit came on them they spake in other tongues, and in so doing they spoke of God's mighty works (Acts 2:11). To speak of God's mighty works does not in itself mean that a group is engaged in a private devotional service. It is true that Peter did not have to preach to them in different languages after the crowd had gathered and heard the different languages, but this does not prove that the tongues were designed for a private devotional service, without reference to the proclamation of the gospel to unbelievers, and that the crowd simply overheard a private devotional. The tongues related directly to the confirmation of the word of God to unbelievers. This is clear from the following scriptures. *First,* tongues, along with other gifts, were signs which confirmed the word. The apostles were confirming the word. In fact, what took place on Pentecost *is included in Mark's statement concerning the confirmation of the word.* After Christ gave the great commission, and after He told them tongues would accompany them that believe, He was received up into heaven. "So then the Lord Jesus, after he had spoken unto them, was received up into heaven, and sat down at the right hand of God. And *they went forth, and preached everywhere,* the Lord working with them, and *confirming the word by the signs that followed.*" (Mk. 16:17, 20.) They did not go forth at the moment of His resurrection, for they were expressly told to wait until Christ sent the Spirit (Lk. 24:46-49). They started after He sat down at the right hand of God, and sent the Spirit (Mk. 16:19). When did this start? On the first Pentecost after Christ's resurrection. Peter said: "Being therefore by the right hand of God exalted, and having received of the Father the promise of the Holy Spirit, he hath poured forth this, which ye see and hear." (Acts 2:33.) The tongues, therefore, which came on Pentecost were not for a devotional purpose, but were to confirm the word which the apostles preached. Christ said it was for this purpose (Mk. 16:17), Mark said God used it for this purpose (Mk. 16:20), and Peter used it as one of the arguments which justified the conclusion that God had made Jesus both Lord and Christ (Acts 2:33-36).

The miracle, of the apostles speaking in tongues, certified to the audience that these men were messengers of God. It was one of their credentials that what they were preaching was from God. The entire sermon did not have to be delivered in different tongues in order to establish, through the use of tongues in the presence of the audience and before the sermon about Christ, that these messengers had a message from God. It fulfilled the purpose of tongues as a sign even if tongues were not spoken during the entire time the crowd was together.

Second, the Holy Spirit came in miraculous manifestations to enable them to begin their work of witnessing in Jerusalem, and then to witness elsewhere (Acts 1:5-8). On Pentecost the apostles began this work of witnessing. Therefore, Peter said: "This Jesus did God raise up, whereof we all are witnesses." (Acts 2:32.)

Third, in a miraculous way God called the crowd together so they could hear the apostles speak in tongues, and then have the gospel preached to them. "And suddenly there came from heaven a sound as of the rushing of a mighty wind, and it filled all the house where they were sitting." (Acts 2:2.) Tongues like as of fire appeared, and they spoke in other languages as the Spirit gave them utterance. The Spirit used the sound to call the crowd together. He was not calling them to a private devotional service, but to come and hear the apostles bear witness concerning Jesus Christ. The Spirit confirmed their word with the miracles of the sound, the cloven tongues like as of fire, and the *foreign languages spoken by inspiration of the Spirit (Acts* 2:3-4). Through Luke the Holy Spirit makes this clear. "Now there were dwelling at Jerusalem Jews, devout men, from every nation under heaven. *And when this sound was heard,* the multitude came together, and were confounded, because that every man heard them speaking in their own language." (Acts 2:5-6.)

Mark, of course, was right. In this way God was confirming the word preached by those whom He miraculously guided from heaven through the Holy Spirit (Mk. 16:20; Acts 2:33, 43). If those who claimed to be miraculously guided by the Holy Spirit today were really guided, they would not so misunderstand the Bible on this and a host of other matters.

NO GIFT OF INTERPRETATION?

Willis' second argument, that Acts 2 referred to devotional tongues and not to the gift of tongues, was that the "gift of interpretation does not seem to have been employed," but that it had to be employed when the gift of tongues was used (265). There was no need for someone to interpret because all of the languages which were spoken were understood by one group or another of those who assembled. In Corinth tongues were being used when no one there knew the tongue, and no one had the gift of interpretation. If the tongues spoken in the assembly of the saints in Corinth had been the native tongues of those assembled, all would have understood and there would have been no need for an interpreter. Since "devotional" tongues were intelligible languages, as Willis admits and as Acts 2:6, 8, 11 proves, they would have been intelligible to anyone in Corinth who understood the languages. It was only when no one understood the language that the speaker was either to be silent or the message was to be interpreted by one who had the gift of interpretation.

ALL SPOKE AT ONCE?

Willis' third argument was that "all those exercised by the Holy Ghost spoke in tongues simultaneously (Acts 2:4; 10:44-47; 19:6, 7) which would have violated perhaps the most stringent rule stated by Paul regarding the regulation of the gift of tongues." (263.) Even if we cannot see the harmony between these two things, there is no reason to conclude that devotional tongues and the gift of tongues were different. However, the two can be harmonized.

Since the same Holy Spirit spoke in tongues through the apostles on Pentecost, who spoke through Paul in the I Corinthian letter, there is no reason to assume that He taught against simultaneously speaking in Corinth in a situation where it resulted in confusion, and yet led the apostles to all speak at once in a situation that would leave things in confusion. There is no indication that anyone objected on the basis that everyone was talking at once and they could not make out anything which was heard. If the apostles had all been standing in one place, and everyone of them had spoken in different languages at the same time, the confusion would have been such that no one would really have understood them in their own language. If twelve people all spoke the same language at the same time, unless they did it as people do when they sing together, it would result in confusion and likely the audience would not understand even though their own language, and only one language, was used.

That all spoke in tongues does not have to imply they did it all at once, or at least all at once in the same spot. Paul said "if *all prophesy;* and there come in one unbelieving or unlearned, he is reproved by all, he is judged by all; the secrets of his heart are made manifest; and so he will fall down on his face and worship God, declaring that God is among you indeed." (I Cor. 14:24-25.) If this meant that the entire assembly spoke at the same time, it would have produced confusion instead of reaching the understanding of the unbeliever and convicting him.

Surely Paul did not say in verses 23-25 that all the believers speaking at once when the whole church was assembled, would instruct and convict an unbeliever, but that when the whole church assembled, those who prophesied were to speak one at a time in turn or otherwise it would be confusion (14:26-27, 33). Does it not follow that "all prophesy" in verse 24 does not mean all at once, but an entire assembly devoted to nothing but prophecy in contrast with one devoted entirely to tongues?

Does Acts 2:4 mean that each apostle had to be speaking at the same time and same place? Just as all could prophesy in Corinth, and do it one at a time (14:24-26), just so all the apostles could speak in tongues and take turns in speaking, and have more than one turn.

Furthermore, although all were in the house—and we do not know what house—when the Spirit came, one does not have to assume they stayed in the house. If they had stayed in the house—unless there were porches from which they could preach, how could they have preached to at least three thousand people? It is likely that far more than three thousand was present. Around that number were baptized (Acts 2:41), but there is no indication that the entire audience obeyed the gospel that day. The ones who received Peter's word were baptized, but there is no indication that all received the word in faith (Acts 2:38, 41). With such a large crowd the apostles could have moved about to different places and spoken to different parts of the audience. There was certainly a difference in addressing such a large gathering, and in speaking to a much smaller assembly in Corinth.

We do not know exactly the circumstances under which the speaking took place, but since the Holy Spirit guided them we know things were done in order and without confusion; for this is the way the Holy Spirit wanted things done and the apostles certainly did as the Spirit willed. Furthermore, everyone understood; so the scene was not one of confusion. Whatever was necessary in order for it to be done orderly, with understanding, and without confusion was done.

Willis thought that around 120 people were simultaneously speaking in devotional tongues. Furthermore, he thought that "even while the 120 continued in their private ecstasy (2:33), the Apostle Peter, in his native tongue, preached a mighty sermon . . . " (266.) How could this be private when it was done in an assembly of one hundred and twenty speakers? This would have been a scene of confusion indeed if, while Peter preached, around one hundred and twenty people were talking in tongues; even though every man heard them in the language wherein they were born. The other apostles were there with Peter when he preached, and if they had been speaking with tongues all during his speech things would have been confused. We know they were with Peter because the audience "said unto Peter and the rest of the apostles, Brethren, what shall we do?" Although Peter did the answering, they must have been beside him at this time to have been addressed by the audience (Acts 2:37-38).

We know no reason why the Spirit would have authorized all of them to speak in devotional tongues during Peter's sermon, and have refused to let all use the same type of tongues—devotional tongues—in the assembly of brethren in Corinth. If all spoke in tongues simultaneously, and in one spot, the entire audience would have surely thought they were mad.

120

DEVOTIONAL TONGUES IN CORNELIUS' HOUSEHOLD?

Were the tongues in Cornelius' household ecstatic utterances? If the Bible said so, we would accept it, but they were languages used as a sign to confirm the word of God; just as tongues were used on Pentecost. Why do we take this position? *First,* the same word is used to describe what took place (Acts 2:4, 11; 10:46). *Second,* if no one there understood the languages, how did the Jewish brethren who came with Peter know that the tongue-speakers were magnifying God? (10:23, 45-46). The people on Pentecost understood what was said and knew the speakers magnified God in that they declared His mighty works (2:11); and the Jewish brethren with Peter knew the speakers magnified God. *Third,* Peter said the Gentiles received the like gift, for they were not only baptized in the Spirit but also spoke in tongues as did those on Pentecost (Acts 11:15-17). *Fourth,* Peter used it as a sign to convince Jewish Christians, who had not yet believed that the Gentiles were to receive the gospel without having to be bound by the law. He said it was God's way of proving that the Gentiles should be saved by the gospel without having to go through the law of Moses. He used it three times to prove this same basic point. (a) To prove to the Jewish brethren, who were with him, that it was right to baptize the Gentiles (10:47-48). (b) To prove to the Jewish brethren in Jerusalem that what he did was right. To have refused to have baptized them into Christ would have been to withstand God. (11:17). The church recognized that the entire incident proved that "to the Gentiles also hath God granted repentance unto life." (11:18.) (c) Peter used it to prove that the Judaizers were wrong in trying to bind the law on Gentiles (15:1, 5). He said that God, in sending the Spirit in the way that He did on the household of Cornelius, bore witness that the Gentiles were to be saved by grace through faith (15:8-11).

ACTS 19:6-7

Willis thinks that the disciples in Acts 19 spoke in devotional tongues and not the gift of tongues. He is wrong in assuming that they all spoke in tongues at the same time. The passage does not say so. There is nothing in this passage which indicates that their gift of tongues differed from the gift of tongues in I Cor. 12. They also exercised the gift of prophecy. What truth was confirmed in this incident in Ephesus? It was made evident that the baptism of John was no longer valid, that the time and place for John's baptism had passed away, and that the baptism of the great commission which Paul administered was the baptism which is binding under the new covenant.

I COR. 12:10 AND 14:2 DIFFER?

It is unscriptural to maintain that the gift of tongues in I Cor. 12:10 and the tongues in I Cor. 14:2 are different tongues. One is not devotional tongues designed for private edification while the other is the gift of tongues designed for the edification of the church and as a sign to unbelievers (14:5-6, 22). Nothing indicates that Paul changes from one type of tongues to another.

Paul mentioned the gift of different kinds of tongues (12:10); that not all speak with tongues (12:30); "if I speak with the tongues of men and of angels" (13:1); "tongues shall cease" (13:8); "he that speaketh in a tongue" (14:2); "wherefore let him that speaketh in a tongue pray that he may interpret" (14:13); "I speak with tongues more than you all" (14:18); "by men of strange tongues" (14:21); "tongues are for a sign . . . to the unbelieving" (14:22); "and all speak with tongues" (14:23), "hath a tongue" (14:26); "forbid not to speak with tongues." (14:39.)

What proof is there that Paul switches back and forth between two entirely different gifts? The tongues of which he spoke were designed primarily to function as a sign to unbelievers, and if interpreted they could edify the church (14:5, 22).If neither condition could be fulfilled, tongues were not to be used in the assembly (14:28).

The following passages also make it crystal clear that the gift of tongues is the same as the gift they call devotional tongues. "If any man speaketh in a tongue, let it be by two, or at the most three, and that in turn; and let one interpret: but if there be *no interpreter*, let him keep *silence* in the church; and let him *speak to himself, and to God.*" (14:27-28). The gift of tongues and the gift of interpretation are mentioned here together, just as they were mentioned together in 12:10. If there is no interpreter this very gift of tongues can be used for personal devotional purposes by the one who has the tongue, but he must do it silently in the assembly and speak only to himself and to God. This is the very thing that Paul had already said about individuals who had what Willis called devotional tongues. "For he that speaketh in a tongue speaketh not unto men, but unto God; for no man understandeth; but in the spirit he speaketh mysteries." (14:2.) These were mysteries because they were not understood by those who heard the sound. The gift of tongues, in other words, could be used for devotional purposes as well as for its main function as a sign (I Cor. 14:22; Mk 16:17, 20). The so-called devotional tongues—as distinguished from the gift of tongues—also could be used to edify the church if one interpreted. "Now I would have you all speak with tongues, but rather that ye should prophesy: and greater is he that prophesieth than he that speaketh with tongues, except he interpret, that the church may receive edifying." (14:5.) He should aim to interpret as well as to speak in tongues (14:13). The gift of tongues can be used for private devotion, when not interpreted (14:27-28); and the devotional tongues can be used to edify the church, when interpreted (14:2, 5, 6, 13-19). Thus they are not different tongues but the same gift of tongues.

Let us underscore this same truth by approaching it from another angle. If the gift of tongues and devotional tongues were two entirely different things, the regulations concerning the gift of tongues did not apply to the exercise of devotional tongues. Therefore, one could use them in the assembly even if no one understood them, and the entire service could be devoted to devotional tongues. Willis said this happened on Pentecost. By claiming that one spoke in devotional tongues, rather than with the gift of tongues, one could circumvent Paul's regulations of the gift of tongues in the assembly; even though the results of the exercise of the devotional tongues were exactly the type of results which Paul taught against when the gift of tongues was used and no interpreter was present. Paul laid down the law that the purpose of tongues and prophecy in the assembly of believers was to edify the saints. Devotional tongues, since they were not understood, would no more edify the saints than would the gift of tongues when it was neither understood nor interpreted. The one using devotional tongues would be speaking to God, and not to man (14:2), he would not be edifying the church (14:3-5), he would be an uncertain voice (14:7-8), he would be speaking into the air (14:9), he would be a barbarian to the audience (14:11), he would not even be trying to "abound unto the edifying of the church" (14:12), the unlearned could not say amen for they would not know what he was saying (14:16-17), ten thousand words in a devotional tongue would not be worth five words in a language the people understood (14:19), they would not be a sign to the unbelievers but the unbelievers would think they were mad (14:22-23). But if Willis is right, they could all use devotional tongues in the assembly.

Furthermore, since the devotional tongue is a case where the individual speaks to himself, and to God, but not to the audience (14:2,28), Paul said that one was not so to speak if no interpreter was present. "But if there be no interpreter, let him keep *silence in the church;* and let him *speak to himself, and to God."* (14:28). The man who used devotional tongues was to be just as silent as the man who used the gift of tongues, unless an interpreter was present.

Paul certainly did not forbid the use of the gift of tongues, because of the aforementioned consequences, unless an interpreter was present, and yet allow the use of devotional tongues which would have just as fruitless and just as dire results.

Devotional tongues and the gift of tongues were the same thing. They had a devotional use for the user even when they were not interpreted, and they had value as edification when they were interpreted. If no one understood them in the assembly, they were not to be used in the assembly. But one could speak unto himself and unto God (14:2). However, this was not to be done in the assembly in an audible way. "If any man speaketh in a tongue, let it be by two, or at the most three, and that in turn; and let one interpret: but if there be no interpreter, let him keep *silence in the church*; but let him *speak to himself, and to God."* (14:27-28.) Since *in the church* is contrasted with being *in the home*, silence in the church had reference to silence in the assembly of the brethren (14:30, 32, 34, 35).

The gift of interpretation and the gift of tongues were both given by the Spirit (14:10). Although not all spoke in tongues, and not all interpreted, it is obvious that the gift of interpretation was given so that tongues could be interpreted to those who did not understand them (12:10). "Do all speak with tongues? Do all interpret?" (12:30). This is also made clear by the fact that Paul said if anyone spoke in tongues in the assembly "let one interpret." (14:27). Interpretation, therefore, meant that the message, which had been delivered in a tongue which was unknown to the listeners, was to be translated so that it was conveyed to the understanding listener. Some say that tongues as a means of speaking to oneself and to God was different from the gift of tongues, but Paul showed that this very type of speaking was to be interpreted if one spoke in the assembly. (14:27-28). The very tongues which some have said were devotional were the ones Paul said were to be interpreted by someone with the gift of interpretation. On what ground, then, can anyone claim that devotional tongues (14:2, 28), and the gift of tongues were different?

Since the gift of tongues was the gift of languages, and since Willis agrees that the devotional tongues were languages (Acts 2:4, 6, 8, 11), there is no distinction between the two. The man speaking a language which he did not know naturally would be speaking unto God and not unto man just as surely as the man who used devotional tongues. The man who had the gift of tongues could not use it in the assembly unless someone understood it, and could interpret it to the rest, and the same thing was true concerning devotional tongues. Why assume that they were two different things? Paul is telling them what is to be done with this same gift under different circumstances; the circumstances being the difference between the times when it was understood and when it was not understood.

WHY THE GIFT OF INTERPRETATION?

The gift of tongues, and the gift of the interpretation of tongues, are not only listed together, but it is natural that they should be so listed (I Cor. 12:10, 30). If the gift of tongues was primarily for personal devotion, as some claim, there would rarely be a need for the gift of interpretation. Did people in their private devotions need an interpreter? If so, they would not be able to carry on their private devotions in tongues except when an interpreter was present to listen to their private devotions. It would be strange if the gift of tongues was primarily for personal, private devotional use and the gift of interpretation was primarily for use in the public assembly. If this were the case, there would rarely be a need for the gift of interpretation.

THE BEST ARGUMENT

Some say that devotional tongues are for all. So far as we can tell the best argument which can be made for all having such tongues, is based on the following statement of Paul: "Now I would have you all speak with tongues, but rather that ye should prophesy: and greater is he that prophesieth than he that speaketh with tongues, except he interpret, that the church may receive edifying." (I Cor. 14:5.) If this mean that everyone should seek the gift of tongues, how much more so does it mean that everyone should seek the gift of prophecy; for Paul said prophecy is greater.

If everyone should seek the gift of tongues, they should at the same time seek the gift of interpretation, for without it the understanding is unfruitful and others are not edified; unless someone else interprets (14:5, 13-19). Without this gift, ten thousand words in a tongue in the assembly were not worth five words with the understanding (14:19).

What good would it do the church for everyone to have the gift if at the most only three could speak in the assembly? (14:27.)

Surely Paul did not want everyone to have the lesser gift instead of the greater; in fact, he had rather they prophesied (14:5).

Paul in 14:5 simply indicates that so far as his desires are concerned, everyone could speak with tongues, but he did not indicate that everyone would. He wanted all Israel saved (Rom. 9:3), but all of his native countrymen would not be saved (Rom. 10:1-4; 11:20-23). Paul knew it was not the will of God that all should speak in tongues, for God gave different ones different gifts (12:7, 10-11, 18). Paul implied

126

that all did not speak in tongues, any more than all were apostles (12:29-30). He showed, in the illustration of the body, that *everyone was not the same member*. All are not the tongue, or the ear, etc. (12:14-27).

"The appeal of Paul is also to the church as a whole. They should desire that the best gifts be manifested in their midst, not that each Christian who has a gift should desire others." (Gromacki, 134.)

A RATIONALIZATION FOR THEIR INABILITY

Since people today do not have the genuine gift of tongues, as did the apostles, *they cannot* use their tongues for the primary purpose for which they were given in the first century, i.e. to function as a sign to help convince unbelievers of the inspiration of the speaker and the truth of the message. Therefore, to justify their "tongues," they search for another purpose as the primary purpose. The Bible made secondary the individual edification which could come from the gift, but made primary its value as a sign. When it could not function as a sign it was not to be used in the assembly (I Cor. 14:1-5, 20-28; Mk. 16:17, 20). At least some of the tongues-speakers today view it as primarily a means of personal, private devotion. R. A. Brooks wrote: ". . . except for its occasional use in a group meeting, speaking in tongues is primarily for private worship, and is therefore a matter between the individual and God. No member of the congregation should call into question or criticism the personal devotional life of another member."

"Use this gift primarily in your private devotions. Paul says that one who speaks in tongues edifies himself. Speaking in tongues opens up a new dimension in personal prayer, which can effect deep changes and blessings in your Christian life. For the most part, this is not a gift to be displayed openly, but as a private language of adoration, praise, devotion, and intercession between you and God." (19-20, 21.)

To this we reply: Since the primary purpose of their gift is for devotional life, and the primary purpose of the New Testament gift was for a sign to unbelievers, it is obvious their tongues differ from New Testament tongues.

If they could speak in other languages by inspiration, they would use it as a sign to unbelievers. Since they cannot do so, they justify the gift on the ground of personal devotion.

If they have the gift of tongues, there should be other people in their congregations with other gifts. They should be able to tell the tongues-speakers that the primary purpose of the gift was not for private devotions, but to convince the unbelievers. The fact that they are so confused as to the purpose of tongues, and make its secondary purpose primary, is proof that they do not have the miraculous gift of tongues from the Holy Spirit. If the Holy Spirit had anything to do with it, He would know the primary purpose of the gift, for He set forth in the New Testament its primary purpose (Mk. 16:17, 20; Acts 2:4, 6, 8, 11; I Cor. 14:22).

If its primary purpose is for devotional life, and if it "opens up a new dimension in personal prayer," it is a shame that the Lord did not give this gift to everyone in the first century. The gift of tongues was given to some, but not to all (I Cor. 12:8-11). Do all speak with tongues, Paul asked? The answer, in the light of the context, is No (12:29-30). What a pity that the gift of prophecy, which was superior to tongues (14:1, 4, 5-6, 23-25), left its possessor without this great means of personal devotion. How sad it is that the one who had the gift of interpretation, could inform the congregation of what was said by the tongues-speaker, but he himself did not have the privilege of being able to open up "a new dimension in personal prayer."

If one Christian is convinced from scripture that something is seriously wrong with the personal devotional life of another Christian, he ought to try to help him directly or indirectly. If we are convinced that tongues such as they use are delusion, that they are self-deceived, it is right for us to try to instruct them more perfectly in the way of the Lord.

Furthermore, those who claim this gift are, as a general rule, going to try to get others to seek the gift also. After all, if it is for Christians today, if it is the gift given in the New Testament, and if it opens up "a new dimension in personal prayer which can effect deep changes and blessings in your Christian life," they ought to try to get others to get this gift. Since we do not believe it is of God, and because it opens the door to other errors, we must not only try to help them, but we must also instruct others so that they will not be deceived in this matter.

CHAPTER IX

THE GIFTS IN ANSWER TO PRAYER?

The author believes that the gifts were given through the laying on of the apostles' hands. When the apostles died, the gifts soon ceased as those on whom they laid hands would pass away also. There are no apostles today, therefore the gifts are not being conferred today. In answer to this argument, which is not the only argument against miraculous gifts today, some point out that Paul said: "Wherefore let him that speaketh in a tongue pray that he may interpret." (I Cor. 14:13.) Therefore, the gifts were given in answer to prayer and not just through the apostles' hands.

As far as the Greek is concerned, the passage, as Wordsworth observed, is "capable of two senses, viz. (1) *Let him pray that he may be endued with the faculty of interpreting* . . . (2) *Let him pray with the design and purpose* (not to display his own gift in speaking in a foreign tongue, but) *to interpret.*" "That" can convey the idea of *"in order that;* thus —*let him who speaks in a tongue pray* (keeping this end in view) *that he may interpret.*" (Boise.)

First let us consider whether it means to pray for the gift, and then whether it refers to praying with the purpose of interpreting. In either case, as we shall endeavor to show, it does not mean that prayer alone brought the gift.

PRAY FOR THE GIFT?

If prayer were the only condition, everyone could receive the gift. But not everyone had the gift of interpretation (12:10, 30). If each speaker had also the gift of interpretation, an interpreter would always be present. However, Paul indicated that an interpreter was not always present (14:28). Therefore, I Cor. 14:13 is not a command which tells how all can get the gift.

If prayer was involved, it would not mean that the prayer would be answered apart from the laying on of an apostle's hands. God may answer a prayer through means. We pray for our daily bread, but we do not receive it as manna from heaven, but through the means God ordains (Matt. 6:11; Eph. 4:28; II Thess. 3:10-12).

Some in Rome had gifts (Rom. 12:6), and Paul could confer gifts through the laying on of hands (Acts 19:6). He wanted to visit Rome that he might impart unto them "some spiritual gift, *to the end ye may be established."* (Rom. 1:11). If gifts came through prayer, why didn't Paul tell them to pray for the gift instead of waiting until he got there? If someone in Rome prayed for the gift Paul promised, the answer would not come until Paul laid hands on them. Why wait for this manner of establishment until Paul got there, if God ordained that it could come directly through prayer?

Some had the gift of tongues and of interpretation (I Cor. 14:5). For some reason, sometimes a gift given through an apostle's hands needed to be stirred into a flame by the one who had the gift (II Tim. 1:6). *Perhaps* this could be done through prayer, and may be what is meant in I Cor. 14:13.

With the exception of the baptism in the Spirit of the apostles on Pentecost, the household of Cornelius, and the implied case of Paul, there is no evidence that gifts were given other than through the laying on of the apostles' hands. *First,* none but apostles were said to have worked miracles until after they laid hands on certain individuals (Acts 2:43; 3:4, 6; 4:29-30, 33; 5:12-16; 6:6, 8; 8:6, 13).

Second, Philip worked miracles, but the Spirit did not come on his converts until the apostles laid on hands (Acts 8:7, 13, 15-16, 17-21). We know: (1) Apostles did confer gifts (Acts 19:1-7; Rom. 1:11; II Tim. 1:6). (2) Peter and John laid hands on those converted by Philip (Acts 8:17). Something then happened for "Simon *saw* that *through* the laying on of the *apostles'* hands the Holy Spirit was given . . . " (8:18.) Simon realized the apostles could do something he could not do. Since the baptized believers are promised the gift of the Spirit on the same condition as the remission of sins (Acts 2:38; 8:12-13), the apostles must have conferred the Spirit in some other sense. (3) They had *power* to do this. Simon said: "Give me also *this power, that on* whomsoever I lay my hands, he may receive the Holy Spirit." (8:19.) If nothing happened when they laid on hands, no power was involved. Simon, or anyone else, could lay on hands without anything happening.

Third, Paul conferred the Spirit, with miraculous manifestations (Acts 19:1-7).

Fourth, did Ananias give the Spirit to Saul in a miraculous way? The Bible does not say he did. In fact, the Bible said he laid hands on Saul that Saul might receive his sight (Acts 9:12). Saul's reception of the Spirit was contingent on Ananias' coming only in that Ananias was to baptize Saul into Christ. (Acts 9:17-18; 22:16).

Fifth, did elders confer a gift on Timothy? Paul expressly said the gift was conferred *"through* the laying on of my hands" (II Tim. 1:6), although it was *"with* the laying on of hands of the presbytery." (I Tim. 4:14.) As H. Harvey pointed out: "The gift is said to be in him *through,* or *by means of (dia)* the laying on of the apostle's hands—language which makes the imposition of Paul's hands, in some sense, the medium of conveying the gift." The "gift was imparted *in connection with* the imposition of the hands of the elders of the church," but it was the "direct result of the imposition of Paul's hands, who doubtless united with the presbyters in the act . . . " This showed their agreement with what Paul did. Furthermore, hands were laid on to set apart or commend people for a work (Acts 13:1-2; 14:26-27; cp. I Tim. 5:22). It could have been their commendation of Timothy to God for the work which he was to do as an evangelist.

Sixth, we again ask: If the gifts could be obtained apart from the laying on of an apostles' hands, why didn't Paul tell the Romans to get the gift in this way instead of promising the gift when he came? (Rom. 1:11-12).

FOR US TODAY?

If the gifts came through prayer, without the laying on of an apostle's hands, this would not mean that the gifts are for us today. *First,* if one gift is available, all are; but there is no group today with all the gifts including the apostleship.

Second, this is a matter not just for argumentation, but also for *demonstration.* Who does the wide variety of miracles, including the wide variety of healing miracles with their amazing characteristics, and who reveals and confirms modern revelations and scriptures?

Third, miracles were for the purpose of revealing and confirming the faith, and this full revelation was made in the first century. There are no more confirmers, for there are no more revealers (John 14:26; 16:12-14; Heb. 2:3-4; Jude 3). God did not have to say miracles would cease at such and such a date in order for them to fulfill their purposes and cease because the purposes were accomplished.

Fourth, Paul said tongues would cease and they did cease (I Cor. 13:8).

Fifth, a parallel can be drawn between the creation and perpetuation of the human race, and the creation and equipment of the church, the one new man, so that it can perpetuate the gospel and carry on its work in the world. No passage says in so many words that "God will not create others as He did Adam and Eve." However, if one is looking for a wife, he will not get one as did Adam. How can we prove God is not creating men today as He did Adam? There is no proof He is doing it. God's way has been to start something by miracle and perpetuate it by law. He created Adam and Eve by miracles, and then instituted the law of procreation (Gen. 1:28). The word of God, the seed of the kingdom, was brought to earth and planted here through miracles (Heb. 2:3-4). The apostles, and others with gifts, equipped the church to carry on its work (Eph. 4:7-12). The word is perpetuated through the seed line—by moral and spiritual laws (Lk. 8:11).

PRAY WITH THE INTENTION OF INTERPRETING

J. A. Beet wrote: *"Pray* denotes all speaking to God, and includes the blessing and thanksgiving of v. 16f. And, since v. 14 is given in proof of v. 13, the word *pray* must have the same reference in both verses, viz. public prayer in church meetings. Consequently, *that he may interpret* is not the matter of prayer, but an end kept in view while praying in public. The word *pray* is therefore equivalent to speak with a tongue; and reminds us that such speaking is speaking to God (v. 2). Since edification of the church is the purpose of all spiritual gifts, he who in an assembly prays with a tongue must do so with the purpose of afterwards *interpreting* his own *inspired,* but unintelligible prayer. If he be unable to do this, this verse enjoins him to keep silence in church, unless (v. 28) an interpreter be present." Singing and instructing were also done in tongues (14:5-6, 15, 19).

That one should pray with the intention of interpreting harmonizes with what Paul said both before and after verse 13.

RELATED TO I CORINTHIANS 14:5-11

Paul is stressing that the tongues speaker should "seek that ye may abound unto the edifying of the church. *Wherefore* let him that speaketh in a tongue pray that he may interpret." (14:12-13.) If he does not interpret, he cannot edify the church. "He that speaketh in a tongue edifieth himself; but he that prophesieth edifieth the church." (14:4.) If he speaks in tongues, and then interprets, he can edify the church. "Now I would have you all speak with tongues, but rather that ye should prophesy; and greater is he that prophesieth than he that speaketh with tongues, *except he interpret, that the church may receive edifying.*" (14:5.) Paul continued this line of thought by saying that tongues without interpretation were as sounds without distinction, as sounds spoken into the air, and as the voice of a barbarian (14:6-11). This being the case, those who spoke in tongues, as in prayer for example, should pray with the intention of interpreting that which they had spoken in tongues. Unless one can pray in a tongue with such an intent, he should not pray in tongues in the assembly. In fact, he would not do it in the presence of one or more believers, since it could not result in their edification either.

PRAYING WITH THE UNDERSTANDING

To pray with the intention of interpreting also harmonizes with what follows this statement of Paul. "Wherefore let him that speaketh in a tongue pray that he may interpret." What if he does not pray with the intention of providing an interpretation after he has prayed? In such a case his understanding is unfruitful. Paul explained this by saying: *"For if I pray in a tongue, my spirit prayeth, but my understanding is unfruitful."*

In order to keep his understanding from being unfruitful, what will Paul do? "What is it then? I will pray with the spirit, and I will pray with the understanding also: I will sing with the spirit, and I will sing with the understanding also." (14:14-15)

134

What does it mean that his understanding is unfruitful? Does it mean that he does not himself know what he is saying? If he does not know, how does he know he is praying and that he is giving thanks well? But he does know these things. (14:16,17) His understanding, therefore, is not unfruitful in that he does not know *anything* about what he is saying in the tongue. However, if a tongue is not followed by an interpretation the understanding is unfruitful in that *it does not bear fruit in so far as the audience is concerned.* It is without any good results for the audience. If he prays with the spirit and the understanding, his understanding is fruitful. Fruitful to whom? To the audience. To pray or speak with the understanding meant the understanding was fruitful. But to pray or speak with one's understanding meant the audience was instructed. "Howbeit in the church I had rather *speak five words with my understanding,* that I might *instruct* others also, than ten thousand words in a tongue." (14-19.) In other words, his understanding is fruitful when he instructs others *when he sings, prays, or speaks with the understanding.* That this is what Paul is saying is confirmed by his statement immediately after speaking of the unfruitfulness of the understanding. "What is it then?" " . . . I will pray *with the understanding also* . . . I will sing with the understanding also." (14:15) That this has reference to speaking so as to be understood is brought out in the consequences which follow if one does *not* speak with the understanding. The audience does not understand and is not edified (14:16-17).

If one thinks it is a peculiar form of expression to say "speak with the understanding," or "pray with the understanding," when one means to speak so as to be intelligible to others, remember that Paul defined in verse 19 what he meant by praying, singing, or speaking with the understanding. It is to speak so that others understand.

Paul's determination, to speak with the understanding, explains what he wanted those who had the gift of tongues to do. It unfolded what he meant when he said: "Wherefore let him that speaketh in a tongue pray that he may interpret." (14:13.) Because if he does not, his understanding is unfruitful in that others are not edified (14:14-19).

Storr concluded that Paul was saying: "I will, as miraculously enabled by the Spirit, pray in an unknown tongue; and I will also pray as a wise man, desirous and aiming to profit those who hear me, i.e. so as to be understood. I will also sing under the inspiration of the Spirit, and I will sing to the edification of my hearers." (As quoted by David Greene)

NOT TO SPEAK UNLESS INTERPRETER ALREADY PRESENT

To pray with the intention of interpreting the tongues to others also harmonizes with Paul's instructions that they were not to speak in tongues unless someone already present had the gift of interpretation. This interpreter could be, in some cases, the speaker himself (14:5), and in other cases it could be someone else. "But if there be no interpreter, let him keep silence in the church." (14:28.)

Paul certainly did not mean that one was to speak in tongues, and then pray for the gift of interpretation. This would violate Paul's instructions that one was not to speak in tongues in the assembly unless an interpreter was present. Unless he could speak with the understanding and instruct others, he was not to speak (14:13-19).

Although Pat Boone stressed more than once that the failure to receive the gifts was due to a lack of understanding and faith on our part, he also recognized that the final decision must be according to the will of the Spirit (I Cor. 12:11). It is the author's conviction that the evidence justifies the conclusion that far more than desire and prayer were involved in whether or not one received a gift. The apostles' hands were also involved.

CHAPTER X

TESTED BY THEIR TEACHING

An unsuccessful sign proved a prophet was not of God, but even the successful sign workers had to be tested by their teaching (Deut. 18:20-22; 13:1-6). For a time Pharaoh's magicians seemed to match Moses, but their teaching was false and before the contest was over even Pharaoh knew who was on God's side (Ex. 7:8-13, 22; 8:7, 15-19, 25; 11:1). Jesus warned against false prophets who showed "great signs and wonders" (Matt. 24:24). On judgment day some, who have not done God's will, will tell Christ that they prophesied, cast out demons, and did many mighty works in His name (Matt. 7:21-23). Paul spoke of the lawless one "whose coming is according to the working of Satan with all power and signs and lying wonders . . ." (II Thess. 2:9-12). Therefore, if men moved mountains with words we must still test them by their teaching (I Thess. 5:21; I John 4:1).

AUTHORITY OF CHRIST

Christ is the head of the church (Eph. 1:22-23). To accept His Lordship means that we must do what He says (Lk. 6:46). We are to be judged by Christ and His word (Acts 17:31; John 12:48). This is the word which He received from the Father (John 12:49-50).

We do not get this word directly from Christ by being personally inspired by the Spirit. How do we get it? *First,* in a special way Christ gave the word to the apostles in His personal ministry. Of the larger group of disciples, Christ had lost many, but of the apostles He had lost only one—Judas (John 6:66-71). It was to the apostles that He gave the word (John 17:6-8, 12, 14). Others were to believe on Him through their word (John 17:20-21). *Second,* Christ was speaking of the apostles when He said the Spirit would bring to their remembrance all that He had taught them (John 13:1-2, 21-30; Matt. 26:20-25; John 14:26). Although we benefit from the truth which was brought to their remembrance, no one today has an inspired remembrance of all Jesus taught in the personal ministry. *Third,* the Spirit was to guide the apostles into all of the truth (John 16:12-13). By the time the last apostle died, all truth had been delivered or Jesus' promise failed. His promise did not fail; therefore, the faith was once for all delivered unto the saints (Jude 3; Col. 2:3-7; II Pet. 1:3). Although we are not personally guided by inspiration into all the truth, we benefit from the promise to the apostles for we have the truth which the Spirit revealed and confirmed. We believe because of their word (John 17:20-21; 20:30-31). *Fourth,* there were other men also whom the Spirit inspired, and through whom He revealed and confirmed truth (I Cor. 12: 28-31; 14:6). *Fifth,* we are to abide in the truth which was revealed and confirmed in the first century (Matt. 28:20; Acts 2:42; John 13:20; I Cor. 14:37; Jude 3; 2 Thess. 2:15). There is no other word from Christ than the word in the Bible; therefore, we continue in it and not in it plus something else. The test on judgment day is not whether we believed that we worked miracles, but whether we did the will of Christ (Matt. 7:20-23).

GOD IS NOT THE AUTHOR OF CONFUSION
AND CONTRADICTION

". . . God is not a God of confusion, but of peace." (I Cor. 14:33). This principle covers not only the confusion in Corinth but any other source of confusion. If what someone is doing, while claiming to be guided by the Spirit, is confusion we know it is not of the Spirit. Of course, one must deal with the question of what constitutes confusion. Confusion may be caused by those who reject God's word, but the preaching of the word itself is not the cause of the confusion (Acts 22:22-24).

God is not the God of contradiction. "Every good gift and every perfect gift is from above, coming down from the Father of lights, with whom can be no variation, neither shadow that is cast by turning." (Jas. 1:17). This principle covers both miraculous gifts and natural gifts. The Spirit of God would not teach one thing through Paul and another through someone today. He is not variable, and so He does not cast shadows by turning from one contradiction to another. Although this author's experience is limited, he has always been able to find, sooner or later, contradictions between the Bible and the teaching of those who claim to be miraculously guided by the Spirit. Any who do not want to subject their teaching to the test of the Bible prove that they are not inspired by the Spirit. If they were inspired, they would not hesitate to contend for their faith, and prove to uninspired men that their teaching is biblical. They would not rely on their experiences, or minimize doctrine. They would recognize that we are to be judged by Christ's word, not by our experiences, and that we must acknowledge the inspired writings—the Bible (John 12:48; I Cor. 14:37; Jude 3).

DENOMINATIONALISTS AND GIFTS

The Full Gospel Business Men's Fellowship, with which Pat has some association, has within it representatives from a wide variety of denominations; including Catholic priests. Tongues speakers are found in different seminaries. A wide variety of gifts is claimed.

God used the miracles to confirm His word (Mk. 16:17, 20; Heb. 2:3-4). God is not the God of confusion and contradiction (I Cor. 14:33, 40; Jas. 1:17). Therefore, God is not giving miraculous gifts to those who teach doctrines contrary to the Bible, and who perpetuate denominationalism. Jesus viewed religious division as a very serious thing. He prayed for the unity of believers, a unity which could influence the world to believe. His prayer includes us, for we believe because of the apostles' word (John 17:20-21, 8; 14:26; 16:12-13). Since the very beginnings of denominationalism—such as loyalty to men around whom a party is built—were condemned in the Bible, how much more so is the open denominationalism of today? (I Cor. 1:10-13).

Paul emphasized the one body of Christ (I Cor. 12:12-13). He taught the one baptism and the one body as surely as he stressed that there is one Spirit, one Lord, one God, and one hope (Eph. 4:4-6). He urged them to give "diligence to keep the unity of the Spirit in the bond of peace." (Eph. 4:3.) They were not to go beyond what is written in their attitude toward faithful teachers of the gospel (I Cor. 4:6). How much more so should we abide within what is written with reference to the one faith, the one baptism, etc.?

There are Roman Catholics who claim the gifts, who do the same type of "wonders" that others do, but who remain in that Church. The Holy Spirit teaches that there is but one head of the church, and we are all to hold fast to Him (Eph. 1:22-23; Col. 1:18; 2:19). Therefore, the Spirit would not leave men in a Church which has another head—the Pope.

There are modernists who claim the gifts, or the Spirit in an unusual way, but who deny the biblical doctrine of inspiration.

Mrs. M. B. Woodworth-Etter began her healing ministry in 1885. She claimed to write books by inspiration, predicted that Christ was coming in just a few years, that through her came the "Last call to the Gentile sinners, the Last Call to the Marriage Supper of the Lamb," that Christ would reign on earth for one thousand years, that her visions were fulfilled and that she worked miracles.

WOMEN PREACHERS

There are women preachers who claim the gifts. Some of them, such as Mrs. McPherson and Beebe H. Patton, founded churches. The Holy Spirit said that women were not to speak or prophesy in the assembly (I Cor. 14:29, 34-35). In I Cor. 11:2-16 Paul corrects their unseemly appearance in the assembly when prophesying, and in I Cor. 14:34-35 he forbids their prophesying. This is parallel to the fact that he first forbids eating meat sacrificed to an idol in an idol's temple on the ground it may lead a brother to stumble (8:1-13), and later forbids it as wrong within itself (10:17-22).

Since other passages authorize congregational singing (Eph 5:19), and since in such a case a woman is not singled out or placed over the man in the assembly, there is no reason to assume that congregational singing, participated in by women, was forbidden.

Ann Lee (1736-1784), the founder of the Shaker community, claimed to speak seventy-two languages. She taught that she was the second coming, that God was male and female, that Jesus was not God manifest in the flesh, and that the Shaker communistic sect was the advent of Christ's kingdom on earth. Dollar said that their "gift of tongues was also accompanied by times of unspeakable joy and dancing during which many of the hymns of the movement were composed, although made up of unintelligible and unheard-of words." (Gromacki, 22.)

Some who claim to follow Paul's teaching on tongues, reject his commandment concerning women preachers (I Cor. 14:37).

ORAL ROBERTS

Pat thinks that Oral Roberts is filled with and led by the Holy Spirit. This does not mean that he agrees with everything Roberts teaches, but he does think Roberts has at least some gifts. We ask: *First,* did the Spirit lead Roberts to join the Methodist Church a few years ago? Much of the top leadership of this church accepts modernism and denies the biblical doctrine of inspiration. This church was founded by man, not by Christ. The Spirit would not have led him into the Methodist Church. Why, if Roberts has been baptized in the Spirit, didn't the Spirit warn him against joining this Church? In this connection a statement by W. E. Mann in *The Christian Century* for September 5, 1956 is of interest. He wrote that Roberts might "start a new sect. Or it may be that, like Charles Templeton, he will come to recognize the limitations of his pentecostal tradition and seek a broader education and a definite church connection."

Second, there were Pentecostals, who have as much evidence of being baptized in the Spirit as Roberts has, who had supported Roberts financially for years. They were not only disappointed, but thought it was wrong for Roberts to join a denomination which had not endorsed, or sponsored, his work during the time the Pentecostals enabled Roberts to get to his prominent position. Which "spirit" was right? The one that told Roberts to join the Methodist Church or the one which told some Pentecostals that Roberts did not do the right thing?

141

Third, has Oral Roberts accepted, opposed, or just ignored the doctrines of faith only, infant baptism, and sprinkling as taught in the Methodist Church?

Fourth, in *Abundant Life* for July 1959 Roberts wrote: "The isolation of the Yemenite Jews continued until 1948, when God spoke to their leaders and caused them to organize an exodus from Arabia to Palestine." (a) What proof does Roberts have that God spoke to their leaders? (b) If God had spoken to their leaders He would have told them to go to Christ, not to Palestine. (c) God speaks today through His Son, and those first century apostles and prophets who were sent by Him (Heb. 1:1-2; 2:1-4).

Fifth, Roberts asked an 85 year old Rabbi to bless him. "He reached over and put his aged hands upon my hands. Then he began to pray, and he blest me in the name of the God of Abraham, Isaac and Jacob. And I tell you that I felt the presence of God in a strangely wonderful way. I could not keep back the tears."

"Then I put my hands upon the hands of the mother, father and children there on the table, and blest them in the name of Jesus Christ of Nazareth. Once again the room was filled with the presence of the Lord . . . What an unforgettable experience!" (6-7.) It is right to pray for all men, but was the presence of God manifested in a strangely wonderful way as a result of the blessing by a Jewish rabbi who did not believe in Christ?

Roberts preached in Israel. Although not every occasion is an opportunity to preach Christ, or to engage in religious discussion, was he moved on any of these occasions to reason concerning Christ with these Jews, and, if necessary, powerfully confute "the Jews, and that publicly, showing by the scriptures that Jesus was the Christ"? (Acts 18:28.)

Sixth, Roberts told Ben-Gurion that he, Roberts, did not have an ear for languages, nor did he know Hebrew (7). If Roberts had the gift of tongues, he should speak some language, or languages, by inspiration.

Seventh, W. E. Mann attended three meetings during a healing crusade by Roberts in Detroit and, among other things, wrote: "The abrupt manner in which Roberts treats many of these failures is disillusioning." (1018.) Gordon H. Fraser told of attending a healing service conducted by Roberts among the Navajo Indians. Many were disappointed for no one was healed.

Eighth, Harland G. Lewis, in the *Christian Century* for September 5, 1956, pointed out that some who came to be healed, and were not, may be left with a sense of guilt. " 'If faith heals and I am not healed, then I am at fault. I am being punished. What's wrong with me?'

"Sometimes this guilt, driven deeper by crowd excitement, is left to fester, and thus the faith-healing campaign produces more pain and illness." (1020.)

Ninth, V. E. Howard wrote that people have died shortly after they were supposed healed at one of Roberts' services.

Tenth, the Bible teaches that the baptism of the believing penitent is into the death, burial, and resurrection of Christ. It is unto the remission of sins, is a part of the new birth, and is into Christ (Acts 2:38; 22:16; Rom. 6:2-5, 17-18; John 3:3-5; Gal. 3:26-27).

There are some who think it is a matter of no importance as to why one is baptized. The Scriptures do not view it in this light. Paul asked some "Into what then were ye baptized?" They had been baptized into John's baptism. They now had to be baptized according to the baptism taught in the great commission (Acts 19:3-5). John's baptism was from heaven, and to reject it was to reject God's counsel (John 1:33; Lk. 7:29-30). When the baptism of the great commission went into force, John's baptism was no longer valid. Surely baptisms today, which are not into Christ are not scriptural baptism. If one thinks he is in Christ and saved before he is baptized into Christ, how can his baptism be the baptism Jesus commanded? Such a baptism was never of divine origin. Since John's baptism, which was of divine origin, was not valid under the new covenant, how much more so is a baptism not valid which is based on man's doctrine.

How long would it take Priscilla and Aquila to teach Roberts, and these other individuals who have not received biblical baptism, more accurately in the way of the Lord on on this subject? (Acts 18:24-26.)

The motives of Mr. Roberts may be left to God's discernment, but the evidence does not justify us in believing that he has been baptized in the Holy Spirit, or is miraculously led by the Spirit, or that miracles take place in connection with his ministry.

Oral Roberts teaches that "It is not necessary to be baptized in water to receive salvation from God . . . we are not saved because we have been baptized, but we are baptized because we have been saved." (Questions and Answers on Doctrine," p. 2.) Pat thinks Roberts has been baptized in the Spirit. The *same day* Peter was baptized in the Spirit, the Spirit through Peter taught that baptism, of the believing penitent, is unto the remission of sins (Acts 2:38). If Roberts has been baptized in the Spirit, why does he not understand what the Spirit saith concerning the purpose of baptism?

Eleventh, was Oral Roberts baptized into Christ? Pat Boone authorized T. G. O'Neal to publish in his bulletin Pat's letter of January 13, 1970 which said, among other things, that: "You may not know that recently Oral Roberts was baptized in water for the remission of his sins calling upon the name of the Lord. I knew this before I went on his program . . . this makes Oral Roberts our brother, unless we have come up with some other standard of membership." When the author received a copy of this bulletin in July, 1970, it was the first he had heard of such a claim concerning Roberts. However, Pat had said in a letter to the author that he had seen Oral Roberts baptize someone unto the remission of sins.

Although the author was confident Pat was sincere in his statement, he wrote Roberts concerning Roberts' position on baptism. In a form letter on July 13, 1970, Roberts said: "Water baptism is not essential to salvation, but it is a testimony to the world that the old life of sin has been forsaken. In other words, we are not saved because we have been baptized, but we are baptized because we have been saved." He enclosed a tract on "Questions and Answers on Doctrine," which said in essence the same thing. If Roberts and Pat are both recipients of some of the miraculous gifts, as they claim, why this contradiction and confusion?

144

Twelfth, Oral Roberts was immersed, and would still choose immersion. "But I have seen too many of God's born again Christians who were baptized by some other mode for me to engage in a controversy on the subject." ("Questions and Answers on Doctrine," p. 2.) The Spirit saith that baptism is a part of the one faith (Rom. 6:2-5, 17-18; compare Acts 8:36-39; Eph. 4:4).

ANCIENT HERETICS

Eusebius quotes an earlier writer's evaluation of the heretic Montanus, which said: "There, they say, one of those who was but a recent convert, Montanus by name, when Cratus was proconsul in Asia, in the excessive desire of his soul to take the lead, gave the adversary occasion against himself. So that he was carried away in spirit, and wrought up in a certain kind of frenzy and irregular ecstasy, raving, and speaking, and uttering strange things, and proclaiming what was contrary to the institutions that had prevailed in the church, as handed down and preserved in succession from the earliest times . . . For he excited two others, females, and filled them with the spirit of delusion, so that they also spake like the former, in a kind of ecstatic frenzy, out of all season, and in a manner strange and novel, whilst the spirit of evil congratulated them, thus rejoicing and inflated by him, and continued to puff them up the more, by promises of great things . . . Those few that were deceived were Phrygians; but the same inflated spirit taught them to revile the whole church under heaven, because it gave neither access nor honour to this false spirit of prophecy." (196-197).

If God were with any of these groups in a miraculous way, the group which held to the true doctrine would so clearly outdo all other groups that it would be evident who was on God's side. But all of these groups do the same type of "wonders".

IGNORE TEACHING REGULATING TONGUES

In spite of the fact they claim inspiration or other gifts, and in spite of the fact that the Spirit regulated the use of tongues in the New Testament, many tongues speakers ignore these regulations. *First,* some of them speak in tongues in groups or in entire congregations. This does not edify (I Cor.

145

14:2, 5; 16-17), the unlearned cannot understand or amen it (14:15-17), it is not worth five words spoken with understanding (14:19), it is not a sign to the unbeliever, but may strike him as madness (14:23), they are refusing to take turns (14:27), and they are not silent when there is no interpreter (14:28).

Second, they often refuse to limit its use to "at the most three." (14:27.)

Third, many of them exalt tongues far beyond what Paul taught in I Cor. 14. Would the Holy Spirit in them emphasize what Paul de-emphasized?

Fourth, some have special meetings where they pray in tongues for their own edification. They are not speaking just to themselves and to God, so they violate I Cor. 14:28, and they are not edifying others (14:4).

Fifth, the use of tongues was to be regulated by love. Love suffers long, so it would not refuse to wait its turn (13:4; 14:27-28). Love envieth not, therefore it would not envy one with a greater gift, nor covet a gift which God did not will to give one (13:4, 12:13, 7, 11, 18). A tongues speaker should not be puffed up (13:4). Love does not behave itself unseemly, so it would not use tongues disorderly (14:23, 40). Love is not manifested in some of the unseemly convulsions or indecent things which have happened in tongues meetings. The Spirit today would rebuke them for such things if He spoke directly through any of them. Furthermore, love which seeketh not its own, would not seek the gift of tongues primarily for self-edification. Although "self-edification may be a by-product of the gift, it should never be the goal" (Gromacki, 121-122; I Cor. 13:5; 14:4, 12).

TONGUES A SIGN

Primarily the gifts were not signs to the individuals who had the gifts, but to the unbelievers in whose presence the signs were used to confirm the message. God "bare *witness* unto the word of his grace, granting signs and wonders to be done by their hands." (Acts 14:3). The written record of the signs was to create faith (John 20:30-31).

Tongues were one of the signs which God used to confirm the word (Mk. 16: 17, 20). They did it on Pentecost (Acts 2:4, 6, 8, 11, 33, 36), and Paul expressly said that "tongues are for a sign, not to them that believe, but to the unbelieving . . ." (I Cor. 14:22). Paul's statement is authoritative (14: 37). The Jews especially sought after signs (I Cor. 1:22). They were present on Pentecost, and at Cornelius' household (Acts 10:45). Jews would have especially been impressed by Paul's reference to the Old Testament in connection with tongues being a sign to unbelievers (I Cor. 14:22). The signs were also for the Gentiles, for they confirmed the word (Heb. 2:3-4). If we have tongues today they must be for the same purpose— to reveal and confirm the word. If we have confirmers today, we also have revealers. Some tongues speakers think that the Bible is the only revelation from God. It is, but if we have the signs today we must also have revelations today, and should have more scriptures being written today.

CERTAIN OF THEIR INFALLIBILITY

Although individuals do not always follow their positions to the logical conclusions, the logical conclusion of their conviction, of a direct and infallible communication and confirmation from God, is that any of their whims, positions, and attitudes are infallible if they are received in connection with, or otherwise seem to be confirmed by, these experiences. Just as their certainty, based on their interpretation of their experience, is beyond the reach of rational examination and rational objections, just so the positions which they take under the same influence are beyond the reach of reason and scripture. They have heard from God, and anything which questions this must be swept aside and ignored. Reason, the Bible, facts of experience; all these mean nothing to them. They have heard from God, their "experience" has confirmed it, and the matter is settled. For them to doubt would be to doubt the very foundation of their religious life and leave them in unbelief, uncertainty, and with the knowledge that they had been self-deceived. It might leave them with doubt as to the very existence of God, or with the desolate conviction that they are now without hope and without God for they are without the "experimental" confirmation which they once thought they had. All this because they built on a false foundation.

There are numerous illustrations where this sense of infallibility has led to immorality and cruelty. R. A. Knox tells us of some incidents around the beginning of the 18th century. Of these he said: "But what lends an added touch of horror to the Camisard murders is that they were not merely in the name of religion but under the direct influence of a religious inspiration. The cynical brutality of governments in crushing out revolt, the mean and hateful revenges taken by an oppressed people, may shock our sense of humanity; but the motives of them are too easily credible, two much akin to the baser instincts in our own nature, to make us feel the full force of Lucretius' Tantum relligio. It is when good men, or what seem to be good men, interpose on the side of barbarism, and preach against clemency as something in itself hateful to God, that we begin to despair of the weak vessels we human creatures are. Such are our feelings when . . . the Camisard prophets override the wishes of their military leaders by insisting that women and children must be put to the sword with the rest. Yet these men, to all appearances, were men of conscience; la Riviere, a pupil of Vivens, justified the massacres when he stood his trial, on the ground that St. Paul told the Corinthians to take away the wicked from among them. That is the worst of it; the Ultrasupernaturalist faced with a moral problem believes that the solution is given to him directly by the voice of God, and from that arbitrament there is no appeal." (363-364.)

In some cases, reality may be so painful that it shatters their illusions. In the late seventeenth century, Gabriel Astier "assured his followers that if they stood their ground and raised shouts of *Tartara* weapons would be powerless against them. At the first approach of the troops they were discovered lying on the ground in ecstacy, or breathing into one another's mouths to produce an inspiration of supernatural courage; it was only as the failure of the prediction became apparent that they began to fire in their turn." (362.)

148

EXTREME ACTIONS

The "Spirit" which some get leads them to carry on in various ways which indicate neither sanctity nor sanity. These people do some of the same things, in so far as speaking in tongues and "miracles" are concerned, that are done by others who do not go to these extremes. Why the difference?

The difference does not seem to be in the "spirit" which they have, for one gives as much evidence otherwise as does the other that they have the same type of "spirit". The less expressive are not restrained by the "spirit", so far as we can tell, but by such as the following: (a) They are less emotional by nature. (b) They have learned self-control in the past. (c) Through their study of the word they have learned more, and therefore act more sanely, than the more emotional and the less informed. (d) They have been taught by others who are less emotional, more informed, and who teach them against such extremes.

SAFEGUARDED BY THEIR GIFT?

To the extent that any of the tongues speakers are safeguarded against error, they are safeguarded not by their gift but by their knowledge of the Bible which they have gained through a study of the Bible and not through the gift itself. The author has known of individuals who were reared in the church and then went into the tongues movement. These individuals, in some cases, continued to hold to the teaching of the Bible concerning baptism, the one church, etc. These things they had learned in their pre-gift days. These things kept them from accepting some of the unscriptural positions which are held by other individuals who claim the gift of tongues and who got their unscriptural positions from the churches in which they were reared. It was not their gift which guarded them from errors on these subjects but their knowledge of the Bible which was gained through study of the word in their pre-gift days. Furthermore, any knowledge of the Bible which they get in their gift days has come, just as the author's has to come, through study. On the other hand, the individuals who have the gifts, but hold to errors in doctrine because of their background, do not get these errors corrected through their gifts or the gifts of others. If they are corrected it has to come through a study of the word. Why, if the Holy Spirit is giving people the gifts today, do not some of them learn their errors either through their own direct inspiration, or the inspiration of someone else today? If the Holy Spirit were giving the miraculous gifts today, as He did in the first century, at least some people would have the gift of discerning the spirits, and they would expose false doctrine. There would be others who would do the same for they would have the gift of knowledge. Why, if they have what the people in the first century had, does the Spirit fail to do through the gifts what He did in the first century? Paul, for example, was inspired by the Spirit to correct the errors present in the church in Corinth. Why don't they have some inspired apostle Pauls, or some other apostles to correct their errors today? How has Pat reacted to this line of thought?

INDIVIDUALS NOT GROUPS?

It has been suggested by Pat Boone that God is dealing with individuals today, and not with groups or organizations throughout Christendom. Although the Spirit is leaving them in different denominations today, He is gradually revealing more and more truth and finally there is to be a great gathering of people. They are being drawn gradually. It will not be done overnight. This position must be evaluated in the light of the following scriptures. *First,* Paul did not tell those in Corinth, who were parties to factions within the church, that they could remain in the factions since God is dealing with individuals and not with groups (I Cor. 1:10-13). He rebuked their division; therefore, how much more so is the open denominationalism of today rebuked by the Bible.

Second, Paul clearly taught that there is but one body (Eph. 4:4-5), and that it is the body, or church, of Christ (Eph. 1:22-23).

Third, the apostles, who were baptized in the Holy Spirit and preached by inspiration, clearly taught the people on Pentecost that they were to be baptized into Christ (Acts 2:38, 40-41). The first gospel sermon told them to be baptized into Christ. They were not left where they were for years, while the Spirit gradually brought them to an understanding

150

of baptism. The Samaritans were not left in the Samaritan religion, but were baptized into Christ (Acts 8:12-13). The eunuch was not gradually led to the truth on baptism, but was taught it in the first sermon Philip preached to him. As a result he wanted to be baptized, and was baptized (Acts 8:36-39). Saul saw the Lord, and although there was a short period of time between the time he saw the Lord and the time when he was baptized, the first Christian who came into contact with him told him to be baptized. From the time he believed until the time he was baptized, he neither ate nor drank (Acts 9:9, 19). He did not continue among the Jews as if he had undergone no great change, and without their knowing about it. "And straightway in the synagogues he proclaimed Jesus, that he is the Son of God." (Acts 9:20). Cornelius and his household received the Spirit before baptism in order to prove that the Gentiles were to come into Christ without going through the law (Acts 10:47; 11:15-18; 15:8-12). There was no long period of time before the Spirit taught them the truth on baptism. For immediately through the apostle Peter the Spirit told them to be baptized (Acts 10:47-48). When Paul found some disciples in Ephesus who knew only the baptism of John, it did not take the Spirit years to lead them to the truth concerning baptism. Immediately, because of Paul's instruction, they were baptized into Christ (Acts 19:2-7).

Although the Spirit did not reveal all the truth on Pentecost, all sinners seeking salvation were told immediately what they must do to be saved. None of them were brought into a denominational body or allowed to continue in denominationalism. Furthermore, we have the complete truth into which the apostles and prophets of the first century were guided. We have the faith which was once for all delivered unto the saints (John 16:12-14; Jude 3). There is no reason why people should wait for years to find out the will of the Spirit on baptism and on the church which is the body of Christ. The Spirit continually speaks to us on these, and on other, subjects in the Bible. He that hath an ear to hear let him hear what the Spirit saith (Compare Rev. 2:1, 7).

Fourth, if anyone is in the Babylon of religious confusion, they should come out of Babylon lest they partake of her plagues (Rev. 18:4-5).

Fifth, how long is it supposed to take? People have been in Pentecostal-type movements in this and other countries for centuries, and yet they have not been guided out of denominationalism and into the one church. Instead, they have either joined denominational churches or established denominational churches of their own.

Regardless of what spirit they may have, it cannot be the Holy Spirit for He would not allow them to perpetuate denominationalism and to frustrate the answer to the Lord's prayer for unity. He would immediately tell them what they must do to be saved if He were speaking directly to them, and speaking through them today.

PERFECT?

Pat thought that the author believed that those who are baptized in the Spirit, and have some of the gifts, should be perfect in life and teaching; including their interpretations of the Bible. *First,* we realize a person can fall below the truth he teaches (Gal. 2:14), but no one should be guided into such a failure. *Second,* no one should be guided into error, nor should the error be confirmed by gifts. But people who claim the gifts are in a wide variety of churches and hold a lot of different doctrines. *Third,* all the truth was not revealed in the first century through one gift and one individual. However, the sum total of the truth was revealed through men with gifts. Why don't these individuals with gifts get together and produce an inspired commentary on the New Testament? *Fourth,* if the people have the Spirit, whom Pat assumes are miraculously endowed by the Spirit, at least some of them should point out the false teachings concerning baptism, the nature of the church, and show denominationalism is contrary to the Spirit's teaching. The Spirit through Paul corrected abuses and false doctrines in Corinth which, if they had already been pointed out by inspired teachers in Corinth, had been ignored by at least some of the Corinthians. Why are not some of the modern prophets as plain as Paul on these matters? Furthermore, those who think themselves to be prophets or spiritual would then acknowledge that what these prophets taught were God's commandments (I Cor. 14:37).

However, in spite of what the Spirit teaches in the New Testament, the men whom Pat thinks are guided by the Spirit continue in their errors in these matters, and think that at least some of their positions are confirmed by their experiences. Would God, who confirmed *His* word in the first century through gifts (Mk. 16:17, 20), confirm error through the gifts today? If some of those with whom Pat deals give up their errors in these matters it will not be through teaching received through their gifts but through someone who learned it from the Bible.

OUR DIVISIONS

Pat indicated we should clean up errors in the church before trying to correct others. Division does exist in the church, but does this mean that we cannot oppose denominaionalism? *First,* if the individual or the church must get rid of all error in teaching or life before trying to teach others, no teaching will be done. We do not have to be perfect in order to teach others. *Second,* perfect unity did not exist in the first century, but division was exposed and opposed (Eph. 4:1-6; I Cor 1:10-13). If these people today had miraculous gifts, the Spirit would teach them that such division is wrong. In fact, the Spirit has already taught this in the New Testament. *Third,* none of us claim we are inspired, or that signs confirm any errors which we hold. *Fourth,* the divisions among us do not require us to perpetuate denominationalism, but if we were in a denomination we would be endorsing and perpetuating denominationalism. *Fifth,* it did not take the Spirit long, through Paul, to oppose religious division (I Cor. 1:10-13; 12:12-14). Why do men, whom Pat thinks to be led by the Spirit, fail to do what Paul did? *Sixth,* it is true that some have not been as kind as they ought to have been in teaching others, but, on the other hand, some are so considerate of the feelings of others that they never teach them more accurately in the Lord's way. *Seventh,* Pat cited John 8:1-11 in connection with denominationalism. These enemies of Christ were trying to trap him. Furthermore, Jesus said for her to sin no more (John 8:11). We are not perfect, and we do not have the power of judicial condemnation, but we are to show that the

Bible is against denominationalism. Does Pat tell denominationalists to go their way and practice denominationalism no more? The author is confident that sooner or later Pat must tell at least some of them that it is wrong. Surely he knows too much Bible to fail to do this. *Eighth*, none of us are perfect. Shall we balance, therefore, our error against their error and cease to oppose their error? No. We should be willing to learn from anyone, even if they are hypocrites (Matt. 23:1-4; Phil. 1:15-18). There is a vast difference between being in Christ's church and being in some church not mentioned in the Bible. As members of Christ's church all truth belongs to us even though we do not see all of it (I Cor. 3:21-23). Therefore, we should be open to truth regardless of who calls it to our attention. We do not have to leave Christ's church in order to accept the additional truths. However, one cannot be open to certain truths and continue in denominationalism (Eph. 4:1-6).

GIVING UP DOCTRINES

Pat wrote that unity is not to be found through our giving up this doctrine in return for that doctrine, but by the surrender of individuals to God's will, by being humble, as was Peter, so that God can show us His Corneliuses. *First*, we must be honest, humble, and studious so that God can teach us through His word. *Second*, doctrines of men can make void God's word (Matt. 15: 1-9), therefore as we learn we must give up such human traditions in order to accept God's teaching on such subjects. *Third*, there are Corneliuses today in the sense of devout people who want the truth. By being diligent in sowing the seed of the kingdom we shall find more and more of these hearts which furnish soil for the seed. *Fourth*, as has been pointed out elsewhere in this book, there are no cases today where through a series of miracles and visions God places an apostle in touch with such a seeker after truth. God established, through the case of Cornelius, the truth that the gospel is for all. Men do not have to become Jews in order to become Christians. This truth was revealed with clarity in connection with Cornelius. There is no other case like it in the New Testament. If there were inspired men today, who through a series of miracles were placed in contact with such as Cornelius, these inspired men would tell them words whereby they were to be saved, and would quickly baptize them into Christ (Acts 11:14; 10:44-48). However, some whom Pat thinks have received the baptism of the Spirit have not yet been baptized into Christ.

POLICING THE CHURCH?

Pat thought that some of us were trying to police the church and the teachings of others. *First.* we are not police with judicial power to enforce the law. *Second,* we are fruit inspectors (Matt. 7:20), wolf detectors (Matt. 7:15-16), contenders for the faith (Jude 3), men who try the spirits and those who claim to be apostles (I John 4:1; Rev. 2:2), and men who must walk circumspectly lest we fall. *Third,* the Scriptures are to be used to make people wise unto salvation, to teach, to give reproof, to bring to the proof, to correct, to rebuke, to exhort, to instruct in righteousness, and to expose sins and false doctrines (II Tim. 3:15-4:4; Rev. 2:1-7, 8-11). We must recognize that all will not endure the sound doctrine, and some will turn from the truth unto fables. We are to uphold truth and oppose error in all longsuffering, while speaking truth in love. *Fourth,* elders are not policemen but they are shepherds who must guard the flock against departures from within and assaults from without. They must give an account unto God. They are watchmen (I Pet. 5:1-4; Acts 20:28-31; Heb. 13:17). The elders at Inglewood were not given much of a chance by Pat to watch over him for they did not learn of his beliefs in these matters until long after he thought he had received the gift of tongues. *Fifth,* we are to be set for the defense of the gospel (Phil. 1:17, 27-28). We need to be taught of Paul's "ways which are in Christ," even as Paul taught everywhere in every church (I Cor. 4:17). Paul was not policing the lives of others when he rebuked sin, exposed error, and told them that under certain conditions they were to disfellowship others. Since we are not to go beyond what is written in our regard for persons, is it any less important that we not go beyond what is written with reference to doctrine? (I Cor. 4:6.)

We are not acting as policemen when we test teachers and doctrines by the word of God. We are obeying the Bible when we test, by both their accomplishments and their teaching, those who claim to have miraculous gifts today. We are convinced that their teaching shows they are not miraculously guided by the Spirit.

Love for God and for His word demands that we try these professed miracle workers not only by their accomplishments, or lack of them, but also by their teaching.

CHAPTER XI

THE HOLY SPIRIT IS NOT A DECEIVER

Deception is of the darkness, but the Spirit guides us in the light (I John 1:5-7). Christ is the truth, and we must walk in the truth and not in deception (John 8:26, 40, 45-47; 8:31-32; 14:6). The Spirit of truth guided the apostles in all the truth, but not into a course of deception (John 14:17, 26; 16:13). It is possible for children of God to be deceived unless they continually evaluate their faith and conduct by God's word. While leaving the judgment of hearts to God, and without impugning the motives of men, we can evaluate actions.

In the course of the conversation with Pat and Shirley Boone on February 18, 1970, which lasted until after 2 a.m., the author pointed out that brethren who had invited Pat to be on programs undoubtedly thought that he had been misrepresented in these matters. The next afternoon the author emphasized that the brethren in Abilene would not have invited Pat for the coming weekend if they had known his position. The fact that Pat's course of conduct in this matter resulted in the deception of brethren was proof that Pat was not miraculously guided by the Spirit. In an effort to impress this on Pat the author also mentioned Reuel Lemmon's defense of Pat.

The author was careful to point out that he was not impugning Pat's motives. Pat thought he was doing the right thing, for reasons which we shall later discuss. However, the Holy Spirit knew that brethren were being deceived, and He would not have guided Pat into a course which resulted in such deception.

DEFENSE BY REUEL LEMMONS

Pat Boone had received some criticism from brethren because of his appearance on Oral Roberts' program, as well as some other appearances. Pat wrote an open letter to Reuel Lemmons, which was published December 2, 1969 under the heading: "A Statement of Personal Faith." This moving statement expressed his determination to utilize whatever opportunities he had, even though he could not always say all he would like to say, to turn the thoughts of people in some measure toward God, Christ, and the Bible. He requested prayers that he might make the right decisions.

In an editorial in the same issue Lemmons expressed his high regard for Pat Boone. He said mistakes are made by all of us in our efforts to teach the gospel, that we ought not to withdraw from such opportunities, and that "I probably would not say what Brother Boone would say, nor what his critics would say, because we are different people." (754.) Reuel defended only the principle of utilizing what one believed to be opportunities.

There was a statement in Pat's article which no one, who did not know what Pat's experiences were, could really understand. The statement seems clear, and unless one knew what Pat meant by "experience," he would not conclude that reference was made to miracles such as the speaking in tongues. Pat said: "Because of those things experienced during the past two years—more than because of any prior knowledge or previous experience—I now understand why 'without faith it is impossible to please Him!' . . .

"To me God's word is suddenly as immediate as yesterday's newspaper. I feel that the tides of 2,000 years have been rolled back and that my God is the God of Adam and the Father of Christ . . . that He has been since the beginning of time: Concerned with man's frailties, willing and ready to bless our feeble efforts with His limitless power." (757.) This is actually a reference to the gifts.

During the conversation on February 18, 1970, the author told Pat that if Reuel Lemmons had known the full story on Pat's beliefs he would not have defended him in the way he did. It was pointed out that, according to one of the author's friends in Austin, there had been protest to the *Firm Foundation* about Reuel's defense. The author told Pat that he was leaving Reuel out on a limb. Pat then said to his wife, "Shirley, I had never thought of that." When the author returned on Thursday afternoon he again stressed this point. It was emphasized that this point was especially important because Pat's position on miracles and tongues had become a matter of public controversy among some brethren throughout the nation. Furthermore, if he had these gifts, they were for

158

public evangelization of the world and edification of brethren. When Pat talked with Reuel a few days after the author's conversation with Pat, Pat did not discuss his position on tongues with Reuel.

ORAL ROBERTS' PROGRAM

In 1969 Pat appeared as a guest on Oral Roberts' program. This created a controversy among some brethren who felt his appearance was an indication that Pat agreed with Roberts. There was some discussion of it in the pages of such publications as the *Christian Chronicle, The Gospel Defender* (Sept. 1969), and the *Firm Foundation* (Dec. 2, 1969).

At the time the author did not know Pat's position concerning miraculous gifts. He had heard that Shirley had been influenced by this type of conviction, and that some were trying to persuade Pat. This was just rumor, but the author had written Pat—without mentioning the rumor—and had sent him some material on the subject; including his book *Miracles or Mirages?* Pat said he was reading the material, and that he would write the author about it. He expressed the belief that the Lord had more for us. He did not say, in what sense, and so the author did not conclude from this that Pat had accepted the idea that the miraculous gifts are for us today. Months later, when Pat was in New·York filming the motion picture on the experiences of David Wilkerson as set forth in *The Cross and the Switchblade*, the author wondered whether portraying this role and working with Wilkerson would have an impact on Pat. When Pat saw the author's daughter in New York, he told her that her Daddy was worried about him, but to tell him he did not need to be worried. At the time the author did not know how to interpret the statement. It could mean that Pat was not being influenced in that direction, or it could mean he had accepted miraculous gifts as being for us today, but this was a good thing and not something to be worried about. The author did not know which interpretation was right; so he drew no conclusion. He now knows, of course, that Pat must have meant the latter.

When the author was asked concerning Pat's appearance on the Oral Roberts' show, he responded by saying that he had not heard what was said. He said it could be that Oral

Roberts had taken advantage of Pat, had caught him off guard, and left some impressions which Pat would not have wanted to leave. On what little the author knew about the appearance, he had tried to put on it the best possible explanation.

It was not until March 1970 that the author secured a partial transcript of the program.

On the program as taken off the tape by a friend's secretary, Pat said he and his wife felt they were "being led by Him again in a brand new and more powerful way." With only this statement before one, questions could be raised as to just what Pat meant. What was this "brand new and more powerful way"? What did "again" mean? Did it mean he had once walked close to God, and was led by Him in His providence, and now was doing the same again? But how was this a "brand new and more powerful way"? In the light of what the author learned the night of February 18, 1970, he now knows a great deal of what Pat included in his statement. It is obvious that Pat knew what he included in this statement, and he knew it *at the very time* some brethren were going out on a limb and defending his appearance. *They would not have defended him if they had known the meaning of Pat's statement.* Pat knew this also. Pat, however, kept it hidden from these brethren, and was "guided" to let these brethren go out on a limb which Pat could know, if he thought awhile on it, would be sawed off from under them when the truth became known.

Here is the context of Pat's statement. Oral Roberts: "Pat, God has moved in on you and Shirley these past few months, tell us about it." Pat Boone: "In the last few months, and partly, or largely to, the help of my better half, Shirley, and through God's own workings I came to realize that God doesn't need me, or my career, or anything else I have. He doesn't need me at all to do His will, but He wants me, He wants my soul and He wants my love, and if I give that to Him in an uninhibited way and unreserved way then He can use me, use anybody He wants to and He will do things with you, and through you, that you never dreamed of yourself. And so we have made this new commitment and the amazing thing is that I was willing to die for (to?) my career, if

160

that's what He wanted. And now I feel new life surging back again, and once again He is in control and He is making the decisions. We find our lives very exciting not just in the entertainment field, but mainly because we feel ourselves being led by Him again in a brand new and more powerful way."

Oral Roberts seems to have known more about Pat's convictions at the time than Pat was making known to his brethren. Roberts at least knew that something different had happened in Pat's life within the past few months. He implied that God had moved in on Pat and Shirley in the past few months in a way He had not done before. Furthermore, it was something which Oral Roberts wanted expressed on his program. Pat told Roberts that God had moved in on them to the extent they were "being led by Him again in a brand new and more powerful way." While *brethren could wonder* about what he meant, *Pat knew* what he meant. He meant that he and Shirley now had miraculous gifts and direct revelations. However, he expressed it in such a way that it would leave the uninformed confused as to what he meant. From what he said, no one could say that he had affirmed that he possessed miraculous gifts. When brethren discussed publicly why Pat appeared on the program, and what he meant by his statements, Pat allowed his defenders to remain in the dark and to make defenses of him which they would not have made if Pat had told them his position on miraculous gifts. We are not saying Pat was conscious of the course of deception he was following, but now he has had time to think it over, he should realize that he was not being led by the Holy Spirit, but by his own inclinations and the false justifications of such a course which he had heard from others or thought up himself.

Did Oral Roberts know that Pat thought he had the gift of tongues? Was this involved in the question which he asked Pat and, therefore, involved in a veiled way in Pat's answer? The author asked Roberts. On April 9, 1970 Roberts wrote the author and, in the first paragraph of his letter, said, "Yes, I knew that Pat Boone had received the gift of the Holy Spirit and tongues. It is what I referred to when I said, 'God has moved in on you and Shirley these past few months, tell us about it'."

Pat knew, Roberts knew, but brethren were kept in the dark.

HARPER'S EXHORTATION

On March 6, 1970, E. R. Harper wrote Pat that he should publicly stand up for what he believed. However, Harper was disappointed that, although the author had told Pat he ought to inform the brethren who had invited him to Abilene the weekend of February 22, Pat had failed to do so. Pat replied that: *First*, there had not been time to arrange a meeting with the Highland elders. *Second*, he had no leading from the Spirit to do so. *Third*, the lack of leading might be due to the fact that a public statement of his position would lead to controversy and choosing sides. *Fourth*, he should be judged by what he did, and not so much for what he believed. His fruits, not so much what he said or did, were the test. These things make it clear that Pat still thought the Spirit was guiding him in the strategy of keeping these beliefs from the brethren. How shall we evaluate his justifications of this strategy? The next chapter is devoted to this subject.

CHAPTER XII

JUSTIFICATION?

The author believes that the course of conduct discussed in the previous chapter involved deception. However, he is convinced that Pat thought he was doing right in trying to keep his beliefs from the brethren until his book was published. What are some of the grounds on which he justified this course of conduct?

PERSONAL MATTER

Pat justified keeping these beliefs from the brethren on the grounds that they inolved an intensely personal matter which he felt no leading to proclaim. Although our relationship with Christ is personal, we should want others to share it and we should use both public and private opportunities to tell others. Paul plainly told others of such intimate details in his joyful relationship with Christ (Compare I Cor. 14:14, 15, 19).

If Christ has these gifts for us today, to preach Christ fully would include teaching people that they should seek the baptism of the Spirit and these gifts which, Pat believes, bring one into a much closer, and more deeply spiritual, relationship with Christ. In fact, Pat said this was the way he came to know Christ as Lord. Didn't he want others to know Christ as Lord?

The apostle Paul publicly taught about gifts. He showed they should be exercised in the assembly of the saints, when they would edify the church, and in preaching the gospel to convince unbelievers (I Cor. 12; 14).

These gifts were used publicly to glorify Jesus through revealing and confirming His word (I Cor. 2:1-5; Heb. 2:3-4). They were not reserved for discussions in confidential conversations.

It was more than a personal matter between Pat and the Lord. Pat's position had become a matter of public controversy. There are brethren who maintain that he has been misrepresented in these matters. In their misunderstanding they were denying that Pat believes what he actually does

163

believe about the gifts. Some of these brethren who invited him to appear on programs thought that he had been misunderstood. When Pat's position became known, these brethren found that Pat had left them out on a limb. Knowing brethren as surely as he must know them, did not Pat realize they would be left out on a limb, and that they would not have invited him, nor defended him as they did, if they had known his beliefs? These brethren were deceived and, we say it with tears, Pat thought he was being led by the Spirit into this course of conduct.

Although Pat is willing to study this subject further, he was not in the condition of a person who was confused and unsettled about his present position. He had deep convictions which he not only practiced in his home, but also taught others on occasion. In fact, he had some influence on Dennis' conversion to the tongues movement. There were cells of tongues speakers, in more than one congregation, which knew of Pat's convictions. Through sharing his experiences with selected individuals, as he did with the author, Pat hoped to convince at least some of them. He thought he would convince the author.

Pat himself made this far more than a private matter, for he publicly proclaimed his position in some denominational publications, in some public appearances, and in some published interviews. Examples will be given in the next chapter.

Some with whom Pat talked made public statements. A minister, who had just been in Pat's home, told the New Life Center in Shreveport, Louisiana, toward the end of 1969, that Pat had been baptized in the Holy Spirit. Sometime in 1969 David Wilkerson made a public statement in Toronto concerning Shirley's experiences with the Lord through the Holy Spirit.

So many statements had been made that it was impossible for these things to be kept as a matter of an intensely personal experience.

MEAT NOT FOR MILK DRINKERS?

Pat thought that tongues and the other gifts were strong meat, and that to try to feed them to babes might strangle them. Therefore, the Boones did not make known publicly their convictions on the gifts. They taught these things only to those whom they thought were sufficiently mature to eat the strong meat. The Bible does speak of milk and of meat, but it nowhere indicates that the gifts were strong meat about which one did not inform immature Christians. In writing to the Corinthians Paul said that they were babes who needed milk, not meat (I Cor. 3:1-2). Did he withhold from them the truth about tongues? No.

First, they knew of the gifts before they became Christians, for signs were performed in their midst to confirm the gospel (Mk. 16:17, 20; I Cor. 2:4-5; II Cor. 12:11-12). *Second*, although they were babes in Christ, they had the gifts (I Cor. 1:4-8; 12:4-31; 14:1-40). *Third*, the spiritually immature were exercising gifts (14:20). *Fourth*, the nature of the gifts demanded that they be used publicly in confirming the word (Mk. 16:17, 20; I Cor. 14:22; Heb. 2:3-4), and in teaching the brethren (I Cor. 14:5-6, 22, 27-28). Pat thought he had several gifts. Why were they not for public use? *Fifth*, even though they were babes, Paul told them about the meat and rebuked their manifestations of childishness (I Cor. 1:10-12; 3:3-4, 5-9). *Sixth*, although one's spiritual condition has to be taken into consideration when one is being taught, Hebrews revealed truths to the people even though they were dull of hearing (Heb. 5:11-14; 6:1). *Seventh*, Paul did not deny, nor did he hide from the babes in Corinth, the existence of meat. He did not, by his silence, leave the brethren in the dark as to his position. When their position was under fire, and being controverted, the Boones by their silence failed to let many brethren know that they believed they had the "meat." They permitted brethren to deny that they believed in and had the "meat." At first Pat was not aware that some brethren were saying that he thought he had certain gifts. However, the Spirit knew, and Pat thought he was guided by the Spirit.

Pat replied that the church knew about the gifts in the first century, but today the church has not seen, or believed in, them. This is true. However, if they are a part of the faith they should be taught and possessed publicly. Furthermore, when one's position is being publicly controverted, one ought not by his silence fail to let brethren know that such important strong meat exists and is for us.

SETTLED OPINIONS

Pat avoided making public statements because people had such settled opinions on these matters. However, if these gifts are for us today, it is important that we have them so that all of us can live in living color instead of in black and white. When people are settled in the wrong things, they need to be unsettled so that they can settle on the right things. Furthermore, in spite of settled opinions, Pat planned to make a public statement through his book.

NOT BEAR THEM NOW?

It may be claimed that Jesus kept the meat from His disciples. Before His ascension He said: "I have yet many things to say unto you, but ye cannot bear them now. Howbeit when he, the Spirit of truth, is come, he shall guide you into all the truth: for he shall not speak from himself; but what things soever he shall hear, these shall he speak: and he shall declare unto you the things that are to come." (John 16:12-13.) Jesus withheld certain things from His disciples, therefore we may withhold certain things from others if we think they are not ready for these things.

Jesus, of course, was inspired, but we do not have any evidence which convinces us that these people today are inspired in what they are doing.

Jesus already had the confidence of His disciples. They were convinced that He was the Son of God (Matt. 16:16-17). Although they did not understand everything that Jesus said, and although some other disciples turned back at certain *hard* sayings (John 6:60, 66) the apostles did not go away. "Jesus said therefore unto the twelve, would ye also go away? Simon Peter answered him, Lord, to whom shall we go? Thou hast the words of eternal life. And we have believed and know that thou art the Holy One of God." (John 6:67-69.) With confidence that Jesus was the inspired Son of God, the apostles were content to wait for Jesus to reveal the things—the many other things—which He mentioned in John 16:12. We do not believe that the ones with whom we are dealing today are inspired, and we cannot simply take on faith in their word that what they are doing is an application of John 16:12.

We do not live in the time of the incomplete revelation, which is mentioned in John 16:12, but in the time of the complete revelation. In order for Jesus' promise to the apostles to be fulfilled, the apostles had to be guided into all of the truth. Unless the complete truth had been revealed within their lifetime, the promise of Jesus failed. His promise did not fail; therefore, the hard things—the many things they could not bear during the personal ministry—were all revealed. The "many other things" have been revealed. They are there for us to read, even though some things may be difficult to understand; for there are profound things as well as simple things in the Bible (2 Pet. 3:16).

We recognize that sometimes a person has to grasp one principle before he can understand another principle. We realize that an individual may not understand why we take a stand for or against a certain thing unless he first realizes the principle which we are applying to the particular case. Therefore, it will be necessary for us to explain to him these principles before he can understand why we have taken such and such a position. In doing this, however, we do not deny, nor do we keep covered up from him, the fact that we accept such and such a position.

It may be that, in a conversation with an individual, there are several things with which we disagree. However, we may believe that one of the things is the basic point of disagreement at this time. Therefore, we may ignore the other points of disagreement and deal with the one which we think is most vital. However, if the individual asked our position on other matters, we would not hide our position from him. Even when asked, and we tell him our position, we may go on to say that we believe the most important point of difference to discuss at this time is such and such. If he insists he would like to discuss the other points of difference, we should deal with them since he considers them more important at this time.

There may also be cases when an individual, who has not obeyed the gospel, is concerned about something in the book of Revelation, but unconcerned about his duty. In such a case we may briefly state what we think the passage in Revelation teaches—if we think we understand it—and then point out that regardless of what the passage teaches, what value is it to him if he has not accepted the Lord? Of course, it may be that from the passage in Revelation we may very naturally and logically work our way to the question of his own relationship to the Lord.

In some cases an individual may ask us a question, and we may believe that his motives are wrong, or that it will be profitless to discuss the matter with him. In such a case we may: (a) Refuse to discuss the matter, but without denying our position. (b) We may tell him we shall answer his question if he will first answer our question. If he refuses to do so, we may refuse to answer his (Matt. 21:23-24). Others who hear of it will realize that he has no just cause for complaint because we did not answer his question. Of course, with a sincere person one may ask a question in answer to his question because his answer may help us to understand him better, or may even provide the principle in the light of which his own question can be answered.

These things, however, are different from a situation in which our position—what we actually believe—has become a matter of controversy. Some people may attack us and say that we hold to such and such a position. Others may defend us, and say that we do not hold to this position. Under such circumstances how can we be justified in letting some deny that we hold a position when we actually hold the position? How can we let them, in their ignorance, *deny our true position* and furthermore, *go out on a limb for us* when we know full well that when our position is known they will have the limb sawed off from underneath them? Although we may be so confused in our thinking that we do not see that this is a deceptive course it is still deceptive. We have allowed others to be deceived in letting them go ahead and make a defense of us against charges which we know to be true. We have allowed them *unconsciously to misinform others* whom they persuade that we do not believe the position. Although we realize that such a confused person may be acting in good conscience, we must let them know that, regardless of their motivation we believe this is the way of deception. While accepting their explanation of their own motivation in pursuing such a course, we must let them know—regardless of how hard it is for them to bear it—that we believe that it is wrong. Furthermore, we believe that their very pursuit of such a course, while claiming to be led by the Spirit in doing it, is positive proof that they are not led by the Spirit of God. And yet, they believe the evidence justifies them in believing they are led by the Spirit in this matter.

JESUS AND HIS QUESTIONERS

Pat thought that the author's approach to these matters would prove that Jesus practiced deception by side-stepping direct answers, answering in ways He knew they would not understand, and sometimes in refusing to answer. As has been pointed out, there was sufficient evidence to show the Jews that Jesus was the Messiah and, therefore, whatever course He followed was right. There is no evidence that Pat was inspired in the course he followed, therefore, we cannot automatically conclude it was right.

Christ was dealing with some people who were not seeking the truth and did not have the love of God in their hearts (Matt. 23:29-37; John 5:38, 41-44, 47). Surely most of the brethren who were concerned about Pat were not of such a condition of heart. Furthermore, such as the Pharisees had had abundant opportunity to know that Jesus was sent of God, but they had hardened their hearts against Him and sought to destroy him. Pat had not given brethren evidence that God was guiding him in these matters.

Pat did not cite concrete cases of "side-stepping direct questions," but perhaps he had in mind such as Matt. 21:23-27. Consider the following: (a) Christ would have answered their question if they had answered His. They refused. (b) The right answer to His question contained a principle which rightly answered their question; for John bore witness to Him. (c) Their refusal to answer Jesus' question revealed that they disqualified themselves as prophet testers. (d) Christ then plainly rebuked them for their rebellion and unbelief, cited a prophecy, and pronounced their coming doom (Matt. 21:28-46). Does any of this parallel the way Pat treated brethren with reference to the concealment of his belief in miraculous gifts?

If Pat had in mind the parables, we observe: (a) Christ did a lot of plain teaching, which they rejected, before He taught in parables. (b) He gave additional information to those who wanted to know (Matt. 13:10-23). Do these parallel Pat's treatment of brethren?

169

PAUL AND EATING MEAT

In connection with his view that the Spirit was not leading him to take a public stand before the brethren, Pat told E. R. Harper on March 19, 1970, that he did not know why the Spirit did things as He does. If the author understood him, Pat is saying this was what the Spirit was doing, but he could not explain. When there is sufficient reason to believe God has done something, one does not have to know why He did it in order to be assured He did it. Pat, to use an example he gave, thought that the Spirit did not lead Paul to make a public statement, in the presence of non-meat eaters, that he did eat meat. This would have been a stumbling block, and the Spirit knew that such an issue was not meant to be a divisive issue among brethren.

The following convince the author that these things do not justify such a course of conduct. *First,* the real issue is whether the Spirit guided Pat in this matter. The author understands Pat's dilemma. This course did result in some brethren being deceived. As long as he believes he was led by the Spirit he cannot believe it was a course of deception. If he comes to believe it was a course of deception he must give up the conviction that it was the work of the Spirit. *Second,* what "spirit" guided him to make so many public statements? *Third,* the Spirit could not have led them to the position that it was just a matter of their private life, for the Spirit teaches that tongues were mainly to confirm the word as a sign to unbelievers and to edify brethren (Mk. 16:17, 20; I Cor. 14:2-5, 22). *Fourth,* if tongues are for us today, the Spirit would rebuke those who reject it and say: "forbid not to speak with tongues." (I Cor. 14:39). This would be authoritative (14:37). *Fifth,* the Spirit led Paul to openly contend against those things which hindered the truth of the gospel (Gal. 2:3-5, 14). If the gifts are for us, Pat should contend for them. *Sixth,* Paul publicly said that it was right to eat meat (Rom. 14:14), unless it involved one in the worship of idols or led others to sin (Rom. 14:15-21; I Cor. 10:18-22, 24-11:1). To forbid to eat meat under other circumstances was a mark of apostasy (I Tim. 4:1-3). One could deny meat to himself (Rom. 14:17), but not to others. Paul did not keep brethren in the dark as to his position on meats.

PAUL BECAME ALL THINGS TO ALL MEN

In keeping his belief in tongues from brethren as a whole, while telling it to others, was Pat following Paul's example of becoming all things to all men? Paul did not remain silent while people denied that he ate meats or believed in becoming all things to all men. He publicly stated his positions on these matters. Paul's flexibility was in the area of his privileges and freedom as a Christian which did not involve his duties. He was under law to Christ (I Cor. 9:21), but wherein Christ had left him free he was flexible so as to avoid casting any unnecessary stumbling blocks in the path of those whom he was trying to win for Christ. Paul's mission was not to make Jews or Gentiles, but to make Christians out of Jews and Gentiles. Therefore, he did all things for the sake of the gospel in order to save men (I Cor. 9:20-23; 10:32-11:1). I Cor. 9:12, 18 gives an example of his refusal to exercise certain of his rights because he thought that, under the circumstances, he could be most effective in winning the Corinthians. Pat's behavior with reference to holding back his belief in tongues from the brethren does not parallel Paul's becoming all things to all men.

FRUIT NOT BELIEFS

Pat thought they should be judged by their fruits, by their lives, and not by their beliefs. However, it does matter what we believe. What we truly believe controls our actions and produces our fruits. Of course, individuals may have some private opinions, which are not to them matters of faith, and they may be very quiet about these. However, Pat believes these things to be a part of the faith, and he had not been very quiet in some quarters about these beliefs.

What we say is a part of our fruits. For example, there is the fruit of our lips, the sacrifice of praise (Heb. 13:15). By our words, too, we are judged (Matt. 12:37. Thank God for His mercies). We are judged by our teaching; whether we teach the word of God.

Those who claimed to work miracles, as well as others, are to be judged by the will of God (Matt. 7:21-23). Pat realizes this.

A part of Pat's actions involves teaching others these things privately, and, in less detail, publicly. Dean Dennis started out to convert Pat, and Pat converted him.

AVOID BEING A BONE OF CONTENTION

One reason Pat concealed his position was that he did not want to be a bone of contention. While we understand Boone's feeling in the matter, the following observations are in order. Pat's own desire and his aversion to controversy—and we can understand this, for controversy within itself is not pleasant—have caused him to conclude that the Lord was leading him in such a way as to avoid being a bone of contention.

The Holy Spirit led Paul to dispute with those who opposed the gospel (Acts 15:2, 6-7; 17:17; 19:8), and inspired Jude to exhort us to contend earnestly for the faith (Jude 3). If Pat is right, these gifts are a part of the faith and he should contend for them earnestly even if it does make him a bone of contention. Why the difference in Pat's guidance and Paul's?

Likely Pat thought he was led to make at least some statements concerning miracles in some of his public appearances, and in certain publications. Didn't he realize these would involve him in controversy? Did he think brethren would not learn of these things—when he must have known that in some cases brethren might be in the audience; or did he think that if they learned of them they would think he meant something else than what he seemed to be saying? It would be impossible for him to make public statements on these matters and at least some brethren not learn about it. The very course he has followed produced controversy, not only about his position, but also about his course of conduct.

Some other things that Pat had done had already produced controversy. Some of the controversy was carried on in the *Christian Chronicle,* in some church bulletins and some other publications. There were brethren who said that his appearance on Oral Roberts' program indicated that he had leanings in that direction, or shared his beliefs, and others have denied it. There were those who maintained that he was speaking in tongues, and there were those who said this was a misrepresentation of Pat.

The course which Pat said the Spirit led him to pursue led some to doubt Pat's motives, and will lead more to doubt his motives when they finally learn how long he has held to these positions. They will not only discredit his motives, but regardless of his motives, they will know that such a course of conduct has discredited the idea that he has been guided by the Spirit and that he actually has any miraculous gift from God. The author is convinced that Pat's course of conduct does discredit the idea that the Holy Spirit has led him in this matter. It also discredits Pat's judgment in this matter. Pat thinks at times he not only has the supernatural leading of the Spirit, but also other gifts such as the gift of wisdom. His course of conduct discredits this, and shows that Pat cannot distinguish between his own inclinations—his aversion to controversy, etc.—and some supposedly divine guidance. Certainly neither he, nor those who have advised him in this matter, nor those who have advocated the type of arguments with which he justifies his course of conduct, have the gift of wisdom or the miraculous guidance of the Spirit. Furthermore, the author does not believe that God would give Pat miraculous gifts which have helped confirm him in his belief that he has been guided by the Spirit in this course of conduct.

The author still believes that Pat is honest, but that he is very confused. Of course, there will be those who do not understand how he has justified these things to himself, and at least some of them will doubt his integrity. The author deeply regrets this.

How long Pat could go on, after his attention had been called to these things more than once, in this course of conduct without being a conscious deceiver, is another question. At the present, however, his strong conviction that this is the guidance of the Spirit will keep him from believing that it was deceptive. For, he can reason, the Spirit is not a deceiver; therefore, it was not deception when he followed the Spirit's leading in this matter! At the rate the evidence accumulated, it finally passed the time when any decision from Pat, or any "guidance" which he thought he had received, had anything to do with whether the brethren as a whole learned of his position.

Pat was puzzled because the author insisted that a public statement was a matter of concern, since, he said, the author knew such a statement would raise a howling debate. He asked whether this was what the author wanted. If the author followed his desires he would rather agree than to disagree. But controversy is inevitable in a world in which there is sin and error. Therefore, the author ought to do his duty even when controversy is painful. Pat is such a lovable chap it is not easy to hit him head on. Furthermore, there have already been debate, confusion, and choosing of sides. Some controversialists have been controverting in the dark because they have defended Pat without knowing his position.

The author's insistence on these matters is a part of his position concerning Pat's claim of miraculous gifts. In spite of his good motives, what Pat has interpreted as the guidance of the Spirit has resulted in brethren being kept in the dark. Under the circumstances this is a course of deception. Surely this cannot be the work of the Spirit who is the Spirit of truth (John 16:12-14). Pat, and the author asks this with tearful heart, can't you see this?

KEEP PEOPLE CONSTANTLY INFORMED?

Pat asked if it is a matter of deceiving brethren if he did not continually and publicly keep people abreast of his private convictions. But this dealt with his position on some matters which brethren deem to be very vital, which he thinks are important, which have become a matter of public controversy, which he has mentioned in some public interviews, and which he taught to others from time to time. Furthermore, he believed the course which he was following may have been the most effective way to prepare people for accepting these private convictions later. In the same paragraph he wrote that if later the things the Spirit had done through them testified to what was then said, people would be more ready to accept the validity of what they said.

IF HE IS WRONG, IT IS BETTER TO KEEP IT QUIET

Pat thought that a public statement was not best because if they changed their convictions, a retraction would be necessary. However, he had already made enough public statements to make it necessary for him to try to correct these, if he decides these experiences are not miraculous experiences from God. Would it not also be important for him to make known publicly to brethren the fact that the current discussion among brethren, as to his convictions on these matters, was not due to some brethren misrepresenting his position when they said that he believed he had some of the miraculous gifts? Having made so many statements, which brethren have gotten hold of, how could he quietly and privately change without some public statement? The brethren who know his present convictions, and those whom they have told, would not know that he had changed, and others would not know that they had not misrepresented him in *these* matters.

PREMATURE?

Since they were still studying, Pat thought it was not time for a statement which would be hasty and ill-thought out. The willingness to study is good and commendable. However, he had already made quite a number of public statements, as well as taught some people privately in sharing his experiences with them. In February Pat told the author that a long, taped interview was being turned into a book. Were there any basic changes in the convictions expressed in it? If not, can it be viewed as a hasty, ill-thought out statement? Furthermore, if he and his family have the various gifts, including inspiration at times at least, these gifts ought to have enabled them to make some very excellent statements. Of course, their judgment was that the Spirit has not yet willed that they make a public statement to the brethren. Pat had been studying this matter for around two years, or more, and had held these convictions for over a year.

MUST RELY ON THE SPIRIT

Pat wrote that he would not use the gift of tongues in the assembly where he attended unless the Spirit led him to do so, since he had to depend on the Spirit's impulses and not on his own. He did not tell how he distinguished between his impulses—for example, his aversion to controversy—and those of the Spirit. Is it done by the Bible? A feeling? A supernatural sign? Or a voice? In the same paragraph he stressed that we must reinstate the concept that Christ is the head of the church. This means that He does the thinking for the

175

church and we must follow His orders. However, much of His leading cannot be anticipated or understood through the word. Pat thought Jesus showed us that we cannot always predict or contain the Spirit's work, since the Spirit is like the wind and no one knows where He comes from or where He goes (John 3:8). What shall we say to these things?

If this is true concerning the impulses of the Spirit to us today, and Pat was discussing Christ's thinking for us today and letting us know what we should do today, how can one measure all things by the word? It is not contained in the word, nor is it predictable on the basis of the word, *how then can it be measured by the word?* If this is the case, there must be some other way in which to decide whether it is of God, than by measuring it by the Word of God. Do we measure it by some modern revelation? Would not a "leading" be a modern revelation, since it is the work of the Spirit and Pat supposedly knows it is the work of the Spirit? Is it confirmed by modern miracles? Does it escape altogether the test of whether it is in harmony with the revelation in the Bible? If it does escape this test altogether, how can Pat reject some of the unscriptural things into which some other people, with so-called miraculous signs, are being led, and have been led in the past?

As has been brought out in the section on questions and answers, John 3:8 does not teach that the Spirit and the Christian are unpredictable. Whether he realized it or not, in the same letter Pat contradicted this position for he predicted that the Spirit most certainly would not contradict the Bible.

THE LORD'S STRATEGY TO PREPARE THE CHURCH?

During the conversation on the phone on February 28, 1970, Pat and Shirley, with Pat as the main spokesman on these particular matters, said that they believed the Lord was leading them day by day in graceful and gentle ways. For them to jump out and go ahead of His leadings would be to rock the boat. Christ is the Head of the church, and He does the thinking for the church. Although we must use our own minds also, the Head, and not the leg or some other member of the body, lays out the strategy. Pat said that if he started taking over, and determining the direction of things, he would be trying to take over the function of the Head. He would be trying to do the thinking instead of letting the Head do it. They would make a public statement now if they felt that God wanted them to do it. They did not feel led to do it. Instead, they shared in the light of their own experience, the leading of the Spirit, and the spiritual condition of other people—whether they are babes who would gag on the meat or are more mature so they can take the strong meat. They did not want to see the church torn asunder. The best way was, first of all, to let people see that they had more dedication than before, and as people see the fruits in their lives, the new idea can come in and be more effective. The people will see that these gifts are nothing to be afraid of, for they do not lead to extremes as in the case of some people. They believe the devil conterfeits these gifts, and that the extremes are due not to the leading of God, but to the work of the devil. Furthermore, they said, only the Spirit can reveal these things to different individuals. They, in following the leading of the Spirit, tell the full story of their experiences only to those who are prepared for it.

Christ is the head of the church. But we can know His thinking only as He has revealed it. No man can know the mind of God except as the Spirit of God has revealed this mind to and through inspired men. Those who learned His thinking through the Spirit then spoke Christ's thoughts to others *in words which the Spirit taught* (I Cor. 2:10-13). Pat thinks that this strategy which he has followed was from Christ. Does he also think that he revealed to the author Christ's thoughts on this subject *in words which the Spirit taught him?* Neither Pat, the author, nor anyone else can *know the thoughts of Christ except* as they are revealed in the Bible. Christ has already done the thinking for the church, and He has expressed His thinking in the words which He wanted used, and all of this thought is in the Bible. We must try to think His thoughts after Him by letting His word dwell in us richly (Col. 3:16). How can Pat know that any thoughts of Christ are coming to him directly from Christ? The strategy which he has followed does not come from the Bible, for it is contrary to the Bible. We agree with Pat that we must use our own minds, but we believe he has wrongly used his in concluding that Christ is doing the thinking for him in this matter.

When the author denies that we can know any thoughts of Christ which are not found in the Bible, he is not denying that Christ may work behind the scenes for the good of His people. But this does not mean that we have revealed to us thoughts of Christ in addition to those in the Bible, nor does it mean that we uninspired men can pull back the curtain and delineate with accuracy and certainty His work behind the scenes. We can see, of course, some of the workings of His moral and spiritual laws.

Christ no more does our thinking for us today, than He does our seeing, our hearing, or our works for us. In all these things, of course, we should be motivated by love for Him and by obedience to His will. All should be done in the light of His mind as revealed in the Bible (Col. 3:16-17).

Pat said they would have made a public statement in February 1970 if they had felt God wanted them to do it. Since they felt they had the mind of Christ on this matter, since this was His strategy, of course they did not feel they should make a public statement. But how did they know that God did not want them to do it then? Did they have a revelation? Was their revelation confirmed in some miraculous way? Furthermore, why were they "led" to make so many statements outside of the context of the brotherhood, but which brethren were bound to learn about sooner or later?

The strategy included, they said, letting people see the renewed dedication and other fruits in their own lives, and that they did not go to extremes. This was to prepare the way for the effective entrance of the new ideas into the minds of the brethren. In other words, they think that the Lord's strategy has been to soften up the church for the reception of these ideas, by their keeping these convictions from the brethren until the time was ripe. The author told them that he did not question their sincerity, but from the angle from which he viewed it, this was a boring from within.

RED FLAG?

In the same phone conversation, Pat also said they did not want their full position known at the time because they felt

178

it would be only partly understood. It would be like waving a red flag before the brethren. They intend to present the full case in the book, and this would be more effective. In other words, in the book the brethren would get the complete sotry, and this would make a greater impact than if only a part of the story were made public now. In effect this says to the author that after the softening up process the full attack comes! In the author's judgment, their strategy will result in more than one red flag being waved before brethren.

During the conversation the author pointed out that in a sense he was being put on the spot. Since the author believed these were serious errors which led to other errors, he had a duty not only to them, but to others also. However, when he decided the time had come to say something publicly about their position, he would let them know first. Unless we changed, the author said, we were on a collision course. The author wanted them to know that when our heads hit, his would be filled with love. Pat said, when we hit we can hug one another! Pat, it is now time to hug!

WHY NO PUBLIC STATEMENT IMMEDIATELY?

How did the author justify his not making a public statement, through some of the religious papers, for example, as soon as he learned of their position? He thought it was worthwhile to study the matter with them through correspondence for a period of ime. If neither one of us changed, a public statement could then be made. If the author changed, he would make a public statement of his change.

The author felt that no greater harm would be done, than had already been done, by waiting a while longer.

The author told Pat and Shirley that such a study would would help him to better understand them and their position, and, if neither one of them changed, to more effectively and fairly deal with their position in print. Or, if the author changed, to more effectively present the new position.

The author planned to speak out publicly before the movie and Pat's book appeared. In fact, his intention has been to get his book out before Pat's, if possible. The author decided that if he had not heard from Pat by April 25 or 26, 1970 he would write Pat and tell him that he had decided it was time to speak out publicly. On April 25 the author received a letter from an elder in Santa Ana, California. Dean Dennis had given him a copy of *Testimony*. The elder saw Pat's article. That Sunday the author revised a letter to Pat which he had written on Saturday, and on Monday morning, the 27th, it was re-typed and mailed to Pat. Shortly before mailing it the author received a letter from Houston, Texas, enclosing a copy of Pat's article in *Testimony*, and a copy of the letter which had been sent to the editor of one of the religious papers.

On Thursday, April 30, the author received a phone call from Pat's secretary relaying a message from Shirley. Shirley said she realized that the author must do what he was convinced was his duty to do, but she would appreciate it if he would wait until Pat got back from Australia and could talk with the author. This request was honored, and on May 4 Pat and the author talked. The author agreed to send the articles, which he had prepared for the *Firm Foundation* and the *Gospel Advocate* to Pat for him to evaluate before they were published. Pat's attitude was highly commendable. These articles, in a much longer form, had been sent to Pat several days before. The short articles were mailed on May 5, 1970. Pat had intended to return them in a few days, but he failed to do so. On July 14 Pat wrote the author that he was terminating our dialogue, at least for the time, on the subject of the Holy Spirit. He did not return the articles with his specific criticisms, although from comments he had made on similar material the author is of the opinion that he knows Pat's main criticisms. What Pat wanted was not to be mentioned at all in print by the author. The author then decided to make some revisions if necessary and send the articles to the *Firm Foundation* and the *Gospel Advocate*. Later Pat returned the articles. He also changed his mind and our dialogue has continued.

CHAPTER XIII

THE HOLY SPIRIT IS NOT BLIND

Pat Boone thought that if the brethren learned of his new beliefs, without the whole story being told to them at one time, it would be like waving a red flag. The force of his testimony would be blunted. He thought the Spirit was leading him to show by his manner of life that he was not a fanatic. When his book appeared the brethren would get the whole story, his testimony would have a greater impact, and the brethren would see that it did not lead to extremes.

However, something was leading him to make some very clear statements in public rallies, newspaper interviews, journals, and in at least one statement in the *Christian Chronicle*. He finally left behind him a trail which made his position clear and destroyed the strategy of keeping it from the brethren until the book appeared. He was so self-deceived that he thought he was keeping something from brethren, whereas he was speaking it from the housetops. Obviously the Holy Spirit is neither blind nor naive; therefore, this was not the work of the Spirit.

ORAL ROBERTS' PROGRAM

Although Pat has an aversion to public controversy, he appeared on an Oral Roberts program which he must have realized would lead to some controversy; especially in view of some of the things which were said and done. *First*, Roberts indicated that something unusual had happened to Pat in recent months. He said: "Pat, God has moved in on you and Shirley these past few months, tell us about it." Pat's reply included the statement that "we feel ourselves being led by Him again in a brand new and more powerful way."

Second, Pat joined in with Roberts in a prayer for the miraculous healing of people. After Pat's statement about being led in a brand new and more powerful way, Roberts spoke of his prayer for the miraculous healing of a man in Jordan, of Jesus' miraculous healing of a man, of his sister's statement years before that God was going to heal him (Roberts), and that "I know how it is to feel the healing touch of

Jesus Christ. Just as I have stood in no man's land and prayed for the healing of Jordan and Israel, I want to stand here and pray for the healing of our country, for the healing of people, and I'm going to ask you to join me . . . Pat, you and I will touch one another in the name of the Lord. And Pat, I know your concern for the healing of our nation, and your faith that God can change men's lives. Let's pray together, and then we are going to touch this map of the world as we pray for our fellow human beings . . . Now I pray that God will heal you as he healed me. God heal your soul, God heal your mind, God heal your bodies. May God heal you from the crown of your head to the soles of your feet in the name of His son, Jesus Christ of Nazareth . . . "

Third, as the program drew to a close, Pat said: "God bless this hour, Oral, and bless me and Shirley, who is here, too. We are very grateful that we could be a part of it." Pat explained to the author that this was not an endorsement of all of the program but an expression of his wish that God would accomplish good through it.

These things were sufficient to stir up controversy, and some of it appeared in such publications as the *Christian Chronicle, The Gospel Defender* (Sept. 1969), and the *Firm Foundation* (Dec. 2, 1969). Although the above statements did not prove it, the author now knows that both Oral Roberts and Pat knew that Pat thought he had already received the gift of tongues (Letter from Roberts, April 9, 1970).

RUMORS CIRCULATING

E. R. Harper told Pat Boone in a letter of March 6, 1970, that he "had heard for several months back that you felt you were speaking in tongues." Although when he first heard it Harper had no confirmation of the charge, this does show that for several months at least there has been controversy over whether Boone claimed such power.

CHRISTIAN LIFE MAGAZINE

The *Christian Life* for November, 1969, carried an interview with Pat Boone in which he definitely affirmed that he spoke in tongues. He said: "I've heard ministers in my Church of Christ worship the Lord in other languages, and I myself do. It appears to me Paul was saying, 'Look, it's better to prophesy, its better to teach, because after all the person who speaks in this prayer language is only speaking to God. He's only helping himself and it's much better to help others.' But in the next verse, (I Corinthians 14:2), Paul also says that when we speak in this prayer language we help ourselves. And man, I need help.

"And besides I want to be able to speak to God and I want Him to understand me. I was a graduate with honors from Columbia University, but I'm still an illiterate ignoramus when it comes to trying to speak to God. And so I don't have the words or the brain power. I have the feelings. I know what I would like to express with my inner self, but I don't have words to do it. So God says, through the prayer language, 'I'm bigger than you are. I understand your problems and I will communicate with you in a way that maybe you wouldn't understand except inwardly and in a spiritual way. You won't understand it intellectually, but I will commune with you and I understand your needs and I will minister to them.' To me that was the birth—not only of a new humility —but of a great new joy and a great new confidence." *(Christian Life,* November, 1969, pp. 59-60.) The author is sure *the Lord can understand* us without having to give us a special prayer language which *we do not understand.*

Although they may hide it from others, those among us who think they speak in tongues seem to be able to find one another; at least in some cases. This is illustrated by Pat's statement that "I've heard ministers in my Church of Christ worship the Lord in other languages, and I myself do." He could not have heard them—with the exception of the rare cases where such beliefs have been made public—do this unless he was in their confidence and in what we assume were private worship services. The author does not know when the interview was taped, but a minister was with Pat and participated in the interview. He was Dean Dennis and was identified as "minister of the Northside Church of Christ in Santa Ana, California." Pat told the author that Dean Dennis had visited Pat with the intention of trying to show him that it was unscriptural to claim to speak in tongues today. As it finally turned out, Pat helped convert Dean on the subject instead of Dean changing Pat. When the elders where he preached found out about it, they worked patiently with him; then, when their efforts were unavailing, they did their duty and took him out of the pulpit over which they had the oversight. The author does not know when this took place in relationship to the time of the interview.

Who are the *ministers* to whom Pat referred? If they have not let brethren know their stand, *they are wolves in sheep's clothing*. Their deceptive clothing should be taken from their backs so that they will no longer be able to have such access to the flock. Of course, they do not regard themselves as wolves, but we suppose that "wolf" never connotates to a wolf what it does to the non-wolves. They view themselves as individuals who have some truth which others do not have. With this "truth," however, they have not kept in mind a very old truth; the truth that one ought to sail under his own colors and not be deceptive. Of course, the author is not talking about a person who is studying the question, and who is having problems. He is speaking of those who think they have such gifts today, but *keep it hidden from those who support them*. Why will they worship in tongues in the presence of Pat, but not in the presence of the elders? As ministers who have had extra time to study the Bible, their knowledge of the word should be superior to Pat's; therefore, in the author's opinion they should not be as naive and self-deceived as Pat has been in this matter. Of course, they may have convinced themselves they are being led by the Spirit in their deceiving those who support them. Regardless of whether they are self-deceived or are consciously deceiving others, if these are their settled convictions they need to sail under their own colors. It is one thing to work with long-suffering with a person who is struggling with the problem, or one who is willing to re-study it, but it is another thing for individuals to believe and practice these things and yet draw their *support* from people who would not support them if they knew these things.

CHRISTIAN CHRONICLE REPRINT

On December 8, 1969, the *Christian Chronicle* carried excerpts from an interview which Lanny Salsberg had with Pat Boone for the *Daily Star* in Toronto, Canada. Among other things it said: " 'It's a story of modern-day miracles, because there's no way to explain these things other than the intervention of God and His Spirit'.

"Pat Boone witnessed what he believes was a modern miracle at one of Wilkerson's youth rallies, where a youth 'who was having a very bad LSD trip' was calmed by the placing of hands on his shoulders. 'I realized at that moment,' Pat Boone recalled, 'that some divine power had actually counteracted chemical actions in his brain'."

Although people sometimes use the term "miracle" in a very loose way, the context in which Pat used it indicated that he believed it was a supernatural event which was a visible sign of divine power at work in a way which was above the natural. Pat did not tell us how he knew that "some divine power had actually counteracted chemical actions in his brain." Did God reveal this to Pat? He certainly could not see some divine power counteracting chemical actions in the youth's brain. If God did not reveal this to him, where is the evidence that this is what took place? If he is being supernaturally guided by the Lord, did the Lord guide him to make such a statement publicly? If not, why has he made such rash statements which help discredit his claims to have miraculous gifts?

We shall further consider this "miracle" a little later in this chapter.

Anyone reading this statement in the *Christian Chronicle* could easily see, in fact could not avoid seeing, that Pat believed that God was working miracles through Wilkerson's work. In this place, however, Pat did not claim any miraculous gifts. He may have thought, and naively so, that an interview with a newspaper man in Toronto would not be picked up and mentioned by brethren. He was supposedly being guided in the strategy of keeping these things from brethren for the time being, but at the same time he was publicly spilling the beans—so to speak.

WILKERSON'S STATEMENT

That portions of the religious world were being told of what was happening to the Boones, is further confirmed by a letter written shortly after Pat visited Toronto, Canada. This letter, a copy of which was given to the author in March, 1970, said: "About six months ago in Toronto, Dave Wilkerson told of the circumstances leading to your playing his part in 'The Cross and the Switchblade', and of Shirley's own encounter with the Lord through the Holy Spirit. I *praise God* for that and the resulting movie—along with your personal appearances with Rex Humbard and Oral Roberts!"

The person who wrote this letter is associated with a group in the Toronto area which meets at Etobicoke. Tongues speakers in Canada seemed to know about Pat, but Pat did not want the other brethren to know.

INDIANAPOLIS CHURCH BULLETIN

On March 22, 1970, in *The Informer*, W. L. Totty quoted a printed interview in which Pat spoke of modern miracles, of a "20th century addition to the Book of Acts," and of David Wilkerson being like one of the apostles.

MONROE

In a public meeting in Monroe, Louisiana, on December 6, 1969, Pat said that Wilkerson prayed for miracles and received miracles just like those in the Bible. Pat said that a year ago he did not believe in modern miracles, but because of what he had witnessed he had no more doubts about miracles in connection with Wilkerson's work. He referred to the same miracle which was mentioned in the *Christian Chronicle* for December 8, 1969. Lowell Brown, in the *Bastrop Bulletin* for January 25, 1970, reported that "Pat told of seeing a 'genuine miracle' . . . "

Brethren were present in the civic auditorium when Pat said these things, and the word was bound to spread. There are brethren there whose business activities, and their church work, carry them to various parts of the United States. One of them gave the author a tape of Pat's statement. If the Spirit's strategy was to keep these things from the brethren, what "spirit" led Pat to make public statements which destroyed this strategy? Pat has obviously been responding to some confusing and conflicting signals and impulses.

DENOMINATIONAL BULLETIN

In January, 1970, in Louisiana, some brethren had copies of a bulletin of The New Life Center in Shreveport, Louisiana, which, in speaking of its pulpit, said: "But oh! how much gospel goes over that pulpit! Even Dale Evans' testimony of

186

the Baptism of the Holy Spirit, as well as Pat Boone's (second-hand)" (Jan. 7, 1970). One radio minister told the author in early March that some of the Pentecostal, and related, journals were claiming Pat as one of their own.

In answer to an inquiry as to what was meant by Boone's testimony being second-hand, the author received a letter from The New Life Center which said: "The occasion to which I referred in the bulletin was a service in which Rev. Kenneth Copeland was the guest speaker. He had just left California, where he was guest in Pat and Shirley's home, and related some of their experiences in prayer there in the Boone home.

"Incidentally, just a few days later I read in the *Christian Life Magazine* this same testimony . . . " (March 31 1970.)

THE VOICE OF DELIVERANCE

Other parts of the denominational world knew it even though Pat Boone did not reveal it to the churches of Christ. *The Voice of Deliverance*, published in Dallas, Texas, carried an ad which had been in other publications also. In advertising Pat's record, "Rapture," it said: "Pat Boone is now filled with the Holy Spirit." (Feb., 1970, p. 10.) They obviously meant he had not been filled with the Spirit in the past but *now* is filled.

The following disclaimer is published in each copy of *The Voice of Deliverance:* "We assume no legal responsibility for the veracity or permanency of reported healings, miracles or other happenings. All supernatural events and blessings are contingent upon spiritual condition, relative to the individual, and any other deviation from the intended Divine plan could result in mental, physical, and/or spiritual set-back." Evidently they could not discern the "spirits"!!

CHRISTIAN CHRONICLE, 1970

The *Christian Chronicle* on February 16, 1970 printed an open letter from Pat Boone to Foy L. Smith. In it he clearly affirmed his conviction that David Wilkerson's work was being backed by God with miracles. He wrote: "Foy, if you can spend an hour with David Wilkerson, or go through a Teen Challenge center, I'm certain your opinion will change. Miracles are happening there every day—life-changing, soul-saving miracles. And I thank God for them, because it took miracles to convince Peter that Cornelius was loved of God. (Acts 11:15-18; Jas. 4:11-12)." This statement affirms that Wilkerson is preaching the gospel in such a way as to save souls.

Pat also affirms that miracles are being wrought in connection with Wilkerson's work. Some may say that he was using the term miracle in a broad and loose sense. He meant only that lives were being changed. However, Pat paralleled the miraculous confirmation of Wilkerson's work with the miraculous confirmation at the household of Cornelius. He called "miracles" that which took place in connection with Teen Challenge centers, and at the household of Cornelius. The reference which he cited in Acts says: "And as I began to speak, the Holy Spirit fell on them, even as on us at the beginning. And I remembered the word of the Lord, how he said, John indeed baptized with water; but ye shall be baptized in the Holy Spirit. If then God gave unto them the like gift as he did also unto us, when we believe on the Lord Jesus Christ, who was I, that I could withstand God? And when they heard these things, they held their peace, and glorified God, saying, then to the Gentiles also hath God granted repentance unto life." (Acts 11:15-18.) How had the 'Spirit fallen on them? They had been baptized in the Spirit and spoke "with tongues, and" magnifed God (10:45-47; 11:16.) Peter said it was like what had taken place at the beginning when the preachers on Pentecost had been baptized in the Spirit and spoke in other tongues, or languages (Acts 11:15-16; 1:5,8; 2:1-4,6,8,11).

Pat, whether he realized it or not, was saying that miracles accompanied, and accredited, the work and teaching of Wilkerson just as they had the work of the apostles on Pentecost, and of Peter at the household of Cornelius.

Pat went on to write: "I pray that soon we'll have a quiet hour together, so that Shirley and I can share with you the beautiful joy that we've come to know. Our hearts are bubbling over with gratitude for what Jesus has done in our lives, and this is truly a gift from God; we could not have manufactured it ourselves. (John 14:26-27)" *(Christian Chronicle,* Feb. 16, 1970, p. 2.)

THE BIRMINGHAM NEWS

Roger Ebert in Chicago wrote up an interview which he had with Pat Boone. This interview was published in *The Birmingham News* for February 20, 1970. In it Pat is quoted as saying, with reference to Wilkerson's book *The Cross and the Switchblade;* that: "Both the book and the movie have been life-changing experiences for me. The book is a 20th century addition to the Book of Acts. Wilkerson is like one of those fellows Jesus chose to be an apostle.

"He had no great qualification but faith. But one day he stood on a tarred rooftop in little Puerto Rico, and a group of young dope addicts told him: 'Man, there's only three ways out of addiction: overdose, suicide, or God.'

"Wilkerson realized they were right. He told me that story one night when I stood on the same rooftop with him. He said that at that moment he spoke to God. He said, 'God, you're gonna have to give me miracles. You gave Peter and James and John miracles, and now you're gonna have to give them to me'."

" 'What happened then'? I asked.

" 'God gave him miracles,' Boone said, 'The first miracle I personally ever witnessed in my life took place at a Wilkerson youth rally last year in Orange County, California. See, the young kids trust Wilkerson. They trust him because they know he walks the streets talking to the junkies, the prostitutes, the homosexuals. They listened to him, and when he had finished, 500 young people came for counseling.

" 'A lot of them were on pills, grass, speed. But he reached out to them right through the dope ,and they heard him. And it was then I witnessed the miracle.

" 'One of the young men was freaking out—literally! He was on some kind of chemical. He was moaning, clawing at his face, screaming. I asked his friends what was wrong with him, and they said he was on a bad trip. How do you give counsel to someone who's freaked out?

" 'Just then two counselors approached the young man. They put their hands on his shoulders and they began to pray.

189

And as they prayed, I saw this young man suddenly slump in his chair. He appeared to go to sleep. His face was tranquil. Prayer had cut right through the drugs and given him instant peace.

" 'It certainly sounds remarkable,' I said.

" 'It was a miracle,' Pat Boone said softly, 'If things like that didn't happen all the time, there'd be no Teen Challenge'."

How could there be a clearer claim that Pat believed miracles were being wrought today in connection with the work of David Wilkerson? Consider the following. *First,* Wilkerson's book is a continuation of the books of Acts, with reference to miracles, for it is "a 20th century addition to the Book of Acts."

Second, "Wilkerson is like one of those fellows Jesus chose to be an apostle." If this is true, what follows? (a) Wilkerson has seen the resurrected Lord in a post-resurrection appearance. (b) Wilkerson should have the authority of an apostle, so we should continue stedfastly in his doctrine as well as in that of the other apostles (Acts 2:42). (c) Wilkerson should know the gospel by inspiration and teach it by inspiration (Gal. 1:11-12). (d) Wilkerson's doctrine should harmonize with that of the apostles. (e) Wilkerson's miracles should have the characteristics of the miracles of the apostles, and should be of the same wide variety. After all, Wilkerson said: "God, you're gonna have to give me miracles. You gave Peter and James and John miracles, and now you're gonna have to give them to me." The interviewer said: "What happened then?" " 'God gave him miracles,' Boone said." We asked: When Wilkerson gets enough faith, will he ask for and receive the power that Peter had to walk on the water? (Matt. 14:28-31.) Speak in tongues, with other ministers, so that everyone in the audience understands in the language wherein he was born? (Acts 2:4, 6, 8, 11.) Miraculous prison deliverances when necessary? (Acts 5:19-23; 12:5-11.) Announce the coming immediate death of a deceiver? (Acts 5:7-10.) Confer the Spirit with miraculous manifestations as did apostles? (Acts 8:14-22; 19:1-7.) Be caught away as was Philip? (8:39.) Raise the dead? (9:40-41; 20:9-10.) Announce the temporary, but immediate, blindness of a false teacher?

(13:8-12.) Healings through handkerchiefs or aprons? (19:12.) Will he write inspired scripture as did Peter, James, and John? If *The Cross and the Switchblade* "is a 20th century addition to the Book of Acts," Pat should recommend that it be included in the next printing of the Bible. What right have we to discriminate against the writings of a man who is like one of the apostles, and who works miracles like they did? Why exclude his writings from the Bible?

Third, concerning the "miracle" which Pat witnessed, we observe: (a) In these "trips" the victim may go from one condition to another; from moaning and even screaming to quietness. A doctor, who has some experience in this field, was asked by the author about this case. He wrote: "The behavior from moment to moment is quite variable, the patient may be relatively quiet or stuporous and then become extremely overactive, and changes from one type of behavior to another would not be unexpected."

Additional remarks of the doctor could cover some other cases. He wrote: "Patients under the influence of LSD or other drugs are very much like psychiatric patients under similar drugs, which have been called for years truth drugs. They are remarkably susceptible to suggestion, and they are almost in a hypnotic state and can be induced to act and behave in many ways, depending upon the persuasiveness of the individual."

(b) The youth slumped, seemed to go to sleep, and his face became tranquil. The young man was unconscious in the chair. Pat's critical faculties seem to have slept, for he apparently could not tell the difference between this and miracles as recorded in the Bible. Why didn't the young man come to and praise God, having received "perfect soundness in the presence" of all? (Acts 3:7-9, 16.) Even the enemies of the gospel could not deny the reality of this miracle in Acts 3. (Acts 4:16.)

(c) In other accounts of the same incident, Pat testified to that to which he could not have been a witness unless the Lord gave him a special revelation. He testified that some divine power counteracted the chemicals in the youth's brain.

191

(d) There are many other miracles, too, Pat said. " 'It was a miracle,' Pat Boone said softly, 'If things like that didn't happen all the time, there'd be no Teen Challenge'."

Fourth, in this particular interview Pat did not claim miraculous powers. However, two things logically follow from this: (a) These things are for us today. Therefore, the brethren have been wrong about the purpose and duration of miracles. (b) If they are for us, it would follow that Pat also should seek and find such gifts.

Fifth, the endorsement of *The Cross and the Switchblade* as "a 20th century addition to the Book of Acts," and of Wilkerson as being "like one of those fellows Jesus chose to be an apostle," is an *endorsement of the doctrines* in Wilkerson's book, and the doctrines he teaches in addition to what is in the book; as surely as it is an endorsement of the book of Acts and the first century apostles. If Pat says that he did not mean it this way, he is being guided by some "spirit" to make statements which do not convey what he has in mind. How could one so endorse the book as an addition to Acts, and Wilkerson as being like an apostle, without endorsing Wilkerson's doctrine? It would be as logical to repudiate the doctrine in Acts, and in the writings of the other apostles and prophets, as to repudiate this 20th century addition to Acts and this modern apostle.

Since we know the Spirit speaks through the Bible, and since Wilkerson contradicts some of the teaching of the Bible, he has a different "spirit" if he has a "spirit." Whatever is leading Pat to make such statements is misleading him, and when he thinks on these things he should be led by the word to abandon the course which he has taken.

Being published in a city where there are numerous congregations, the interview in *The Birmingham News* was immediately seen by brethren. For example, it was quoted in an article by Rubel Shelly in the March issue of *Words of Truth,* a paper put out by some brethren in Jasper, Alabama. The author received his copy of this issue on March 21, 1970.

THE VOICE OF DELIVERANCE

The April, 1970, issue of *The Voice of Deliverance,* was mailed in March. In a full page ad of songs by Pat Boone it said: "Read Pat Boone's testimony in *Christian Life,* how he

has received the heavenly language and sings for the Lord."
(p. 12).

As far as the author can tell, all of these statements of
Pat Boone, including the interview that was printed in *The
Birmingham News*, were made before the author visited Pat
February 18th and 19th, 1970. Even the references in the
April *Voice of Deliverance* were based on statements which
Pat had made previously to the author's visit. These statements show that Pat believed miracles were being wrought
today as they were in the first century, and that he had the
gift of tongues. However, he still wanted to keep these positions from being known among the churches of Christ. He
still thought he was being guided by the Lord in doing this.

TESTIMONY

The issue of *Testimony* for the First Quarter, 1970, was
published in March. It carried an article by Pat Boone with
the title "I received the Holy Spirit and Tongues!" The
following illustrates the fact that this Pentecostal journal was
being widely circulated. On April 8, 1970, Benjamin Franklin,
who is a tongues speaker, mailed a copy to the author. On
April 15 one was received from someone in Memphis. On
April 25 the author received a letter from an elder in Santa
Ana, California. He said that Dean Dennis had given him a
copy of *Testimony* and he mentioned the article by Pat.
On April 27 the author received a copy of the article from a
friend in Houston. This friend had also sent a copy to the
editor of one of the religious papers. The editor of this paper
had received many copies. The afternoon of April 27 a friend
from Los Angeles called about another matter. Although the
author had not mentioned Pat Boone's name, this friend told
the author that an article on Pat Boone's position which
appeared in *Testimony* was circulated privately among some
people at the lectureship at Pepperdine College the week before. Pat's beliefs, in his own words, were now publicly circulated. Pat had written the article for another journal for
publication later in 1970. He and Shirley were very surprised
when, without his knowledge or permission, it was published in
Testimony. Who or what led the publisher of *Testimony* to
publish this article? Who led Dean Dennis to give a copy to
an elder in Santa Ana? Who led Benjamin Franklin, who

thinks he has gifts, to send a copy to Perry Cotham who then published an article on Pat and others in the *Gospel Advocate* and other journals?

Until the appearance of *Testimony,* Pat thought the brethren would not realize that he believed in modern miracles. He was blind to the clarity of his own statements, and the fact that material originating outside the brotherhood sometimes quickly circulates in the brotherhood. On February 28, 1970, the author told Pat that he had made his position clear in the November, 1969, issue of *Christian Life.* Pat asked how many in the church would know about that article, and pointed out that the author had not known about it until Pat gave him a copy. However, with a circulation of around 89,000 copies, one would expect brethren to know about it sooner or later. As a matter of fact, Foy L. Smith had already quoted from it in his open letter to Pat, which was dated February 16, 1970, and which Smith was circulating. It was mentioned in the December issue of a Pentecostal journal which later was quoted in the May 31, 1970, issue of a bulletin of the church in Manchester, Tennessee.

In the same conversation the author told Pat that brethren would interpret the remarks in Monroe, Louisiana as expressing belief in modern miracles. Pat did not think so; instead, he thought they would interpret it as a broad use of the term which conveyed the meaning of changed lives. However, such an interpretation was impossible in the light of the fact that Pat had believed in changed lives for many years, but not in modern miracles. He said that until a year ago he did not believe in modern miracles, but now because of what he had seen he had no more doubts about miracles in connection with Wilkerson's work. As a matter of fact, brethren who heard Pat's statement rightly interpreted it. Lowell Brown, in the Bastrop bulletin for January 25, 1970, said that "Pat told of seeing a 'genuine miracle' . . . " Other brethren who were there told the author of Pat's statement, and they rightly interpreted it. One of them gave the author a tape of Pat's statement.

THE SPIRIT IS NOT BLIND

While Pat thought the Spirit was guiding him into the strategy of keeping from the brethren his beliefs until the book appeared, he was making statements which defeated this strategy. Furthermore, he was so blind that he did not realize that brethren were understanding, as they learned of these things, his true position. The Spirit is not blind, and if the Spirit had been guiding him the Spirit would not have guided him to defeat the Spirit's own strategy. Furthermore, the Spirit would have known that the brethren would have rightly interpreted Pat's statements. Pat has been so naive in this that the author is not surprised that he has swallowed so many other things. It hurts the author to say this, but it must be said for Pat's sake as well as for the good of others.

Pat has a keen mind, but he was not using it effectively in these matters. As has been indicated in the chapter on "Silence the Intellect," he is letting someone else do this type of thinking for him, and that someone else is not Christ or the Spirit.

The author also believes that this case illustrates the fact that God, working behind the scene and without any miraculous demonstrations, in His providence helps those who study the word, and dig up what information they can, to detect and expose those errors which would lead us away from the faith once for all delivered to the saints. We are neither promised nor do we receive direct inspiration and miraculous confirmation in order to prove all things and hold fast that which is good. We do not require miraculous gifts in order to contend earnestly for the faith once for all delivered to the saints (I Thess. 5:21; Jude 3). But we must keep honest and studious hearts in order to be open to correction from the Word, from evidence, and from straight thinking.

195

CHAPTER XIV

WHAT CAN BE DONE?

When we understand why people seek the gift of tongues, we may be able to do one of two things. First, show them how their legitimate longings can be satisfied. Second, show that some of the longings which led to the quest for tongues may not be at all commendable.

It is right to be filled with God, Christ, the Spirit, and the Word, but it is not right to seek for a miraculous filling which God has not promised us, and which these people do not actually receive.

It is right that the emotional life be enriched, but it is not right to give it high priority nor to conclude that an emotional experience is within itself a guarantee that one has had a genuine spiritual experience. There may be emotional reactions to some of our spiritual experiences, but we may have spiritual experiences without having those emotional reactions. On the other hand, we may have emotional reactions which are not at all related to spiritual experiences.

ASSEMBLY

Everyone cannot take a public and leading part in our worship services, and although our worship services are but one part of our total life of service to God, we need to keep our hearts in the services to keep them from becoming unconscious routine. Congregational participation is very active in singing, and in each of us when partaking of the Lord's supper. We also participate, but with less physical expression, when we follow the prayers, and when we listen to the teaching. We further participate in contributing of our means. In fact, we participate in one way or another in every act of public worship. Whether this becomes for some of us lame, tame, and same (as Andrew Blackwood put it) depends on whether we worship sincerely and with the understanding. It will not so much depend on what is done by someone else, but by what we are and what we *will* to do in the assembly.

There are some who seek tongues because someone has drawn them into a small group which expressed concern for them, and in which they did not feel isolated as they may feel in a larger group. As congregations grow larger, there is a real need for people to get together at times in smaller groups to be associated with one another in a way which many do not associate in connection with assembly on the Lord's Day.

STUDY THE BIBLE

Some have gone into the tongues movement because they were taught very little concerning the Holy Spirit and His work. When they realized that something on this is taught in the Bible, they began to study it and due to their ignorance they may not handle aright the word of truth, and therefore they may conclude that something is promised to them when it is not promised to them.

We know nothing about the mind of God except as He revealed it through the men inspired by the Spirit in the first century, and who left us the New Testament; the only word of God which we have. It is Christ's word, and by His word men shall be judged (John 12:48). Therefore, we must continually apply ourselves to the study of His word. We must measure all claims, doctrines, and experiences by the truth into which the apostles and prophets were guided in the first century. If it is not a part of their teaching, it is not a part of the faith once for all delivered unto the saints (Jude 3).

In the Old Testament men were told not to add to God's word (Deut. 4:2; 12:32). No wonder Isaiah said: "To the law and to the testimony! If they speak not according to this word, surely there is no morning for them." (Isaiah 8:20).

Under the New Covenant we must be just as strict in obeying God's word. If we do not harken to the word spoken by the prophet like unto Moses, it will be required of us (Deut. 18:15-19; Acts 3:22-23). In fact, Hebrews argues that since men had to be careful under the law, how much more so under the gospel (Heb. 2:1-3; 12:25). The inspired men bound the will of God (Matt. 16:19) and, therefore, instructed men to observe all that Jesus commanded because He has all authority and power (Matt. 28:19-20). His word is the judge of our experiences, instead of our experiences being the judge of His word. Men must continue in the apostles' doctrine (Acts 2:42), not go beyond what is written (I Cor. 4:6), speak oracles of God (I Peter 4:11), hold that which the apostles

197

delivered (II Thess. 2:15), they are without authority to add to the book of Revelation (Rev. 22:18)—and surely we have no right to add to any other inspired writing, they are to let the word *of Christ* dwell in them (Col. 3:16), they are to acknowledge that what Paul wrote is the commandment of Christ (I Cor. 14:37), they are to oppose all that opposes the knowledge of God (II Cor. 10:5), they are to bring "every thought into captivity to the obedience of Christ," (II Cor. 10:5), and they are to contend earnestly, not for human experiences or traditions, but for the faith once for all delivered to the saints (Jude 3).

CULTIVATE ZEAL

Even when spiritual gifts were given to some, the important thing was to use them to edify the church. Therefore, Paul wrote: "So also ye, since ye are zealous of spiritual gifts, seek that ye may abound unto the edifying of the church." (I Cor. 14:12.) Everyone in Corinth did not have the same gift, nor did each one of them have all the gifts; in fact, there is no evidence that everyone had a gift. And yet, it was possible for everyone to be zealous to do what he could to edify the church in one way or another. We do not have to have miraculous works in order to abound in building up the church.

Christ "gave himself for us, that he might redeem us from all iniquity, and purify unto himself a people for his own possession, *zealous of good works.* (Titus 2:15.) Some people are more emotional than others. They show more visible signs of enthusiasm than do less emotional people. However, one does not have to be an emotional volcano in order to be zealous of good works. Zeal is manifested in devoting ourselves to the will of God. He who continually engages in good works is zealous of good works. He who is enthusiastic in his talk, and dilatory in his deeds, is not zealous of good works; regardless of how strong he may be in making emotional appeals, or how he may thrill at times as he contemplates some truth, or meditates, or prays, or sings. There are people who can sing enthusiastically and emotionally, in fact they may be so stirred that it stirs even their feet to movement, and yet they would not lift a hand or walk out of their way to do a good work.

While it might be nice—or on the other hand it might burn one up emotionally—if we could always live on the mountain peaks of emotionalism guided by truth, as a matter of fact much of life must be lived regardless of how we feel about things at the moment. We may feel like being unkind, but if we are guided by principles and good will we shall curb this feeling and do or say the kind thing. How wonderful it would be if our emotions and impulses were always behind our principles! However, unless we are to depend on the ebb and flow of physical emotional experiences we must will to do God's will and follow the path of duty, set forth in His will, regardless of the strength or weakness of our emotions at the time.

If we meditate on the love of God as demonstrated in the cross of Christ, we shall experience sufficient emotional impact. In addition to this there are so many things on which we can think which stir our emotions in a good sense. Why should we have to seek some sort of mysterious experience in order to enrich our emotional life?

Be zealous of good works. Get up and get busy! Do the next thing at hand which it is our duty or privilege to do. In the every-day experiences of your life demonstrate your zeal by being full of works. A needle, thread, and some skill, and determination can make you into a Dorcas. Deep emotional satisfactions can come from such acts of service (Acts 9:36, 39). The more you walk in the path of duty and privilege, the more you are engaged in good works, the less need you will feel for some sort of emotional jag to try to bring you closer—as some imagine—to God. The less your life is filled with good works, and with the satisfaction of doing God's will, the more you will feel the need of something to get you into what you think is a religious "mood." While we are not saying that those who seek the experience of tongues are not interested in good works, we are saying that even in the first century people had tongues without having the right attitude toward the use of tongues or toward the service of others.

Enrich your emotional life, but keep it under the control of the word of God.

EXTREMES NOT NECESSARY

R. P. Haakonson well said: "Fanaticism is no remedy for formalism. Jumping into a steaming kettle over a hot stove is not much better than sitting stiff in the freezer. Let God thaw us out to a normal, healthy, Christian activity in a great world of darkness and sin." We need zeal, but zeal according to knowledge is one thing, and zeal without proper knowledge is another thing. Because the Jews had zeal for God, but without knowledge, they did not subject themselves to God's way of making men righteous through Jesus Christ. They rejected the salvation which is found in Him (Romans 10:1-4; 9:31-33). They were cut off because of their unbelief, even though they were extremely zealous (Romans 11:20).

That the presence of zeal is not a necessary result of the work of the Spirit of God, is also evident from the fact that Paul's zeal for the law was demonstrated in his persecution of the church. He was so zealous that he was willing to go far and wide, and to do anything he thought necessary, to try to stamp out that which he viewed as false (Acts 9:1-2; Phil. 3:6). To certain Jews who were opposing him, Paul said, I was "zealous for God, even as ye all are this day: and I persecuted this way unto the death . . . " (Acts 22:3-4). Zeal without knowledge led him to persecute Jesus in persecuting Jesus' disciples (Acts 22:7-8, 4).

The zeal of those who claim to speak in tongues, or perform other miracles, does not prove they actually have the miraculous gifts or that their zeal is always according to knowledge.

EPH. 5:15-21

Christians must be taught that the proof of their being filled with the Holy Spirit is not to be found in miraculous gifts, but in their manner of life. To the Ephesians Paul said: "Look therefore carefully how ye walk, not as unwise, but as wise; redeeming the time, because the days are evil. Wherefore be ye not foolish, but understand what the will of the Lord is. And be not drunken with wine, wherein is riot, but be filled with the Spirit; speaking one to another in psalms and hymns and spiritual songs, singing and making melody with your heart to the Lord; giving thanks always for all things in the name of our Lord Jesus Christ to God, even the

Father; subjecting yourselves one to another in the fear of Christ." (Eph. 5:15-21).

There is some discussion as to whether reference is made to the Holy Spirit, but, even if it is not, the work here discussed is the work we are to let the Spirit do through us as we abide in His will revealed in the word of God. G. C. Martin pointed out that: "The rendering of the text is the common one and obviously refers to the Holy Spirit, but the reading of the margin, 'in spirit,' demands attention. It signifies, 'let your desires be after spiritual and not carnal repletion.' The higher nature, not the lower, is to be satisfied. The latter rendering much more satisfactorily meets the demands of Greek grammar, and also seems to yield, at least, as satisfactory a sense as the ordinary interpretation." The parallel passage in Colossians reads: "Let the word of Christ dwell in you richly; in all wisdom teaching and admonishing one another with psalms and hymns and spiritual songs, singing with grace in your hearts unto God. And whatsoever ye do, in word or in deed, do all in the name of the Lord Jesus, giving thanks to God the Father through him." (Col. 3:16-17.) Certainly if we do not let the word of Christ dwell in us, we are not going to let the Spirit instruct us, and we shall not be able rightly to instruct others in songs and otherwise.

Instead of being possessed by wine, we are to be under the Spirit's influence. We can do this only if we yield ourselves to the will of the Spirit as revealed in the Bible. If we live in the Spirit, Paul said, we must also walk in the Spirit (Gal. 5:25). Anthony A. Hoekema pointed out that the verb, "be filled" "is in the present tense in the Greek. Since the present tense in Greek signifies continuing action, the specific thrust of the present imperative is to indicate that something which has already begun is to continue, or that something which has not yet begun is to be done from now on as a continuing action. The command, therefore, could well be translated: 'keep on being filled with the Spirit,' or 'be continually filled with the Spirit.' 'The present imperative "be filled with the Spirit" . . . indicates not some dramatic or decisive experience which will settle the issue for good, but a continuous appropriation'." (143.) Although they had been sealed with the Spirit, they needed to put forth effort to be filled continually with the Spirit. Being led by the Spirit means that we walk by the Spirit, and we know nothing about how the Spirit wants us to walk except as He has revealed it in the Bible. And He set forth in bold outlines what it means when he contrasted the works of the flesh with the fruit of the Spirit (Gal. 5:16-26). To put this in another way, we are not only to offer our bodies unto God as a living sacrifice, but we are also to do so continually (Romans 12:1-2).

In addition to the general moral principles Paul mentioned in Gal. 5:16-26, what are some of the results of being filled with the spirit; of being indwelt by the word of Christ? He told the Ephesians that it included such things as: (1) Walking as the wise who redeem the time. (b) Understanding the will of God (Eph. 5:15-17). (c) Abstinance from drunkenness (5:18). (d) Speaking to one another in psalms, hymns, and spiritual songs. (e) "Singing and making melody with your heart to the Lord." This certainly includes, among other things, something of joy, as well as of praise and adoration. (f) Continual thankfulness. How many Christians concentrate on complaining! If we are guided by the Spirit as we ought to be we shall give "thanks always for all things in the name of our Lord Jesus Christ to God, even the Father." (g) "Subjecting yourselves one to another in the fear of Christ." (Eph. 5:19-21.)

Paul then set forth something of what was involved in subjecting ourselves to one another in the fear of Christ. *First*, it involved the relationship of the wife to the husband. *Second*, the relationship of the husband to the wife (Eph. 5:22-23). Some think that being filled with the Spirit is proved by having perpetual, or at least regularly, highly emotional experiences in speaking in tongues or having some other sort of sensation. Paul said it is proved in part by the way you live in all the stress and strain, the ups and downs, the joys and the sorrows, and all the other things which occur in marriage. *Third*, it involves the right relationship between the children and the parents (Eph. 6:1-2). *Fourth*, it deals with how the fathers treat the children (Eph. 6:4). *Fifth*, it includes the servant's attitude toward the master, and his working not by "the way of eye-service, as men-pleasers; but as servants of Christ, doing the will of God from the heart; with good will doing service, as unto the Lord, and not unto men." (Eph. 6:5-7.) In other words, how we treat our employers is one of the tests as to whether we are filled with the Spirit. *Sixth,* it also includes the way in which the master —or, in our day, the employer—treats the one who serves him (Eph. 6:9).

Furthermore, Paul tells the Ephesians that they must put on the whole armor of God and fight the good fight of faith (Eph. 6:10-20).

The proof of our loyalty to the Lord is not found in even a legitimate emotional experience, but in how we conduct ourselves in the day-to-day pressures, duties, and opportunities of life.

GRIEVE NOT THE SPIRIT

Those who are filled with the Spirit, those in whom the word of God dwells and controls, should not grieve the Spirit. Paul said: "And grieve not the Holy Spirit of God, in whom ye were sealed unto the day of redemption." (Eph. 4:30.) This is not in the context of spiritual gifts, but of one's manner of life. One was to walk as he had learned Christ, and not in the former manner of life in which the Gentiles walked. (Eph. 4:17-31). Through sin we grieve the Spirit, but not through the absence of miraculous gifts. Whether we are filled with the Spirit is testified to not by miraculous manifestations, but by whether we let the Holy Spirit's will control our lives.

CHAPTER XV

THERE IS GROUND FOR CERTAINTY

Although some search for certainty in a way, and on grounds, which God has not promised to us, there is certainty available to the Christian. Luke wrote to Theophilus "that thou mightest know the certainty concerning the things wherein thou wast instructed." (Luke 1:4) It may be objected that we are not Theophilus, and did not live in the time when there were living witnesses to the resurrected Christ. Luke, however, said that certainty can be conveyed through written testimony as well as through oral testimony. John wrote that the written record can produce faith. (John 20:30-31)

We shall very briefly sketch some of the things which enter into the certainty which the Christian can have. However, this certainty does not replace faith.

FAITH IN GOD

First, we exist. Of this we have direct, personal, immediate and experimental knowledge. Those who doubt their own existance are either insane, or trying to play tricks on themselves. They may even feel offended if one suggests that something is wrong with *them,* but, of course, they would have to exist to feel offended, or even for them to doubt their own existence!

Second, the external world exists. Those who deny it continue to stub *their toe* on the material world. Futhermore, they continue to eat food to perpetuate the existence of their own bodies.

Third, there are two possible explanations of our existence. We know that we have not always existed and that we are not the cause of ourselves. Whatever has existed eternally caused us and others. All who think on the matter agree that someone or something is eternal. Something now exists. Out of nothing comes nothing, therefore, if at one time nothing existed there would not be anything now. Something is, so something has always been. The eternal reality is either of the nature of Mind or Spirit, or of matter. The eternal reality is either a Being or a thing. God or Matter is the eternal reality.

Fourth, those who deny God must believe as follows: (a) The nonliving created the living. This is a greater miracle than the resurrection, and the only miracle worker the deniers of God have is dead matter. (b) The non-conscious created the conscious. (c) The non-moral has created man with his moral sensitivities. Man believes that good exists, that evil exists, that there is a difference between the two, that man is obligated, and that man is obligated to the good and not the evil. Even those who deny the reality of good make distinctions, sooner or later, between justice and injustice, for example. If materialism is right, man is but matter in motion, and the person who says "I ought" is saying the same thing as the person who says, "I itch." In both cases, one is describing a physical sensation, physically produced. (d) The non-thinking created man with his power of thought. (e) Matter which cannot worship created man with his capacity for worship. (f) Matter which cannot purpose and plan, or realize when an objective has been achieved, created man (or the particular arrangement, viewed from their standpoint, of matter called man) who can purpose, plan, and know when he has achieved his purpose. (g) Matter which has no goal or purpose in life created man who seeks for purpose and meaning for life. (h) Matter which cannot have concern or compassion for anyone or anything created man with compassion and concern. (i) Matter which cannot be shown to create a dead machine, supposedly created the marvelous mechanism—or combination of many mechanisms—called the human body.

It is far more reasonable, being in line with the evidence that we have, to believe that an Intelligent Being is behind it all than believe matter did what we cannot prove matter has ever accomplished by itself. Furthermore, if matter is the ultimate reality, and the only reality, nothing is reasonable. He who says "I think" is describing a physical sensation as surely as the man who says "I itch". Thinking would be a vibration in the brain and nervous system produced by internal and external pressures of matter. If this is true, and it must be true if materialism is true, all reason is discredited. Therefore, instead of bringing reasons against faith in God, the unbeliever is merely sounding off mechanically and describing his physical vibrations. If God is discredited, man's reason is discredited. Furthermore, if there is no God, if materialism is true, there is no moral law. If there is no moral law man is a thing and not a being with rights and responsibilities. Man himself is degraded. Without God, man is merely an animal, and an animal is but a peculiar arrangement of matter in motion. When one is logical in his thinking, to believe in man we must also believe in God, and to deny God means ultimately the denial of man's value.

ALL STAKE THEIR ALL ON THEIR FAITH

Certain questions come to man because he is man, even though he is an atheist. Such questions as Who am I? What is my origin? My duty? My destiny? Is there any meaning to life? Does my life, or can my life, count for anything? For what can I hope, if anything? Atheism cannot provide answers for *life*, but Christianity can and does. Everyone has some sort of answers to or attitudes toward these questions.

Everyone believes something, although not all beliefs are adequately founded. Furthermore, everyone stakes his all— his present life and the future—on what he believes. If the atheist is right, and man is but matter and death ends all, he will never know that he was right; and the Christian drops out of life on even scores with the atheist. No atheist will ever arise in eternity and say: "I told you so, there is no life to come." If the Christian is wrong, he will never know it. Death, which he thought was a doorway, was the end; but he who dies never lives to know that death was the end! If the atheist is wrong, he will always know that he was wrong, while the Christian will always know that he was right.

If it is not possible to go right, one cannot be any more wrong for putting his life on the highest that man has known —Jesus Christ. If it is possible to go right, one cannot go wrong in placing his life on Him to whom even eminent unbelievers have paid the highest tribute.

There are some difficulties involved in faith in God and Christ, but there are far more difficulties involved in unbelief. There are also some good reasons for faith. Once when Jesus had taught some difficult things, certain disciples went back and walked no more with Him. "Jesus said therefore unto the

206

twelve: Would ye also go away? Simon Peter answered him, Lord, to whom shall we go? Thou hast the words of eternal life. And we have believed and know that thou art the Holy One of God." (John 6:66-69.) Peter realized some things were difficult, but in this place he set forth two firm convictions. (1) If they turned from Christ they not only did not solve the difficulties, but were left in a hopeless situation. There was no one else to whom they could turn. Although we do not have the space to present it here, the author is convinced that the evidence shows that if God has spoken anywhere He has spoken through Christ, and that if He has not spoken through Christ it is futile to look elsewhere for a message from God. (2) The evidence which Peter had convinced him that Jesus is the Christ. We could also add: (3) As one learns and lives by the principles of Jesus, more and more of the difficulties are resolved.

SOME CREDENTIALS OF CHRIST

What are some of the credentials of Christ which abundantly justify faith in Christ? Briefly stated some of them are: (1) His miracles which even His enemies admitted. (Acts 2:22.) It has well been said of Him that, being a miracle it would have been a miracle if He had wrought no miracles. A higher being demands higher manifestations. Man, a higher being than an animal, can do things which, if done by an animal, would rightly be considered miracles. Christ is so superior to man, and even many unbelievers have acknowledged His uniqueness and superiority that it was "natural" for superhuman manifestations to accompany the ministry of Christ. Furthermore, the record of His miracles is contained in historical documents which pass the tests that documents must pass in order to be acceptable. Some unbelievers may not be impressed with the written record of these miracles, for they likely have not studied the record closely; and to them—as well as to others—some other aspects of the credentials of Christ may be more impressive. However, the documents are reliable and he who rejects their testimony rejects it on some ground other than on the lack of historical testimony. The record, however, when fairly examined does furnish one with sufficient reason to believe in the miracles of Christ. Surely no believer in Christ can say that the written record can have nothing to do with producing faith; for the inspired apostle John said that the miracles were recorded that we might believe (John 20:30-31).

(2) The fulfilment of prophecies which were made centuries before He lived; for example, Isaiah 53.

(3) The testimony of His moral and spiritual teachings which have never been surpassed.

(4) The testimony of his marvelous personality and life.

(5) The testimony of His resurrection for which we have reliable witnesses who have left reliable accounts of their testimony.

(6) The impact of His life and teaching on the world, i. e. by His fruits you can know Him.

(7) The fact that in a very real sense His way of life works, and that other ways really do not work. They leave out something which should be included, and include some things which should have been excluded. This could be viewed as a part of the fruit test, as could also the following argument.

(8) There is a testimony which comes in the crucible of experience as we live the Christian life. There is the deep of His teaching which calls forth the deep in our own beings. He calls forth in us possibilities of which we were really unaware, or only vaguely realized. There is reason to partake of the pudding, and there is also the proof of the pudding to be found in the eating thereof. As we live the Christian life we become more and more convinced that He who made us made the Book to guide us and sent the Christ to save us. There is evidence which comes from experience. There is experimental proof, but it is not found in just an emotional experience, but through living by faith in Christ, and involves walking in the light of His word.

A powerful argument for Christ is found in what happens to men and to civilizations, over the decades, when they abandon Christ or the principles for which Christ stands. We are not saying, and the Bible does not teach, that no moral and spiritual truth was taught before Christ came to this world; but we are saying that He catches up within His message the complete truth, and His Person furnishes us not just with abstract principles to which we become coldly attached, but with the living Person whom we love, trust, and obey.

He underwrites truth and furnishes us the Perfect Example, as well as the highest motivation to act on the truth.

(9) Christ is inexhaustible. What the mind of man has written, the mind of man can fathom, exhaust, and move on to something else. The Bible, of which Christ is the central figure and theme, is inexhaustible. It is the mighty ocean on whose shores the child can wade, but whose mighty depths no man has completely fathomed. It is a vast universe that regardless of how deeply we penetrate it, there is still more to explore.

FAITH IS INVOLVED

The certainty which we seek, and find, in Christ is not a certainty which places everything in the realm of sight, and nothing in the realm of faith. Reason is involved in hearing, understanding, and evaluating the credentials of Christ. Reason is involved in studying His word so we may know what we are to do. Reason must be utilized in applying the principles of Jesus, such as the Golden Rule. Although Christianity does not discredit reason, it does teach that reason, without the light of the Divine Revelation found in the Bible, is insufficient. What happens to man when he turns from divine revelation further argues for the need for the revelation made in Jesus Christ and His word. There are reasons why we must go beyond reason. Once we see that the evidence justifies faith in Christ, we trust Him even in those things we cannot see and which reason cannot arrive at by itself. If Christianity were just a life of unaided human reason, there would be no need for God's revelation.

Furthermore, if the certainty which we have involved no faith at all, we would be proving that Paul was wrong when He said we walk by faith and not by sight. The evidences justify our having faith, and walking by faith further convinces us that we are on the right track. "Being therefore always of good courage, and knowing that, whilst we are at home in the body, we are absent from the Lord (for we walk by faith not by sight) . . . " (II Cor. 5:6-7).

The nature of man is such, the nature of faith is such, and the nature of Christianity is such, that faith cannot be coerced. We cannot be forced to believe against our very will. It is in the good and honest heart, not in the hard heart, that the seed can take root and bring forth fruit (Lk. 8:11-15).

This life is a pilgrimage and the pilgrim is not already at home without any of the temptations and struggles of the pilgrimage. There are some who want a certainty that raises them above *all* temptations, trials, difficulties, problems and perplexities. God has not promised us such a faith. As we grow, through trust in Christ and the application in life of the principles that produce growth in character and knowledge, our faith grows and many perplexities are solved. We more and more arrive at a practical, and increasing, certainty but we never arrive at such a theoretical certainty that there are no unanswered questions, no unsolved difficulties, and no objections which cannot be raised in one way or another to Christianity. In this sense, we no more arrive at a perfect certainty than we arrive at perfect love, perfect faith, perfect obedience, and complete and perfect knowledge of all that is found in the Bible. Although there are sufficient reasons for faith, we must still walk by faith in Jesus Christ as we go on into the future which cannot be penetrated by human reason, but light upon which is shed by Christ and His word.

THE MIND IS INVOLVED

There are some who seek for certainty which so transcends this life that our own minds are not involved in reaching and in holding to this certainty. This, too, is impossible. Without the use of our minds we would not know that we are seeking for certainty, or think that it was to be found in a certain way, or know when we had arrived at whatever certainty we were seeking. We cannot get outside of ourselves and our minds so that our minds have nothing to do with evaluating and understanding the grounds for faith, the need for faith, and the reality of faith. If an individual claims to be inspired so that he does not have to depend on his mind at all, he has deceived himself. He must use his own mind to think that *he* is inspired, to understand the nature of that inspiration or at least the fact of it, and to justify his conclusion that he is inspired instead of being insane. He must use his mind to conclude that he is inspired, and is right about the matter, instead of accepting the reasons which others bring against his claim of inspiration. If he is inspired, there must be some reasons why he believes he is inspired, and he cannot deal with these without using his own mind. If he claims that God has completely taken over his mind and life, he must have some reasons—which his mind thinks adequate—to believe that such has taken place. Furthermore, if someone else claims to be inspired, and by their inspiration says that he is not inspired, he must use his mind to tell why he is right and his critic wrong.

In other words, he must accept, and expect others to accept, his position for some reason or for no reason at all. It is foolish to say that he accepts it, and others should accept it, for no reason at all. For if he accepts it for no reason at all, he has made an arbitrary and irrational choice and he has no grounds on which to affirm that there is any security in his certainty. If there are no reasons, the mind must still decide that one is justified in accepting the experience and the certainty for no reason. On the other hand, if there are reasons, the mind must pass on them.

The Christian has some security, but the informed Christian does not seek a security based on some personal experience unevaluated by the word of God. Furthermore, he is obligated by the Scriptures not to try to escape from having reasons for his hope. Peter expressly said: " . . . sanctify in your hearts Christ as Lord; being ready always to give answer to every man that asketh you a reason concerning the hope that is in you, yet with meekness and fear." (I Peter 3:15.) Paul defended his faith and gave reasons for the hope which was within him, and we need to do the same; even though we did not see the Lord.

We neither saw the resurrected Christ, nor the signs that confirmed the revelation and confirmation of the gospel. We are not in the position that Thomas was, but we are of those blessed ones of whom Jesus spoke. "Jesus saith unto him, because thou hast seen me, thou hast believed: blessed are they that have not seen, and yet have believed." (John 20:29.) We have sufficient evidences, drawn from several fields of study, to assure us that the faith which was revealed and confirmed in the first century is from God. We are not like those

Jews who asked for signs and without them would not believe (John 4:48; 6:30; I Cor. 1:22); even with the signs most of them did not believe. We are of those who, although they are convinced faith has a firm foundation, walked by faith and not by sight.

CHAPTER XVI

I CORINTHIANS 13: QUESTIONS AND ANSWERS

Paul said tongues shall cease, *"will come-to-nought:* become inoperative, cease to produce results." (I Cor. 13:8. Beet.) *Why?* Because they were part of the incomplete stage (13:9). *When?* When they fulfilled their purposes in revealing and confirming the gospel. When the complete came, and the truth was revealed in all of its parts (13:10; John 16:12-14; Jude 3).

Do the three gifts Paul mentioned—prophecy, tongues, knowledge—represent all the gifts? Paul does not say that these three gifts will cease, but the others will continue. *First,* those who claim that the "perfect" is Christ at His second coming, agree that all, not just three, gifts will cease then. *Second,* all the gifts were involved in the revelation and confirmation of the truth (Mk. 16:20; Heb. 2:3-4). Why would only three gifts cease, but the rest continue, when their objectives were accomplished? *Third,* why would the gift of interpretation continue when the gift of tongues ceased? *Fourth,* other gifts, as well as tongues, were signs (Mk. 16:17, 20). Why would some signs cease, and others continue? *Fifth,* in illustrating the more excellent way, the way of love, Paul mentioned four gifts—tongues, prophecy, knowledge, and miraculous faith (13:1-2). Surely Paul is not saying that *only* these gifts when used without love do not profit one. Instead, he uses these gifts as illustrations of the entire category of gifts. *Sixth,* if any gifts continue, we must also have apostles of Christ today (I Cor. 12:28; Eph. 4:7, 11).

THE GIFTS, NOT THE GOSPEL

In what sense would prophecies, tongues, and knowledge be done away? (a) The *gift* of prophecy (12:10), not the truth delivered through the gift, would cease. (b) The gift of tongues ceased, but not the truth which was delivered through tongues. Furthermore, speaking human languages which one had learned would not cease on earth. The tongues of angels will surely not cease in heaven. When tongues ceased, they ceased. Paul did not say they would cease for a century, or more, and then start again. (c) The gift of knowledge would

213

be done away (12:8; 13:2, 8), but not the knowledge delivered through it. If knowledge in itself is done away, then everyone will become blank—knowing nothing—when that which is perfect is come! (d) The gifts, not the gospel which they revealed and confirmed, would cease when they had fulfilled their purposes.

THE PART AND THE PERFECT

The time of the part was the time when the gifts were functioning. All the truth was not found in one place, for the full New Testament had not been revealed. It was in the process of being revealed. From one prophet one could learn some truth, and from another one could learn some more. There was no place, however, that one could go *to find all of the truth*. While the gifts were revealing and confirming the truth, the truth was in part. That which was in part, in the very nature of the case, would cease to be in· part when the entire truth was revealed and confirmed. The partial revelations would finally add up to the total revelation. ". . . when that which is perfect is come, that which is in part shall be done away." (13:10.)

Was there a time when only part of the truth was revealed, or was it all revealed at one time? First, the Old Testament was an incomplete revelation which pointed to the New (Heb. 1:1-2; 2:1-4; 10:1; Col. 2:17; Matt. 5:17-18). *Second,* the complete truth was not revealed in Christ's personal ministry, but the Spirit was to guide the apostles into all the truth (John 16:12-14). ". . . the order of the original is remarkable; *the truth in all its parts* . . ." (Westcott). *Third,* even when the Spirit came, all the truth was was not revealed at one moment (1 Cor 13:9). For example the full truth concerning the Gentiles, the law, and the gospel was not revealed before Cornelius' conversion (Acts 11:1-18; 15:7-11). Fourth, by the time the last apostle died, the truth in all of its parts had been revealed or Jesus' promise failed. His promise did not fail, the faith has been delivered (Jude 3), the word of God abides forever (I Pet. 1:23, 25), and we have the apostles and prophets, in that we have their teaching, as surely as the Jews had Moses and the prophets (Lk. 16:29-31).

What was the part? First, it is the partial, or the incomplete, in contrast with the complete (Lk. 11:36; Rom. 11:25-

26; I Cor. 12:27, "members each in his part.") *Second,* the thing which is in part is of the same nature as the whole. Knowledge in part would not be contrasted with fullness of stomach, although a partly filled stomach could be contrasted with one which was full in all of its parts. The truth in part would be contrasted with truth in all of its parts. Knowledge in part would be contrasted with knowledge in its completeness. *Third,* Paul contrasts the partial revelation, which was delivered through the gifts—a part now and a part then, with the complete revelation.

When would the part cease? It naturally follows that "when that which is perfect is come, that which is in part shall be done away." (13:10.) Paul is discussing the purposes, the nature, and the duration of the gift-stage of the church when the partial revelations were being made. The part is contrasted with "the perfect, the full-grown (telos, end), the mature." (A. T. Robertson.) The gifts were never an end within themselves, and when they filled their purposes of revealing and confirming the truth they ceased. If we are still in the time of the "part" we must have all the gifts, including apostles, and inspired men must write and speak new revelations from God today.

What does perfect mean? H. K. Barrett translated it: "For we know in part, and we prophesy in part, but when *the totality* comes, that which is partial shall be done away with." He commented: "The adjective (in the neuter gender, and with the article, *to teleion)* rendered *totality* is fairly common in Paul; see ii 6; xiv. 20. It takes its precise meaning from the context, and here, in contrast with *in part* . . . it means not perfection *(in quality)* but *totality*—in particular the whole truth about God. This totality is love; in comparison with it, other things (true and valuable in themselves) may be left behind like the ways and achievements of childhood." As the total truth, in so far as God's revelation to man on earth is concerned, about God it would be the total truth about love. The partial and the total are of the same nature. The partial knowledge is contrasted with the total knowledge, for example. The gifts, including prophets and apostles, were given in order to perfect or equip the church so that it could carry on the work of ministering and of building up of the body of

215

Christ (Eph. 4:7, 11-12). The truth which they revealed and confirmed enables the church to speak the truth in love, and "maketh the increase of the body unto the building up of itself in love." (Eph. 4:15-16.)

IS CHRIST THE "PERFECT"?

Does "that which is perfect is come," refer to Christ at His second coming? *First,* Christ and the second coming are not discussed in this context. *Second,* "The word *teleion* does refer to the end of a process or development . . . is never used in the New Testament to depict the second coming, the millennium, or the eternal state. Also, since *teleion* is set in contrast to that which is 'in part' *(ek merous),* it must refer to the culmination of a process. The second coming is not a process; it is an instantaneous event." (Gromacki, 122-123.) To perfect something was "to bring an end by completing or perfecting . . . of accomplishing . . . of bringing to completion . . ." *Perfect* "signifies having reached its end *(telos),* finished, complete, perfect." *(Vine.)* ". . . *full grown,* or *mature:* that which has reached its full development ·or goal . . ." (Beet). Gilbert B. Weaver wrote: "Logically, *to teleion* must refer to completeness or perfection in the *same realm* as that referred to by *to ek merous.* Since *to ek merous* refers to the transmission of divine truth by revelation, the other term *to teleion* must refer to God's complete revelation of truth, the entire New Testament (taken of course with its foundational book, the Old Testament)." (Quoted by Gromacki, 126.) The partial ceases because the total has come. Since the whole is the result of a process, a process which involved the stage of the fragments, the totality or perfect must be of the same nature as the part. This does not suggest that Christ is the whole in contrast with the partial revelation. The time of the fragment, however, naturally came to an end when the time of the whole arrived. *Third,* if the gifts were to continue until the second coming, one should be able to trace the gifts—including apostles and prophets and new scriptures—from Paul's day until now. However, this cannot be done. The gifts did cease, therefore that which was perfect has come. *Fourth,* "perfect" is an adjective which is here used as a noun. It is in the neuter gender and nothing in the context suggests that it refers to a person, Jesus Christ.

CHILD TO MAN

Paul gives two illustrations of the fact that "when that which is perfect is come, that which is in part shall be done away." (13:10.) One should not take these illustrations and prove something different from the principle Paul is illustrating. "When I was a child, I spake as a child, I felt as a child, I thought as a child: now that I am become a man, I have put away childish things." (13:11.) "This reference to childhood is an illustration, suggested by the use of the word *totality*, which, in other contexts (ii:6) denotes maturity." (Barrett.) The childhood stage is essential, but it is not the perpetual state. It is part of a process which culminates in maturity. Just as the child becomes the man, just so the partial revelations finally add up to the complete revelation.

FROM REFLECTION TO FACE TO FACE

Paul's second illustration is: "For now we see in a mirror, darkly; but then face to face: now I know in part; but then shall I know fully even as also I was fully known." (13:12.) The mirrors of those days were of "polished metallic surfaces reflecting objects, but imperfectly; and since the figure seems to be *behind* the mirror, the observer seemed to see 'through' it." One saw dimly, or darkly; or, as the Greek literally means, in a riddle. (David Brown.) *First,* the contrast between the partial and the total is illustrated by the contrast between the mirror-image and the face-to-face view. The time when one knew in part was the time when the revelation was partial because it was in the process of being revealed to man (13:8). At first the church did not clearly see the relationship between the Gentile and the law, but with the revelation at the household of Cornelius they were enabled to see it clearly or fully (Acts 11:1-18; 15:7-11; Eph. 3:3-6).

Second, "If the mirror (glass) is metaphorical for something, then the 'face to face' experience is also metaphorical. If the mirror represents imperfect (or incomplete) knowledge, then the face to face encounter is metaphorical for the complete state of knowledge." (Weaver as cited by Gromacki, 127.) Face to face does not mean, unless the contexts demand it, that an individual literally sees God. The closeness of a manifestation of God to Israel was called face to face even though Israel did not see God in reality (Deut. 5:4-5; Num.

14:14; compare Genesis 32:24, 30; Ex. 33:20). Moses knew God face to face although literally he did not see God's face (Ex. 33:11, 19-23; Deut. 34:10). It meant a clearness and fullness of revelation to Moses, beyond that which had been made to the other prophets. ". . . with him will I speak mouth to mouth, *even manifestly, and not in dark speeches . . .*" (Num. 12:2-8). I Cor. 13:12 darkly, or "in a riddle," was "in an obscure saying in an enigma." (James Robinson Boise.) It was obscure because incomplete, and it was obscure to the extent it was incomplete. The partial revelation is contrasted with the plainness of the full revelation. As Broadbent observed: "Numbers 12:2-8 is dealing with a comparison of two forms of Revelation in Old Testament days, and so also is I Cor. 13 dealing with a comparison of two forms of Revelation in New Testament times." (26.) The first word for "know" in I Cor. 13:12 is different from the second "know." Barrett suggested that "the change is probably intended to bring out not a different kind of knowing—I shall recognize—but the completeness of future knowledge; man's present knowledge will be done away not in the interests of ignorance but of fuller understanding . . . " In other words, "then I shall know-well . . . as also I was well-known." *(Expositor's Greek Testament.)*

What does Paul mean by knowing "fully even as also I was fully known"? (13:12). Paul would know who or what? *First,* what was known in part? The revelation of God's will. What, then, will be known fully when the perfect is come? The complete revelation of God's will. *Second,* did it mean that Paul would know God even as God fully knew Paul? Is Paul saying that when he gets to heaven he will know God as God knows him? Omniscience is not promised to man, so the author does not believe man will ever know God as completely as God knows man. However, even on this earth we can know about God that which He has revealed to us. *Third,* it may be that Paul is saying that with the full revelation one will know himself fully as God knows him; at least to the extent God reveals to man His view of man. In this sense, in the light of the full revelation, we see ourselves as God sees us. God has revealed to us in His word His view of man's nature, plight, needs, duty, and destiny. With the full revelation one passes from an in-

218

complete knowledge of man to a full knowledge of man, including one's knowledge of himself.

Didn't Paul die before the full revelation was made known, and, therefore, the perfect, which he was to know fully, could not refer to the complete revelation? First, some think Paul is saying that the gifts were only for a few years at the most, but that when one died and went to be with Christ he would have complete knowledge. In this case, Paul was not saying how long the gifts would or would not last, but was saying that our incomplete knowledge would give way to complete knowledge when we die and go to be with the Lord (II Cor. 5:6-8). *Second,* this is true, but the author does not think this is Paul's point. *Third,* much was revealed *before* it was written. For example, Paul taught orally some things to the church in Thessalonica some time before he wrote them of the same things (II Thess. 3:10). The complete revelation could have been made known to Paul, before he died, without it having been recorded at that time; and without having to be recorded by Paul himself. *Fourth,* Christ promised the apostles they would be guided into all the truth, but this did not mean that each apostle had to live until it was all revealed (John 16:12-15). The promise was made to them as a group, and it was fulfilled if all the truth was revealed by the time the last apostle died. Paul may have been referring to himself not as an isolated Christian, but as a member of the church. Thus he could pass from using "we" to "I." "For we . . . I . . . For we see . . . now I know . . ." (I Cor. 13:9-12.) Paul could simply be identifying himself with the church, and not necessarily be saying he would live until the complete revelation was made known. For example, in I Thess. 4:14, 17 Paul identified himself with the ones who would be alive at the second coming. However, other passages show that he expected to die before the second coming (II Cor. 4:14; II Tim. 4:6-8). The church existed when Paul was alive, and it would exist at the second coming. Paul simply identified himself with the church. We say that we became an independent country in 1776, we fought the Civil War in 1860-1865, and we later fought World War II. This does not mean that we were alive in 1776. It was not necessary for Paul to live until the complete revelation had been made in order to illustrate with himself, as a member of the church, what the situation would be like when the complete revelation had been made.

WHAT ABIDES?

"But now abideth faith, hope, love, these three; and the greatest of these is love." (13:13) *To what does "now" refer?* "Now" can refer to this present time, but it can also refer to a logical sequence. The context, the author believes, indicates that "this adverb is not temporal, but logical, meaning *in this condition of things, these things being so.*" (Gould.) " 'But now' considering all the gifts that shall be put away completely . . . how about love? We have already learned that love never fails, v. 8." (Lenski.) David Brown wrote: " 'Now' —in contrasting the supernatural *gifts*, which were soon to disappear from the church, with the permanent *graces* of 'faith and hope and love:'—'All these supernatural gifts were designed only for the first starting of the church, and are gradually to cease; but the cardinal graces of faith and hope and love, without which the Christian character cannot exist, will abide on earth as long as the church itself is left there'." Although, in our judgment, Godet did not draw the right conclusion—conclusions which we are not quoting—from his premises, we believe he was justified in saying that although *but now* can be used in a temporal sense, it is not so used here. "The three virtues are contrasted with the three preceding gifts, which are to cease with the future era, and not to enter into the perfect state. Now, if these three virtues also only belonged to the present epoch, there would be no contrast to be set up in respect of duration between them and gifts. We must, therefore, give the particle a logical sense; comparison of charity with the two other virtues contains the indication of a new element, of the true state of things. 'In reality, this is what abides, and by no means what you suppose.' The contrast between the virtues and the gifts is likewise emphasized by the apposition . . . that is to say: '*these three,* and not the three gifts of which we have been speaking'." "Gifts will be done away at the coming of the perfect state; but these three virtues will remain in the perfect state iself." ". . . the perfect state is represented in it as one single era from which gifts only are excluded."

220

WHEN IT ABIDES

The author believes this contrast between the gifts and the graces indicates that the graces abide in the church on earth, after the gifts have ceased. It does not refer to the gifts lasting throughout the existence of the church on earth, with the graces lasting not only on earth, but also in heaven throughout eternity. *First*, the gifts fulfilled their purpose of revealing and confirming the truth, therefore they ceased. But faith, hope, and love never fulfill or complete their purpose on this earth. Here there is always need for the faith which comes by, and is guided by, the word of God. We need the hope founded on God's promises. And love should always characterize our conduct. *Second*, the three graces abide on this earth, but all three of them do not continue in heaven. The three graces existed during the time of the partial revelation, and they continue to exist during the time of the complete revelation. Although love never ceases, and will continue after the second coming, faith and hope as we know them now will not continue in heaven. (a) Now we believe even though we have not seen (John 20:25-29; I Pet. 1:8-9), but then we shall see Him as He is (I John 3:2-3). On earth we walk by faith and not by sight, but we shall walk by sight when we are present with the Lord (II Cor. 5:6-9). Although we shall always have confidence in God, when Christ comes our faith will no longer be the assurance of things hoped for, or the conviction of things not seen (Heb. 11:1). For we shall both see and have that for which we have hoped. Then we shall not believe that He will reward us, but we shall have actually received the reward (Heb. 11:6; I Pet. 1:3-9). (b) Hope will not continue when Christ comes, for hope will be replaced by realization. Hope ends in the attainment of that for which we have hoped. Paul is clear in saying that we do not hope for that which we have. ". . . hope that is seen *is not hope:* for who hopeth for that which he *seeth?*" (Rom. 8:24.) This life is the time when faith waits with patience in hope for that which we see not (Heb. 11:1; Rom. 8:25).

David Brown dealt with this when he said some may ask: "But what . . . is to become of 'faith' and 'hope' hereafter? A reasonable enough question *in itself*, but one on which no light is cast by this verse, as we understand it; the one object being to affirm that those three *graces* will outlive all mere *gifts*. As to the future of those graces, the truth would seem to be that since 'faith' and 'hope' will certainly pass into sight, and so be lost in any distinctive sense, they are to be viewed as, in their very nature, temporary means towards something else into which they are destined to pass; while love, from its very nature, though admitting of indefinite increase, can never pass into anything else and higher, and so is necessarily eternal." Love, itself, as dealt with in this chapter pertains to love on this earth. For this life is the time when love must suffer long; when love must resist the temptation to envy, to be puffed up, to vaunt itself, to behave itself unseemly, to seek its own, or to be provoked; now is the time when love "beareth all things, believeth all things, hopeth all things, endureth all things." (I Cor. 13:4-8.) Love, of course, never fails (13:8); therefore, even when faith is lost in sight and hope is swallowed up in attainment, love will continue as the basic principle in heaven itself. Although love is eternal, I Cor. 13 deals with love in relationship to life on this earth.

The graces existed when the gifts existed, but they continued after the gifts ceased. The gifts, therefore, cannot continue until the second coming; for the graces outlast the gifts, but the three graces do not abide *after* the second coming. Therefore, the gifts cease before the second coming, while the graces continue on earth until the second coming. It follows that that which is "perfect" did not refer to Christ at the second coming.

IF

If the gifts continue until the second coming, what contradictions and conclusions follow? *First,* only a part of the truth was revealed in the lifetime of the apostles, even though Jesus said they would be guided into all of the truth (John 16:12-14). *Second,* instead of being once for all delivered in the first century (Jude 3), the faith is still in the process of being delivered and this process will not cease until Christ comes. *Third,* faith, hope, and love will continue in heaven for they were to outlast the gifts. *Fourth,* apostles of Christ must be on earth today. *Fifth,* new scriptures should continue to be added to the Bible which will be completed only at the second coming. *Sixth,* the perfect is not the culmination of a process

222

which involved the stage of the part—the childhood stage, so to speak, of revelation, but is a person—Christ—whose coming is not the culmination of the process of partial revelation.

The author does not imply that everything in I Cor. 13:8-13 is easy to understand. He does believe, however, that the explanation which has been given is in harmony with the immediate context, that it harmonizes with other scriptures, and that it has far fewer difficulties than any Pentecostal explanation.

CHAPTER XVII

PAT BOONE: QUESTIONS AND ANSWERS

Pat wanted us to approach our study as if we had not studied the question before. Is this possible? *First,* over thirty years ago the author's Uncle Charles Davis tried to convert him to the Reorganized Church of Jesus Christ of Latter-Day Saints. He claimed they had all the gifts, apostles of Christ, modern revelations, and new scriptures. He was more consistent in his errors than is Pat. The author determined to be honest in the study, and to become a Latter-Day Saint if the evidence justified it. The author could not void his mind of the two-year discussion with his uncle who used arguments which Pat used. *Second,* although the author could not have a blank mind as he studied the subject with Pat, his determination has been to be honest.

ARGUMENTS

Pat said that, unlike the author, he did not think of himself as having arguments for his position. *First,* magnifying the Lord includes giving reasons for faith (Acts 2:36), being set for the defense and contending for the gospel (Phil. 1:16; Jude 3), and giving reasons for our hope (I Pet. 3:15). *Second,* regardless of what he called them, Pat made arguments on scriptures and experiences.

AUTHORITY OF PAT?

Pat said he hoped he never thought of himself as an authority. *First,* if he has any gifts, anything which comes through or is confirmed by the gifts is authoritative (I Cor. 14:37). *Second,* his denial of authority is in effect a denial that he has any gifts. If he has gifts, why is he so confused?

WHAT IS PAT'S PRESENT VIEW OF BAPTISM?

First, he teaches Acts 2:38; 22:16; Rom. 6:2-5; Gal. 3:26-27; I Pet. 3:21. *Second,* however, he believes that some people who have not done this have been baptized in the Spirit, have put on Christ, and are his brethren; even though they teach contrary to Acts 2:38. *Third,* the author has not seen the complete manuscript of Pat's book, but there is a reference in one chapter which has been published. He took a man to the pool. "There he acknowledged again that he was putting his life completely in the hands of Jesus Christ. I baptized him as a testimony to his act of faith."(Quoted in *Christian Life*, July 1970, p. 8). This does not affirm that it is an act of faith which is involved in coming into Christ. After this was in type, the author learned that Pat would not have expressed it this way. The author assumes an editor worded it, and that it was not noticed by Pat and appeared in the book *(A New Song, 177)*. *Fourth*, will Pat change his belief concerning baptism? The author is not a prophet, so he does not know how much Pat will allow his subjective experiences to override the Bible. Pat's present determination is to teach his present conviction as he has opportunity.

BORING FROM WITHIN?

Do some tongues speakers quietly spread their beliefs without letting the church know about it? *First*, Joyce Dennis was studying with Pat, and seeking the baptism of the Spirit, as early as February 1969. Well over a year later, Pat was still trying to keep his beliefs from the brethren as a whole. It is one thing to struggle with a problem, but it is another thing to propagate one's firm convictions while letting people deny that you have these convictions. *Second*, in some meetings of the Full Gospel Business Men's Fellowship, people were told to remain in their churches and influence them. *Third*, Sherrill, whose book influenced Pat, decided that he would remain where he was, refrain from saying anything unless it came up naturally and keep company with Pentecostals on the side. He finally wrote: "Yet this is not a good solution either. If I believe in the importance of the Baptism of the Holy Spirit, as I do, do I not have an obligation to talk about it wherever and whenever I can?" (134-135.) The gifts were to edify brethren, and to publicly proclaim and confirm the word (Mk. 16:17,20; I Cor. 14; Heb. 2:3-4).

COMMUNICATION?

Pat thought he and the author had communicated very poorly. He had not had time to read all that the author had sent him, much less to digest and respond in full to it. He felt the author had not understood much of what Pat tried to say, and very little of the experiences of Pat and Shirley. *First,* the author felt that our problem was not a lack of communication, but a lack of agreement. *Second,* in the *Christian Life* article, November 1969, Pat said it was better to communicate with others and edify them than to have the gift of tongues for private devotions. Since Pat thinks the gifts are for us if we ask in faith, why did he not receive the gift of prophecy so he could more adequately communicate with the author? (I Cor. 14:5-6). Pat did not specify which parts of his letters and conversations were the products of, or confirmed by, his gifts and thus were inspired. Instead, he denied that any of them were inspired. *Third,* the author does not have a gift of discernment, therefore, if he did not understand Pat it was because Pat was not clear at times, or the author did not think straight on what Pat said, or that the author was prejudiced or dull of hearing for some reason or reasons (Heb. 5:11).

CONFIDENCE BETRAYED?

Pat said he would not have been as frank and open in the correspondence and conversations if he had realized that at least some of his arguments and experiences would be mentioned in the author's book. The author did not keep Pat in the dark as to his intentions, and he does not believe he has betrayed any confidence. *First,* from what the author has seen of Pat's book, and from what the editor of *Christian Life* wrote, Pat has been very frank, on some matters, in his book. "Difficult as it was, he chronicles his downfall morally and spiritually. By the late 1960s it was apparent that Pat Boone was virtually bankrupt: financially as well." (July, 1970, p. 7.) Our exchange did not deal with such intimate matters, but with scriptures, reasons, and experiences which Pat thought proved that the miraculous gifts are for us today.

Second, the author thought that he made his intentions clear. (a) On February 18 he said he would not make a public statement *concerning Pat's position until* we had corresponded. He said if Pat changed him, he would still make a public statement. If Pat did not change him, the exchanges would enable the author to better understand Pat and to help others better through the author's book; which, he told Pat, he was in the process of writing. The author thought this made clear that he would deal publicly with Pat's position *after* we had corresponded. (b) On February 27, 1970 the author mailed Pat an article on: "Is This The Work of the Holy Spirit?" It did not call Pat's name, but it was easy for Pat to see that it dealt with him. The article told of recently telling a friend, who thinks he has the gifts, but has not informed the brethren that he was leaving some brethren out on a limb; that the friend's motives were good because he thought the Spirit was leading him in this course of conduct which, the author said, would deceive the brethren; that tongues were not mainly for private edification; and that the author believed we needed to speak out publicly, when necessary, concerning tongues speakers among us. These were all things which the author had told Pat on February 18 and 19. (c) On February 28 on the phone Pat and Shirley spoke of revealing their beliefs to brethren as they felt they were led by the Spirit and the Lord to do so; and they did not feel led at this time to make public statements. The author said, and by it meaning in the providence of God, that they needed to consider whether it might not be the Lord's purpose to reveal these things, concerning their beliefs, to the brethren through the author. The way they told the author to remember this six months from then, led the author to try to make clear, what he meant, in a letter of March 1, 1970. (d) During the correspondence the author built entire chapters around quotations from Pat's letters. He thought this also made clear his intentions. After awhile Pat mentioned this, and said he did not want to be quoted. (e) In a phone conversation on May 4, 1970 the author told Pat that Pat could pass on quotations which the author planned to use in the book, or that he could revise them for the book, or that the author would give the gist of Pat's arguments without using direct quotations. He stated that he never felt that arguments were confidential. (f) Pat has long known that the author writes books, including books on controversial subjects and in which names are mentioned.

Third, when the author talked with Pat February 18, Pat did not start out by saying that the conversation was confidential. As far as the author recalls, the only thing the author said that related to it being confidential was that he would not say anything publicly *until* they had corresponded. When Pat and Shirley called February 28, and wanted it kept confidential, the author understood this in the context of the time limit, i. e. until we had corresponded, and when this was done the arrangement concerning matters being kept confidential would terminate. Later Pat did make it clear that he did not want to be mentioned at any time in anything which the author wrote. This request could not be granted because the author was convinced that duty demanded that Pat's arguments and experiences be publicly examined since Pat is now an open advocate of these things.

Fourth, does the reader think that the Holy Spirit would be so dead set against being quoted, or His work through Pat and Shirley being publicly mentioned and examined, if the Holy Spirit had anything to do with this in a direct and miraculous way? If Pat has what he thinks he has, he ought to be more confident about what he has said and experienced. His very attitude indicates confusion and contradiction and is one of the proofs that he does not have what he thinks he has. If one of the parties to this discussion was going to be fearful about being quoted, why wouldn't it be the one that knows he is uninspired? Why is the one who has a number of gifts, and thinks he can get the rest of them if he asks in faith, so fearful?

Fifth, although the author had tried to make his intentions known to Pat from the beginning, Pat seemingly did not understand. However, it is obvious that the Holy Spirit understood from the beginning what the author's intentions were. If the Spirit were in such direct communication with Pat why, after the author had failed to get Pat to understand his intentions, didn't the Spirit clearly reveal these intentions to Pat? Surely this discussion was more important than some of the matters on which Pat believes he has gotten revelations either directly, through his family, or through someone else.

Sixth, the entire question of gifts and direct guidance must be tested not just by theoretical discussion, but also by how it operates in practice. If Pat and his family have various gifts, why did they not operate better in this discussion which Pat considered to be of great importance? Why has Pat been unable to tell the author when he was inspired, and when he was not, in his conversations, letters, and arguments? Pat concluded that we had not communicated well in the discussion, that it was getting nowhere, and, in fact, that it was not turning out well, but was being used to create division because of the way the author was handling it. If the gifts operated on Pat's side in this discussion, why is he so dissatisfied with the outcome? He not only regrets that he did not convert the author, but he now regrets that he told the author as much as he did. In fact, Pat and Shirley concluded that it was not wise to have discussed the matter at all with the author. What proof is there they had any miraculous guidance at all in this discussion? If they did, why do they feel as they do now? If they did not have such guidance, why didn't they; if their position about the gifts is correct? The author believes that the entire discussion, and its outcomes so far, show that it is better to depend on the use of the mind, the prayerful study of the Scriptures, and the providence of God than on assuming that one has miraculous gifts of the Spirit today. God has not left us orphans just because He does not give us the miraculous gifts, including the gifts of inspiration and discernment. Pat certainly doesn't think that in this discussion he had the gift of discernment!

Seventh, if Pat did not think that his arguments and experiences would help convert the author, why did he use them? If he thought they would, why does he object to others knowing about them? If God has done with Pat, for Pat, and through Pat these things in a miraculous way, what is wrong with others knowing about them? Why were not his arguments and experiences used for the purposes of spreading and confirming the gospel? What is wrong with others knowing what Pat thinks helps prove that the gifts are for us today? The author is convinced that Pat sincerely believes these things, but Pat is so confused that he does not act like a person who had much confidence in these arguments and experiences. It may be said that perhaps Pat feels the author will not adequately or accurately represent his arguments and experiences. The author has not quoted Pat's arguments because Pat did not want to be quoted. Pat did not accept the author's offer to let Pat re-state the arguments. If, after trying, the author has failed to represent what Pat actually believes, perhaps Pat would like to have a written dialogue, which would be printed in book form, with the author.

The author does not believe he has taken advantage of Pat. He does feel, however, that if Pat had the gifts, Pat would have done a lot better job than he did. He would not have misunderstood so many scriptures. Furthermore, no uninspired man could be a match for an inspired man, so if Pat had some of the gifts it would be impossible for this uninspired author to wield the sword of the Spirit against some of Pat's teachings.

CONTROVERSY

What is Pat's attitude toward controversy? He does not like it, and is strongly opposed to his being involved in public controversy in these matters. *First,* when one takes a stand on a matter it is an invitation, in effect, for others to investigate one's claims. If one does not want to be involved in controversy he should not advocate a position. *Second,* it is impossible for someone as prominent as Pat to make such a radical change in his beliefs and practices, and avoid public controversy. *Third,* those who believe he is involved in serious error, and that he will have an influence on some in the church, have the duty both to try to teach Pat and to try to keep him from leading others into the same errors. *Fourth,* inspired men engaged in controversy (Matt. 23; Acts 15:2, 7; Gal. 2:5, 14). *Fifth,* Christians are to give a reasoned defense to those who ask concerning their hope in Christ (I Pet. 3:15), to test teachers (I John 4:1; Rev. 2:2), to guard against apostasy (I Tim. 4:1), to uphold the sound doctrine against fables (II Tim. 4:3-4), to detect and expose wolves in sheep's clothing (Matt. 7:15), to be fruit inspectors (Matt. 7:16-20), and to contend for the faith (Jude 3). These things cannot be done without being involved in public and private controversy. Why should any Christian feel that he should be exempt from these things because he has an aversion to controversy? Why should one feel that his own positions should not be subjected to public examination when they involved positions which he publicly proclaims? *Sixth,* years ago a Baptist, John A. Broadus, wrote: "The Reformation involved a revival of controversial preaching. Religious controversy is unpopular in our day, being regarded as showing a lack of charity, of broad culture, and, in the estimation of some, a lack even of social refinement and courtesy . . . it must not be forgotten that religious controversy is inevitable where living faith in definite truth is dwelling side by side with ruinous error and practical evils." "His (Christ's) teachings were to a great extent *controversial,* polemical. He was constantly aiming at some error or evil practice existing among His hearers . . . Truth, in this world oppressed with error, cannot hope, has no right, *to keep the peace.* Christ came not to cast peace upon the earth, but a sword. We must not shrink from antagonism and conflict in proclaiming the Gospel, publicly or privately; though in fearlessly maintaining this conflict we must not sacrifice courtesy or true Christian charity."

Charles Porterfield Krauth, a Lutheran, affirmed that: "The life of a Church may be largely read in its controversies . . . so may the glory or shame of a Church be determined when we know what it fought for and what it fought against; how much it valued what it believed to be truth; what was the truth it valued; how much it did and how much it suffered to maintain that truth and what was the issue of its struggles and sacrifices . . . A Church which contends for nothing either has lost the truth or has ceased to love it. Warfare is painful, but they whose errors create the necessity for it are responsible for all (?J.D.B.) its miseries." *(Christian News,* May 4, 1970, p. 4.)

CORRESPONDENCE TERMINATED

On July 14, 1970 Pat terminated, at least for the time being, the dialogue on the Spirit. *First,* after the author mailed the letter to Pat on June 19 he told his wife he would not be surprised if this did not terminate it. *Second,* the author plans to conduct a monologue, the Lord willing, by sending material to Pat from time to time. Pat has already responded with two long letters. *Third,* the author asked if Pat thought the Spirit guided him into this decision, and into the reasons which he gave for the decision. If Pat thought so, this would be strange for the Spirit knew these reasons before the correspondence started. Why would not the Spirit have kept him from the correspondence? Pat thought we really did not get anywhere. If Pat does not think the Spirit guided him into these things, why, if Pat has miraculous guidance at times, does not Pat wonder why the Spirit did not guide him not to enter into the correspondence? The reasons he terminated the correspondence would be good reasons why he should not have started it. Surely Pat must wonder why his guidance system has not worked any better than it seems to have worked so far in these matters. The author is convinced that if the gifts are for us today, and if we have them, we would not be misguided as Pat has been; at least would not the Spirit have warned against some of the things Pat has done? The author has continued to hear from Pat.

DENOMINATIONALISM

Sometimes at meetings of the Full Gospel Businessmen's Fellowship International they sing: "I Don't Care What Church You Belong To." *(Christianity Today,* August 1, 1969, p. 997.) Jesus prayed for the unity of believers. Paul taught unity and taught against division (John 17:20-21; Eph. 4:1-6; I Cor. 1:10-13). Pat has some associations with the FGBMFI.

GOD SURPRISES MEN?

When the author insisted that if we have these gifts today they *must* be for the same purpose as in the first century—to reveal and confirm the word of those who worked the miracles (Mk. 16:17, 20), Pat shuddered because he was scared by the idea that we had God so pinned down that we could say with absolute certainty what He will and will not do and for what reasons. We could study what God had done in the past, but God has continually surprised man throughout history by doing what men thought was unusual.

First, why wasn't Pat frightened by the consequence of his position that we *must* have these gifts today if we are open to all God has for us?

Second, since Pat goes to the Bible and claims these gifts, what is wrong with the author going to the Bible to find the purposes of these gifts? How can Pat separate them from their purposes? We can know God's mind only as He has revealed it in the Bible. (I Cor. 2:10-13; John 16:12-14; Jude 3.) Therefore, we have no right to say God is granting the gifts today but for different purposes.

Third, we are not trying to pin God down *when we insist that men be pinned down by what God has revealed.* "To the law and to the testimony! If they speak not according to this word, surely there is no morning for them." (Isa. 8:20).

If Pat had been there, would he have said: What are you trying to do, Isaiah, pin God down? When Luke said that they continued stedfastly in the apostles' doctrine (Acts 2:42), would Pat have asked: Were you suggesting that we can pin God down to the apostles' doctrine? When Paul said men were not to go beyond that which is written, would Pat have asked: How can you be so certain as to what God permits and what He does not? (I Cor. 4:6.)

Fourth, (a) the revelation of God to man involved not merely *events* in human history but also *God's inspired interpretation* of the events which He revealed to inspired men. Event plus the divine interpretation equals the revelation of God's will to man. Although outside of the Bible we can see the working of God's moral and spiritual laws, none of us can make an inspired interpretation of God's work in human history outside of the Bible. Righteousness exalteth a nation, and sin is a reproach to any people. God has revealed this, and we can see its truth confirmed in human history over the centuries, but none of us are inspired interpreters of God's action in history today so that we can say: We have the inspired interpretation of this or that event in history. And certainly we cannot take something in history, which is not connected with God's moral and spiritual laws and say: This is very unusual, but it is of God because God has "continually surprised us throughout human history." Or, one cannot say, if Pat is right, it is not of God, for Pat said think how God has surprised man in history in times past. (b) When God surprised men in human history in the Bible, God revealed through His prophets that it was God's action. Furthermore, He gave His prophets the proper credentials so that the people could know that the prophet's interpretation was in reality God's revelation through the prophet. (c) Therefore, if God is surprising us in human history today, in order for us to know it is God, it is not sufficient to say that God has surprised men in the past. If this were sufficient, anyone could validate any doctrine today as being from God. The more surprising it is, the more it is different from what we expected when we based our expectations on the Bible, the more it could be argued that God has continually surprised men so how do you know He is not surprising men in this

233

act or teaching today? In order for us to know it is of God, the Lord would have to send His prophets today, with miraculous confirmation of their word, to reveal to us that this surprising thing is of Him. If God does this, we have additional revelations. If we have additional revelation, we have additional inspired material to put in the Bible. God's surprising ways, revealed by the prophet and confirmed by God through signs, became a part of the Scriptures in times past; so why not put the modern surprises in with the Scriptures?

Fifth, we are confined by the Word of God as to the range, the nature, and the purposes of the miraculous gifts. For us to know God gives them for some other purpose or purposes, or for more limited purposes, God would have to make a modern revelation to inform us of this fact. If He makes and confirms such a revelation we would be bound to put it in with the Bible. We are bound by what is revealed, and if God authorizes more the only way we can know it is by God making and confirming an additional revelation. We are not trying to pin God down to our rules when we discern the rules He has revealed.

JUDGE?

Has the author set himself up as an expert so that he can with certainty pass on the experiences of others and decide who is and who is not acceptable to God? *First,* does one have to claim to be an expert in order to decide that certain doctrines are unscripural? Do they claim to be the expert when they claim you are wrong in your claim that their doctrine is false? *Second,* Pat and others will say that some individuals have not experienced with God what they claim to have experienced. Mrs. Eddy, the founder of Christian Science, claimed to have experiences with God, but she taught that there is no sin, sickness, nor death. Therefore, Jesus Christ did not die for our sins. All those who believe in the gospel, and Pat does, must affirm that her message is not the true gospel (Gal. 1:6-9). *Third,* in *Testimony,* No. 30, Pat claimed that certain people, at least two of whom preach for different denominations, had such experiences with God that they were living the Christian life in living color. How did he become such an expert that he knows this is the case? *Fourth,* we did not write the Bible, and we cannot change it. We cannot repeal what God has legislated, nor can we scripturally promise what God has not promised. When Jesus says one must be born of water and the Spirit in order to enter the kingdom (John 3:2-5; Gal. 3:26-27), we have not set ourselves up as judges when we accept His statement. If God wants to make exceptions on judgment day, it is within His prerogative as lawgiver and judge, but we do not have the authority to make exceptions.

How can one failure condemn or judge other failures? *First,* we are not the judge who can send man to his fate. Christ is the judge (Acts 17:30-31). *Second,* we all stand in need of God's mercy. *Third,* we must point men to the word by which we shall be judged (John 12:48). *Fourth,* if one failure excuses another failure, is one just as well off outside the church as inside the church? *Fifth,* our need for God's mercy does not exempt us from trying the spirits (I John 4:1; Rev. 2:2), disputing when necessary (Acts 15:2, 7), standing firm and contending for the faith (Gal. 2:5; Jude 3), rebuking publicly when necessary (Gal. 2:14), and exposing commandments which are not from the Lord (Acts 15:24).

JUDGING?

Pat thought that brethren were judging him in denying that he has the Spirit, and in being unable to fellowship him in these things. *First,* we are not the judge of man, but we do seek His judgments in the Bible. *Second,* although we are not to be hypocritical mote-finders who refuse to cast the beam out of their own eye, we are to make judgments and distinctions so that we distinguish between loaves and stones, fishes and serpents, the narrow and the broad, the sheep and the wolves in sheep's clothing, good and evil fruit, and the rock and the sand (Matt. 7:1-27). *Third,* if we are judging him, is he not judging us in claiming that we are judging him? If we are judging him in rejecting his interpretation of his experiences, is he not judging us in believing we are rejecting something which is scriptural? *Fourth,* Pat made a judgment concerning the author in saying that the author had absolute confidence in his mental capacity to almost infallibly interpret the Scriptures, the mind of God, the working of the Spirit, and the inevitable consequences of the actions and beliefs of others. This evaluation did not offend the author, and he appreciated Pat's frank expression of his impression. It furnished the author with an opportunity to examine himself anew, and also to evaluate Pat's impression.

MIND—BUDDHISM

Do any pagan religions minimize the mind? Zen Buddhism, for example, minimizes the mind and the rational. Through inward meditation and some sort of direct insight as one turns the mind in on itself, one comes to enlightenment. Lit-sen Chang asked: "What is Zen? Perhaps this is the most difficult question to answer. Zen is considered to be 'extremely elusive' and as a 'bottomless abyss'. It is beyond perception, description, definition and grasping. Dr. Suzuki says, 'The only truthful answer is 'that's it'." *(Zen-Existentialism, p. 29.)* Pat, and others, are held back from extreme irrationalism by their Western heritage and Biblical background. However, if one follows, to its logical conclusion, their emphasis on some sort of experience which by-passes the mind, there is no *reason*—for how could one depend on any reason—to stop short of complete mysticism (See also I Cor. 2:7, 10-14).

What about I Cor. 2:7? Pat, in minimizing the mind, wrote that even God's recorded word was more profound than our finite understanding. In this connection he quoted Paul's statement that "we speak God's wisdom in a mystery . . . " (I Cor. 2:7). *First,* there is always more for us to learn from the Bible, but what we learn involves the use of the mind. *Second,* Paul stressed that what had been a mystery, in that it was hidden in the mind of God, has now been revealed by the Spirit through inspired men (2:8-16). *Third,* how had the Corinthians learned the mystery which was now revealed? (a) The gospel was preached to them so that they could have the faith which comes by hearing God's word (I Cor. 1:21; Rom. 10:17). Paul said: "We preach Christ crucified . . ." (1:23-24). (b) The Corinthians, to whom Paul wrote I Cor. 2:7-14, had been reasoned with by Paul and through the preaching of the word had been converted to Christ (Acts 18:4-11). " . . . and many of the Corinthians hearing believed, and were baptized."

Although the finite mind of man never exhausts the divine revelation, what man does grasp involves the mind.

What about I Cor. 2:10-16? In minimizing the mind, Pat

236

said that Paul taught that the things of the Spirit of God are discerned spiritually; not naturally, or intellectually. He granted that the intellect is useful and that the mind is involved. Does Paul minimize the mind and its power to understand God's revelation? Our chapter on the intellect deals with this, but here we make some brief comments. *First*, the Corinthians had been converted through the preaching of the gospel to their minds (Acts 18:4-11).

Second, the epistle was directed to their minds, they were told "in mind be men" (14:20), and to prove themselves whether they were in the faith (II Cor. 13:5).

Third, man could not know of himself the mind of God. The Spirit knows God's mind, and revealed His mind through the words of the men whom He inspired (I Cor. 2:10-13). They had the mind of Christ for it was revealed to them. And we have this mind to the extent that we accept and understand what God revealed through the Spirit (2:10, 16).

Fourth, the natural man in I Cor. 2:14 does not refer to the mind itself, but to those who have determined that all must be known through man's uninspired, and unenlightened by divine revelation, insights into reality. Such rule out the divine revelation as foolishness (I Cor. 1:18-25). The natural man of whom Paul speaks *"receiveth not* the things of the Spirit of God: for *they are foolishness* unto him; and *he cannot know them*, because they are spiritually judged" (2:14). The things of the Spirit are the things which God has revealed through the Spirit and which were taught by the inspired men (2:10-13). They were foolish to the wise and disputers of this world who viewed the cross as foolishness (1:18-25). The believers, however, have accepted this wisdom of God (1:21; 2:6). God put His laws—and He did it through the teaching of the inspired men—in their minds and wrote them on their hearts (Heb. 8:10). They, of course, had to furnish receptive hearts (Lk. 8:11-15). *The natural man is not a part of the Christian man, such as his mind.* If the natural man included the mind of the Christian, we would have to affirm that "the mind of the Christian receiveth not the things of the Spirit of God: for they are foolishness unto him; and he cannot know them, because they are spiritually judged." (2:14.) Pat will be unwilling to affirm, and rightly so, that his mind receiveth not the things of God, and that they are foolishness to his mind. They are foolishness only if we use our minds to look at them from the standpoint of man's wisdom, but this is not the way we look at them for our minds have been instructed by the word of God and we have accepted this instruction. To my mind the gospel is not unreasonable, but is the only view of reality which really makes sense. When our minds are enlightened by God's word, we can see how really foolish is the wisdom of the world which views all things from the standpoint of man's speculations and without the acknowledgement of the reality of the divine revelation. The natural man *of I Cor. 2:14 is not some part of the Christian man*, but the one who rejects divine revelation and views things in the light of human speculation. It is true that the church in Corinth had in it people who were not spiritual in that they had jealousy and strife (3:1-3), but they were not this natural man, for they had accepted the gospel (1:23-24; 2:1-5), and the natural men had not accepted it (1:18-21). The natural men depended on their own wisdom, and thus knew not God, "for seeing that in the wisdom of God *the world through its wisdom knew not God,* it was God's good pleasure through the foolishness of the preaching to save them that believe." (1:21.)

Fifth, by the expression "the spirit of man" Paul includes the intellect. "For who among men knoweth the things of a man, save the spirit of man, which is in him?" (2:11.) This is true not just of the Christian man, but of the un-Christian man; for it is his spirit that knows his own things. What does any man know unless his mind is involved? The natural man knoweth not the things of God, but it is given to the good and honest hearts to know (Lk. 8:15). Such hearts have not waxed gross; instead they see with their eyes, hear with their ears, and understand with their heart (Matt. 13:15-16). The Samaritans evidently willed to know God's will, for after hearing the woman and Jesus they knew that Jesus is the Saviour of the world (John 7:17; 4:42). In Ephesus Paul reasoned and persuaded, and through the word of the Lord led people to faith in Christ (Acts 19:8-10). To these Ephesians he wrote: "When ye read, ye can perceive my understanding in the mystery of Christ." (Eph. 3:4.) And he told

238

them not to be foolish "but **understand** what the will of the Lord is." (5:17)

The author believes that Pat is confused as to the use of the mind, but that if he will continue to study the Scriptures, and use his mind in the service of a good and honest heart, the Spirit will instruct him more perfectly in the way of the Lord on this as well as on other subjects.

PAUL—SOME LETTERS MISSING?

Are many letters of Paul missing? *First,* we do not have to have every case where a particular type of miracle was worked in order to have samples of all the types (John 20:30-31; 21:25). We do not have to have every sermon an apostle or prophet preached in order to have every truth which they taught. We would not have to have every epistle Paul wrote in order to have every truth he taught. *Second,* however, there is no evidence in the Bible or outside the Bible that many of Paul's epistles were not preserved. If there is any such reference in the Bible, the most likely one is I Cor. 5:9. However, the author is not convinced that this refers to a lost epistle. We have discussed this matter in *The Book of Mormon?,* pp. 20-59.

PRESUMPTUOUS?

Pat thought it was presumptuous for an uninspired man to check those who claim to be inspired. It was as presumptuous as a self-trained mechanic challenging the statements of an IBM trained computer expert. The mechanic might be right, but the odds were against it. *First,* unless Pat claims inspiration, which he does to the extent he claims to have and exercise the gifts, it would be presumptuous for him as an uninspired man to say that some are inspired today. With his minimization of the mind, how could he presume to pass judgment either way?

Second, this author made it clear that those who claimed to be inspired today can be shown to teach false doctrine when measured by the word by which we shall be judged (John 12:48; Jude 3). Is Pat presumptuous in following I John 4:1-2 and Rev. 2:2 and rejecting Mormon prophets and apostles? Why are we to put on the whole armor of God, and take the sword of the Spirit which is God's word, if we are not to defend truth and defeat error? (Eph. 6:10-16.)

Third, on Pat's logic it would be presumptuous to think we can learn any truth from the Bible and expose any error; unless we are inspired. Does Pat think that he is the IBM trained computer expert, because he has gifts, and the author is the self-trained mechanic? However, Pat granted the author "the right to test those statements in practice." If God made Pat the expert, it is satisfactory with the author, but what proof can he give that he has gifts? Why has the author been able to detect at least some errors in Pat's teaching? Pat never did tell the author which of his explanations were inspired— that is, which came through or were confirmed by the gifts.

Fourth, Paul was inspired although his audience at first did not believe it. They used their uninspired minds to study the Bible, and found that Paul was right (Acts 17:11-12). If the author learns that Pat is inspired, it will have to be learned through using the mind to examine the evidence.

Fifth, neither Pat nor the author desire to compare their "humilities" to see which has the most humble "humility." However, if it is "the height of presumption" for this uninspired student to believe he can use the Bible to detect error, is it the depth of humility for one to claim that he is supernaurally taught by the Spirit so he can understand the Bible? Pat thinks that without such teaching our minds can grasp but a little portion of the Bible. If very little of the Bible can be understood by uninspired men, very little of the Bible is the revelation of God's will to man.

Sixth, the author prays concerning Bible study, and he believes God is so powerful that He can work behind the scene through others and help the author. The author has been instructed by unbelievers when they have called his attention to something in the Bible he had overlooked or forgotten. They did not have to be inspired in order to instruct the author, nor did the author have to be inspired in order to be instructed.

DOCTRINE ONLY?

Pat said one of his troubles was that much of his view of Christianity was doctrine only—a set of rules. This had not worked for he still had problems to which he had no answers. *First,* Christ is the heart of Christianity. *Second,* the will of this Person should be written on our hearts (I Cor. 9:21; Heb. 8:10). His grace teaches us rules and principles for living (Titus 2:11-14). *Third,* too many think Christianity should banish all problems and immediately answer all questions. If they continue in this attitude, they either give up Christianity, or adapt Christianity in such a way that they get a guidance system which is supposed to answer all questions and solve all problems in some direct, inspired way. Christ has not promised us a problem-free life. We have to keep walking by faith even when we do not have answers to some problems. If Pat had to turn to a different concept of Christianity because he had problems, does not this mean that now his problems are solved and all of his questions answered? Does he really not have some of the same problems and some of the same questions which he once had? Have his new experiences and beliefs brought him no new problems and perplexities? Has he no problems as to how to harmonize some of these experiences, which some of his friends have, with the false doctrines which they teach? What problems has he solved, and questions answered and answered rightly, which could not have been solved, without the claim of inspiration and miracles, through Bible study, living by the principles of Christ, study of the problems, consultations, and prayer?

DOGMATIC?

Pat felt he must reject what he viewed as the final and dogmatic way in which the author wrote, and the positive and judgmental positions the author supposedly took concerning others who love God and study and serve God to the best of their ability and understanding. *First,* the author felt that he had made no more dogmatic statement on any matters than Pat made in the above. *Second,* the author does not know if Pat felt guided to make this sweeping judgment. *Third,* if Pat thinks the evidence justified such a statement, what is wrong with the author making a positive statement when he thinks the evidence justifies it? *Fourth,* the author is willing for his statements to be evaluated and to honestly study the evaluation. *Fifth,* Pat thinks that some modern miracle workers are of the devil. The author has not been this positive or judgmental, because he has not seen a case which he thought was a miracle. However, if a miracle worker did appear and contradicted the Scriptures, it would be by the power of the devil. *Sixth*, how could one try false prophets and teachers, Mormon apostles for example, without someone accusing one of being dogmatic, positive, final, and judgmental? Yet, we are to try them (I John 4:1-2; Rev. 2:2). *Seventh*, the destiny of man is determined by God, and not by the author. *Eighth*, the author was not upset by Pat's evaluation. It furnished an opportunity for reflecting on how to express things, and to let Pat know the author's reaction. *Ninth*, it is difficult to find people who are more dogmatic than some of the Pentecostals. For example, see the charges which Mrs. Joyce Dennis brought against elders in Santa Ana, California, and against the author.

FELLOWSHIP?

Pat wants to be fellowshipped while he teaches publicly and privately, in print and on the platform, Pentecostalism. If fellowship is as broad as Pat teaches, we must fellowship a wide variety of denominationalists and take a different view, from what we have taken in the past, of the new birth, the church, the Bible and the gifts. In such a case, the author is guilty of factionalism in disfellowshipping the Pentecostals. Therefore, he should be disfellowshipped by Pat, after admonitions and instructions, if the author does not change. Is Pat's concept of fellowship scriptural?

First, if the Bible is not the standard, fellowship can be as broad as the authority one accepts allows.

Second, it is one thing to bear with a person who has problems and it is another thing to fellowship an advocate of Pentecostalism.

Third, the unity of the Spirit, which we are commanded to keep, is not perfectly attained by Christians, but Pentecostalism makes it impossible for us to hold some of the things Paul briefly mentioned in Eph. 4:3-6. (a) How can we fellowship those who advocate and belong to different bodies? There is one body of Christ, which is the church (Eph. 1:22-23; 2:14-16; 4:4). Sooner or later the Pentecostals among us view the church as a sect, and contend for a larger body of Christ which includes those who have not been baptized into Christ. If Pentecostals were baptized in the same Spirit in

242

whom the apostles were baptized, they would not establish or teach that there are different bodies. (b) All that we know about the one Spirit is found in the Bible (Eph. 4:4). Pat teaches that even with the Bible before us we cannot say with finality what the Spirit will or will not do. The Spirit, Pat said, is unpredictable. This means that we cannot prove from the Bible that the Spirit did not do certain things. If this is the case, how do we know we can depend on what the Spirit taught in the Bible? (c) The one hope is a part of the unity which we are to keep (Eph. 4:4). (d) We must hold to and obey the one Lord (Eph. 4:5; Acts 2:36; Lk. 6:46). His will can be found only in the Bible. Pentecostals who claim direct revelations sooner or later contradict the Bible. (e) We must hold to the one faith which was delivered once for all in the first century (Eph. 4:5; Jude 3). It is the truth in its completeness, and we must oppose that which is not sanctioned by the faith (John 16:12-14; Jude 3). If the gifts operate today we must have modern apostles, prophets, and scriptures. This would mean that the faith was not revealed in its fulness and finality in the first century. We could not measure all things by it. As a general rule, when Pentecostals cannot follow both the Bible and their experiences, they follow their experiences. Pentecostalism destroys the Bible as the final authority. If this does not constitute grounds for disfellowship, there can be no grounds for each individual could appeal to his modern experiences, supposedly produced by the Spirit, to justify what he has said or done. So-called modern gifts are used to sustain unscriptural doctrines. These individuals have as much evidence and argument for their "gifts" as Pat does for his. On the other hand, if the full gospel—the one faith—includes the gifts, as Pat believes that it does, we should be disfellowshipped for not holding to this one faith and for refusing to walk in the doctrines of modern apostles and prophets. If they are sent by Christ, to reject them is to reject Christ (John 13:20; Acts 2:42). We must mark the Pentecostals for causing division contrary to the New Testament faith (Rom. 16:17; I Cor. 16:13). (f) There is one baptism which makes up a part of the unity of the faith (Eph. 4:5; Matt. 28:19; Acts 2:38; 22:16; Rom.

6:2-5. 17-18). Modern Pentecostalism contains people who reject what the Bible teaches concerning who can be baptized, what is the act of baptism, and baptism being into Christ. It accepts those not baptized into Christ. As Reuel Lemmons pointed out, to be consistent, those who accept Pentecostalism must "break completely with the idea of a 'plan of salvation' which one must obey to become a Christian . . . " (*Firm Foundation*, May 19, 1970, p. 306). This plan centers in, and draws its meaning and value from, the Person, Jesus Christ. (g) The unity of the faith includes the one God who is our Father (Eph. 4:6). Although we can discern His existence without the Bible (Rom 1:19-21), we can know His mind only as He has revealed it through the inspired men who wrote the Bible (I Cor. 2:10-14).

Fourth, Pat said that John gave broad guidelines to fellowship and brotherhood. Although John is not the only writer who deals with fellowship, what are some of the things which he taught? (a) Don't abide in darkness (I John 1:5-7). (b) Admit that you sin (1:8-10). (c) The test of knowledge is found in obedience (2:3-6; 3:22-23). (d) Love the brethren (2:7-11; 3:10-12; 4:20). This, too, is tested by our works (3:16-18). (e) Love God, not the world (2:15-17). (f) Oppose those who deny Jesus is the Christ (2:18-23). (g) Abide in the truth (2:24-27). (h) Guard against being led astray (2:26). (i) Do not be lawless (3:4). (j) Do righteousness (2:29; 3:10). (k) Test those who claim to be prophets. One test, but only one, is whether they confess that Jesus Christ came in the flesh (4:1-3). (l) The spirit of truth listens to the inspired teachers, the spirit of error does not (4:6). (m) Keep the commandments (5:3). (n) Guard against idols (5:21). (o) Reject those who deny Christ came in the flesh (II John 7-11). These verses teach at least this much, if not more. (p) Oppose the Diotrepheses (III John 9-11). (q) Jesus told John that He disfellowships those who persist in leaving their first love and who continue in immoral doctrines and practices (Rev. 2:4-5, 6, 14-15, 16, 20-23). He said He would spew out the lukewarm (Rev. 3:15-16). Since we are unable to measure the temperature of another Christian, we must leave this spewing to the Lord.

244

DIVISION INEVITABLE

Why is division inevitable when men try to spread Pentecostalism in the church? *First,* those who sincerely believe in Pentecostalism will sooner or later teach it. When they drive the wedge of Pentecostalism into the log called the church, they will accuse others of causing division and of persecuting them.

Second, if they are right, we are guilty of opposing the work of God and His modern apostles, prophets, and revelations. Would the church in Jerusalem have continued to fellowship those who continued to oppose the apostles? (Acts 2:42; John 13:20).

Third, how can we continue to worship together in the assembly when we are in such disagreement? When we control the assembly, we refuse to let them exercise their gifts. If they have these gifts from God, it is their duty to use them to edify the church and convert unbelievers; and we would be rejecting Paul's authority and what he authorized (I Cor. 14:37-39). Sooner or later they would have to disfellowship us. If they are wrong, we must forbid them to exercise their delusions in the assembly.

Fourth, Pat and the author differ as to where the line of fellowship should be drawn. But would Pat accept the author as a member of an evangelistic team, if the author continued to oppose Pentecostalism in such joint meetings? If he were an elder, how long would he fellowship someone in the congregation who opposed Pentecostalism as vigorously as does the author? Although Pentecostals among us may be broad in their fellowship as they ask us to fellowship them where they do not control the congregation, we wonder how long they would fellowship us if they did control the congregations?

Fifth, we disfellowship because we love the truth, love the souls of those who might be misled by false teachers, and love the one whom we disfellowship (II Thess. 3:15). God can correct, chastize, and re-direct individuals through disfellowship as well as within fellowship (I Cor. 5:1-13; II Cor. 2:5-11).

Sixth, it is true that one must work out his own salvation, but not independently of the Bible. Pat stands or falls before

God, but so does the author. He, too, must decide on the basis of the Bible whom he can fellowship and whom he cannot. Pat cannot go beyond our love, but he has gone beyond the author's fellowship.

FELLOWSHIP AND OTHER CONGREGATIONS

Pat raised the question as to whether it is right for ministers or elders in one congregation to try to get another congregation to disfellowship someone. *First,* a public figure such as Pat has a wide influence and what he believes and does can be the legitimate concern of many congregations. If an individual by his conduct or beliefs brings reproach, or advocates false doctrine, which hurts a lot of congregations, they have the right to *ask* his congregation to look into and do something about the matter. No congregation can dictate to another. Each must make its own decisions, and this also involves the decision of the relationship of one congregation to another. We cannot dictate, but we can affirm what we believe we must do in upholding truth and opposing error. *Second,* each of us has the freedom to use his influence as widely as possible. Although Dean Dennis approached him first Pat did help convert Dennis even though Dennis was a member of another congregation. *Third,* it should be realized that those who are closest to a problem may not move as fast as those who are not close to it. There may be internal problems which make it wise to move slowly in some cases.

INTERFERING WITH THEIR FREEDOM?

First, false teachers, both sincere and insincere (and we think Pat is sincere), will complain that their freedom is being interfered with when they are opposed or fellowship is withdrawn. Conscious wolves in sheep's clothing will complain when one refuses to give them a hunting license, or refuses to finance them, while they devour the flock. Any wolf, from whom one pulls the sheep's clothing, is going to howl. *Second,* they have the freedom to advocate their beliefs and we have the freedom to oppose them and to disfellowship them. They cannot bind us to cooperate with, back, or encourage them. They cannot bind us to silence or require us to fellowship them. *Third,* although the Pentecostals among us want the freedom to freely circulate their doctrines among us, without our withdrawing fellowship from them, we can rest assured that Pentecostal groups are not going to fellowship us so that we can freely circulate among them our opposition to their doctrine. *Fourth,* if anyone denies that Pat will try to teach these things in the church and out of it, they are denying that Pat sincerely believes that these things are of real importance. They are overlooking the fact that Pat approached Wilkerson about making the film *The Cross and the Switchblade.* Pat did this because the book convinced him that, among other things, signs accompanied Wilkerson. Furthermore, Pat was teaching these beliefs privately as long ago as February 1969, if not before; he is teaching them publicly now, and has written a book, the advanced orders for which have convinced Pat that it will become a best seller.

GAMALIEL'S ADVICE (ACTS 5:33-40)

Is the ideal attitude toward the tongues movement one of wait and see? (Sherrill, 137.) *First,* the tongues speakers are not waiting, but are joining in and affirming that it is the work of God. *Second,* why don't they have the same attitude toward opposition to tongues, i. e. wait and see who prevails. Instead, they teach tongues and oppose those who oppose them. Why does not Pat wait until he sees how things are going to turn out? Pat refuses to take Gamaliel's advice. *Third,* Gamaliel's advice made enough sense to the council that they beat, but did not kill, these apostles. *Fourth,* Gamaliel was not an inspired man, although we do have the word of the inspired writer, Luke, that Gamaliel gave this advice. We must measure his advice by what inspired writers teach. *Fifth,* we cannot wait until the end of time, and the judgment, to see how things turn out before we make a decision. If we wait until the end of time, it will be too late to make the right decision. Gamaliel cited cases where the temporary success of a movement was quickly undone, but not all error is shown to be error by its failure in one generation. Error can be perpetuated for centuries, and may prosper while truth suffers. Judaism has lasted longer than Christianity, but we do not become Jews. The Islamic faith has spread for centuries, but this does not make it true. Communism has been highly successful as a movement of deceit, destruction, and conquest, but it is false. The church has suffered apostasies, and has even been driven underground, but the faith is not false. Stephen's enemies outlasted him, and the church was scattered, but the faith is still true (Acts 8:1, 4, compare with the scattering mentioned by Gamaliel, Acts 5:36-37). *Sixth*, Gamaliel's advice is that of the neutralist who wants to sit above the battle until he sees who is going to win. Instead, one should try to determine what is right and what is wrong and then back the right and oppose the wrong. This should be done regardless of who seems to be winning. *Seventh*, instead of waiting to see how things turn out, we should be willing to listen, studious in study, prove all things, hold fast that which is good, and contend for the faith regardless of how unsuccessful it may seem to be at times (Acts 17:11-12; I Thess. 5:21; Jude 3; II Tim. 4:14-18). *Eighth*, Pat and others want to use Gamaliel's advice to stop our opposition to the tongues movement.

Did history prove Gamaliel was right? Pat thought history proved Gamaliel right because, in opposing the apostles, history shows that they would have been fighting God. *First*, Gamaliel's advice was neutrality; that is, neither to support nor oppose the apostles. "Refrain from these men, and let them them alone." (Acts 5:38.) Both the credentials of Christ, and the additional credentials furnished by history, prove that Gamaliel's neutralism was wrong. The author again asks: If Pat has some of the gifts, and at times is miraculously guided by the Spirit, *why does he misinterpret so many passages of scripture?* *Second*, Gamaliel supported neutralism with two arguments. (a) "If this counsel or this work be of men, it will be overthrown." He cited two examples where this had happened (5:36-37). (b) "If it is of God, ye will not be able to overthrow them; lest haply ye be found even to be fighting against God." Regardless of which way things went, *one* of the alternatives had to be true. However, neither one of them proved that neutralism was right. Gamaliel was advocating neutralism concerning a work of God. *Third*, Gamaliel did not say that at the moment we do not have enough evidence on which to make up our minds; therefore, let us examine the credentials of the apostles and of Christ. If we find them adequate, let us accept Christ. If we find them inadequate, let us oppose their false teaching with true teaching from the Old Testament. No, instead of proposing such an examination he said let us sit above the battle to see how it is going to turn out. As far as we know, Gamaliel never accepted Christ and thus his neutralism resulted in his condemnation. Gamaliel's decision to be neutral about Christ placed him against Christ. "He that is not with me is against me; and he that gathereth not with me scattereth." (Matt. 12:30.)

Does Pat follow Gamaliel's advice? Pat's confusion is further made evident by the fact that he does not follow Gamaliel's advice. *First,* he does not tell unbelievers to be neutral about Christ. If one waits to see how things turn out it will be too late to decide for Christ. The evidence was sufficient in Gamaliel's day, even though we have the additional confirmation of history.

Second, Pat did not follow Gamaliel's advice with reference to the tongues movement. Instead of waiting and seeing how it will turn out, he rejected neutrality and became a participant in, and an advocate of, tongues and the other gifts. *Third,* Pat told the author that through the gifts the Spirit is working to ultimately bring people of different denominations into the unity for which Christ prayed. He did not want the author to be neutral, and to wait to see whether unity is achieved by the Spirit through these means. Instead, he wants the author to accept this as the Spirit's way of doing it. *Fourth,* Pat does not say that he will be neutral concerning the question as to whether the author is right or wrong. He thinks the author is wrong. He does not say that he will not take a stand concerning my positions because if the author is wrong it will come to naught, and if the author is right he would be opposing God in opposing my position. However, his letter of July 14, 1970, indicated that he was discouraged with the author, in so far as correspondence at least is concerned, on this subject. This is not because he is neutral, but because so far he has failed to convert the author, because he thinks he is not getting anywhere, and because he is afraid that anything else he says might also find its way into one of my books.

The author is confident that Pat wishes that the author like Gamaliel would be neutral since he does not accept Pat's position. However, too much is at stake for one to adopt neutralism as his position. It is one thing for a person to be undecided for a period of time, and it is quite another thing for him to adopt neutrality as his position.

HILLTOP EXPERIENCE

First, the author has attended Pentecostal services where the ministers got the people involved physically through standing up, testifying, raising hands, shouting, and then finally some of them got the Spirit. Once in Toronto, Canada, the building was so cold that no one got the Spirit that night! Pat's frame of mind had prepared him for the hilltop experience related in his book. The first time he met Bredesen, Bredesen took him outside to pray, suggested they run to clear their minds, and started praying out loud as they ran. He would pray and he would talk to Pat, and it was hard sometimes to tell which he was doing. As this continued for hours, the sun sank and darkness came. Pat began to feel the Lord's presence as he had never felt it before. They wept, talked and prayed and Pat viewed Bredesen as a brother.

Second, Pat undoubtedly had a highly emotional experience. All of us have likely had some emotional experiences when we felt closer to God than at some other times. When one willingly follows along with men like Bredesen, and does some of the things Pat did, it would be amazing if he did not get his feelings deeply involved. This does not prove it is of God. Our feelings flow from our faith, and the state of mind in which we become involved. Sometimes the author has felt chills run up and down his spine as he sang songs of Zion. These feeling overtones are not a sign of spirituality or of God's presence. He can worship God just as scripturally and sincerely when he has no such feelings.

Third, we should have joy, but joy and experiences are not the ultimate test of our relationship to God. The ultimate test is God's word. Some Pentecostals recognize this. In an official publication of the Assemblies of God, Willard T. Cantelon rightly stated that we are not saved by joy. "When you were saved, you felt the joy of salvation *after* you believed. Faith comes first, then feeling."

"Of course, I believe in feelings! But feelings should never be equated with faith. We are not saved by joy, but by faith. Feelings are a by-product of faith. Faith is a man's first step toward God in taking Him at His Word and acting upon His promise." *(The Pentecostal Evangel,* Springfield, Mo., April 2, 1967, p. 5.)

Undoubtedly Pat would say we are not saved by joy. However, Pat needs also to measure his beliefs and those of Bredesen by the Word of God. His hilltop experience does not prove what is right or wrong.

INFALLIBLE?

Pat thought the author had absolute confidence in his mental capacity to almost infallibly interpret the Scriptures, the mind of God, the working of the Spirit, and the inevitable consequences of the actions and beliefs of others. *First,* did the Spirit guide him into this evaluation? Was it the product of the gift of discerning the spirits? (I Cor. 12:10.) If it were, Pat's evaluation of the author was infallible. He, not the author, would be claiming infallibility. *Second,* if this view of himself is implied in the fact that the author is positive about some things, what does Pat's confidence in his own experience, in his own evaluation of the author, indicate concerning Pat's view of himself? *Third,* that the author does not view himself as almost infallible is evident from: (a) He has changed his mind on some things. (b) He cannot command as did Paul (I Cor. 14:37). (c) He has engaged in numerous discussions in an effort to learn from others as well as to teach others. The author's aim, which is not always easy to carry out, is to be studious and honest in dealing with the Bible and with the positions of others. *Fourth,* the author knows that nothing can be known about the mind of God except as God has revealed it in the faith (I Cor. 2:10-13; Jude 3). *Fifth,* if it is impossible to know anything, one could not know that another thought he was infallible, or even know that one held this view of the other. If it is possible to know any truth, someone who does not agree with that truth may accuse one of claiming to be infallible. *Sixth,* since Pat thinks he has some of the gifts, he should think he is infallible in everything which comes through the gifts, or is confirmed by the gifts. A difference between Pat and the author is that the author knows he is not infallible, but that Pat must either believe he is *infallible at times or he must doubt that he ever has or exercises any of the gifts. Seventh,* one may know the outcome of certain positions, when

251

carried to their logical conclusion, regardless of whether some people carry them to these conclusions. *Eighth,* regardless of such charges, Christians should study the Bible, be open to truth regardless of who calls it to their attention, contend for the faith, and prove all things and hold fast that which is good (John 8:32; I Thess. 5:21).

JESUS AS LORD

How do you evaluate Pat's claim that he only recently came to know Jesus as Lord? Pat wrote: "About a year ago, on my knees, I met Jesus as my Lord." Although he had been "an outspoken Christian for twenty-two years," he has "just come to really know Jesus." He had been a guest in Jesus' house for twenty-one years, but only now has he "come to know my landlord Himself, Jesus of Nazareth." He had been saved all during this time, but now he actually knows Jesus as the Lord of his life. *(Testimony, 7.)* Pat confuses knowing the Lord with emotional experiences and miracles.

First, it is essential to know God in order to be saved (John 17:3). To accept Jesus as Savior means accepting Him as Lord, for if we did not accept His Lordship we would not accept, as authoritative, His word concerning salvation. The great commission indicates that sinners seeking salvation must accept Jesus' Lordship. They must become His disciples and submit to Him by being baptized into Him. Then they are taught the commandments which they must obey in living the new life (Matt. 28:19-20). The Lordship of Jesus was preached at Pentecost. (a) The exalted Christ to reign until all enemies were conquered (Acts 2:33-35). (b) Ruling as "Lord" at God's right hand (2:34). (c) The sermon proved that God had made this same Jesus "both Lord and Christ." (2:36.) Those who accepted Jesus as Lord were baptized into Christ (2:38-41). The very act of baptism involved submission to His authority.

The Lordship of Jesus was implied in the fact that people must hearken to Him or be cut off (Acts 3:22-23). After saying this, Peter spoke of Christ turning people away from their iniquities (3:26). Paul taught the Saviorship and the Lordship of Christ in the same context (Eph. 1:20-23; 5:22-32). " . . . Christ also is the *head* of the *church*, being himself the *saviour* of the *body*." (5:23)

252

Second, the acceptance of the Lordship of Jesus does not mean that we understand all that is involved in it, any more than we fully understand all that salvation means. As babes we have much to learn. However, we accept additional truths, as we learn them, because we have accepted His right to teach and command.

Third, it is possible to rebel against His Lordship (Acts 5:3-4).

Fourth, it is inconsistent to call Him Lord and to refuse to obey Him (Lk. 6:46). The test of whether we know Him as Lord and Savior is not in an experience, or by a miraculous gift, but by whether we keep His commandments. John shows there are other tests, but this is one of them (I John 2:3-6).

Fifth, acceptance of His Lordship no more implies that we do a perfect job of obedience, any more than acceptance of Christ as Savior means that we are saved never to commit any more acts of sin. To accept Him as Savior includes letting His grace teach us how to live (Titus 2:11-14).

Sixth, as brought out elsewhere in this book, the author is convinced that Pat's way of knowing Christ as Lord led him into a course of unconscious deception and blindness.

Seventh, Pat thinks that some who have not been baptized into Christ have the baptism of the Spirit, miraculous gifts, and even the gift of inspiration. Is not this unconscious tampering on his part with the authority, the Lordship, of Jesus for Jesus in His word teaches that individuals must be born of water and the Spirit to enter the kingdom? (John 3:3-5.) Furthermore, if these men had the Spirit in a miraculous way, at least some of them would realize and teach that the Lordship of Jesus necessitates the abandonment of denominationalism and the submission to the Head in the one body of Christ (Eph. 1:19-23; 5:22-32). These men who contradict one another in some of their doctrines, and who contradict some of the New Testament, are all supposedly guided by the Spirit. And yet, Pat himself wrote: "We don't have to fear that the Holy Spirit will lead us into doctrinal error: how could God's Spirit contradict Himself? He will help us to understand God's Word, to love it, and to cherish and trust it." *(Testimony,* p. 10.)

253

Pat's confusion about accepting Jesus as Savior without accepting Him as Lord, is one of the proofs that he is not miraculously guided by the Spirit.

LAWSUIT: THREAT AND REPENTANCE

The author has debated, written about, and corresponded with atheists, modernists, Buddhists, and others. The only time he has been threatened with a lawsuit was in a telegram of May 15, 1970 from Pat Boone's attorneys who said that he would be sued if he published any part of the correspondence from Pat Boone. Concerning this we observe: *First*, this threat shows that Pat's guidance system was not working. He thinks he has some of the gifts, and that other gifts such as that of wisdom, operate in his family circle. Why didn't he get at least a warning against making such a threat? (a) It was contrary to I Cor. 6:1-8. (b) It was harmful, since it would give Pat more unfavorable publicity than anything which the author could have quoted from the correspondence. (c) It would have given national publicity to the author's book. (d) It was useless since the author had told Pat on May 4 that, if Pat did not want to be quoted, the author would state in his own words the gist of Pat's arguments. (e) It was futile for there is no law against stating Pat's position in the author's own words.

Second, Pat repented and withdrew the threat after the author told him how it hurt him personally and why he thought it was wrong. Pat's change of mind did not come because of any miraculous guidance, but because of the author's letter, the scriptures, and Pat's own re-thinking of the matter.

Third, Pat has been forgiven. The author did not hold it against him in the first place. Why has the author mentioned the threat of a lawsuit? (a) The threat of a lawsuit was not a private matter, and the author had told several people about it before Pat withdrew the threat. The author had called Reuel Lemmons and told him not to run an article which had quoted Pat without using Pat's name. The article, however, had just been printed. The news spread and both Pat and the author received some questions about it. Mentioning it in this book makes it a matter of record that Pat was big enough to change his mind and withdraw the threat. (b) Peter evidently repented of his failure to walk upright according to the truth

254

of the gospel. He later referred to the beloved Paul, and expected to die faithful to Jesus (II Pet. 3:15; 1:12-14). However, Paul mentioned the case in a *public* letter not to bring Peter to repentance, for he had already repented, but to drive home a lesson concerning the Gentile and the law (Gal. 2:11, 14). The author believes that the threat of a lawsuit helps demonstrate that Pat does not have the guidance sysem which he thinks he has. By mentioning this case, we may help keep some from being led into Pentecostalism. (c) The author has tried to follow the golden rule in this matter. He wrote Pat the pros and cons, as to whether or not to use this case, and asked Pat what he would do if he were in the author's place. The author decided that the golden rule did not forbid Paul's use of Peter's case (Gal. 2:14), and that if Pat was in the author's place, and the author was in Pat's place, it would be Pat's duty to use it to show that there was something wrong with the claim that various gifts, including that of wisdom, were operating in him and his family. (d) The author does not think that it will hurt Pat's reputation, for many people will not see anything wrong with such a threat, and those who do will appreciate Pat's being big enough to withdraw the threat. (e) After pondering over the matter, praying about it, and advising with others, the author's decision was triggered by Mr. Nickel, a Pentecostal, who indicated that at least some Pentecostals would use Pat's conversion as an opening wedge in churches of Christ *(Testimony,* No. 31, pp. 14-15). Mentioning the threat of a lawsuit was one of the legitimate things the author could do to help blunt the force of the wedge. Pat also has Mr. Nickels to thank, if thanks be the word, for publishing Pat's statement in *Testimony,* No. 30 in March, long before Pat meant for it to be published. (See p. 375 also.)

MIND MADE UP?

Is it wrong for one to have his mind made up on this or on any other subject? *First,* it depends on what one means and the basis on which his mind was made up. If he means he will not change even if truth shows he is wrong, he is not being honest. We should try to make up our minds and to make them up on the basis of truth. Through laziness, or dishonesty, or the lack of information an individual may refuse to make up his mind on some subjects. *Second,* we should make up our minds to be honest and diligent, to worship God and to serve humanity, to have faith in God and to live the new life in Christ. We do not have to claim to be authorities on all matters in order to know that God will not contradict Himself, and He will not command us to worship idols. He will not command His people to repudiate moral law. *Third,* obviously all things are not as clear as the above matters. However, since the faith has once for all been delivered to the saints (Jude 3), we can know what God approves or disapproves only by what is revealed therein. To go beyond the faith and say that God does thus and so is to go beyond what is revealed and is to speak without authority from God.

Does I Cor. 4:3 mean that Paul could not make up his mind and be certain about anything? Paul said: "But with me it is a very small thing that I should be judged of you, or of man's judgment: yea, I judge not mine own self. For I know nothing against myself; yet am I not hereby justified: but he that judgeth me is the Lord. Wherefore judge nothing before the time, until the Lord come, who will both bring to light the hidden things of darkness, and make manifest the counsels of the hearts; and then shall each man have his praise from God." (I Cor. 4:3-5.) *First,* Paul is not speaking of making up one's mind on a host of matters. If he were, none of us should make up our minds on anything until the Lord comes, and then it will be a bit late; to say the least. Paul had made up his mind about the gospel, and about certain conditions in the church in Corinth. The "spiritual" of whom he spoke were to judge whatever Paul included in "all things" (I Cor. 2:15). He authorized some to judge certain disputes between brethren (I Cor. 6:2-5). He wanted the Corinthians to be men, not children, in mind (I Cor. 14:20). *Second,* the context of Paul's statement shows that he has reference to judgment as to the faithfulness of his stewardship. Faithfulness is required (I Cor. 4:2). The judge of our faithfulness is not man—whether us or someone else—but Christ. Although we should exercise ourselves to be void of offense (Acts 24:16), although we should try to so live that our heart condemns us not (I John 3:21), although we can have assurance, but not arrogance, it is still true that even if we do not know anything against us it does not mean that Christ does not know something against us. The final judgment is His. In faith and obedence we need to rely on the mercy of this Judge who will do right. Our determination should be to honestly examine our lives in the light of the word of God. "Try your own selves, whether ye are in the faith; prove your own selves. Or know ye not as to your own selves, that Jesus Christ is in you? unless indeed ye be reprobate. But I hope *that ye shall know that we are not reprobate.*" (II Cor. 13:5-6.) Just how faithful we are in our stewardship, God only knows. That we can be faithful unto death, however, is an assurance which we can have as we live in the light of the Word.

ROMANS 14:14

Does Rom. 14:14 apply to Pat's beliefs? *First,* it is clear that Rom. 14:14 is not unlimited. *Second,* Paul is dealing with weaknesses of individuals and not with things which are, if Pat is right, a vital part of the faith once for all delivered to the saints. *Third,* these things were not to be bound on others (Rom. 14), but if Pat has the gifts they are to be used to preach and confirm the gospel and to build up the church. *Fourth,* on the other hand, if we are right, Pat has embarked on a course which will end in the undermining of the church and the acceptance of false doctrines. So, again, Romans 14 does not apply to these matters.

USING PAT'S NAME

Since Pat did not want his name used in connection with the book, why did the author use it? *First,* when the author told Pat on the phone early in May that he planned to call the book *Pat Boone and the Gift of Tongues,* the only objection which he raised was that limiting it to the gift of tongues was too narrow. Pat later informed the author that he thought the author was joking. Here again Pat's guidance system failed to help him. *Second,* Pat is the most prominent one among us to go into the tongues movement. Since he will be defending his position, in one way or another, publicly and privately, it is important that brethren know there is a book available which deals with some of the arguments which he makes. *Third,* if the author does not mention Pat's name, others will do so. Of course, if it was wrong to do so, their mentioning it would not make it right for the author to do so.

Fourth, even if his name was not mentioned in this book, most brethren would know that at least some of Pat's arguments and experiences were being examined. If the author did not label the arguments and experiences which involve Pat, they might attribute to him arguments and experiences mentioned in this book which do not pertain to him. *Fifth,* the author has no objection to his name being used in a book in which his positions are fairly presented; especially, if the individual who writes the book has been as fair, open, and honest with the author as he has been with Pat. *Sixth,* the author asked Pat to put himself in the author's position. If he believed someone was involved in as serious errors as the author believes Pat is involved in, and if he believed that they would have an influence in leading others into these errors, would Pat not believe it was his duty to try to instruct and warn others? *Seventh,* the author is not quoting Pat because he asked not to be quoted. However, he told Pat that he never considered arguments to be confidential. Furthermore, Pat has been given the opportunity to see what the author planned to publish. *Eighth,* some may think the author's experience in debating and teaching gives him an advantage over Pat. The author has made no claims concerning any credentials, but puts forth material to be evaluated by the reader. However, it should be kept in mind that the author is not inspired at any time, that he does not have the miraculous guidance of the Spirit, but that Pat claims some of the gifts and direct guidance from the Spirit in at least some things. The sword of the Spirit in the author's uninspired hands would never be a match for the Spirit speaking through an inspired man. The advantages would all be on the side of the inspired man. *Ninth,* the author does not see how that the public use of Pat's name can hurt him professionally. Those who are not concerned about his religion will still not be concerned. Those who like him as an entertainer will still like him. Brethren who object to his new positions will object whether the author mentions Pat's name or not. *Tenth,* in effect what Pat is saying is that he should have the right to teach these doctrines both publicly and privately, but that the author should not publicly examine his arguments and experiences which he thinks confirm his new positions. When Pat sets forth his arguments and experiences in an effort to convert someone, as he did in trying to convert the author, he should not be surprised at a public examination of these things. When Pat takes controversial positions he is no more exempt from controversy than anyone else. *Eleventh,* are there any of his arguments and experiences, which he has related to the author, of which he is doubtful, or ashamed, or which he does not want others to know? *Twelfth,* the author told Pat in February that he planned to do his duty, God helping him, if it bathed his heart in tears. The author is pained to cause Pat pain. He told Pat that he plans to continue to love Pat regardless of the outcome, and that the use of Pat's name against his wishes could well be an occasion on which Pat's love for the author is tested. Perhaps this will not be as painful an experience for Pat as he anticipated it would be. It may be that one day he will express his appreciation to the author for having disregarded his wishes in these matters.

WHEN DID PAT GET THE GIFT OF TONGUES?

In a letter on March 12, 1970 he indicated that it had been within the last two years. It was before February, 1969, since at that time Pat, Shirley, and George Otis were in the process of converting Joyce Dennis *(Testimony,* No. 31, Second Quarter, 1970, pp. 9-10). This means he had kept his change of convictions hidden from the brethren for a long period of time.

According to a speech Shirley made in New Jersey in the autumn of 1969, she got the baptism a couple of months before her Father died. This would put it in the summer of 1968. At the same gathering Pat said that he had been handing out *The Cross and the Switchblade* for four years. He guaranteed the audience that their lives would never be the same after they read it. Pat said that he had not believed these things could happen. This was what he had been taught in the church of Christ. When he first read it, half way through the book he became convinced that these things had to be true. He said during the last half of the book he was crying and trembling. By the time he had finished it, he wanted to make a movie of it. He called Wilkerson right away. This shows that Pat came to believe in modern miracles, and that he thought Wilkerson worked miracles, around 1965. It was not until some time later that Pat thought he got the "baptism" and tongues. Why didn't Pat give some of us an opportunity to help him before he became so deeply involved in Pentecostalism?

WISDOM—PAT HAVE GIFT OF?

Pat believes he has some gifts, and that the others are available if we have enough faith. He thinks he has tongues for private devotions. Since it is important to teach others, and not just to have private devotions, surely he should be able to get the gift of wisdom which is important in teaching others and making countless decisions in life. The conversation on February 18, out of which came the extensive correspondence, was an important one for such reasons as: (a) Pat thought that he would be used of God to convert the author. (b) The author was writing a book on the subject and what was said could have an influence on the book. (c) Several people had asked the author to let them know what he learned about their beliefs. Although Pat knew nothing of these requests, and the author did not think to mention it, the Holy Spirit knew and, if He had been guiding Pat and Shirley, would have taken this into consideration.

They considered it of sufficient importance that they evidently talked about it and prayed about it in their family circle. Certainly wisdom was needed, especially in light of their view that the strategy of the Spirit was to keep their beliefs on gifts from the brotherhood as a whole until Pat's book appeared. Do they now think that the gift of wisdom, or the supernatural guidance of the Spirit, was manifested in their conversation with me? They do not.

First, the author made the appointment with Pat, which Pat went to considerable efforts to keep, before he went to California. He thought and prayed about how to best approach Pat. He told the Lord he did not know how best to raise the subject, he left it with the Lord, and, as it turned out, Pat raised the question as to what the author thought the "perfect" in I Cor. 13:8 meant. The author's answer took but a few seconds. He stated, but did not argue, his position. Pat immediately went into a discussion of the gifts and experiences which he and Shirley, who had joined us, thought they had.

Second, Pat, in what he later called his naive human enthusiasm, told the author his experiences; the validity of which he thought I would be convinced, and which would lead to my rejoicing that the gifts are available today. As things stand at this writing, they feel their efforts did not accomplish anything worthwhile. The author asked some questions as the hours went by, he did not try to argue with them, but listened in an effort to understand them and to try to get the full impact of their message. The author sensed that Pat thought he was going to convert him, and the more the author listened the more pessimistic he became of changing Pat any time soon. The conversation lasted until a little after 2 a.m. The author thought that his long-listening might have indicated to Pat that he was being convinced, so just before he left he stated that love listened as well as talked, that the author was trying to understand them, that he would study the matter honestly, but he did not want Pat to get the false impression that he was being convinced. The author then left deeply touched emotionally, and also sad.

Since Pat had prayed about the matter, and did need wisdom in this matter, if he was not guided by the Spirit to proceed as he did, why didn't the Spirit tell him not to do it? He surely did not speak or act like one who thought he was going contrary to what the Spirit wanted him to do.

Third, the author later learned that Shirley did not share Pat's enthusiasm about sharing these things with him, and therefore prayed earnestly before she did so. She must have thought that it was the will of the Spirit that she do so, for she gave no indication at all that she was doing what the Spirit did not want her to do. If they were guided by the Spirit, they must have done the right thing. Obviously the Spirit foresaw the consequences of the conversation, and the correspondence, up to now and beyond. If they were not guided by the Spirit why, with all their gifts, were they not guided to refrain from sharing their experiences? Would not this indicate they need to re-examine this question of direct guidance?

Fourth, Pat said that another member of the family received the prophetic instruction, which he called God's wisdom, to share only what was in the Bible since the author would not accept personal experiences which seemed to conflict with his understanding of God's word. What about this? That all things must be measured by God's word is a basic conviction of the church, and is often taught. In a letter on June 18, 1969, the author told Pat and Shirley that we must walk by faith in what the Spirit has revealed, and not by our feelings. He enclosed two chapters from *The Finality of The Faith*, and one of these chapters emphasized that we can know nothing about the work and mind of the Spirit except as revealed in the Bible. The same truth is emphasized in *The Holy Spirit and the Christian*, 110-116-137-139, and *Miracles or Mirages*, 223. The author does not know whether the other member of the family, through whom the prophetic instruction, as Pat viewed it, came had read any of these or whether her parents had discussed it in her presence. However, it is quite obvious that it would be exceedingly difficult to be in the services of the church, and in a Christian home, from one's very first recollections and not learn that all things must be tested by the Bible. The authority of the word of God is stressed in the church, and rightly so.

Furthermore, it was impossible for them to follow the so-called prophetic guidance to share with the author only God's word and not also personal experiences. The circumstances being what they were it was impossible for the conversation to deal with just what the Bible teaching on miracles is without also dealing with whether they are for us today, and whether the Boones thought they had some of the gifts. If they had talked just about the Bible, and not about whether the gifts are for us today and whether they think they have them, the author would have asked them point blank whether they thought they had any of the gifts. They would have answered him honestly and the author would have learned of their beliefs. If they had refused to answer, or if they had dodged, the author would have told them that he drew the conclusion that they thought they had at least some of the gifts, or that they believed the gifts were for us today. Under the circumstances silence would have been consent. However, just as the author expected, they made no effort to hide their beliefs.

Fifth, the author's beliefs are such that even in his own home he would not ask his wife to lead in prayer in the presence of men. Whether he is right or wrong about this is not here discussed. Since he holds this position, the author does not believe the gift of wisdom led Shirley not just to suggest that we pray, at the beginning of our conversation, but also to lead the prayer. The prayer was sincere and the author was deeply touched by her fervor. The "Spirit" some Pentecostals have leads some women to become public preachers in contradiction to Paul's instructions (I Cor. 14:33-36, 37).

Sixth, Pat and Shirley did not make clear to the author, when he talked with them in California, that they wanted the conversation to be kept confidential. Therefore, he mentioned it to a very few people whom he thought ought to know, including those who had asked him to let them know what he found out. He told Pat he would not make a public statement until we had corresponded. But he would later make a public statement even if Pat did not do so. Since Pat said he told people who asked him what his beliefs were, the author thought it was all right to mention it to a few who had an interest in the matter. When Pat and Shirley called the author on February 28, they were disturbed because he had mentioned it to some, and the author said he would refer to them for the answer any who asked him until we had corresponded further. Their spirit was excellent in this conversation, as it has been in other conversations.

Seventh, toward the beginning of the correspondence on the gifts, the author told his wife that he wondered if Pat wouldn't finally conclude that it was not wise to have discussed the matter at all with the author. At the time this is being written, they have concluded that it was not wise. However, all the way through the author has made it clear that he was writing a book, and dealing with their arguments. In fact, he told them that even if they converted him, he would still bring out a book on the subject, the Lord willing.

CHAPTER XVIII

LANGUAGES BY INSPIRATION

Although Sherrill came to believe in tongues, he was puzzled by the following. *First,* the interpretations were stereotyped exhortations to stand fast, etc. Why were these more adequate when expressed in a tongue instead of in English? *Second,* interpreters whom he heard used King James English exclusively. Why were the socalled heavenly languages so much more like the King James? The author believes this indicates they simply wove together fragments of scripture as they came to mind. *Third,* ". . . there was often no correlation between the length of the message in tongues, and the length of the interpretation." (87) Although some languages are more compact than others, no known language packs into such few expressions so many statements in another language. One speaker used two phrases in the author's presence, and the interpreter used many sentences.

HAVE LINGUISTS ANALYZED TONGUES?

First, Sherrill taped around forty examples of tongues. The linguists could not identify any of them. One tongues speaker said it was a mistake to try to isolate a language in the tongues, and that when he met the Spirit the problem would not bother him any more (102-103). *Second,* Eugene Nida and others have analyzed scores of tongues without finding a human language (*Christianity Today,* Nov. 24, 1967, p. 40). *Third,* would Christ have submitted to such close examination? (a) Those who claim to work miracles are inviting investigation. (b) Christ does not want us blindly to accept truth (I Thess. 5:21). (c) He invited Thomas to investigate closely (John 20:24-29). (d) Luke traced things accurately (Lk. 1:3). (e) How can we obey I John 4:1-2 and Rev. 2:2 without close investigation? Pentecostals admit that some falsely claim to work miracles, so they must grant that it is right to investigate closely. (f) Unbelievers in Christ were commended for examining what the inspired Paul preached

(Acts 17:11). How much more so should we examine un-inspired men and those who claim to work miracles today.

ACTUAL CASES?

In all of his wide reading and contacts, Sherrill thought he found around five individuals who had spoken in human languages. One person thought his name, another thought his Father's name was called. What about these? *First,* if the gift of tongues operates today, why is it extremely rare that anyone even claims a human language was spoken? All understood on Pentecost (Acts 2:4; 6, 8, 11). All the tapes which have been analyzed, and all meetings which linguists have attended, have not produced a case of a known language. *Second,* why are so many unscriptural things done in tongues meetings: such as several praying in tongues at the same time, supposedly under the impulse of the Spirit? (Sherrill, 90-91). Long ago, the Spirit prohibited this (I Cor. 14:26-33). *Third,* tongues speakers teach some false doctrine. *Fourth,* records, radio, TV, motion pictures, newscasts, travel, and the presence of foreign languages in our own country make it extremely difficult for anyone to keep from hearing at least some snatches of foreign languages. These make an impression. Although we cannot consciously recall these, when delirious or in a highly emotional state some people have repeated what they heard years before. Out of the millions of cases of speaking in tongues in the United States in the last two hundred years, the wonder is not that this may have happened a few times, but that it has not happened more often. *Fifth,* we sometimes mis-hear. Out of the millions of cases of tongues, it would be amazing if someone did not think he heard a language, or a name, but it was his own subjective interpretation or mis-hearing of sounds. *Sixth,* why do missionaries have to learn languages? Orson Pratt, a Mormon, said the gift was needed to preach the gospel to foreign people (*Works,* 99-100), but their missionaries had to learn the languages (*Millennial Star,* 1854, Vol. 16, pp. 188, 190-191, 223, 236, 239, 254, 257, 365).

Sherrill told of a missionary who was captured by an unfriendly tribe in Africa. On trial for his life (he assumed), he was given an opportunity to speak after the witch doctor spoke. He prayed, shook violently, felt the Spirit was near, remembered Jesus' statement about taking no thought as to what one was to say, became bold, and spoke words he did not understand, and he was released. *First,* he did not know what he said. The natives did not tell him he spoke their language. How, then, did he know that he spoke their language? *Second,* a superstitious people hearing a white man—and likely this was the first one they had seen—speaking strange sounds, could be impressed even if they understood none of the sounds. Witch doctors have spoken in tongues, and they may have decided this man was a witch doctor. *Third,* the man's wife was sick and he was trying to get medicine for her. Why didn't he or some of his fellow workers have the gift of healing? *Fourth,* if he was inspired by the Spirit, why wasn't he inspired at some other time to forsake denominationalism?

Harald Bredesen claimed that in one case one person said he spoke in Polish, and in another case an individual said he spoke in old Arabic (Sherrill, 19-20). *First,* the author knows of no way to check with these two individuals. *Second,* linguists have checked Bredesen's tongues without recognizing a human language *(Christianity Today,* Sept. 13, 1963). Eugene A. Nida, a linguist with the American Bible Society, analyzed some tapes of Bredesen's tongues and concluded that they were not languages but were ecstatic speech without the essential characteristics of human languages (Letter to the author, May 13, 1970). Tongues were a sign to convince unbelievers (Mk. 16:17, 20; I Cor. 14:22). Why, where he has been checked, did he fail to speak a language known by the listeners? The two individuals Bredesen mentioned must have either mis-heard or Bredesen recalled some foreign words which were stored in his unconscious. *Third,* why hasn't the Spirit—if Pat is right in saying Bredesen has been baptized in the Spirit and is being led and used by God in mighty ways *(Testimony,* No. 30, p. 8)—led him out of denominationalism? He once preached for the First Reformed Church in Mt. Vernon, New York, and now is a minister for a Lutheran Church *(Testimony,* No. 31, p. 1).

Pat thought he heard Shirley use a Latin phrase in a prayer in his presence, and two other phrases were used in the presence of someone else. These were "praise God," "we love you, God," and "I love you, Lord." As much as anything else, this led Pat to believe tongues are for us today. *First,* Pat does not believe that Shirley's prayer language is composed principally of Latin or any other earthly language. *Second,* a mutual friend, to whom Pat related this same experience, said it did not sound like Latin to him. *Third,* tongues were a sign to unbelievers (Acts 2:4, 6, 8, 11; I Cor. 14:22). Why have only three phrases been detected in Shirley's frequent uses of tongues? Biblical tongues were not non-intelligible sounds with three intelligible phrases on two occasions. *Fourth,* tongues were not primarily for personal devotional services, but to convince unbelievers and edify believers (I Cor. 14:4-6, 22, 27-28). *Fifth,* likely we forget nothing beyond the possibility of recall under some conditions. At times scenes, which the author saw only once decades ago, have flashed across his consciousness. It is almost impossible today to escape hearing some foreign languages. The author has heard portions of Catholic services in Latin, and some songs in Latin. To an untrained ear some expressions in languages which are akin to Latin—especially French, Italian, and Spanish—may sound alike. Praise or glory to God is in the Mass. People in a highly emoitonal state may use words which have been recorded in the unconscious. *Sixth,* Shirley has spoken enough times in tongues that it is not surprising that some instances may occur where some of the sounds may sound like words in some languages. The day the author wrote this statement, but when he did not have it on his mind, he heard a bird sing twice—as clear as a bell—DDT, DDT. He did not think the bird was pinpointing one aspect of the pollution problem. Who has not heard "bob white" sung in the meadow? *Seventh,* one mis-hears at times. In some cases, when the statement was repeated, the author understood easily why he had mis-heard. The author believes the three brief Latin phrases were either picked up unconsciously by Shirley, or that in the numerous sounds she makes in speaking tongues, the three phrases showed up— one on one occasion and two on another—which sounded like Latin. *Eighth,* if she spoke a foreign language at length, her teaching would still have to be tested.

Dr. Donald Liedmann said he heard Demos Shakarian, President of the Full Gospel Businessmen's Fellowship International, pray the following in ancient Aramaic: "Dear Lord, I thank you for the years I have been privileged to serve you. Forgive me Lord, for the shortcomings that I have, and please let me serve you even if I am a little man." (*Voice*, Jan.-Feb., 1970, p. 12). The author is trying to get additional information on this case, but at this time he evaluates it as follows: *First*, this could not have been a devotional exercise of tongues which enabled one to more adequately express what was in his heart. The prayer is just as adequate in English as in Aramaic. It must be viewed, therefore, as a sign. If they have the Biblical gift of tongues, why are the claims, of a human language being employed, so very rare? *Second*, this message, which could have been stated without any gift, was hardly something for the edification of the church "by way of revelation, or of knowledge, or of prophesying, or of teaching" (I Cor. 14:5-6). *Third*, Dr. Liedmann said an interpreter was present, but he had been unable to locate him. The author does not know whether the interpreter gave an interpretation, or whether it harmonized with Liedmann's. If he did not give an interpretation he failed in his duty, or Shakarian should not have spoken in tongues. *Fourth*, Liedmann said that ancient Aramaic is spoken by a few people today, and he has heard it. However, as far as the author has been able to learn, no one today knows what ancient Aramaic sounded like. *Fifth*, Shakarian said he did not know Aramaic or any language similar to it. Liedmann thinks that ancient Aramaic sounded somewhat like Hebrew. The author is trying to find out whether Shakarian may have heard a prayer in Hebrew—the prayer was one an unconverted Jew could have prayed, for it did not specifically mention Christ—and in a highly emotional state it came back into his consciousness. Shakarian's rendition may have sounded like the Aramaic Liedmann knows. *Sixth*, Liedmann may have mis-heard. *Seventh*, if Shakarian has the gift of tongues, why are there not numerous occasions in which he speaks in a language? If he has the gift of Aramaic, others should be able to verify it. He has spoken in tongues at least from the time he was thirteen, when he spoke for four hours on one occasion (Morton T. Kelsey, *Tongue Speaking*, N. Y.: Doubleday & Co., Inc., 1964, p. 87). It would be amazing if in all these years someone did not think that he said something intelligible on at least one occasion. *Eighth,* if the gifts of tongues, revelation, and prophecy have been manifested in the Shakarian family since 1880, why is it that the Full Gospel Businessmen's Fellowship, which Demos Shakarian founded as a formal organization in 1953 (Kelsey, 86-88), does not care what church you belong to, and does not set forth the New Testament teaching on baptism? *Ninth,* Shakarian spoke at a meeting where Kathryn Kuhlman preached. Why didn't Shakarian, *if* he spoke by the Spirit, rebuke her in harmony with Paul's instructions in I Cor. 14:33-35? When the author asked Dr. Liedmann how he harmonized her preaching with I Cor. 14:33-35, he replied that the author's question was a carnal one. *If* the author understands what he meant (and he has written to try to find out), he meant that these were spiritual matters and in Christ there is neither male nor female. However, we must acknowledge that what Paul wrote was the commandment of God (I Cor. 14:37). The same Paul who penned Gal. 3:26-29 also wrote I Cor. 14:33-35.

At this stage of the investigation of this case—and Dr. Liedmann has not yet replied to the author's additional inquiries as he may be out of the country—the author is not certain of the correct explanation. However, he is confident that it is not the work of the Spirit. If it were, Shakarian would know that tongues were always languages, every case would actually be a language known to some men instead of unintelligible sounds, and they would not teach doctrines of men. The author is convinced there is a natural explanation. He would exhaust all possible natural explanations before he would cnclude that it was a direct work of the devil. Nothing the author has heard or read has been sufficient to accredit modern tongues as the work of the Spirit.

CHAPTER XIX

THE GIFTS: QUESTIONS AND ANSWERS

ALL THE GIFTS

Pat thinks that at least some members of each congregation should have one or all of the gifts, but that our lack of faith hampers God's will in this matter. *First,* if Pat himself does not have all of the gifts is it because of his lack of faith? *Second,* apostles of Christ were not found in all congregations. *Third,* if there are modern prophets they should teach by inspiration and not just from a study of the Bible (I Cor. 14:3-4, 29-31). *Fourth,* all did not have all the gifts (12:8-10, 29-30).

Oral Roberts believes that when "you receive the baptism with the Holy Spirit, four things will happen in your life: (1) You will speak in tongues; you will be given a new level of communication with God. You will be able to speak to God not only in your own language, but in the languages created by the Holy Spirit inside you; (2) you will have continuous use of this new level of speaking to God in tongues for the rest of your life, and through it you may edify yourself daily; (3) you will receive power to witness of Jesus Christ; and (4) you will have a release into the charisma, or the nine gifts of the Holy Spirit." *(Commentary,* 745).

"The gifts are given in times of crisis . . . Rather than say that we have one gift or another gift, we need to recognize that we have the Giver of gifts, the Holy Spirit, dwelling within us. Then, whenever we come against a need, we can expect the Holy Spirit to operate a gift through us to meet that particular need or crisis. I believe the nine gifts of the Spirit are included in and are part of the river of living water which Jesus promised would flow through us after we have received the Holy Spirit. These gifts could be termed 'tools for crisis time'." (746)   (a) If the gift of tongues is permanent, it should be used daily for its fourfold purpose. Or at least, whenever there is need. Roberts should have many cases where he has spoken in a human language by inspiration. (b) Paul said both the gifts and the Spirit were given to them (I Cor. 12:4-11). (c) Paul clearly taught that not everyone had all the gifts (I Cor. 12:4-11, 29-30). Roberts is taught by a different "spirit" in these matters than was Paul. Paul spoke of persons having different gifts, and not of one having the different gifts on different occasions or crises. (d) If these are tools for crisis times, then every crisis should find one or more of these gifts functioning. Is it not strange that Roberts does not face more crisis wherein there is a need for the gift of languages?

Christians in the first century, who had miraculous gifts, used these gifts to reveal and confirm the word of God (Mk. 16:17-18, 20; Heb. 2:3-4). The Spirit would not work through Oral Roberts today and confirm doctrines which are contrary to what the Spirit has already revealed in the Bible. We must continue steadfastly in the apostles' doctrine (Acts 2:42), and not in Oral Roberts' doctrine.

APOSTLES OF CHRIST?

Pat thinks there are modern apostles like Peter, James, and John, and as they are willing to exercise their faith they have the same powerful gifts from God. When asked to name some apostles of Christ, he mentioned Batsell Baxter, George Bailey and Otis Gatewood as men given special assignments and abilities. From the standpoint of his human understanding, he also listed David Wilkerson and Billy Graham. *First,* if they are apostles of Christ, why do these men disagree on some very important doctrinal points? *Second,* do they do the mighty works of Paul, teach by inspiration, write scripture, and speak with authority? (I Cor. 14:37). Did they see the Lord, as did Paul? Do all the modern apostles teach the same doctrine Paul taught? *Third,* Pat pointed out that the word "apostle" is applied in the Bible to more than the special apostles of Christ. This is true, since the word meant a messenger, or one sent (II Cor. 8:23; Phil. 2:25; Heb. 3:1). Thus Paul and Barnabas were messengers of the Spirit and of the congregation in Antioch (Acts 13:1-3; 14:4, 14, 26-27). Paul, however, was also an apostle of Jesus Christ, but Barnabas was not (Gal. 1:1). See chapter one for the brief discussion on the apostles of Christ. *Fourth,* where are modern apostles like Peter, James, and John? *Fifth,* if Pat has several gifts,

271

and if several are operating in his family, he should know the qualifications of the apostles of Christ. Knowing these he would not think there are such apostles on earth today. One does not have to be inspired in order to learn these things from the Bible. *Sixth,* if Pat will ask any of these men, or men such as Harald Bredesen, whether they are apostles of Christ—like Peter, James, John, or Paul—the author is confident they will answer in the negative.

CESSATION?

Why are there specific scriptures concerning the gifts, but none concerning their cessation? First, there are many scriptures concerning the gift of apostleship (Eph. 4:8, 11; I Cor. 12:28), but none which say in so many words that the apostleship would end. Where are the men today with the qualifications, power, authority, and functions of the first century apostles of Christ? All we have ever tested have been false apostles, for it takes more than the claim to make an apostle (Rev. 2:2). We know this apostleship has ceased for no one today can qualify, various passages show that in the nature of the case the gift was temporary, and our apostles are in the foundation, not the walls, of the church. We no more need new apostles each generation than we need a new cornerstone, Christ, on earth each generation (Eph. 2:20-23).

Second, there is no passage which says in so many words that no more inspired scriptures would be written and added to the Bible. No scripture says the gifts would continue, but without producing scriptures as they did in the first century. Pat, where are the modern scriptures? Will you write some with your gifts? Were any of your letters to the author inspired? Pat said that in recent months he had seen or experienced knowledge, wisdom, tongues, *and* interpretation, prophecy and healing. If this is the case, what is said or written in such instances is as inspired as the Bible. Where are the modern Marks, Lukes, Johns, Peters, and Pauls? Shall we bind *The Cross and the Switchblade* in with Acts as a 20th century edition of Acts of Apostles? If not, why do the gifts fail to produce today as they did in the first century? What passage says the gifts will continue until the second coming but that their purposes will change and, among other things, no inspired scripture would come through these modern gifts?

Third, Paul did say tongues would cease (I Cor. 13:8-10). An entire chapter is devoted to this passage.

Fourth, the passages which show the purposes of the gifts indicate that when these purposes were fulfilled the gifts would cease.

Fifth, no scripture says that: "No more men or women will be created as were Adam and Eve." However, if one is seeking a wife it will be best not to wait until one is created from material taken from his side. Man and woman were created by miracles but the race is perpetuated by the natural law of procreation. Miracles created the church, and revealed and confirmed the word (Eph. 1:19-23; Heb. 2:3-4). The Word is perpetuated through the spiritual seed line, and not through being re-delivered and re-confirmed each generation. The Word when preached and obeyed produces today what it produced in the first century. The miracles were not an end within themselves but were designed to reveal and confirm the Word. Having done this, their basic purpose was fulfilled, and they ceased.

COMMANDED?

Is Pat right in saying that Paul's command to desire spiritual gifts is as specific as any other command that he makes (I Cor. 12:31 and 14:1)? This has been commented on in the section on whether desire and prayer bring the gifts. From Pat's standpoint, how can he explain that all who desire the gifts do not get all the gifts, including the apostleship? Since the gift of tongues plus interpretation was equal to the gift of prophecy, why cannot all tongue speakers interpret? (14:4-6). This question is all the more impressive when we recall that Paul said that the prophet is greater than the tongues speaker, and Paul had rather that they prophesied. (14:5.) The very verses Pat mentioned said: "But desire earnestly *the greater gifts*." (12:31.) "Follow after love; yet desire earnestly spiritual gifts, *but rather that ye may prophesy*." (14:1.)

CONFIRMATION?

Do we have sufficient Scriptures, but an insufficient confirmation of these Scriptures if we do not have gifts today? Pat said we have sufficient scriptures, but the miraculous confirmation is needed today as in the first century. *First,* the gifts were not given to confirm a written message given centuries before, but to confirm the message *then* being delivered (Heb. 2:3-4). What new message is being confirmed today? *Second,* the prophets received revelations, and these revelations taught the church the will of God, (I Cor. 14:4-5, 30). If men are receiving revelations today these revelations are words from God when *spoken* and when *written.* They would be as much a part of the divine Word as the revelations made in the first century. *Third,* to dispute or to deny the word given through modern revelations would be as much of a denial of God's word as the denial of the Bible. *Fourth,* if there are modern apostles and prophets, they could say of their word, whether written or spoken, that: "If any man thinketh himself to be a prophet or spiritual, let him take knowledge of the things which I write unto you that they are the commandment of the Lord." (I Cor. 14:37.)

COUNTERFEITS

Because the gifts are counterfeited today, does it mean there are no genuine gifts? *First,* counterfeits by themselves do not prove there are no genuine gifts. On the other hand, because some falsely claim the gifts does not mean there are others today who have the gifts. *Second,* if some have them they should: (a) so outdo the others that it will be clear who is on God's side, (b) and they should harmonize with the New Testament in their teaching. *Third,* since it is acknowledged that there are counterfeits, it means that we cannot accept something just because it is claimed by someone. We must prove all things and hold fast to the good and the truth (I Thess. 5:21). *Fourth,* the false apostles of today do not prove there are genuine apostles also today.

DRAW UP A CREED?

If we are going to draw lines, Pat thought it would be better to have a written creed drawn up, instead of an unwritten one, so one could know on what grounds he will be acceptable to the church in different places. *First,* no one has authority to speak authoritatively for the church either through an unwritten or a written creed. *Second,* human creeds have not brought unity. Consider the controversy in the Roman Catholic Church today. *Third,* some complain about unwritten creeds because they want to accept something without getting any opposition from others. Their unwritten creed says that others ought to accept them regardless of these beliefs. *Fourth,* we believe in Christ and, therefore, we accept His word as the authoritative statement of the faith. We are to contend for the faith. We must use the word of God not only for exhortation and consolation, but also for teaching, reproof, correction, and for instruction in righteousness (II Tim. 3:16; 4:2-4), and to find the lines for fellowship. *Fifth,* mistakes will be made. Some will be too broad in their fellowship and some too narrow. If one is disfellowshipped by some brethren, it does not necessarily mean that Christ has disfellowshipped him (III John 9:12). The fact that mistakes will be made at times does not release us from the obligation of studying and, when we are convinced it is necessary, of withdrawing fellowship while loving the one from whom we have had to withdraw. The final judgment belongs to God, but we have the responsibility for making decisions on the basis of love, study, discussion, and prayer.

EDIFICATION NEEDED, SO GIFTS NEEDED?

First, the truth revealed and confirmed through the gifts edified the church. We have the truth in all of its parts, the faith once for all delivered to the saints (I Cor. 14:3, 4, 6; John 16:12-14; Jude 3). *Second,* if we have the gifts they must reveal and confirm new revelations as well as re-affirm New Testament revelations. *Third,* the gifts, if available, are not for private edification only, but for the church; yet some claim they are mostly for private edification.

ARE WE DEPENDING ON HUMAN EFFORT?

Pat said that before he was baptized in the Spirit, "my Christian life was too much effort . . . " He spoke of others, now "Spirit-filled," who "had known the emptiness of dedicated, but human, Christian service . . . " This baptism of the Spirit was "a whole new dimension, and I wanted it! I wanted everything that God had for me! I was tired of trying to 'do it myself' " *(Testimony, No. 30, 7, 8)*.

First, we are not depending on human effort as the source of our salvation; but it is not "doing it ourselves," and "human, Christian service," when we human beings act in surrender to and obedience to God. God opened the door to salvation to the people on Pentecost, but they had to be willing to listen, to learn, to believe, to be exhorted, and to obey (Acts 2:14, 22, 37, 38, 40, 41). When Peter said: "Repent ye," they did not say: Peter you are calling for human effort and we do not want to do it ourselves. When he said: *"Save yourselves* from this crooked generation" (2:40), they did not say: We want God to do it, we are tired of trying to do it ourselves. But God works through us and our efforts (Acts 14:17, 21, 25, 27).

Second, Paul said that *"we walk by faith,* not by sight." (II Cor. 5:7.) God does not *believe* for us, nor does He *walk* for us. He does not *walk us* as puppets on strings. He does not take over our bodies and without effort on our part use them as instruments of righteousness (Rom. 6:12-13, 19). He does not take the steps for us. He has given us the opportunity to believe, reasons for faith, motivation to belief, but we must hear and believe. He has told us to walk, He has given the narrow way in which to walk, and He has promised to walk *with* us. However, God has not negated human effort. *We* must walk by faith. We must take care lest we fall (I Cor. 10:12). We must walk "in the steps of that faith of our father Abraham." (Rom. 4:12). We must walk in newness of life, and not after the flesh (Rom. 6:4; 8:1). We must walk according to the rule that what avails is a new creature; which involves faith working through love (Gal. 6:16; 5:6). God created Adam, but he had to do the work God ordained for him after he was created. Although we had to do something in becoming a Christian, God through the gospel, and our response to it, created us in Christ Jesus as new creatures. He does not do our works for us, but "we are his workmanship, created in Christ Jesus for good works, which God afore prepared that *we should walk in them."* (Eph. 2:10.) He does not walk worthily of the calling for us, we have to do our own walking (Eph. 4:1). "Look therefore carefully how ye walk, not as unwise,

but as wise; redeeming the time, because the days are evil."
(Eph. 5:15.) Perhaps you get tired of having to walk carefully? Therefore, be baptized in the Spirit and let God do the
looking out for you as well as the walking? God helps us, but
if we do not use *our* ears to hear, *our* eyes to see, and *our*
hearts to understand, He is not going to take over and do
these things for us. We must walk in the light (I John 1:7).

Third, it may be asked: But is it not God doing the work?
If God does all the work, and human effort is not involved,
anyone who is not converted, or any converted one who does
not work, is not to be blamed for it; since the work is all done
by God, any failure is a failure on the part of God. A premise
which leads to such a conclusion is false. But, didn't Paul say
that it was God who did the working? Paul told the Philippians: "So then, my beloved, even as ye have always obeyed,
not as in my presence only, but now much more in my absence,
work out your own salvation with fear and trembling; for it
is God who worketh in you both to will and to work, for his
good pleasure. Do all things without murmurings and ques-
tionings . . . that I did not run in vain neither labor in vain."
(Phil. 2:12-16.) The Philippians obeyed. God did not obey,
nor did He obey for them. " . . . *ye* have always obeyed."
The Philippians were to work out their own salvation. The
Philippians were told to *"do* all things without murmurings . . . " God was not told to do all things without murmurings. Paul had labored in order to save the Philippians, and he
wanted them to continue to obey so that *his labor* would not
be in vain. On the other hand, Paul was working for God, and
with God, so that he could speak of "all things that God had
done with" him. God had opened the door of faith to the Gentiles, but Paul had to preach (Acts 14:27). The Philippians
had to work out their own salvation, with fear and trembling.
However, we are weak. Perhaps we cannot make it. We can
because God works with us and through us. This reminds us
that we are not working alone. We are fellow-workers with
God; but it was God who created man with the capacity for
faith and obedience, it was God who provided the gospel of
salvation, it was God who took the initiative to save man, and
it was God who furnished us with reasons and motivations for
working. He works through us, but not apart from our will,

our consent, and our efforts. If God does it all, then all that we do is done by God without any blame or credit—for good or evil—due us. God bestowed grace on Paul. Without it Paul could have accomplished nothing. But God's grace did not work in Paul without Paul's consent and efforts. We must always give credit to God, but we must not think that God will work in us apart from our work. "But by the grace of God I am what I am," Paul said, "and his grace which was bestowed upon me was not found vain; but I labored more abundantly than they all; yet not I, but the grace of God which was with me. Whether then it be I or they, so *we* preach, and so *ye* believed." (I Cor. 15:10-11.)

As Bloomfield remarked in his commentary: "In short, to sum up the doctrine contained in this most important passage, it is said of *God,* that of his good pleasure He worketh in us both to will and to do; and it is said of *man,* that he is to work out his salvation, i. e. to do *his part,* whatever that be, in effecting it. Nothing can be more marked than the distinction which is here made between the agency of God, and the agency of man. Nothing is more certain on the one hand, than that, without the assistance of God, man cannot be saved at all; nothing can be more certain, on the other hand, than that by his own voluntary cooperation, with such aid from above, man *ultimately is saved* . . . In short, to·use the words of Mr. Scott . . . 'He worketh in us effectually, that we may effectually work'."

It is true that sometimes we fail to give God the credit as we ought, it is true that sometimes we may forget that though we be little men we have the Mighty Fellow-Worker, but it is still true that as Christians we must render *dedicated human effort* to God. It is not always easy, and the Lord knew it would not be. Therefore, we are exhorted: "Wherefore, my beloved brethren, be ye stedfast, unmovable, always abounding in the work of the Lord, forasmuch as ye know that *your labor* is not vain in the Lord." (I Cor. 15:58.) There are seasons when the author feels like working and there are seasons when he does not feel like working. However, whether he feels like it or not the author tries to make all seasons working seasons for the Lord.

INSPIRATION AND ERROR

Did inspiration mean that the apostles lived perfect lives?
No, but it did mean their teaching is true.

Did inspiration keep the apostles from teaching false doctrine? Yes, for Jesus promised that the Spirit would guide them into the truth in all of its parts (John 16:12-14). Therefore, we know that the Spirit never guided them into any error. If some of what they wrote in the Bible is not true, how can we tell what is true and what is false? If part of the Bible contains their opinions, when they thought they were teaching God's word, how can the Bible be the standard today against which to check all teaching? Pat agreed that all things must be checked against God's word which never lies.

Does I Cor. 7:25, 40 indicate that Paul was not always sure when he was speaking by inspiration? Pat wrote that although Paul, Peter, and others had the gifts in an unlimited measure, they were capable of mistakes and Paul did not always seem sure whether he was speaking by inspiration (I Cor. 7). It was not until later, Pat said, that it was clearly known that God was speaking through Paul. Pat might ask why, on his own logic, some in the first century had gifts in an unlimited measure, but very few today even claim gifts to this extent.

Concerning Paul and inspiration we observe: *First,* if this passage does indicate that Paul was not always sure when he was speaking by inspiration, this is the only case where he was not sure. *Second,* Paul let the reader know that such was the case. Will Pat let us know when he and Wilkerson, or others, are speaking by inspiration, and when they are not? *Third,* Pat agreed that these passages do not mean that Paul was not inspired in this case. *Fourth,* Christ did not teach everything in His personal ministry; however, He promised that the Spirit would guide them into the complete truth (John 16:12-14). Paul was taught by Christ and the Spirit (Gal. 1:11-12; I Cor. 1:23, 15:3). Paul showed that Christ had legislated on certain matters concerning the marriage of two believers, but that Christ had not legislated on this same matter with reference to the marriage between a believer and an unbeliever (I Cor. 7:10, 12). Paul legislated on this, and it was binding for he was an apostle. Therefore: "And so ordain I in all the churches." (I Cor. 7:17.) *Fifth,* concerning virgins and their marriage under certain circumstances, Paul said "*I have no commandment* of the Lord." The Lord inspired him to give a judgment which, since it was not a commandment, was not required of them although it would be better for them to follow it. So Paul said, "I give my judgment, as one that hath obtained mercy of the Lord to be trustworthy. I think therefore that this is good by reason of the distress that is upon us . . . " (7:25-26.) This is a trustworthy judgment, for Paul had "obtained mercy of the Lord to be trustworthy." It was also a judgment inspired by the Spirit, for Paul said: "But she is happier if she abide as she is, after *my judgment:* and I think that I also have the Spirit of God." (7:40.) No one who accepts the inspiration of the Bible, can think that Paul thought wrongly and that he did not have the Spirit of God. Therefore, his judgment in this matter is trustworthy.

Does Paul's fear of being a castaway mean that he taught error? Weakness and fear do not mean that the teaching of either Paul or Peter was wrong. By becoming a castaway Paul did not mean that he taught false doctrine, but that he had to exercise self-control in all things, and keep his body under subjection, lest he fall from grace (I Cor. 9:25-27; 10:1-13).

Did the apostles sometimes teach false doctrine? Pat said that they did not exhibit perfection in life *and teaching.* Of Paul's confrontation with Peter, Pat said we had only Paul's side so we do not know what arguments Peter used to defend himself. God, however, worked out the conflict eventually. Pat also thought that Paul demonstrated in his writings that inspiration did not keep him from all kinds of human errors including the teaching of error and of things which could not be tested by Scripture.

This author has noticed many times that individuals, like Pat, who claim to be inspired at times, and to have the Spirit as did the apostles and prophets, will end up convicting Scripture of error. Can it be that since their "inspiration" guides them into error, they conclude that the Spirit must have done the same thing in the first century?

Our comments are as follows: *First,* Peter did not teach a false doctrine. Peter was the main one through whom the revelation was made which established—and established it with finality and without the need for such a demonstration again—that the Gentiles were to be saved by the gospel apart from the law of Moses (Acts 10). Peter knew this, as well as Paul. Peter agreed with Paul about this matter (Gal. 2:1-10). When Peter failed to live up to the truth which he, Peter knew, Paul rebuked him for it. The only sense in which Peter taught false doctrine was that his own *conduct* in this case was contrary to what he himself taught and what he knew to be right. The circumstances under which Peter refused to eat with the Gentiles was due to fear on Peter's part, and set the wrong example. It would give encouragement to those who wanted to build up something which Peter himself, as well as Paul, had previously destroyed (Compare Gal. 2:14-18).

Second, what did Paul say? "Let us keep this matter quiet so brethren will not choose sides, so division will not take place." There had already been a lot of dissimulation, and even Barnabus was carried away with their dissimulation (Gal. 2:12-13). Did Paul say: "I ought not to feed them this strong meat, especially in the presence of others"? No. This was having its impact on the church and their *conduct* was contrary to the truth of the gospel. Therefore, Paul publicly rebuked this public dissimulation. "But when I saw that *they walked not uprightly according to the truth of the gospel,* I said unto Cephas before them all . . . " (Gal. 2:14). We have only "Paul's side of the story," but this is enough because Paul's side of the story was God's side of the story. Pat said "we don't know what arguments Peter put up in his defense to Paul . . . " How do we know that he put up any defense? He had none except fear, for "he drew back and separated himself, fearing them that were of the circumcision." (Gal. 2:12.) Certainly Peter did not put up any arguments to justify his failure to walk upright according to the truth of the gospel. There is no reason to think that he ever taught that he was justified in what he did.

Pat should give us some examples where Paul amply demonstrates in his other writings that it is possible to have the Spirit of God even in a supernatural measure or in a gift, and still be subject to all kinds of human error, including teaching things that are not true or cannot be tested by Scripture. If this is true, we cannot know what to trust in the Bible, and Pat cannot know what he can trust in the things into which the Spirit supposedly guides him today. Surely it is not the Holy Spirit which has guided him into such a sea of uncertainty, and such a casting of doubt on the Bible.

A difference between Pat and the author is not that Pat is inspired some of the time, and the author isn't. A difference is that the author is not inspired at any time and he knows it, while Pat is not inspired any of the time, but he does not know it.

PERMANENT BECAUSE PROMINENT?

Pat asked, if the gifts were temporary, why was there so much space devoted to them in the New Testament? *First,* why is so much space devoted to non-repeated events such as the creation, the flood, Israel's captivities, her deliverance from Egypt, wilderness wanderings, experiences in the promised land, the personal ministry of Christ, the qualifications and works of apostles of Christ, the old law, the tabernacle, the priesthood, etc.? Although God speaks to us through His Son, the Old Testament has many values to the Christian (Heb. 1:1-2; 2:1-4; Rom. 1:2; 16:25-26; I Cor. 10:1-12).

Second, it is neither necessary nor possible for all stages, in the divine plan of redemption, to be perpetuated or repeated. Although they were necessary in the unfoldment and confirmation it does not mean they would be perpetuated after the faith was fully revealed and confirmed (Heb. 2:3-4; Jude 3). The incarnation, the personal ministry, the death, the resurrection, the ascension, and the coronation of Christ do not have to be repeated; nor does the miraculous confirmation.

Third, the principles Paul applied to eating meat sacrificed to idols, can be applied to other problems. Just so, the principles regulating miraculous gifts can regulate natural gifts. For instance, they should be used to build up others.

Fourth, Pat might ask himself: "Why the instructions to Peter to walk on the water, unless I also can so walk?" We are convinced, and we say this both lovingly and laughingly, that it will take more than white, buckskin shoes to walk on the water. Tongues speakers sometimes tell others: Start speaking in sounds other than English, and the Lord will take over and the Spirit will speak through you. Why not step out on one's own and then expect the Lord to take over so that one can continue to walk on the water? Tongues speakers improve with practice; would Pat improve with practice if he practiced on his own backyard swimming pool? If the individual begins to sink, will it be because of his little faith? Will the Lord reach out and keep him from sinking in spite of his little faith? (Matt. 14:22-23.) We accept the Scriptures but will our friends accept and act on their own logic? However, all that the author knows shows that *if* this record was designed to instruct us how to walk on the water, it is wasted space for we cannot do it regardless of the strength of our faith.

Is the record of any value to us just because we cannot walk on water? Yes. (a) It is another example of Christ's power over the elements. It is a part of the record which was written that we might believe (John 20:30-31). (b) It furnishes us with a good example to refute the reasoning of some of our friends concerning miraculous gifts. (c) It shows that some things can have a once-for-all character. (d) One can draw some analogies about walking on the troubled sea of life, and of being able to make it safely if we keep our eyes on Christ instead of just looking at the fearful difficulties.

Fifth, if we have the gifts, they must serve the same purposes. To turn their own logic against them we ask: Why were the purposes recorded if they were not to be the purposes for the gifts as long as the gifts lasted? Therefore, today the gifts must be for signs (Mk. 16:17, 20; I Cor. 14:22), to reveal and confirm old and new truths (John 16:12-14; 14:26), and to write inspired scriptures. The gifts were not given for their own sake, but to reveal and confirm the gospel. It has already been revealed and confirmed. The gifts ceased, having accomplished their purposes.

If we have the gifts, we have the same instructions concerning their use. Tongues speakers, taken as a whole, have often violated the instructions in I Cor. 14. If the same instructions do not apply today, why was the space taken to record them?

It was important that many regulations and instructions be given during Christ's personal ministry, which were not to be perpetually repeated. Just so, while the gospel was being revealed and confirmed, it was important that instructions be given concerning, and instances of, the gifts regardless of how long the gifts were to last.

In constructing a building a tremendous number of things, including scaffolding, are used which are not necessary once the building is constructed. The house called the faith, in the sense of the revelation and confirmation of the doctrine, has already been built.

SETTLE BY MAJORITY OPINION?

Pat indicated that these things were not to be settled by majority opinion in the church. *First,* the author has appealed not to majority opinion, but to the Bible. *Second,* it is not to be settled by minority opinion either. *Third,* Pat has the freedom and responsibility to be fully persuaded in his own mind, and we have the same freedom and responsibility. He has the freedom to advocate his beliefs, and we have the freedom to oppose them. He is free to accept these things, but he is not free to bind us to say that we must fellowship these things. Each stands or falls before God, and each is also responsible to God for how he deals with error. *Fourth,* we are not trying to do his thinking for him when we tell him why we cannot accept his positions. To give reason for the hope which is in us (I Pet. 3:15), and to try to instruct others more accurately in the way of the Lord (Acts 18:25-26), is not to try to do their thinking for them, but to try to get all of us to accept God's will.

REVELATIONS TODAY BECOME
A PART OF THE BIBLE?

Pat wrote that modern revelations are not new revelations but things which usually have to do with the private needs or the edification of individuals or groups, in much the way that Agabus and others spoke in the Book of Acts. *First,* since revelations needed to be made to congregations in many different places, their own prophets would receive revelations which were identical with revelations received in other congregations. However, even these revelations could be quoted by others as "thus saith the Lord." Can we do this with modern revelations? *Second,* if we have prophets like Agabus, why not apostles with the authority and power of Paul? *Third,* there are words of Agabus which constitute a part of the Bible

284

(Acts 11:28-30). Why not write a 20th Century Book of Acts, or at least a 29th chapter for Acts, composed of the utterances and works of modern prophets?

UNITED ON THE GOSPEL

Pat thinks that because we are united on the gospel we ought not to be divided over matters of deeper spirituality. *First,* the issue is whether these are matters of deeper spirituality or whether they involve serious errors. *Second,* the gospel is the death of Christ for our sins, His burial, and His resurrection (I Cor. 15:1-5). However, there are other matters which are rooted in and sustained by this gospel and are a part of the new covenant which is dedicated with Christ's blood. (a) After accepting the gospel, we are also to do what Jesus commanded (Matt. 28:20; Acts 2:42). (b) We are to contend for the faith (Jude 3). (c) We are to walk upright according to the truth of the gospel (Gal. 2:14). (d) We are to try the spirits (I John 4:1; Rev. 2:2). (e) The epistle to the Corinthians not only set forth the gospel, but also dealt with their numerous errors.

UNITY AND THE GIFTS

Are the miraculous gifts and miraculous guidance essential for unity? Although Pat said the full revelation of God's will is in the Bible, the divisions in Christendom show the need for miraculous guidance. He thought that only the Lord Himself, through His Spirit, will ever be able to teach us all that He wants us to know and to believe. *First,* there is always need for growth in knowledge, but is the lack of gifts the reason for division? *Second,* Mormons claim that each believer must be inspired if we are to achieve unity. They do not claim that each individual receives revelations, however, for the entire church. Mormonism is divided. When the author has had about five Mormons talking with him in a group discussion, he has found it possible to have them arguing among themselves. We do also, but we don't claim to be inspired. *Third,* the Pentecostal groups have claimed the Spirit for many, many decades, yet they are divided in doctrine and organization. The tongues movement today has in it individuals with many conflicting doctrines on very important subjects. Many of them will not accept some of the scriptural

285

doctrines to which Pat holds; for example, his position on Acts 2:38. *Fourth,* some of the causes of division are: (a) Accepting authorities other than the Bible. (b) Traditions of men. (c) Acknowledging what the Bible teaches, but failing to follow it. (d) The lack of love. (e) Ignorance. (f) The lack of patience. (g) The failure to understand and apply Rom. 14. *Fifth,* we have not only Moses and the prophets, but also the apostles and prophets of the New Testament. If we will not hearken to them in the Bible, would we hearken if one arose from the dead today? (Compare Lk. 16:27-31.) *Sixth,* perfect unity was not attained in the first century, but this does not mean that we should not strive to answer more fully Christ's prayer for unity (John 17:20-21; Eph. 4:1-5). One of the wonderful things about being a member of Christ's church is that one does not have to be bound by another's position, even if that individual disfellowships one. One is still a free man in Christ and ultimately responsible to Christ, not man. Of course, no one is bound to fellowship another regardless of what they believe or teach. *Sixth,* the Spirit brings unity to the degree we yield our lives to God, study and practice His word, and give "diligence to keep the unity of the Spirit." (Eph. 4:3; I Cor. 1:10-12.)

CHAPTER XX

MIRACLES: QUESTIONS AND ANSWERS

What are some of the questions which are raised, and scriptures which are cited, concerning miracles? A good many of these questions have been dealt with in other chapters, but here we shall consider some which either have not been dealt with or as fully as they are in this chapter.

ASA A. ALLEN

Do some healers use doctors? Asa A. Allen, a prominent "healer" and President of Miracle Valley Bible College in Arizona, died June 11, 1970, in San Francisco, California. The coroner's report revealed the following: *First*, on the left knee there were old surgical scars. In times past Allen had been treated "for arthritis of the knee." *Second*, Allen had an appointment arranged with *his personal physician*, "because of severe pain in the knees. A decision was to be made whether to operate on the second knee because of continuing severe pain." *Third*, "two prescription bottles were found alongside the television—one contained 10 yellow tablets and one contained 18 pink and white capsules." *Fourth*, "the deceased had been taking relatively large quantities of painkiller, and medication for sleep. These consisted of Percodan and Seconal." *Fifth*, the "alcohol blood level was found to be 0.36%." A study published by the U. S. Department of Transportation on *Alcohol and Highway Safety*, August, 1968, said that some states adopted as the standard, by which to determine whether a driver was driving while his ability was impaired by alcohol, as more than 0.5% and some 0.10%. (p. 105). *Sixth*, "the cause of death was acute alcoholism and fatty infiltration of the liver." *Seventh*, "the apparent mode of death was Natural vs. Accident, undetermined."

ACTS 4:29-31

Does not this passage show that the entire church worked miracles? *First*, Paul expressly said all did not work miracles (I Cor. 12:4-11, 29-30). *Second*, Acts does not say it was the entire church. The two apostles, Peter and John, when re-

287

leased reported "to their own company" (Acts 4:23). It was surely not the five thousand (Acts 4:4), for there is no evidence that they all gathered together in one place, which was shaken, as was this company to whom the two apostles reported (Acts 4:31). It would be natural for these two apostles to report to the company of the apostles. *Third,* if more than the apostles were in this company, it is strange that no one other than the apostles were said to work miracles until after apostles later had laid hands on the seven. (a) "And with great power gave the apostles their witness of the resurrection of the Lord Jesus . . . " (4:33). "And by the hands of the apostles were many signs and wonders wrought among the people . . . and they were healed every one." (5:12, 16). (b) If more than the apostles were involved in the company of Acts 5:23, and others were also the servants through whom the signs were done (5:29-30), this is no reason on which to base the contention that they got the power apart from the laying on of the apostles' hands. The apostles were there and could confer the gifts on any additional ones to whom the Lord wanted them to give gifts. Just as Christ stretched forth His hand to heal (4:30) through healing through the hands of the apostles (5:12), just so He could confer this power through the hands of the apostles. *Fourth,* there seems to be a distinction between the "they" of 4:23-31, and the "multitude of them that believed" in verse 32. If it was the identical group why did it not continue by saying: "And *they* were of one heart and soul . . . ?" *Fifth,* that not all the multitude of believers were included is indicated by the fact that not all of them were preachers of the word. The prayer (4:29), and the results (4:31) had to do with those servants who were all preachers of the word. And in this context it has been the apostles whose ministry of preaching was mentioned (4:20, 33). *Sixth,* this was not the original endowment of the apostles with the baptism of the Spirit, for it is obvious that Peter and John, whom we know were there (4:13, 23), received the baptism on Pentecost (Acts 2:1-4). They had already done signs and wonders in Jesus' name, and they had already spoken with boldness (2:43; 4:9-11, 12, 13). They asked God to continue to give

288

them boldness and confirm the word which they preached (4:29-30). Their being filled with the Spirit in this case did not add anything to what they had already done, but they did continue to speak with boldness (4:31), and great power (4:33). *Seventh,* do those who claim that they get the Spirit, in a miraculous way, in answer to prayer match this account? (a) Do they have any apostles of Christ? (b) Do they have a miraculous shaking of the place where they are meeting (4:31) (c) Do they do the works—the miracles—which the apostles did? (d) Do they teach the same doctrine the apostles taught?

ASK IN FAITH?

Does Heb. 11:6 mean that we shall receive specific rewards if we ask for them in the faith that we shall receive them? Pat thinks it means that we must not ask for the gifts in order to create faith, but that we should ask with the conviction or faith that we shall receive them. *First,* even if it means this, we must use the gifts to convince others (Mk. 16:17, 20; I Cor. 14:22). *Second,* if we can get one gift this way, we can get them all this way. If one cannot get all the gifts this way, it means Pat has limited the application of the passage, and he should not be surprised when we study the Bible to see what rewards are *promised to us. Third,* why not ask for the gift of apostleship, and the power to write inspired scripture? These people reason that if they ask for it in faith they shall receive it, and receiving it they should have enough faith to exercise it. Therefore, one should launch out and write scripture, tell the church to continue in his doctrine, speak authoritatively (Acts 2:42; I Cor. 14:37), do the miracles of an apostle, and confer miraculous gifts as did the apostles. *Fourth,* one should ask for the knowledge and wisdom necessary to explain difficult scriptures, and then explain them. *Fifth,* this makes it easy for one to be deceived. He thinks he receives the gifts when he seeks them in faith, and having sought in faith he has received them. Those who have the gifts ought to use them, so they use them. With reference to some of the gifts, they cannot keep from deceiving themselves with this approach. If they can make sounds at all, they can make sounds in other than English. They think this is speaking in tongues. If they can talk about religion, they can call this the gift of prophecy. Irenaeus (A. D. 120-202) tells of a heretic named Marcus who taught women to prophesy. "Open thy mouth, speak whatsoever occurs to thee, and thou shalt prophesy." And she did! (Ante-Nicene Fathers, Vol. 1, pp. 334-335). *Sixth,* what does Heb. 11:6 mean? (a) We can neither come to nor please God without believing in His existence (Comp. Rom. 1:18-25; 10:14-17). (b) If we do not believe He rewards those who seek Him, we do not believe in His love. If we think God is unconcerned, it would be futile to seek, for what could we do to make Him concerned? (c) This passage does not tell us how to come to God through Christ, it does not tell us what rewards God promises men, and it does not tell us on what conditions these rewards are promised. We learn these things from other passages. We must grow in faith so we are firmly persuaded that what *God* has promised He is able to perform (Rom. 4:20-21), but this is vastly different from saying that what men have promised us, or we have promised ourselves, God will give us.

ATONEMENT—HEALING IN IT?

The way Isaiah 53:5 was used in Pat's book, it was implied that healing here and now was included in the atonement, for with His stripes we are healed (Christian Life, July, 1970, p. 50). At this writing, Pat has not responded to the author's letter asking whether this is Pat's belief. *First,* the redemption of the body takes place not on earth, but when we receive the heavenly body at the resurrection (I Cor. 15:26, 42-57; Phil. 3:20-21; I John 3:2; Rom. 8:22-23; Rev. 21:4; 22:3).

Second, if the healing of the body here and now is included in the atonement, we are healed if our sins are remitted. If a saint is sick it means that he has not been forgiven. However, redeemed people suffer sickness and it is not said that this proves they have sinned (II Cor. 12:7-9; I Tim. 5:23; II Tim. 4:20; Phil. 2:26-27; Jas. 5:15).

Third, death is the most destructive thing that happens to the physical body. If healing is included in the atonement, why do we die? (Heb. 9:27). Our outward man is decaying, but not our inward man (II Cor. 4:16). Death entered because of sin, the atonement for sin has been made on the cross, but the body is still subject to disease, decay, and death (Rom. 5:12, 17, 21; I Cor. 15:20-28, 42-57).

Fourth, Luke 4:17-19 does not teach that healing is included in the atonement. Jesus showed that even in the Old Testament healing was the exception, and not the rule (Lk. 4:25-27). Isaiah's prophecy was fulfilled in Christ's work (Lk. 4:2). Physical sickness may be a *type* of the sickness of sin, and Jesus' healing miracles constituted one of His credentials which showed that He had the power to forgive sins (Mk. 2:9-11).

Fifth, if any passage teaches that healing is included in the atonement, it is Matt. 8:14 and Isa. 53:4. Do they teach it? (a) Our first three points have shown that healing is not included in the atonement. (b) Christ's healing miracles were performed during his personal ministry. None of them were performed by the Christ when He bore our sins (I Pet. 2:24). Matthew says that in the healing miracles in His personal ministry, Isaiah's prophecy about diseases and infirmities was fulfilled (Matt. 8:16-17). Matthew made no reference to Isaiah's predictions about Christ's atonement for our sins. (c) The modern healers, who claim to be redeemed, will not claim that none of them have any diseases or infirmities. (d) The apostles preached remission of sins as included in the atonement, but never the present healing of the body. (e) If healing is included in the atonement, healing would take place whenever one accepted the atonement. Why would one have to do anything to get bodily healing in addition to what he did to get spiritual healing? (f) Why were there special gifts of healing (I Cor. 12:9, 30), if healing is in the atonement? There were no miraculous gifts of salvation. (g) R. V. Bingham observed that Matthew used a word for "bear" which differed from the one which Isaiah used, which was associated with atonement. The word Matthew used expressed sympathetic bearing; as bearing one another's burdens (Rom. 15:1; Gal. 6:2). When Peter said Jesus bore our sins, he used the word Isaiah used and not the word Matthew used (I Pet. 2:24). Peter used the word for healing which can be used for spiritual or physical healing, while Matthew used a word associated with physical healing. The Holy Spirit must have had some reason for having Matthew make these changes. Bingham concluded that "Matthew is guided to use the spiritual figures of Isaiah 53 *illustratively* of the physical healing ministry of Christ, but that in doing this he is carefully guided to a change in language which indicates this. *The Bible and the Body,* pp. 55-58; James D. Bales, *Miracles or Mirages?,* pp. 10-112). (h) We are baptized into Christ's death, burial, and resurrection and unto the remission of sins, but we are not baptized unto the healing of the body (Acts 2:38; 22:16; Rom. 6:2-5, 17-18; Gal. 3:26-27).

BODILY PROCESS MAY STOP THE DISEASE

We do not know enough about the human body to know why in some cases a disease is stopped, nor do we know what triggered the cessation and even cure of the disease. There are cases where this has happened, and yet not even faith healing was involved. A small percentage of cancerous tumors have failed to grow. Drs. Tilden C. Everson and Warren H. Cole, Professors of Surgery, wrote a book which documented cases where growth in cancers had stopped spontaneously. The book is called: *"Spontaneous Regression of Cancer."* (Walter C. Alvarez, "Cancers That Stop Growing," *Arkansas Democrat,* 9-16-68). A spokesman for the American Cancer Society said: "It can be pointed out that the remissions in cancer are common even without treatment, and the society does not regard remission in one patient as necessarily significant." *(Arkansas Democrat,* 4-2-67, p. 2A).

Dr. Alvarez also wrote: "Yes, I remember cases in which although the cancer had scattered—even without treatment, the patient lived for years. I was much impressed once when, at the autopsy on an old patient of mine who died of an accident seven years after a black cancer had flared up, my friend, the pathologist, found a nodule of black cancer in the 'liver. Why hadn't it grown? No one could say.

"Many times in my life I have seen a cancer quit growing, probably because the natural defenses of the body became so great that the cancer cells could not grow." *(Arkansas Democrat,* 4-30-67).

CEASED WHEN FULFILLED THEIR FUNCTIONS

The miracles which made possible the deliverance of Israel from Egypt were not essential to the wilderness wanderings and were not repeated there. The pillar of cloud ceased when it fulfilled its function. There did not have to be an express statement, that they would cease, in order for the miracles to accomplish their purposes and come to an end.

CONTEST?

Moses engaged in a contest with Pharaoh's magicians and won (Exodus 7:18; 12:36), Elijah put to shame and silence the false prophets at Mount Carmel (I Kings 18:17-40), and Simon the sorcerer realized that Philip could actually do miracles and was converted (Acts 8:9-13). However, Oral Roberts declined an opportunity to match a Moslem. An AP dispatch from Nairobi, Kenya, said: "American Evangelist Oral Roberts, who has told Kenyans to 'expect a miracle' from his current crusade, has turned down a challenge from Moslems to a 'faith healing contest'."

"Khadi proposed that he and Roberts divide the number of cripples in Kenya and see who could heal them fastest. The winner's prize, the chief conceded, would be 'the first sign from Almighty God which is the true religion.'

"Roberts' press officer, Wayne Robinson, said Friday: 'We do not indulge in side shows. We want nothing to do with razzle dazzle. It's not a part of the Christian religion'."

At one of his meetings, one woman laid aside her crutches and walked away with a stagger. Hands were laid on fifty other infirmed people, but there "was no sign of change in their infirmities."*(Los Angeles Herald-Examiner,* July 20, 1960 or 66. The date on the clipping was indistinct).

DEVIL EVER PERFORMED MIRACLES?

Since the devil has performed lying wonders, it is necessary for God's people to test all things by the word of God (Jer. 23:25-32; Matt. 7:21-23; 24:24; II Cor. 11:13-15; II Thess. 2:7-11; Rev. 13:13-14; 16:13-14; 20:10).

DIDN'T JESUS SAY, ASK BELIEVING?

"And all things, whatsoever ye shall ask in prayer, believing, ye shall receive" (Matt. 21:18-22). Does this mean that if we ask in faith we shall receive the miraculous gifts for which we ask? In addition to our comments on "Ask in Faith?" we observe: *First,* Jesus was speaking to the apostles (Mk. 11:1, 12, 15, 19, 20, 22-24).

Second, He did deal with the miraculous for at His word the disciples had seen the fig tree wither *immediately* (Matt. 21:19-20).

Third, the apostles and some others had a gift of faith which involved the miraculous; but not everyone had this faith (I Cor. 12:9). However, without love the faith that moved mountains was profitless (I Cor. 13:2).

Fourth, as far we know the apostles never miraculously cast a mountain into the sea (Matt. 21:21), so evidently it was not God's will that this be done miraculously.

Fifth, if this passage is unlimited, why do modern "miracle" workers fail so often to work miracles?

Sixth, why have they *never* cast a mountain into the sea? Surely they have faith as "a grain of mustard seed;" which was a proverb for something very small. If they have a very small faith, they must be able to miraculously move mountains; if they have rightly interpreted Jesus' statement (Matt. 17:18-21). Instead of arguing about this passage, they should demonstrate; but they move no more mountains than does the author. If they move the first mountain, and if their teaching harmonizes with the New Testament, the author will be encouraged to try to move the next mountain.

Seventh, "a grain of mustard seed" was a proverbial expression for something very small (Matt. 17:20), and moving a mountain could indicate something tremendous. The apostles did great miracles, but they never literally moved a mountain. John did no miracles, but spiritually speaking he moved mountains (Isa. 40:4-5; Lk. 3:5; John 10:41).

Eighth, a well known principle of Bible study is that a passage, which seems unlimited when taken by itself, may be limited by another passage. (a) Are we to give to everyone who asks? (Matt. 5:42). No. (II Thess. 3:10,15). (b) Are we forbidden to work for our food? (John 6:27). No. One is to work and eat his own bread (II Thess. 3:12), provide for one's self and help others (Eph. 4:28). The people in John 6:26-29 were seeking Christ for the wrong purpose. The sign of the multiplication of the food should have led them to recognize that Christ had a message from God to which they should hearken. "Instead of seeing," Lange wrote, "in the bread the sign, they had seen in the sign only the bread." The work of God which they wanted was physical in nature, and the work which God wanted to do for them had to do with faith in God and Christ. Jesus was not discussing whether one should work for a living. (c) One may pray, and not receive, because he has wrong purposes in mind (Jas. 4:3). (d) How one treats one's wife can hinder his prayers (I Pet. 3:7). (e) There is mercy with the Lord, but no amount of faith can enable us to pray away the law of sowing and reaping (Gal. 6:7-9). We must change the sowing in order to change the reaping. (f) Wives are to submit to their husbands in all things (Eph. 5:24), but not if it leads them to disobey God (Acts 5:29). (g) In the very context of the promise that they would receive what they asked in faith, Jesus showed that it took more than one's personal conviction. One would not be forgiven when he prayed for forgiveness, if he did not forgive (Mk. 11:25). (h) Matt. 17:20-21 is limited even by those who argue as if it is unlimited. They do not move mountains. The *unmoved mountain* stands between them and their arguments. Even when miraculous power was granted, it was limited by God's will. We do not have miraculous power today, so the passage was limited by the purposes and duration of the miracles. The faith has been revealed and confirmed. No matter how strong our personal conviction about our receiving the very thing we ask for, we must remember that the decisive factor is God's will and what God has promised—not what we or others have promised ourselves (Rom. 4:20-21; I John 5:14).

Ninth, some come to doubt whether they have the Spirit, and they may feel they generated the tongues themselves. Some of them are told that after His baptism, Jesus was tempted (Sherrill, 127-128). Jesus was not tempted to doubt that He had the Spirit or that He was the Messiah (Matt. 4). Instead of re-examining their position in the light of the Bible, these individuals believe this doubt is of the devil and must be put away through faith in God. Of course, it is difficult to reason with people who view your arguments from the Bible as temptation from the devil!

Tenth, if one interprets Matt. 21:22 without considering other passages which limit it, Pat is involved in the following dilemma. He said if he had realized the author was going to mention his name and arguments in his book, he would not have been as frank and open with the author on an intimate and personal basis. However, he would have had to tell the author all he asked, and more too, on the basis of Matt. 5:40-42; unless a passage, which taken by itself seems universal in its application, may be limited by another passage. In speaking of a young man's desire for healing, Mk. 11:24 was cited, and Pat wrote: "All he had to do was to believe it." *(Christian Life,* July, 1970, p. 50).

FAILURES?

Since not everyone was healed in the first century, why should we be so negative in our attitude toward modern miracles when everyone is not healed today? *First,* we have already dealt with this elsewhere. *Second,* there is no record where any miracle worker, after the establishment of the church, tried to work a miracle and failed. *Third,* since Pat thinks that we get the gifts if we sincerely ask for them, why do the gifts sometimes fail to work when men sincerely try to use them? The way Pat has interpreted scriptures on asking in faith, he should interpret the following scripture to mean every sincere request will be granted. "And all things whatsoever ye shall ask in prayer, believing, ye shall receive" (Matt. 21:22). We have discussed this verse elsewhere. *Fourth,* the fact that God did not will to give everyone the gifts, or to give each one all of the gifts, or to heal everyone, is one of the proofs that the purposes of these gifts were neither in themselves to make the individual spiritual or to heal everyone, inspire everyone, etc. They were to reveal and confirm the truth and when these purposes would not be accomplished, there was no reason for them to be used. The revelation and the confirmation went hand in hand, and if we have confirmation today we also have revelation today (Heb. 2:3-4).

FAITH AND RECEIVING A STONE?

Since God will not give us a stone, instead of bread, when we ask for the gifts we shall receive them. God will not allow us to be deceived. This argument is based on Luke 11:11-13. *First*, their use of this passage assumes that God will not permit them to be deceived. God does permit men to be deceived. (a) Jews had a zeal for God, but not according to knowledge, and many of them accepted false Messiahs (Rom. 10:1-4; Matt. 24:11). They accused those who accepted the true Messiah (Acts 26:6-7). (b) One can be deceived even though he claims to work miracles (Matt. 7:21-23). (c) Mrs. H. W. Smith told of some whose system of guidance led them into immorality. "I expressed my horror at this and tried to show her how dangerous it was and to what abuses it might lead, and she seemed to begin to see it, but she exclaimed, 'Oh, Mrs. Smith, I dare not look at it in that light or I shall lose all my faith in God. What am I to do if in my most sacred moments, when I am most consecrated to God, and most fully abandoned to His will, the command comes to me to do this sort of thing? How can I believe that at such moments He would let me be deluded into evil, and how can I refuse to obey His voice?" (Ray Strachey, Editor, *Religious Fanaticism*, London: Faber and Gwyer, Ltd., pp. 198-199). (a) A girl was led to walk into the river, and before she drowned she said: "Faith is the victory." Her sister made a step to stop her "and was pushed back by the Spirit," she said. *(Toronto Telegram*, September 17, 1948).

Second, God must judge each individual heart, but He has told us that it is possible for men to want something so much that He lets them receive according to the fruit of their thought, and the idol which they have set up in their hearts (Jer. 6:19; Ezek. 14:4-5). Hearts can be prepared for the reception of lying wonders (II Thess. 2:9-12; II Tim. 4:3-4).

Third, the Book of Mormon tells the reader to ask God, with sincere heart, whether the book is true, and through the power of the Spirit God will manifest the truth of it unto them. The passage tells one not to deny the gifts of God, that God is the same today and tomorrow and forever, and that the gifts will never be done away (Moroni 10:4-19). Mormons

297

think that God will not allow them to be deceived, and that He tells them the Book of Mormon is true. They claim that no one who has rightly applied this test has failed to believe the Book of Mormon.

Fourth, unless God makes a promise, and unless we meet the conditions on which the promise is made, we do not have faith in God's word, but in man's promises, when we seek to obtain these promises. (a) One can have the wrong purpose in mind, and thus not obtain (Jas. 4:3). (b) One can ask for something which is not for him (Acts 8:18-24). Biblical faith is a firm persuasion that what God has promised He is able to perform (Rom. 4:21). There is often a vast difference between what others promise us, or we promise ourselves, and what God has promised.

Fifth, Luke 11:13 says nothing about miraculous gifts, nor do other passages teach that Christians today will receive these gifts if they pray sincerely for them. We receive the Spirit, but not miraculously, when we are baptized into Christ (Acts 2:38; I Cor. 6:19, 20). God will not deceive us, but it is possible for us to be deceived. Those who trust must also test all things by the word of God so they can guard against, or overcome deception. We must love God with all of our minds and prove all things (Matt. 22:37; I Thess. 5:21; I John 4:1; Rev. 2:2). In a passage parallel to Luke 11:9-13, Jesus warned us to keep alert because there are false prophets, there is bad fruit, and there are those who will depend on their assumed power to work miracles and yet be deceived (Matt. 7:7-11, 15-21). Perhaps these thought that God would not permit them to be deceived.

Sixth, the "pray-through" test, which is found in the Book of Mormon and used by at least many who seek the baptism of the Spirit and the gifts, is not scriptural. This approach in itself shows they are not guided by the Spirit. No sinner seeking salvation, no one seeking faith in Christ, was told to pray through. Faith comes by hearing the word of God with an honest heart which seeks the good (Rom. 10:17; Lk. 8:11-15; John 7:17; 5:32-47; 20:30-31). In Acts, Peter gave people four reasons for faith—prophecy, Jesus' miracles, the resurrection and the miracles on Pentecost—and on these grounds called for faith (Acts 2:36). Prayer is not a substitute for Bible study, nor for testing those who claim to have a message from God, or a gift from God. Jesus' statement in Luke 11:11-13 must be considered in the light of other statements in the Bible, and not in the light of man's promises.

FULL GOSPEL BUSINESSMEN'S FELLOWSHIP INTERNATIONAL

Ralph J. Conroy wrote that: "I have attended many healing meetings. I have also attended the meetings of the Full Gospel Business Men's Fellowship. My business partner is an enthusiastic member. And yet I have never seen anyone get healed. The claimed healings are so vague and emotional that one cannot be honest with oneself and accept them as fact" (*Christian Life*, October, 1967, p. 15).

HOW TO BE HEALED—ORAL ROBERTS

Oral Roberts is so confident that he has written an article entitled: "Exactly How You May Receive Your Healing." He tells of one man who he says was cured: "Bob picked up my book, EXACTLY HOW YOU MAY RECEIVE YOUR HEALING . . . THROUGH FAITH. And the message entitled EXACTLY HOW YOU MAY RECEIVE YOUR HEALING was the key to Bob's divine, instantaneous deliverance. It can be yours, too.

"The guarantee of healing for body and mind is everywhere evident in the Word of God." (6). There are six steps. *First,* "Know that God wants to heal you." *Second,* "You must want God to heal you." *Third*, "Approach God for healing through faith." "More than prayer, more than desire, more than hope is needed. You must have faith that God will actually heal YOU." (7). *Fourth,* "Use a point of contact to make your believing a single act of faith." "A point of contact is anything you do whereby you release your faith, letting it go instantly to God for a specific desire or a specific answer to your prayer." It may be the laying on of hands. "My touch was her point of contact for the release of her faith, which instantly went to God and brought her the desired healing." (8). "Through your point of contact you also set the time. It is necessary to set the time, for the time you set is the point of expectation. You must expect a miracle if you want one to occur." (8-9). *Fifth,* "How to receive help through my (Oral Roberts') prayers." When Roberts reaches out his hands toward the audience at the close of his TV programs, "touch your own body as your point of contact and accept my prayer as if it were for you exclusively." Literature can be the point of contact. "Remember, as I write these sermons, magazines, and books I pray to God to heal you as you read; believe God will heal you at this moment." His answer to your personal letters is also "my point of contact. When the recipient reads the letter it becomes his point of contact." (9). *Sixth,* "Give the Glory to God."

Since Roberts knows *exactly* how it is done, he must think his prayer for such knowledge has been answered. "For 23 years I have prayed that God would give me both the knowledge and the simplicity to reveal to the people exactly how they may receive their healing."

"This is God's hour to heal YOU and make YOU 'every whit whole'. This is YOUR hour to release YOUR faith in Him." (Oral Roberts, "Exactly How You May Receive Your Healing," *Abundant Life,* August, 1970, 9).

Of course, to explain his numerous failures, Roberts can always say they did not exactly apply this exact formula. In striking contrast with this, there is no case where the apostles or prophets, or others who had gifts, in the New Testament ever failed after the coming of the Spirit. The only failure was during the personal ministry, and then Christ blamed it on the disciples and not on the one on whom they failed (Matt. 17:19-20).

HYPNOSIS

There are cases of patients who responded to hypnosis when other things failed. (1) Skin conditions. (2) Speech difficulties. (3) Continuing pain following an operation. (Douglas N. Rhodes, "Medical Hypnosis: Trick or Treatment?" *American Mercury,* October, 1955, pp. 59-64).

JAMES 5:14-15

First, physical sickness is here dealt with, although such an individual may or may not have sinned (5:15). All sickness is not the result of one's sins.

300

Second, the elders—not a woman preacher or a man preacher—were sent for; as there were some pastors or elders who were such by gift and would have gifts (Eph. 4:7, 11).

Third, the elders came to the sick. The sick were not taken to a healer's meeting, nor did they have to get permission to get in the healing line.

Fourth, during the personal ministry of Christ, the apostles anointed with oil some whom they were about to heal (Mk. 6:13). Why? We are not told, but the following is a reasonable explanation. When individuals were sick, mourned, or fasted, they did not anoint their hair and faces as was customary in that day (Ruth 3:3; II Sam. 12:20; 14:2; Dan. 10:2, 3; Micah 6:15; Matt. 6:16, 17). "When, therefore James enjoins the elders to anoint the sick—that is, at once make his usual toilet—after prayers for his restoration, he really says just this, 'Pray for him with full faith, and show that you have such strong faith, *by acting towards him as if he really were recovered*'." (Robert Tuck, *A Handbook of Biblical Difficulties,* pp. 348-350). Whitaker said: "Let them anoint with oil who can procure health for the sick, and let those who cannot, abstain from the vain symbol."

Fifth, the prayer of faith. James P. Lange wrote: "Not faith in general, but miraculous faith as a special charisma . . . I Cor. 12:9." James McKnight said: "In scripture *faith* some--times signifies the spiritual gifts in general, Rom. 12:3, sometimes the gift of working miracles, I Cor. 12:9; 13:2, and sometimes the gift of healing diseases miraculously, Acts 3:16, in which sense it is to be understood here. The gift of working miracles was called *faith*, because they were always performed in consequence of an impression made by the Spirit on the mind of the person who was to perform them, moving him to undertake the miracle, and working in him a full persuasion that it would be performed. Wherefore, 'the prayer of faith' is a prayer which the elder, moved by the Spirit of God, was to make for the recovery of the sick, in the full persuasion that the Lord would raise him up." There is no case after Pentecost, where the apostles or prophets tried to work a miracle and failed. Since some were not miraculously healed (I Tim. 5:23; II Tim. 4:20; Phil. 2:26-27), it is reasonable to conclude that God let them know when they were to work a miracle.

Sixth, the Lord shall raise him up. There was no provision for failure. Those who have failures should not claim to be able to pray this prayer of faith.

Seventh, some think that James has reference to ordinary prayer, the use of oil for medical purposes, and that the promise of healing is no more universal than the promise of Christ to draw all men (John 12:32). We are to pray for the sick, and God in His providence may answer the prayer with "Yes," or "No." If this is the case, why send for the elders? Why not send for the physicians and let them prescribe? Surely James' reference to oil is not for the purpose of giving a general prescription for all manner of sickness. Oil is not such a cure-all! When Paul prescribed medicinally, he was more specific than prescribing oil (I Tim. 5:23).

LIMITING GOD'S POWER?

First, the issue is not God's power, but what has God willed? Although able, He has not raised up children unto Abraham from stones (Matt. 3:9). He can, but He does not, create men today as He did Adam or translate them as He did Enoch. *Second*, we are not limiting God's power, but observing and accepting what God has revealed, when we maintain that He raises up children to Abraham through moral and spiritual means. It is done by God through men preaching and obeying the gospel (Gal. 3:26-29; I Cor. 4:14-15; Jas. 1:18; I Pet. 1:22-25). *Third*, some seem to question God's power in assuming that He cannot work behind the scenes in providence without working miracles. *Fourth*, the issues are whether God is granting miraculous power to the church, whether those who claim such power really have it, and whether they teach what the Bible teaches.

LOURDES, A ROMAN CATHOLIC SHRINE

Dr. Alexis Carrel said that he witnessed a miraculous healing at Lourdes of a woman who he was convinced was dying. He witnessed some of the changes. She was still left weak and in the hospital for awhile. "The Voyage to Lourdes," *Reader's Digest*, September, 1950, pp. 147-162).

First, there is an extended discussion of this passage in James D. Bales, *Miracles or Mirages?* pp. 233-257. *Second,* the so-called modern miracle workers do not do all the things mentioned in Matt. 16:17-18 and embraced in Mk. 16:20; which covers all the miracles done by the miracle workers in the first century. *Third,* the promise of Mk. 16:17-20 is limited by the purpose and duration of miracles as revealed in this and other passages.

Oral Roberts teaches that the serpents in Mk. 16:18 are enemies such as in Lk. 10:19 *(Commentary,* 646-647). There is no more evidence that this meant figurative serpents than there is that drinking any deadly thing meant drinking in false doctrine. Paul was not hurt by a viper (Acts 28:3-6).

Anthony A. Hoekema wrote: "As we examine the Greek text of Mark 16:18, however, we find that, though the statement about drinking poison is put in a conditional form ('If they drink any deadly thing, it shall not hurt them'), the statement about taking up serpents is not put in a conditional form, but is in the future indicative: 'they shall take up serpents,' as is the statement about tongues: 'they shall speak with new tongues,' . . . If the speaking with new tongues is to be taken as a sign which confirms believers in their faith, why must we not further conclude that taking up serpents is also to function as such a sign? There is as much reason for accepting the one sign as the other, since in both cases the Greek verb is in the future indicative . . . " (55-56). If we should have the sign of tongues, why not the sign of taking up serpents?

Roberts believes he can lay hands on the sick and they will recover (Mk. 16:18). "I know that I have a command of God to lay my hands upon the people, and God uses my hands. I look on them, not as endowed with any special virtue or power, but as an extension of the hands of Christ. When I touch someone I try to envision my hands as an extension of the hands of Christ. I see Him touching you. And when He touches you, you are made whole—in soul, mind and body!" *(Commentary,* 648). If Mk. 16:18 applies to him, and if his hands are extensions of the hands of Christ, and if you are healed when Christ touches you, why does Roberts have so many failures? Jesus said: "They shall recover." (Mk. 16:18). The author received a letter in July 1970 from a cripple who told him of a spastic who went through Roberts' healing line and is still a spastic. If, in effect, Roberts' hands are an extension of the hands of Christ, there is special virtue or power in them. He should know this, if he knows that God gave him a command to lay on hands and if God uses his hands.

MATTHEW 13:58

Was Christ's power limited by unbelief? First, He did heal those who were brought to Him (Matt. 13:58; Mk. 6:5). Since Christ could work a miracle on even the unwilling, these passages do not mean He was without the power to work miracles here. Since miracles were designed to lead to faith, there would be no reason to work miracles when men were so hardened that nothing could reach them. Furthermore, where unbelief prevailed, not many people would be brought to Him to be healed. *Second,* it is clear that Christ never tried to work a miracle and failed.

MIRACLES MATCHED?

What are some of the miracles in the Bible which people today, at least as a general rule, do not claim to match? Of course, they would need to prove as well as to claim to do such miracles. (1) Miraculous creation of men and women. (2) Rod into serpent. (3) Water into blood, or into wine. (4) Smiting a country with a plague of frogs. (5) Thick darkness such as in Egypt. (6) Death of the first born, but with the sparing of those who followed God's instructions (Ex. 3:20, 7:17). (7) Pillar of cloud by day and of fire by night (Ex. 14:24). (8) Going through the sea on dry land (Ex. 14:15; Joshua 3:13). (9) Clothes and shoes not waxing old (Deut. 8:4, Neh. 9:21). (10) An unwilling prophet conveyed to his destiny via a great fish (Jonah). (11) Leprosy cured after dipping seven times (II Kings 5:10). (12) Multiplication of loaves and fishes (Mk. 6:37-44). (13) Translation so one does not see death (Gen. 5:24; Heb. 11:5; II Kings 2:1-11). (14) Miraculous transportation (Acts 8:39-40). (15) Manna from heaven (Ex. 16:4). (16) Meal and oil miraculously increased (I Kings 17:14). (17) Someone turned into a pillar of salt (Gen. 19:26). (18) Walking on the water (Matt. 14:25). (19) Unconsumed by the fire (Dan. 3:20). (20) Sun and moon standing still (Joshua 10:12). (21) Deliverance from prison (Acts 5:19; 12:7; 16:26). (22) Missing members of body restored (Lk. 22:51; Matt. 18:8; 15:30-31). (23) The combination of the sound which all heard, of tongues which all understood, and cloven tongues which all saw (Acts 2:1-4, 6, 8, 11, 33). (24) The resurrection of someone who has been dead four days (John 11:39-44).

What do they more than others? If God were giving one group miraculous power, they like Moses would so outdo their competition that it would be easy for even Pharaoh to see who was on God's side. However, groups with conflicting doctrines—ranging as widely in doctrines from those of the Christian Scientists to those of Roman Catholics—do the same type of thing and claim the same type of thing so far as the author has been able to learn. All the author has checked neither measure up to the miracles in the Bible nor harmonize in their teaching with the Bible. Instead of these individuals and groups asking us to explain their miracles, why don't they explain why they do not do more than others, and why they do not harmonize with the teaching in the Bible?

Do the Lord's disciples do greater miracles than He did? (John 14:12). No. They did nothing greater than raising the dead, walking on the water, and miraculously multiplying loaves and fishes. What did Jesus mean? *First,* He was speaking to the apostles (John 13:1-30; Matt. 26:20-25; John 14:1-12, 16, 26). *Second,* they were to do these things because Jesus went to the Father (John 14:12). He went, and as a result He sent the Spirit who brought to their minds all that Jesus had taught and guided them into all the truth (John 14:26; 16:12-14). They had the power to reveal and to confirm the truth. This they did. They did greater works than Jesus did both geographically, nationally, and racially. Their ministry was longer in its duration, and it was not preparatory to the New Covenant as was that of Jesus. They were guided into the complete truth, but Jesus revealed only a part of it while on earth. Their message was greater for while the kingdom was emphasized in the preaching during His personal ministry, the person of Christ was more emphasized after the Spirit came. The apostles proclaimed the risen and reigning Christ.

305

They proclaimed Him as the One who died for our sins, while Jesus proclaimed this only in anticipation. Christ's ministry was under the old law, but the ministry of the apostles was under the greater covenant; that of Christ. Their works were greater in their numerical results. Of course, all of their work was the work which Christ did through them. *Third,* does anyone today claim, and then do, greater miracles than did Jesus?

POWER?

Sometimes failures today are excused by saying they do not have the power. Did the apostles, and other miracle workers in the New Testament, have the power? Yes. Although the power was from God, He gave it to certain men. *First,* He promised that the apostles would receive power when the Spirit came on them (Acts 1:2-3, 5, 8). *Second,* they did receive power when this happened. They spake in other languages (Acts 2:1-4, 6, 8, 11), God wrought miracles *"by* their hands" (14:3), *"through* them" (2:43; 15:12), "God wrought special miracles *by the hands of Paul"* (19:11), Paul spoke of the miracles *"Christ* wrought *through me"* (Rom. 15:18-19), and the Spirit was imparted in a miraculous way *through* the laying on of the apostles' hands (Acts 8:17-19; 19:1-6; Rom. 1:11, II Tim. 1:6). *Third,* God gave the gifts, but He gave them *to men* (I Cor. 2:8-11, 29-30). *Fourth,* if God inspires men today, and gives them power, He would let them know when they were to work a miracle so that they would not try and fail and then blame, as it were, the failure on God! *Fifth,* Oral Roberts used Lk. 24:49, Acts 1:8; 2:4 to prove that when you are baptized with the Spirit, "you are supernaturally endued with power from on high." ". . . power that dwells inside you and which you can feel inside." ("The Baptism With the Holy Spirit" pp. 2-3). Roberts views his hands as an extension of the hands of Christ *(Commentary,* 648). He also claims to tell people "exactly how you may receive your healing" *(Abundant Life,* August, 1970, pp. 6-9).

PRISON—MIRACULOUS DELIVERANCES?

Pat said there were such cases. The only one he cited was Richard Wurmbrand and his experiences in Communist prisons. *First,* the author has met Wurmbrand; he admires his courage and dedication, and if one wants to see what communism would like to do to all who profess faith in Christ, they should listen to his experiences. The author does not know what he himself would do if he had to undergo what Wurmbrand experienced. However, all teaching must be measured by the word of God. *Second,* there were no such miraculous deliverances as Acts 5:19-23; 12:1-19. *Third,* Wurmbrand thought that the fact that he is alive, in spite of all the physical punishment he endured and the TB which he had, is a miracle *(Tortured For Christ,* Old Tappan, New Jersey: Fleming H. Revell Co., 1969, p. 41). It may be amazing, but it is not a miracle. He was not healed instantaneously, and he did not receive perfect soundness.

PRAYER

Don't you believe in praying? Yes. However, prayer is not a substitute for other duties and privileges of the Christian. *First,* we pray for our daily bread, but we also work without expecting Manna from heaven (Ex. 16:15, 35; Matt. 6:11; Eph. 4:28; II Thess. 3:10-14). A miracle was a supernatural, superhuman work done by God through inspired men in order to confirm their message. God is not so limited that He cannot answer prayer without working a miracle. He can work behind the scenes in His providence and, without any supernatural manifestation, answer prayer. David prayed that God would turn the counsel of Ahithophel into foolishness. David then did what he could. God overruled and answered the prayer, but there was no supernatural sign. He did it, but we do not know how (II Sam. 15:31, 32-34; 16:23; 17:7, 14). God carried out His promise to protect Saul in Corinth, but there was no supernatural manifestation, as there was in the deliverance of Peter (Acts 18:9-10, 12-17; 12:7-11).

Second, the author prays concerning Bible study. He is not enlightened by a direct revelation. If he were, to challenge the author's interpretations would be the same as challenging God's word. When the author understands a passage those who differ with him are differing with the Bible, not because he is inspired, but because the Bible is inspired. Since the author is not inspired, he must always be willing to study with an honest heart so that misunderstandings may be corrected and correct understandings will be strengthened.

Third, the author does not know how God answers his prayer for help in Bible study. He knows he is not inspired, and he knows he must not substitute prayer for honest, diligent study of the Word. However, working behind the scenes, God can overrule so one is brought into touch with information and individuals who *can* help one understand. In many cases we are confirmed in our understanding by the fact that people from many different religious bodies may utilize the same scriptures, and same type of arguments, and arrive at an understanding of Scripture in the same way we do. Furthermore, they may explain the passage in contradiction to their own practice. This helps increase our conviction that we have understood such passages rightly. We continue to read and study that we may understand more (Eph. 3:4).

Should we expect almost instant, direct, and miraculous answers to our prayers? A mutual friend told a tongues speaker that he heard she was getting mystical. This remark stabbed her, as it were, and she spent much time in prayer that night and asked God to show her whether it was from Him or from the devil. She thought she got the answer it was from God. He bore witness in some way with her spirit, she thought. *First,* there may be a vast difference between what we promise ourselves and what God has actually promised. Faith should be based on what He has promised (Rom. 4:20-21). He has not promised to solve our problems by some direct revelation or "witness." *Second,* when one believes he will get such answers, he usually has some sort of feeling or experience which confirms his beliefs. *Third,* Mormons teach that the answer to whether the Book of Mormon is true comes through prayer (Moroni 10:4-5). One is laying down human conditions for God to meet if he expects some direct answer to his request that God show him whether the Book of Mormon is from God, from man, or from the devil. *Fourth,* this is the old pray-through-at-the-mourner's-bench approach to salvation and truth. The more emotional ones pray through quicker. *Fifth,* the method is unscriptural and those who use it show they are not guided by the Spirit in these things. Sinners seeking salvation were never told to pray through, but were given reasons for faith (Acts 2:22, 32, 33, 3-4, 6, 8, 11, 17, 34-35, 36). Those seeking truth were taught by the inspired word, whether written or spoken, and not by praying through (Acts 17:11-12; 18:25-26; Eph. 3:4; Rev. 2:1, 7). *Sixth,* one of the signs of maturity is the willingness to wait. We must not demand of God that He show us instantly and directly the answer to problems. We should pray and then we should do all we can to learn. If we do not learn the answer as quickly as we would like to, we must patiently continue our quest.

Do different groups use the pray through method? Yes. *First,* a Roman Catholic priest told the author to pray, Lead Kindly Light, for six months and he would see this matter differently. One must not only pray, but also keep his eyes open to see where the light of the word is leading. *Second,* the Roman Catholic De Montfort wrote: "As the Saints say, never has it been heard since the world was the world that anyone has confidently and perseveringly had recourse to our Blessed Lady, and yet has been repelled." *(The True Devotion to The Blessed Virgin,* p. 59). *Third,* Pentecostals of various beliefs use the pray-through method. *Fourth,* Mormonism uses it. "And when ye shall receive these things, I would exhort you that ye would ask God the eternal Father, in the name of Christ, if these things are not true; and if ye shall ask with a sincere heart, with real intent, having faith in Christ, he will manifest the truth of it unto you, by the power of the Holy Ghost. And by the power of the Holy Ghost ye may know the truth of all things." (Moroni 10:4-5). *Fifth,* over thirty years ago members of Moral Re-Armament told the author that one got the answer to problems and questions by asking God when one was confronted with these problems. The emphasis of these particular individuals was not on prayer and Bible study, but on prayer and direct answer. *Sixth,* the pray-through method is not of God since men pray through to such different positions, and they all have the same type of proof to prove their position is right. *Seventh,* the pray-through method is not scriptural, and those who use it show they are not guided by the Spirit either directly or through the written word.

Is not prayer supernatural, and if God answers it in any way is it not a supernatural answer? *First,* our prayers are neither inspired nor supernatural manifestations. Our speaking to the Supernatural Being is not in itself supernatural. *Second*, if God answering our prayer, without working a miracle, is a supernatural answer, there is no distinction between the natural and the supernatural. In such a case everything is natural and everything is supernatural. How could there be any supernatural manifestations which were signs? As we have pointed out elsewhere, the miracles were supernatural events, which functioned as signs, and which could be seen even by the unbeliever. *Third*, there is surely a difference between God answering in a natural way a man's prayer for a wife, and God taking something from the side of man, fashioning him a wife, and presenting the wife to him when he awakes from the operation. *Fourth*, God can work behind the scenes and answer prayer. He answered David's prayer without a miracle (II Sam. 15:31; 15:34; 16:23; 17:1-5; 14). He can protect His disciples without working a miracle (Acts 18:9-17). Surely there is a vast difference between this case and the miraculous deliverance of Peter from prison (Acts 12:1-19). *Fifth*, God enabled Peter to walk on the water, and then kept him from sinking. It is our conviction that regardless of how strongly Pat believes, and regardless of how fervently he prays, he will have to find some other means of crossing bodies of water.

The author has been asked if he would pray for the gift of tongues. First, it is right to pray, but prayer is not a substitute for Bible study. If one prays for an honest heart that he may learn the truth on baptism, he must also fulfill his responsibility of keeping his heart honest and studying the Bible. *Second*, since the author does not believe God has promised us such gifts, he cannot pray for these gifts (Rom. 4:20-21). He can, and has, prayed that if they are for us he would be glad to have any gifts which are available for him. *Third*, if these gifts are for us, the author must learn it from the Bible for it is the truth which God has revealed to man. The truth about tongues will not come through some direct revelation or inward feeling. *Fourth*, the author would no more try to discern the truth about tongues by trying to speak in tongues, as some Pentecostals teach others to do, than he would try to learn the truth on baptism by being baptized and observing what happened. *Fifth*, something out of its place can be dangerous. Air is necessary in the lungs, but deadly in the blood stream. Prayer and emotionalism are not substitutes for learning the truth from the Bible. *Sixth,* how does one know when he has prayed through? Does he learn it from the Bible? Is it on the basis of feeling or some other human experience?

SAME?

Does the sameness of God and Christ prove that miraculous gifts are given today? (Heb. 13:8). If so, creation, the flood, the virgin birth, the personal ministry, the crucifixion, the resurrection, the coronation of Christ, all the miracles, and the writing of new scriptures should take place in every generation. All men should be created as was Adam and women as Eve. All who walk with God should be translated as was Enoch (Heb. 11:5; 9:27). God could not have changed dispensations. His first dispensation would have been the last, but this is not true (Heb. 1:1-2; 2:1-4). God is the same in His nature, but He reached different stages in His dealings with man. We live in the time of the new covenant when the faith has already been delivered to earth and confirmed (Heb. 13:20; Jude 3).

SIGN SEEKERS?

If we ask those who claim miracles to work miracles are we evil sign seekers? (Matt. 12:39). No. *First,* these Pharisees had acknowledged supernatural works of Jesus which were directly against the devil, yet they attributed them to the devil (Matt. 12:24; Mk. 3:30). We have neither seen nor admitted their performance of such miracles. *Second,* we are satisfied with the signs in the Bible (John 20:30-31), so we are not sign seekers. They are the sign seekers who say one must do these signs. When we ask some of them to do what they claim they must do, they insult us by quoting Matt. 12:39. *Third,* they should finish the quotation. This would obligate *them* to give us the sign of the prophet Jonah, i. e. the resurrection. If they say Jesus has already given this, we say He has already revealed and confirmed the word (Mk. 16:17, 20; Heb. 2:3-4). *Fourth,* their misuse of this passage proves they are not miraculously guided by the Spirit.

SNAKE HANDLERS
"Oscar Franklin Pelfrey, 65, lay minister of the snake-handling Church of Christ in Jesus Name sect; in Big Stone Gap, Virginia, of rattlesnake bite during a service." *(Christianity Today,* Sept. 13, 1968, p. 1226. Obituary column).

VISIONS?
Lit-sen Chang, who was for decades a Buddhist, but who turned from it, wrote that: "Most experiences of mystical consciousness have come after spartan prayers, fasting, and mortification of the flesh . . . Now, we are told that through the use of LSD and other psychedelic drugs it is possible to produce the same experiences. Physicians have long suspected that the visions of religious mystics were the result of some change in body chemistry brought on by self-hypnosis, pain, breath-control or intense hunger." *(Zen-Existentialism,* Nutley, New Jersey: Presbyterian and Reform Publishing Co., 1969, p. 13).

In some cases individuals work themselves into such a state that they have all sorts of unusual sensations, or may suddenly feel transported and released into a higher level of life. This happens to Buddhists as well as to some followers of Christ who become deceived. Toda was a leading figure in Nichiren Shoshu, the most militant sect of Buddhism in Japan. "Early in 1944, Toda began chanting the *daimoku*— that is, the sacred phrase 'Nam-myoho Renge-kyo'—more than ten thousand times a day. After two million repetitions, an 'extremely strange sensation' seized him, and 'a world which I could never see before unfolded itself in front of me.' His body shaking with ecstatic joy, Toda stood in his cell and shouted to 'all Buddhas, all bodhisattvas, and all common men of the world' that he had now found, at the age of forty-five, 'the true meaning of life'." (Kiyoaki Murata *Japan's New Buddhism*, New York: Walker/Weatherhill, 1969, p. 89). "Nam-myoho Renge-Kyo" means Devotion to the Lotus Sutra (51).

WALKING ON WATER
The Hindu Fakir Sandra Rao demonstrated the depth of his faith by stepping on the top of the water before around 5,000 believers in Bombay. He only sank up to his whiskers,

according to one report. He did not sink further because he found something more substantial than his faith, i. e. the bottom of the tank. *(Newsweek,* June 27, 1966, p. 48; *Arkansas Gazette,* June 16, 1960.)

WHY DO SOME PEOPLE TODAY TESTIFY THAT THEY HAVE BEEN HEALED?

Why do some sincere people testify today that they have been miraculously healed? *First,* they may have been so emotionally and psychologically stimulated that they temporarily ignored the sickness. *Second,* their illness may be internal. They feel better at the moment, so they think that they are healed. *Third,* they ignore the distinction between a slow natural recovery and a miraculous recovery. Thus because they are gradually feeling better, and actually are gradually getting better, they think that a "healer" has miraculously healed them. But how could this be a miracle, a manifestation of supernatural power, if it is just like the natural recovery? How can it be a sign, when it does not differ from other cases where the people have gradually gotten well without the "healer's" help. *Fourth,* mental attitude does have an important relationship to getting well in many, many cases of illness. We do not fully understand the power of the mind. *Fifth,* some are deceived by the healer into believing the following: Claim the healing in faith and you are healed. If you claim it in faith, you have it! Since you have it, in gratitude— as well as to help others—to God you should testify and thus glorify God, giving Him the credit. You still have the symptoms? The devil put them there to shake your faith in your healing. Are you going to believe God or the devil? If you believe God, testify. If you believe the devil, and conclude that you have not been healed, you will lose your healing! (See Mrs. Fitch, *The Healing Delusion.) Sixth,* there are, of course, conscious deceivers. *Seventh,* we do not understand many things about bodily processes. There are cases where for some reason the body has stopped cancer and other diseases.

CHAPTER XX

PRACTICAL TESTS: QUESTIONS AND ANSWERS

It is not sufficient to discuss miraculous, direct guidance and the gift of wisdom in theory. One must also consider how these things work in practice. This chapter will deal with some of the things which they think show that the changes in their lives must be due to the miraculous reception of the Spirit and of at least some of His gifts. We shall also deal with some of those things which we believe show that their theories do not work in practice. In fact, there are numerous demonstrations in their lives which show that they do not have what they think they have. There are people who will not take the time to follow an argument, but who quickly see those things which demonstrate that these people are deceived.

ACTIVE ALWAYS?

Does not their increased activity prove that they have miraculous gifts? Some assume that Christians must always be on the go. Sherrill said the baptism of the Spirit filled people with energy which, if not channeled into constructive areas, was likely to be spent in frenetic running around. He spoke of people who constantly boarded jets on missions for the Spirit. Somehow this undirected hyper-activity ended up egocentric (135). *First,* if they were really Spirit-guided, they would not have engaged in what Sherrill called egocentric activity. Why can't they tell the difference between their own impulses and the Spirit's? *Second,* a false doctrine when believed has the same emotional impact on one which it would have if it were true. Believing that they have received some sort of power, they are stirred to greater activity. They have been emotionally stirred. A new-found faith, whether true or false, brings a sense of mission and helps drive one to work. It can finally have a bad impact physically unless one learns moderation. *Third,* if travel is an index to spirituality, the more spiritual one is the more he travels, and vice versa. *Fourth,* we are active spiritually when studying, praying, and meditating. Some keep so busy physically that they do not think deeply nor properly expend their time and energy.

Fifth, Christ sometimes withdrew from people. Paul spent some time in Arabia (Gal. 1:17). If he was very active there, we do not know it. Prison curbed his activities in various degrees. We are physical beings, subject to God's physical laws, and we should properly use our physical bodies. For spiritual and physical reasons we may need time off from persons and projects. It is right, not wrong, to aim at moderation in all things. To do nothing at times, or to do something different, is not a sign of laziness. One is not guilty just because he is not involved in more projects than he can handle!

CHRIST IS GLORIFIED?

If one's beliefs about the gifts and miraculous guidance help one to teach others about Christ, is not Christ glorified? *First*, truth is truth even when taught by hypocrites (Matt. 23:1-4; Phil. 1:15-18). Any truth taught by misguided individuals is still truth, but it does not sanction their errors. *Second*, a shy student came to the author last year to try to teach him. He said the baptism of the Spirit had given him boldness. Yet, this student repudiates some of the scriptural positions which Pat holds on other matters. He was bold because he thought he was inspired by the Spirit. There are other ways to be motivated than through self-deception. Think of the disillusionment some will suffer when they find they have been self-deceived or deceived by others in these matters. *Third*, thinking that one is inspired and miraculously guided by the Holy Spirit opens the door to all sorts of errors. It led Pat into a course of deception, in keeping these things from brethren, into which he would not have been led if he had depended on his study of the Word. He has been led into many errors, as this book shows. False teaching does not glorify Christ.

DOPE ADDICTS CHANGED

Does the fact that dope addicts have been changed prove they have received the Spirit in a miraculous way? We commend the zeal and dedication of those who work with dope addicts, but we do not believe that even the good things which they accomplish prove that they have the gift of tongues or that their doctrine is thereby accredited. Whether we can explain what they have accomplished with dope addicts does not mean that their explanation is right; that is, that these have actually received the miraculous gifts of the Spirit. Do we have any explanation?

First, they teach the truth on some subjects. It is true that men ought to believe in and love Jesus Christ. They ought to surrender their lives to Christ. To the extent that we surrender our lives to Christ, and to the extent that we know and do His will, to that extent transformations will take place in our lives. This is true, even though an individual may be confused about many other things.

Second, a tremendous emotional experience can have a tremendous impact on one's life. This is true even when he has misinterpreted the nature of the experience. Jacob misinterpreted the testimony of his son and of the blood-stained coat of Joseph. A tremendous emotional experience followed the false conclusion concerning the death of his son. (Gen. 37:33-35.) The impact of this experience continued with him for many decades. When dope addicts, or others, are stimulated—by teaching and by the atmosphere—to try to get the gift of tongues, and when they find themselves actually speaking in what they have been told is a supernatural experience, they are convinced that they have entered a new realm of reality. The emotional impact on them is the same that it would be if they actually had the gift of foreign languages.

Third, in coming to faith in Christ, which may be strengthened at the time by their thinking they have a genuine gift of tongues, and to love for Christ there is what has been called the "expulsive power of a new affection."

Fourth, being without meaning for life, or for some other reason, some of these people had taken to dope in order to find some new experience, to find some thrill in life, or to escape from their own lives of uncertainty and meaninglessness. They find meaning through their faith in Christ, and they find emotional experiences through what they think is the baptism of the Holy Spirit.

Fifth, the conviction that their body is now the temple of the Holy Spirit surely has a tremendous impact on them.

Sixth, those who are under the influence of some drugs are highly susceptible to suggestion, as are people under hypnotism. They, as well as highly emotional people, could re-

316

spond to the suggestions of the religious workers, and even seek and find the gift of tongues through following instructions. This could happen in at least some cases, and such individuals could be influenced by such experiences; especially if these were repeated when they were not under the influence of drugs.

EXPERIENCE AND ARGUMENT

Is it true that a man with an experience is never at the mercy of a man with an argument? *First,* some defend their beliefs with an appeal to experience and rule out the need for justifying their beliefs by scriptures, reasons, and arguments. Some say: "I would not swap my feelings for a thousand Bibles." *Second,* if one has only an experience, without evidence and scripture, he cannot properly evaluate the experience. He cannot determine whether the experience of someone else is good, bad, or indifferent. (a) A man, while carrying on a sinful experience with another woman, told his wife what a beautiful experience it was. She had only arguments and scriptures on her side, such as "Thou shalt not commit adultery," so how could she refute the satisfying experience of her husband; even though she was experiencing misery? (b) A girl committed adultery and said it was a beautiful experience concerning which she had no sense of guilt. Through the experience she said she learned that the arguments against adultery were wrong. (c) She found drugs, at least for the time, to be a terrific experience. What counted, she said, was what one was experiencing. This type of trust in experience says that the way of man is in himself, that we can trust the arm of flesh; but the Bible contradicts this (Jer. 10:23-24; 17:5). *Third,* we must recognize we shall be judged by Christ's word (Matt. 7:21-23; John 12:48). *Fourth,* the man who trusts in argument only, experiences only verbalization of his faith. As he becomes conscious of how hollow his life is, he may yearn for the experiences others have, and in an emotional experience may think that some false doctrine is confirmed as the truth. *Fifth,* evidence, argument, scripture, and experience are necessary. On the basis of four lines of evidence— prophecy, Christ's miracles, the resurrection, and the miracles on Pentecost—the apostles reasoned and drew the conclusion that Jesus is Lord and Christ (Acts 2:1-4, 6, 8, 11, 16, 22, 25-

28, 30, 32, 33, 34-36). Through the truth the Spirit convicted them of sin, righteousness, and judgment. They experienced this conviction and asked what they must do. They were instructed, accepted the apostles' teaching, and underwent the experience of coming into Christ and living in Christ (2:37-42). They experienced the new life in which the grace of God instructed them (Titus 2:11-14). Through serving God, the proof of the pudding was found in the eating thereof as well as in other evidences and arguments (Rom. 12:1-2). Our experience in our everyday lives of the principles of Jesus, through living by them, along with evidences of other types, arguments and scriptures, enables us to give reason for the hope which is within us (I Pet. 3:15). We should also experience what it means to contend for the faith (Jude 3).

FRUIT OF THE SPIRIT?

Since some tongues speakers manifest some of the fruit of the Spirit in their lives, does not this prove the reality of miraculous gifts? *First,* the Bible does not teach that the fruit of the Spirit is the result of miraculous gifts, but of walking by the teaching of the Spirit (Gal. 5:6, 13-14, 16, 22-24).

Second, a Buddhist monk from Burma spoke of the need for love. George Appleton asked him whence this love came, and he "replied that there was a divine seed of it in all men. Then, perceiving the point of my question, he said, 'I suppose you Christians would say that it came from God.' St. Paul says: 'The fruit of the Spirit is love, joy, peace, good temper, kindness, goodness, faithfulness, meekness, self-control.' Surely this must also be true in reverse, that where love, joy, peace are found, there is the Spirit of God at work." *(The Christian Approach to the Buddhist,* London: Edinburgh House Press, 1958, pp. 53-54). There are Buddhists who have peace of mind.

Any truth which they teach is truth, and any truth when followed produces fruit after its own kind. God works through His physical laws in any and all places, and God works through His spiritual laws any time any of His spiritual laws are obeyed by man. Any spiritual law when followed makes the person, to that extent, more like what God wants him to be. Any spiritual law when violated, makes the person that much less than what God wants man to be. The pagans who refused

318

to retain God in their knowledge, and who turned to idols and immorality became more and more degraded until God gave them up (Rom. 1:18-32). God's laws were at work here, even though they either denied or ignored God.

Any of God's spiritual laws when followed bring some results, whether the one who practices these laws believes in God or not. These results help validate the spiritual law, but they do not validate the system itself, which may be composed of many falsehoods. Romans 2 teaches that even the pagan had some understanding of moral law, but this did not accredit paganism as the true religion.

What Appleton observed in the Buddhist was not a special and direct work of the Spirit of God, but was simply the out-working of some of God's psychological, moral and spiritual laws.

If one must find a specific scripture to locate the source of whatever light there is in any pagan religion, would it not be better to go to John 1 and Romans 2? The Word is the Light. John the Baptist "was not the light, but came that he might bear witness of the light. There was the true light, even the light which lighteth every man, coming into the world." (John 1:8-9). As Westcott observed: "No man is wholly destitute of the illumination of 'the light.' In nature, and life, and conscience it makes itself felt in various degrees to all." To some extent and to some degree the Gentiles who did not have the revelation of the law "do by nature the things of the law, these, not having the law, are the law unto themselves; in that they show the works of the law written in their hearts, their conscience bearing witness therewith, and their thoughts one with another accusing or else excusing them." (Rom. 2:14-15.) Since moral law is real we would expect that man, without divine revelation, should be able to come to an understanding of some aspects of moral law. To some extent the author has dealt with this in *Communism and the Reality of Moral Law*. In addition to this, man may have preserved to some extent some aspects of the revelation which God made to man in the dawn of human history.

However, these things are not sufficient. (a) Because through sin and rebellion man has perverted moral law in many cases. (b) The revelation of God's reality in nature, and of the reality of moral law as discernible by human reason and experience, is not sufficient. (c) Man has sinned and therefore needs the Saviour. He needs to be redeemed as well as to know truth. Although Christ is in some sense the Light which lighteth every man, John emphasized that although "the world was made through him," the "world knew him not." (John 1:10.)

Third, is Buddhism accredited by God because some of God's spiritual laws may be apprehended and obeyed to some extent by some Buddhists? Certainly not. What are some of the doctrines of Buddhism? (a) It leaves out faith in God. There are those who maintain that Buddhism is atheistic, while there are others who claim it is agnostic. Agnosticism says that the question of the nature of the ultimate reality is beyond the power of man to comprehend, he cannot solve it; therefore, there is no need for man to bother himself with the question. The Spirit of God tells us that God is the Eternal Reality. (b) Buddhism denies the reality of the self. (c) Buddhism rejects the doctrine of mercy which is found in Christ, for Buddhism affirms that there is a universal law of karma which says that one must pay for every wrong one does. (d) Buddhism denies that we can be saved through Jesus Christ. Instead, a man must build up enough merit to overcome all the evil which he has done, so that man finally becomes his own savior. In fact, man is his own savior all the way through. Buddhism thus denies that Jesus Christ is God's Son and the Savior of the world.

Buddhism is not accredited in its various beliefs because of the good results in an individual life which comes from following to some extent a moral or spiritual law.

Pat Boone's beliefs concerning the miraculous gifts of the Spirit are not accredited because he lives by moral and spiritual principles which are set forth by the Spirit in the Bible. The reality of these gifts will have to be decided on other grounds. See the section on "Joy," "Work," and "Happiness."

FALSE WITNESS

Mrs. Joyce Dennis believes that she has been baptized in the Spirit, that each day is a miracle as she and her husband (Dean, who preached for the Northside church in Santa Ana, California) are guarded and guided by God, and that God's

Spirit filled her with supernatural love *(Testimony,* No. 31, 2nd Quarter, 1970, pp. 9-11). She said her husband received the gift of tongues a few weeks after February, 1969, and she received it on Memorial Day, 1969. She said: "We plunged into our new commitment to Jesus, telling everyone who would listen about the new Lord of our lives. Then lines were drawn, and we were on one side and our elders on the other." (10.)

"No one would have believed that during the first week of October, Dean would be fired, our car taken away, his name publicly slandered from the Northside pulpit, his salary severed and be asked to leave our home in thirty days, but all of this *did* happen!" (10.)

The Holy Spirit does not bear false witness, and the Spirit said: "Against an elder receive not an accusation, except at the mouth of two or three witnesses." (I Tim. 5:19). If Joyce Dennis has such miraculous guidance from God, and is baptized in the Spirit, why the following?

First, if they told everyone who would listen, why was it that her husband did not tell the elders, when he first got the gift of tongues, and then offer to resign? Why was he not fair with them instead of hiding his convictions and evading the issue from the spring of 1969 until October, 1969? When the elders began to get some understanding of his beliefs, they tried to help him. Being unable to do so, they had to let him go. Even then they did not know how deeply he was involved in Pentecostalism.

Second, why did she find it so unbelievable that a church of Christ would refuse to support a Pentecostal preacher? Would Pentecostals continue to support one of their preachers if he came to agree with us?

Third, the author has known two of these elders for decades. They did not slander Dean Dennis either from the pulpit or elsewhere. A brief history of the situation was presented from the pulpit. If the elders had known, and had told, the full story of his Pentecostalism, is Pentecostalism of such a nature that such a statement would constitute slander?

Fourth, although Dean Dennis was formally dismissed October 7, and rendered no further services to the church, his salary was continued through October. Does Joyce Dennis think a church should be required to support a preacher so that he could propagate Pentecostalism at their expense?

Fifth, the car did not belong to them, but to the church. Why did she put the elders in a bad light by accusing them of taking away "our car"?

Sixth, they were permitted to remain in the church's house not just thirty days, but almost twice that long. They were allowed to stay through November with all utilities paid except the telephone. They wanted to stay on the same basis through December, and put on some pressure in order to do so, but they were not successful.

Seventh, if she had not thought she was filled with supernatural love, the author shudders to think what she might have said! There was something wrong with her guidance system which let her publish false testimony against the elders.

Eighth, the editor of *Testimony* carries the following statement inside the front cover of the magazine. "Testimonies that glorify the Father, the Son, and the Holy Ghost are welcomed for consideration, subject to the leading of the Holy Spirit as to use, including adaptation or condensation." Why did his guidance system lead him to publish this false witness against the Northside elders?

Ninth, brethren need to know how misguided Joyce Dennis is, for she and her husband think they have a call from God to go to Hawaii and teach people, including any members of the church whom they think are interested in Pentecostalism (*Testimony,* No. 31, p. 11).

HAPPINESS

Does the happiness experienced by some tongues speakers prove they have miraculous gifts? Christians should grow in happiness, but happiness does not prove they have the gifts.

Nichiren Shoshu, which regards itself as the orthodox sect of Nichiren Buddhism, is the faith of the Soka Gakkai movement in Japan. They believe that the most important proof of the truth and superiority of their religion is that it "is borne out by reality—for example, by the fact that people who are committed to it are happy." (Kiyoaki Murata, *Japan's New*

Buddhism, New York: Walker/Weatherhill, 1969, p. 49.)
Christ's word, not our happiness, is the standard (John 12:48;
Jude 3).

HUMAN JESUS?

Dean and Joyce Dennis were among the first converts
whom Pat Boone helped make to Pentecostalism. In a Pentecostal journal, whose editor thinks he is led by the Spirit to
publish testimonies, Joyce Dennis tells some things about her
conversion. For nine or ten years she had felt, most of the
time, that *"something* was wrong . . ." Finally, "I gave up.
Very little really mattered to me, any more."

"With nowhere else to turn, I cried out to God, someone
I didn't really know. I remembered a warm Jesus who had
come to me years before in a novel I read, *The Last Temptation of Christ. That* was the Jesus I wanted—the real, human
One; the One that would just hold me and love me just as I
was. Into His arms I went, and said, 'Teach me, Lord!' His
plan for my life since that time has been quite painful, but
growth *is* painful!" *(Testimony,* No. 31, 1970, p. 10.) We can
sympathize with her despair, but this reference to "a warm
Jesus who had come to me years before in a novel I read . . ."
sickens the author and discredits her guidance system and
that of the editor who would print such a statement. Although
Joyce Dennis refused to give a friend the name of the author
of the novel, when the author phoned her and asked if this
was the novel by Nikos Kazantzakis, she said that it was.

Who was Kazantzakis? He was a Cretan whose lies are
well described by an ancient Cretan prophet: "Cretans are
always liars . . . This testimony is true." (Titus 1:12-13.) Out
of the dark depravity of his reprobate mind, which refused to
retain and honor God in his knowledge (Rom. 1:28), he created a Jesus. Of him we say, "yea, let God be found true, but
every man a liar . . . " (Rom. 3:4.) His teachers, whom he
followed at different times, were Homer, Nietzsche, Bergson,
Buddha, and Lenin *(Saturday Review,* Oct. 14, 1967, p. 51).
Then, it seems, he became his own disciple. Out of the depth
of his arrogance and pride this blasphemous sinner decided to
create a new Christ. "Thus at the age of fifty, he threw all his
energies into what he considered his sole duty—to forge, like

Joyce, the uncreated conscience of his race; to become a priest of the imagination."

"He was not primarily interested in reinterpreting Christ or in disagreeing with, or reforming, the Church. He wanted, rather, to lift Christ out of the Church altogether, and—since in the twentieth century the old era was dead or dying—to rise to the occasion and exercise man's right (and duty) to fashion a new saviour and thereby rescue himself from a moral and spiritual void." *(The Last Temptation of Christ,* New York: Bantam Books, 1968, pp. 491, 495-496).

What kind of Jesus did Kazantzakis create in his novel? His Jesus is not our Jesus, so we shall label his the K-Jesus, or K-J. *First,* K-J beat himself with a "strap studded with two rows of sharp nails . . . " On one occasion he scourged himself until the "blood spurted out and splashed him" (13,79). *Second,* K-J said: "It's my fault that Magdelene descended to prostitution; it's my fault that Israel still groans under the yoke . . . " (14). *Third,* someone came to K-J one night, but he did not know whether it was God or the devil. "Who can tell them apart?" (15). *Fourth,* at his mother's bidding K-J went to Cana to choose a wife. He saw Magdalene: " 'It's her I want, her I want!' he cried, and he held out his hand to give her the rose. But as he did so, ten claws nailed themselves into his head and two frenzied wings beat above him, tightly covering his temples. He shrieked and fell down on his face, frothing at the mouth. His unfortunate mother, writhing with shame, had to throw her kerchief over his head, lift him up in her arms and depart." (25). *Fifth,* after a perverse dream under a tree, K-J said to the tree: " 'Farewell, my sister,' he murmured, 'Last night under your shelter I brought shame upon myself. Forgive me'!" (79). *Sixth,* K-J told Magdalene the whore, at her place of prostitution, that he had many sins; he begged her for forgiveness, and was going to the desert to expiate his sins (80-88). *Seventh,* K-J opened the door to the five foolish virgins, but Jesus Christ left it shut in the parable (210-211; Matt. 25:12-13). *Eighth,* K-J dreamed he was suckling with the lion cubs, his mother appeared in the dream, screamed, and woke him up. K-J then said to his sleeping mother: " 'Why did you wake me up?' he shouted at her. 'I was

324

with my brothers and my mother'!" (240). *Ninth,* K-J committed adultery with Magdalene and said their son would be called "Paraclete, the Comforter!" (440-442). *Tenth,* K-J insanely thought on the cross that he had wives and children, and then realized he was on the cross and that he had not succumbed to the temptation to marry and have children (473-487).

How can these things be? Joyce Dennis thinks she is miraculously guarded each day, and that she has at least some direct guidance *(Testimony,* 10-11). *First,* why, then, would she speak of a "warm Jesus who had come to me years before *in a novel I read* (italics by J.D.B.), *The Last Temptation of Christ. That* was the Jesus I wanted—the real, human One; the One that would just hold me and love me just as I was." *Second,* when the author talked with her on the phone on July 25, 1970, she said the novel showed her the humanity of Jesus. The author replied: "Kazantzakis' Jesus is not our Jesus." We learn of the humanity of Jesus Christ from the New Testament, and not from a blasphemous creation of a reprobate mind. *Third,* Joyce wrote these things *after* she was supposedly baptized in the Holy Spirit. The editor of *Testimony* printed her statement, and he, supposedly, adapts and condenses testimonies as he is led by the Spirit. This case demonstrates that neither he nor Joyce Dennis have any miraculous guidance of the Spirit. If they did, surely the Spirit would have at least warned them against including the reference to the "warm Jesus" in Kazantzakis' novel, and her statement *"That* was the Jesus I wanted . . . "

How does the author explain such a reference? The author does not know the explanation, but he does know it is a demonstration that she does not have the guidance which she thinks she has. The author does not know how she explains it to herself. He told her he planned to write an article on this reference. In her letter of July 26, and obviously before she had seen the article for it was not then completed, she said: "I can only give glory to God that he has counted me worthy to bear this reproach for his name, knowing that through it he will be glorified. I also claim the many blessings that will come to me as a result of what you do." How can a horrible blunder like this be called the bearing of reproach for the name of God? She can get a blessing out of this, if it helps her to re-think and to abandon Pentecostalism. She also wrote: "I will look forward to reading your description of God's work in my life." Obviously, this incident has nothing to do with God's work in her life, but deals with her own terrible blunder.

JOY?

If we really know the Lord, shall we always know joy? Pat tells us that until he received the baptism of the Spirit, he was "more or less a typical Christian: the kind that is determined to be good, no matter how miserable it makes him!" However, he went on to say that "it is not accurate to refer to myself as 'miserable'," but that he had "too little joy." He was living in black-and-white TV while men like David Wilkerson and Harald Bredesen were living in "glorious color." "We are living in color now, with power and peace in our lives that does 'surpass understanding'!" (*Testimony*, 7, 8, 10). *First*, a part of this color was dark; the darkness of the deception of brethren.

Second, if the baptism in the Spirit and the gift of tongues are essential to joy in Christ, there were Christians in the first century who did not have access to this joy, for all did not have these things. The author has salvation in Christ, he has the hope of heaven, he is continually cleansed by the blood of Jesus as he walks in the light, his body is the temple of the Holy Spirit, but the life of joy is lacking because he has not been baptized in the Spirit and does not speak in tongues! He can have all that is essential for salvation, he can have faith, hope, and love, but he must live a drab black and white Christian life because the living color does not come without Holy Spirit baptism. The author is not always on the mountain peaks of joy, but he believes there are other reasons for this than the fact that he does not have the miraculous gifts.

Third, joy is not necessarily an intense emotional experience. If this were so, a life of continued emotional excitement would burn us up emotionally, and would leave on less emotional people the impression that living color is not for them.

Fourth, we may not experience as much joy as is available to us because we need to grow more in faith, because we con-

326

centrate on life's irritants without thinking of our blessings, because we sometimes lose sight of our goal, because we have not grown in love as we ought, because we become discouraged, because we think God has called on us to guarantee the crop instead of asking us to be faithful in sowing, because we do not serve people as we ought, etc. If one must be on the mountain peaks all of the time, would it not be far better to achieve the gift of the more excellent way rather than the gift of tongues and of joy? The more excellent way is the way of love (I Cor. 12:31; 13:1-13). Yes, the author lacks in joy, but he has a greater lack in love. Love, not as an emotion, but as the attitude which actively wills good towards others, and which works no ill. If he were fully mature in this love, he would have constant joy, and that overflowing. He wishes that it were as easy to become mature in love, as it is to deceive one's self into thinking he has the gift of tongues. If an individual follows the instructions Pat followed—to start out speaking in sounds which are not English, and be convinced the Lord will then take over—he cannot miss getting the gift of "tongues." Anyone can start out and then get better as he is encouraged by the results, and by someone else. One loves by willing good, and doing good, but it is far easier to keep uttering sounds without significance than it is to continue to work good and avoid working evil.

The basic lack in the author's life is not miraculous gifts, it is not emotional experiences, it is the lack of maturity in love. The love which suffereth long and is kind, which envieth not, which vaunteth not itself, which does not behave itself unseemly, which seeketh not his own, which is not provoked, which taketh not account of evil, which rejoiceth not in unrighteousness, but rejoiceth with the truth, which "beareth all things, believeth all things, hopeth all things, endureth all things. Love never faileth . . . " (I Cor. 13:4-7). Lord, give us this love and this will be all the living color we need. The author knows, of course, that this is not just a gift to *bestow* but a life in which to *grow;* and, with God's help, the author must do the growing.

Fifth, the miraculous gifts were designed, not to be the source of joy, but the means through which the gospel was revealed and confirmed in order that through Christ men may have the joys of salvation. Furthermore, the gifts themselves could not be utilized in the most profitable way unless they were utilized in love (1 Cor. 13).

Sixth, joy in Christ does not mean that we are always excited, eager, and bubbling. Jesus lamented over Jerusalem (Mat. 23:39). There were times when he was "sorrowful and sore troubled," yea, "exceeding sorrowful." (Matt. 26:37-38). Paul knew the Lord, was baptized in the Spirit, had the miraculous gifts, taught that we are to rejoice in the Lord, but he knew what it was to be tempted and he needed to buffet his body (I Cor. 9:27; 10:1-13).

Paul also knew what it was to suffer tribulation. He did not enjoy the tribulation itself, but, looking to the outcome of tribulation when successfully endured, he rejoiced not only "in hope of the glory of God," but also rejoiced in tribulation (Rom. 5:2-5). The sufferings are real, but are not worthy to be compared with the glory which shall be revealed to us (Rom. 8:17-18). Viewed in this light, we can rejoice in spite of sufferings.

The Christian life is not one life-long shout of joy. It is a life which also involves groaning. "And not only so, but ourselves also, who have the first-fruit of the Spirit, even we ourselves groan within ourselves, waiting for our adoption, to wit, the redemption of our body." (Rom. 8:23). We are now in the body of our humiliation (Phil. 3:21).

Paul knew the Lord, but he also knew the anxiety for the souls of others. "Besides these things that are without, there is that which presseth upon me daily, anxiety for all the churches. Who is weak, and I am not weak? Who is caused to stumble, and I burn not?" (II Cor. 11:28-29).

Paul was sore troubled because of the conduct of the woman with a spirit of divination (Acts 16:16-18).

Although we should not fret ourselves because of evil doers (Psa. 37:1), if the emotions which accompany joy are the only emotions we know, something is lacking in our Christianity.

Paul knew the Lord, yet such is the weakness of man that even Paul had to be encouraged at times so as not to be afraid. If he did not need such encouragement, why did the Lord say: "Be not afraid, but speak and hold not thy peace: for

I am with thee, and no man shall set on thee to harm thee: for I have much people in this city." (Acts 18:9-10).

Seventh, Christians should grow in joy, but joy in itself does not prove that what one believes is true. There are people who have found joy in different and differing things. Some people think that they have been saved because they feel good. The Biblical position is that one knows that he is saved, and as a result he feels good. The Lord has promised the remission of sins to the believing penitent who is baptized into Christ (Acts 2:38; 22:16; Rom. 6:3-5; Gal. 3:26-27). The eunuch was baptized into Christ. He knew that Christ would fulfill His promise. Therefore, he knew that Christ had forgiven him. As a result of this knowledge, based on his faith in God's integrity, he went on his way rejoicing (Acts 8:39). He did not know he was a Christian because he felt good. He felt good because he knew he was a Christian.

Eighth, a lie when believed, or an experience when misinterpreted, will have the same emotional impact on one that it would have if the thing were true and rightly interpreted. Some of Jacob's sons set the stage so that they knew that Jacob would draw the conclusion that Joseph was dead. It had the same emotional impact on Jacob that it would have had if Joseph had actually been dead. But Joseph was not dead. Yet Jacob said: "It is my son's coat; an evil beast hath devoured him; Joseph is without doubt torn in pieces. And Jacob rent his garments, and put sackcloth upon his loins, and mourned for his son many days . . . he said, For I will go down to Sheol to my son mourning. And his father wept for him" (Gen. 37:33-35). The individual who believes he has the gift of tongues will have the same emotional reaction that he would have if he actually had the gift of tongues. For it is his conviction that he actually has the gift.

JUDGING THE AUTHOR

The author does not think that the following indicate that Joyce Dennis has miraculous guidance from God. *First,* in a phone conversation on July 25, 1970 she told the author that Pat Boone had been sending them the material which the author is putting in his book, and that the author was slandering Pat. Pat has never even hinted to the author that he believes such a charge. He does not believe it, but Joyce made

329

the charge. She also said the author was telling lies and slander about her in his proposed article. *Second,* when she wrote the author on July 26 she said she was in the flesh when she talked with him, but that God had forgiven her. The author had not held it against her, for he realizes how confused these emotionalists are. Her confusion was also evident in the letter. The second sentence said: "I come to you now not in eloquence of words or speech, but in the power of the Holy Spirit." She did not come in the power in which Paul came (I Cor. 2:1-5; Rom. 15:18-19; Heb. 2:3-4). In the same letter she said: "I can understand your discomfort as you see such tremendous things happening in lives today. As we talked it was so evident to me the lack of the fruits of the Spirit in your life. You have no peace, joy and love, and if you have a marriage, it is a miserable one lacking in spiritual and physical communication." She was not certain that the author was married, but she was confident of what his marriage would be like if he were married. Neither the author's wife, nor their six children would agree with this evaluation of our marriage. People like Joyce are so misguided they confuse their impulses sometimes with the leading of the Spirit. When the author asked her to sustain her charges concerning slander and his marriage, etc., she quoted and paraphrased Col. 1:3-14, said she had need of the author's prayers and love and she also said: "Praise God I cannot be so positive about your spiritual condition nor you of mine! That again, frees each of us to love one another and to God who alone is our judge." We are free to love, and we must leave judgment to God, even if we have evidence concerning a person's spiritual condition. *Third,* the author believes that this type of accusation helps prove that these people do not have the guidance which they claim. Furthermore when they correct errors of this kind it is not the result of supernatural guidance.

LIVES CHANGED?

Tongues speakers sometimes argue for the reality of their gift by affirming that their lives have been changed; therefore, this must be a genuine gift from God. *First,* the author had an uncle who supposedly was baptized in the Holy Spirit and performed and witnessed miracles. He left the church and became a member of the Reorganized Church of Jesus Christ of Latter-day saints. He could make some of the same arguments about changed lives; but anyone who understands the Bible, and the finality of the New Covenant, realizes that God did not lead him or anyone else into a movement founded by Joseph Smith, Jr. The reign of Christ, which was proclaimed to the world on the first Pentecost after Christ's resurrection continues until the end of time (Acts 2:34-35; I Cor. 15:24-28; Rev. 20:11-15). Smith claimed that the reign of Christ, which was going on in Paul's day (Col. 1:13; Eph. 1:19-23), was ended by apostasy, and a different dispensation began with the work of Joseph Smith, Jr.

Second, there are those whose lives have been changed morally speaking, and who have become more zealous. They think they are new creatures in Christ, but they have not yet been born of water and the Spirit (John 3:1-5).

Third, the individual who thinks he has the gift of tongues, believes that it is from God. He thinks it has brought him into the presence of God, and into a relationship with God, which he has never before experienced. He thinks it is a miraculous proof, in his own life, of the truth of Christianity. In the light of other scriptures, he realizes that he ought to be grateful to God for His gifts. Furthermore, from the Scriptures he has already known, or can shortly know, the kind of moral life God wants him to live. Motivated by all of these considerations, he makes even a greater effort to yield his life to God. His conviction of the reality of the gift results in the same impact on his manner of life that would result if he actually had the gift.

An individual who was sick, but had no organic illness, can be healed by a modern "healer." He is convinced that he has been miraculously healed. He may then live a changed life. However, his conviction, and the results which flowed from it, do not prove that he had experienced a miraculous healing.

Fourth, on the other hand, there have been individuals whose lives were far from what they ought to be, who actually had the gift of tongues. There were tongues speakers in Corinth who were childish, proud, and disorderly. Did this prove they did not have the genuine gift of tongues?

331

Fifth, our lives should be changed, but a changed life does not prove the reality of the gift of tongues today. Pattison observed that: "Glossolalia does not miraculously change people in a supernatural sense, but participating in glossolalia as a part of a larger social and personal commitment may play an important role in the change of direction in participants' lives." (85).

Pattison also observed that: "Many adherents of the glossolalia movement assert that the experience has made a change in their lives, has improved their style and quality of personality and life. Clinicians have been hesitant to accept such testimonials. Yet a careful study of non-pathological mystical experiences, such as the work of Deikman, Ludwig, Underhill, Sedman, and Salzman, have illustrated that mystical experience often in a religious context, can be an integrative emotional experience that results in an altered life style with subsequent improvement in life adaptation" (77). It should be observed that he indicates that although it is often in a religious context it is not necessarily in such a context. Therefore, this change in itself is not proof that the experience is supernatural in origin.

Some may ask: Since you admit that some people have changed for the better on the basis of this experience, why not recommend that some seek such experiences; or at least, why do you oppose these experiences? *First,* we realize that some people have been changed for the better because they have become Buddhists, but we do not therefore recommend Buddhism, nor cease to deny that Buddhism is God's message to man.

Second, we are not concerned just with what works for some people regardless of all other considerations.

Third, the good can be accomplished by the Lord without these misleading experiences.

Fourth, much harm has resulted from people seeking, and finding, such experiences. When one bases his life on this type of experience, he does not have an adequate foundation on which to judge truth and falsehood. Of course, some of these individuals have had enough of a background in the Bible to try to justify matters by the Bible, and they do not usually go to the excesses that some others go. But excesses of one type or another can be found in all of these groups. Furthermore, on the basis of "experience" one could not oppose these excesses, for they are "justified" by the "experiences" of those who engage in them.

Fifth, it is always right to uphold the teaching of the Bible regardless of what is done by some of those who misunderstand these matters.

PAT AND THE GIFTS

As has been pointed out more than once, the question of the gifts involves not only discussion, but also demonstration. It is one thing to talk about them and to reason that they are for us today, it is another thing to demonstrate them in one's own life. Pat believes that all of the gifts are for us if we ask in faith. In commenting on a prayer for a miracle, which a young man based on Mk. 11:24, Pat said: "All he had to do was to believe it." *(Christian Life,* July 1970, p. 50.) Therefore, if Pat does not have *all* of the gifts, he lacks them only because he has not asked for them in faith. If Pat has any or all of the gifts they will demonstrate themselves in his teaching, powers, and life. Does Pat claim and demonstrate that the following gifts are manifested in his life?

First, is Pat an apostle of Christ with the authority, powers, and qualifications of a Peter or a Paul? The apostleship was a gift (Eph. 4:8-11; I Cor. 12:28). Has Pat seen the Lord? Can he confer gifts through the laying on of hands? Does he write epistles which are the commandment of the Lord? (I Cor. 14:37). If he is not such an apostle, why does it take so much more faith to get the gift of apostleship than that of tongues? Where is your faith, Pat?

Second, is Pat a prophet? (Eph. 4:8-11; I Cor. 12:28). "But he that prophesieth speaketh unto men edification, and exhortation, and consolation." Does he speak "either by way of revelation, or of knowledge, or of prophesying, or of teaching?" And these by inspiration? (I Cor. 14:4, 6). Has this author been carrying on a discussion with apostle or prophet Pat, and yet an apostle or prophet who does not want to be quoted or mentioned in the author's writings? Furthermore, Pat concealed, not revealed, his beliefs from the brethren for a time.

Third, even Pat does not think that the word of wisdom was manifested by him in our discussions (I Cor. 12:8). See "Wisdom."

Fourth, does Pat have the "word of knowledge"? (12:8). What does Pat understand about the Bible that the author either does not understand or cannot learn without any special gifts? Although the author has made no such claims in our discussion, Pat has indicated that he thinks the author has a greater knowledge of the Bible than he, Pat, has. How could this be? If Pat has a greater knowledge of the Bible than does the author it would be due to one or more such factors as the following: (a) He has outstudied the author. (b) He has a keener mind and grasps things quicker than the author. (c) He is less prejudiced than the author. (d) He has had better teachers than the author. It would not be because Pat has the gifts and the author does not.

If Pat has ·the gift of knowledge, as well as other gifts, why is he so confused on some passages of Scripture? Why has he misinterpreted at least some of them? Why is he so confused concerning the qualifications of apostles of Christ? Was Paul, or one of the prophets, confused?

If Pat has the gift of knowledge, and other gifts, why does he not infallibly interpret some of the hard scriptures for us? The majority of passages which other Bible students have found hard, are hard for Pat. If he learns their meaning, he must learn in the same way we learn—by perspiration and not by direct inspiration!

Fifth, does Pat have the miraculous gift of faith? (I Cor. 12:9). If so, perhaps he will walk on the water (Matt. 14:28-32). Pat, read Mk. 11:24 and remember that: "All he had to do was to believe it." The swimming pool is in your back yard, Pat, so start walking in faith. Does he believe that if after walking for awhile his faith diminishes that Jesus will be there to take hold of him and say: "O thou of little faith, wherefore didst thou doubt?" (Matt. 14:31). This is plain speaking, but what else should be said to someone, even if he is very dear, who neither demonstrates nor desists?

Sixth, does Pat have "gifts of healings"? (I Cor. 12:9). Does he do any better than some of the pagan healers? Than healers such as Asa A. Allen? Than some psychologists? Than

334

some nutritionists? Does he match the wide variety and the characteristics of, the healing miracles in the Bible?

Seventh, does he have the gift of "working of miracles"? (I Cor. 12:10). If so, does he match the wide variety, and the characteristics of the miracles of Christ? If he has the power to work miracles, why is he so confused that he calls some things miracles which obviously were not miracles? For example, the quieting, but not the cure, of the young man who was on a drug trip; and the gradual recovery of a boy from asthma? *(Christian Life*, July, 1970).

Eighth, as we have already asked: Does he have the gift of prophecy, and is he therefore a prophet? (12:10, 28).

Ninth, does he have the gift of "discernings of spirits"? (12:10). If so, what false teachers, who claimed to be inspired, has he exposed? Why has he been so deceived as to think that some people who have not been baptized into Christ, are baptized in the Spirit and endowed with miraculous gifts?

Tenth, does Pat have the gift of tongues (languages)? (12:10). So far as the author knows, he never has claimed to have spoken in a foreign language by inspiration. He can make non-English sounds, but so can the author.

Eleventh, does Pat have the gift of "the interpretation of tongues"? (12:10). If so, will he tell us what he says in tongues, and what others say in tongues, so that men may be edified? (14:1-6, 26-28).

The author is not a prophet. However, he does predict that for the time being, Pat will neither put up by demonstrating any and all of the gifts, nor will he hush up by ceasing to say that all of the gifts are for us and all we need to do is to ask in faith. For if Pat does hush up, it means that he has ceased to believe that if we ask for them in faith all of the gifts, or even part of the gifts, are for us here and now. It would mean that he must abandon Pentecostalism.

The author hopes that no one is offended because he insists that if Pat has the gifts he ought to demonstrate that he has them, and use them to edify the church, evangelize the world, and miraculously confirm the gospel.

RELATIONSHIP?

Aren't they seeking relationship with Jesus, and not just an experience or so? *First*, their motives cannot be evaluated by us unless we know what their motives are. *Second,* our relationship with Jesus must be sought through responding to Him as He has directed in His word.

SHAKARIAN

"Shakarian forecasted both the collapse of the American economy within two years and the possibility of a Communist takeover. The root of the problem? 'Poor people (especially Negroes) are being gouged'." *(Christianity Today,* August 1, 1969, p. 997.) Time will soon test this prophecy.

TESTIMONY ARTICLE

There were those who bought copies of *Testimony* and mailed it to many ministers and churches on the West Coast. Since the article had been published without Pat's knowledge and consent, someone who defended Pat charged that those who did this were the ones who were sowing discord and making an issue out of the matter. *First,* the article was written by Pat, it expressed his beliefs, and the claim of the gift of tongues had already been made known by Pat in *Christian Life* for November 1969. Pat had written the article for publication at a later date, so the only thing about which he had to complain was that it upset his timetable for the disclosure of his beliefs to the brethren. *Second,* does Pat think the Pentecostal who published it in *Testimony* was led by the Spirit. If he was, why object? If he was not, why, since this was an important matter, didn't the Spirit prevent it? Why didn't the Spirit warn Pat about letting the article out of his hands, *if* Pat has the direct guidance of the Spirit which he claims? *Third,* what led Dean Dennis, whom Pat helped convert to the tongues movement, to circulate it by giving it to an elder in Santa Ana? What led Ben Franklin to send a copy of *Testimony* to the author, and to Perry Cotham who wrote an article on it for the *Gospel Advocate?* Were they guilty of sowing discord and making this an issue? *Fourth,* how were the brethren, who circulated this issue of *Testimony,* to know it had been published prematurely and without Pat's consent? The article made clear Pat's position, and settled the controversy among brethren as to what his true position was. What, then, was wrong with mailing it to others? *Fifth,* because a Pentecostal let the cat out of the bag earlier than Pat intended, it is unjust to accuse brethren of creating discord by circulating Pat's article. No one guided by the Spirit would make or endorse such an accusation. But Pat included this accusation in a letter to the author. He mentioned it as having been made by a minister, and Pat passed it on to the author without any indication that he in any way disapproved of it. *Sixth,* the confusion over the article in *Testimony* is compounded by information contained in issue No. 31 of *Testimony* (Second Quarter, 1970). Thomas R. Nickel, the editor, wrote that he had prepared other material for that issue. "Then, in a lightning-like maneuver, God took over and completely changed the issue." (No. 31, p. 14). Among other things, George Otis called and read Pat's testimony to him over the phone. "The Lord directed us to run the testimony in the forthcoming issue. We asked George if he could get Pat's permission, which he did, along with that of Robert Walker, who is bringing out Pat's book, *A New Song,* in cooperation with Bible Voice, in August . . . and *Testimony* No. 30 soon became a reality, by the Hand of God!" (p. 15). He then spoke of the response and said: "Yes, God did do such a thing as this, and to Him belongs the Glory!" (p. 15). (a) George Otis is the one who was studying and praying with Pat when Pat supposedly was baptized in the Spirit and received the gift of tongues (No. 30, p. 8). Pat told the author that he did not give permission for the testimony to be published in *Testimony.* The author believes Pat. The author assumes that George Otis, who is supposedly "Spirit-filled" was confused and that he did not realize that he did not have Pat's permission; or else Nickel was confused and did not rightly understand Otis; or Otis assumed that he had the authority to speak in Pat's name. (b) The author knows that Pat and Shirley were caught off-guard by the appearance of their article in *Testimony.* (c) Pat and Shirley thought they were being led by the Spirit to make their beliefs public later. If the editor of *Testimony* is right, God directed him to publish the article which destroyed the Spirit's timetable (if Pat and Shirley are right). If this is true, God failed to inform the Spirit of the change of plans, or the Spirit failed to inform Pat. How can Pat explain these things to himself? If he rejects Nickel's claim that God led him to publish Pat's testimony, how can he explain his belief that God did lead him to do it? Nickel has as much proof as Pat that he is directly guided by God. On the other hand, if Pat accepts Nickel's claims, how does Pat explain his belief that he was guided by the Spirit in a course of action which was defeated by Nickel's action? Pat has as much evidence as Nickel has that he is directly guided by the Spirit, at times at least.

One does not have to know much about the Bible in order to know that this confusion is not the work of God. God, in His providence, does let self-deceived and misguided human beings interpret their own impulses as the voice of the Spirit. This is because God has left them free to do as they will. It is the testimony of the Spirit in the Bible that such confusion is not of God.

Would it not have been better to have worked this problem out quietly and without all the disturbance that came through the circulation of the article in *Testimony? First,* it would have been better for Pat to have studied with some of us before he accepted the Pentecostal position. *Second,* it would have been better if, once he came to these convictions, he had let the brethren know instead of trying to keep them in the dark until his book comes out. *Third,* it would have been better if Pat had talked with the elders at Inglewood long before he did. *Fourth,* once Pat's position was made public by his own statement in *Testimony,* although it was published without his permission, what were brethren to do? Hide it? Deny it? Act as if they did not know Pat's position? *Fifth,* should brethren really be disturbed at what, in essence, is Pat's complaint—that *Testimony* upset Pat's timetable of the disclosure of his position to the brethren? *Sixth,* Pat ought to ask himself whether in the providence of God this was not God's way of upsetting his timetable so as to keep his book, and the later publication of the article, from having as great an impact on brethren as Pat planned for them to have.

WORK

Hasn't the baptism of the Holy Spirit made Pat Boone a harder worker? Pat spoke of his Christian life having no real power, and that "witnessing was an embarrassing affair, especially among my show-business friends, and I felt a need to prove that I was no 'square,' that I could fit right in any-

338

where, between my Church World and my Career World!" (*Testimony*, No. 30, 7). *First*, we have already commented on the emotional impact of even a misinterpreted experience.

Second, none of us are witnesses in the sense the apostles were (Acts 1:8; 2:32).

Third, the Spirit through the word, did not lead Pat into a strategy of deception, such as the supposed guidance of the Spirit, since he was "baptized in the Spirit," led him into with reference to the brethren. In the midst of controversy over his position, he did not reveal his convictions, but deliberately left the brethren in the dark because he thought this was what the Spirit was guiding him to do. Pat may have been embarrassed at times when it came to declaring his faith among his show-business friends, but he declared it anyhow. The courage of a man is even greater when in spite of embarrassment he declares his faith. He should be far more concerned about the deception into which he was "led" than about the fact that "witnessing was an embarrassing affair." The author is pained to be so plain in speaking of his beloved friend, but the tears which are in his eyes as he writes cannot wash out these words which need to be written. The author loves Pat and Shirley enough to bear this pain and even to run the risk of hurting our personal friendship.

Fourth, Pat put his finger on the real problem, the problem which confronts and tempts us all, and it was not the problem of a lack of baptism in the Spirit. In the paragraph which followed the above quotation, he said: "I know now that this was the real heart of the problem. I was more concerned about what the public, the industry, and my church brethren expected of me than I was about what my Lord expected of me! I hoped that, if I could somehow work out a compromise between church acceptance and public acceptance, maybe Jesus would accept me, too.

"But my compromise didn't work! Jesus said, 'Seek ye first the kingdom of God and all of these things will be added unto you.' He also said, 'You cannot serve God and mammon.'

"After several years of compromise, half-hearted occasional obedience, wavering faith, some grievous mistakes, and a growing awareness of separation from my Heavenly Father, I finally found myself on my knees, begging God to take over

339

my life completely, to become my Lord, to give me the peace, the joy, the power that Jesus had promised those who would truly seek Him." *(Testimony,* No. 30, 7-8).

The author knew of some of Pat's faults, but he felt that Pat had borne up under his temptations better than some preachers had with theirs. Of course, this does not justify anyone. We believe Pat, in spite of his mistakes, did a lot of good and showed a lot of dedication. However, it is a shame that when he decided to cease seeking compromise, and tried to make a complete surrender beyond what he had at least done for some time, that he also sought the gift of tongues which, in the way that he was taught to seek it, was the easiest thing in the world about which to be self-deceived. Thinking he has miraculous gifts, he has now become bolder, but this no more proves him right than Jacob's deep sorrow, based on a misinterpretation of events, proved Joseph was dead.

ZEAL?

There are those who maintain that their increased zeal and devotion prove that the experience is the real thing. *First,* more zeal is certainly needed in most congregations. Although there are many people with zeal, there are too many who are bench warmers. If we reflect sufficiently on who we are, whose we are, what are our privileges and responsibilities, the needs of man, and the love of God, our zeal will increase.

Second, zeal within itself does not prove that one is on the right track. Unbelieving Jews had a zeal for God, *but not according to knowledge* (Rom. 10:1-4). Saul thought he ought to do many things contrary to the name of Jesus of Nazareth, and his zeal was such that he even went beyond Jerusalem with the determination to stamp out the church as a heretical movement (Acts 8:3; 9:1-2; 22:3; 26:9-11; Phil. 3:6).

Third, the individual who thinks that he has been given a miraculous gift, would find it very natural to conclude that he ought to be grateful and do more work for Christ. Of course, we ought to have this gratitude because of what Christ did for us on the cross, and all that this, His resurrection, His reign, and His coming mean to us.

Furthermore, the individual who thinks that he has a gift, and because it has had such an emotional impact on his own

340

life, is apt to become more zealous for he wants others to have this intense and thrilling experience.

Fourth, in some cases it brings increased zeal because it involves the stimulation of a change of pace. When one becomes a Christian he may have a good deal of zeal. It may be that he became a Christian in his youth. As time goes on, however, it is easy to become involved in so many things that we lose some of our zeal, and Christianity may have lost its freshness to us. We may tend to become stale. Problems may develop within our own families. We may feel frustrated. Then we may get something, or hear something, which is a bit new to us, and it quickens us. Individuals may have found their spiritual life has become a humdrum habit. They realize that this is not what it should be. As a result they begin to look for something new. They hear that some believe the miraculous gifts are for us today. By letting go and speaking in something which is not English they become stimulated further and out flow the sounds. They think that the Spirit has taken over, and that they now have the gift of tongues. Thrill and excitement again become a part of their religion; or maybe they find excitement for the first time. This is so different from what they have been experiencing that they think everyone else ought to know about it. So they go to work with renewed zeal.

They begin to read the Bible again. They may be motivated by many things. They may be motivated by gratitude, they may be searching to see if there are deeper things that God has for them, they may be hunting for additional confirmation that they have the gift of tongues, and they may be searching for reasons and scriptures which they can use to convince others that the gifts are for us today.

In a phone conversation on February 28, 1970 with the author, Pat Boone said that he knew he had become "incredibly devoted to God," and this could not be of the devil. Now when he reads the Bible, on a plane, for example, he sometimes weeps, whereas in the past he would go to sleep. The author thinks that Pat had played down too much his past spiritual life, because he is so impressed with his emotional experiences now. The author does not think that Pat is inspired by the devil in these things. Instead, they are a very natural reaction

341

to his conviction that God has given him some marvelous gifts. The emotional impact of this belief and the gratitude have moved him to try to be more devoted.

Pat also mentioned his willingness to sacrifice his career if necessary. We do not doubt this, but we have seen this splendid type of conviction in Pat in more than one case in his "pre-gift" days.

CHAPTER XXI

THE HOLY SPIRIT: QUESTIONS AND ANSWERS

ACTS 19

"Did ye receive the Holy Spirit when ye believed?" (Acts 19:2). Does not this indicate they could have received the Spirit without Paul's help? Yes. *First,* if they had been baptized under the great commission they would have known about the Spirit and would have received the gift of the Spirit when they were baptized (Acts 2:38). *Second,* if Paul had in mind the miraculous gifts of the Spirit, there were other apostles who could bestow the Spirit in a miraculous way. *Third,* we have no Pauls to lay on hands and to confer the Spirit in a miraculous way.

BAPTISM OF THE SPIRIT

Does Pat think the baptism of the Spirit, of Matt. 3:11, is miraculous and that he has received this baptism? Yes *(Testimony,* No. 30, p. 10). *First,* some think Matt. 3:11 does not refer to anything miraculous, but simply to the idea that the Spirit fills the body of Christ, and those in Christ's body are in this sense covered by the Spirit. The author does not accept this interpretation of Matt. 3:11.

Second, some think that all are baptized in the Spirit, but that only in certain ones in the first century did the Spirit will to work in a miraculous way. The author is convinced that this baptism involved the miraculous (Acts 1:5, 8; 2:1-4; 11:15-17; 10:46-47).

Third, if all have it, and if it is miraculous, then all who are God's children are baptized in the Spirit. If we are not thus baptized and perform miracles, we are not God's children. Furthermore, this is not a matter just for *argumentation* but for *demonstration.* Each individual, or at least individuals in each congregation, must possess all these gifts and match the miracles of the New Testament as well as harmonize with New Testament teaching.

Fourth, if Matt. 3:11 were the only passage on this subject, the author would conclude this baptism was for all. The promise, however, was limited by other passages. (a) The promise was not universal to everyone who heard John speak, for some were chaff who would be baptized with fire (Matt. 3:11-12). (b) When Jesus mentioned this promise, He promised it not to everyone, but to the apostles not many days hence (Acts 1:4-5).

Fifth, how do we know He had reference to the apostles?

(1) He was speaking specifically to the apostles (Acts 1:2-5).

(2) It was promised to those who would do the work of witnessing when they received the power (Acts 1:8). The apostles were the special group of witnesses. Although Justus had seen the Lord he was not the one who became "a witness with us of his resurrection" (1:22-26). The apostles were the witnesses (2:14, 37, 32).

(3) The apostles were Galileans (1:11), and the ones who were Galileans were the ones on whom the Spirit came (2:7).

(4) Acts 1:26 identifies the apostles as the ones who in the next verses received the baptism (1:26; 2:1-4).

(5) Mockers accused the tongues speakers of being drunken, and when Peter denied this charge he denied it concerning the apostles; so they were the ones thus charged (2:12, 14, 15).

(6) The ones who received the baptism of the Spirit received power, and the apostles are the only ones mentioned as working miracles until after the apostles had laid hands on the seven (2:43; 3:1; 5:12).

(7) Those who received the baptism of the Spirit spoke in tongues which everyone understood (Acts 2:4, 6, 8, 11). Who understands Pat's tongues? As far as we know, even Otis, who persuaded him to get the gift, did not understand when Pat was baptized in the Spirit, supposedly, and spoke and sang in tongues *(Testimony,* No. 30, p. 10).

(8) Those who were baptized in the Spirit on Pentecost preached the gospel by direct inspiration. The Spirit came in miraculous manifestations, and inspiration, in order to enable them to do this (Lk. 24:46-49; Acts 1:4, 8). Is Pat preaching the gospel by direct inspiration? Can we quote him as we quote the apostles and prophets of the New Testament? Can we continue stedfastly in Pat's doctrine, as well as that of the apostles? (Acts 2:42).

(9) When they received the baptism of the Holy Spirit the apostles immediately started working under the great commission and publicly proclaimed the gospel. This was what the Spirit came to enable them to do. Pat thinks he received baptism and tongues, but only Mr. Otis was there. Instead of publicly preaching the gospel with the public's realization that he had received miraculous manifestations, Pat used his tongues in secret. He kept this hidden from the brethren for around a year and a half. When brethren were engaged in controversy concerning his beliefs in these matters, when some were saying he was off on these matters, Pat stood by and made statements which deliberately left brethren in the dark. He knowingly and consciously let brethren publicly and in print defend him when he was aware of the fact they would not have defended him as they did if they had known his actual beliefs and practices. He let brethren deny his actual beliefs. When he was on Oral Roberts' program both Pat and Oral Roberts knew that Pat believed he had the gift of tongues. This was what Oral Roberts meant when he asked Pat to tell them how God moved in on him and Shirley. Pat answered in such a way that the truth about Pat's position was hidden from the audience, including brethren who listened to the program. Pat was so self-deceived that he thought the Spirit was leading him in this path of deception and therefore it was not really a path of deception.

The author does not know whether Mr. Otis has been baptized into Christ, but if he has not, when Pat received the baptism of the Spirit and spoke in tongues, why didn't he do like Peter did and tell his audience—in this case Pat's audience was Mr. Otis—to repent and be baptized in Jesus' name unto the remission of sins? (Acts 2:38). Why didn't he exhort Mr. Otis to save himself from that crooked generation? Why didn't Mr. Otis receive the word and enter Christ through baptism into Christ? (Acts 2:40-41).

(10) When the apostles went forth under the great commission preaching the gospel by inspiration, God confirmed their word by miraculous signs. These fulfilled Jesus' promises that: "And these signs shall accompany them that believe: in my name shall they cast out demons; they shall speak with new tongues (languages men understood if these

were their native tongues or one they had learned, Acts 2:4, 6, 8, 11) ; they shall take up serpents, and if they drink any deadly thing, it shall in no wise hurt them; they shall lay hands on the sick, and they shall recover." (Mk. 16:17-18). "And they went forth, and preached everywhere, the Lord working with them, and confirming the word by the signs that followed. Amen." (Mk. 16:20).

Pat did not go forth, he did do some work in secret in so far as the brethren throughout the country were concerned, and there was no such public confirmation of his preaching.

Sixth, the next case of baptism in the Holy Spirit is implied, but not expressly stated. After Saul became a Christian he evidently was baptized in the Holy Spirit for he was not a whit behind the other apostles, and had all the miraculous signs of an apostle as well as the other qualifications. He learned the gospel by inspiration (Gal. 1:11-12), and taught by inspiration (I Cor. 14:37; II Thess. 2:15). Paul straightway *publicly* proclaimed the gospel (Acts 9:19-20). Pat, before he preached it to the brethren, left them in the dark for around a year and a half. His plan was to first let them know about it in a book which was scheduled for publication around August (which, by design or coincidence, was the same period of time his movie, *The Cross and the Switchblade,* about Wilkerson's work was scheduled to be released). The strategy and timing, Pat thought, was due to the leading of the Spirit.

Seventh, the only other case of baptism in the Spirit, recorded in the Bible, is that of the household of Cornelius. As in Saul's case, God inspired someone else to know about it, and there was therefore additional confirmation of the reality of the event. An apostle and six Jewish brethren were present and heard the tongues speakers magnify God (Acts 11:12; 10:46). These individuals were baptized (Acts 10:48). If Mr. Otis, who was with Pat, had been baptized in the Spirit in times past, but had not been baptized in water into Christ, why didn't Pat baptize Mr. Otis since Otis, not Pat, needed water baptism? When what Peter had done was questioned by some brethren, Peter publicly explained the situation, and the church accepted it (Acts 11:1-4, 15-18). To have refused to have done so would have been to withstand God (Compare Acts 11:17). When brethren were in controversy about Pat's

346

beliefs and conduct, he made some public statements which left the brethren in the dark. Was Pat afraid we would withstand him and thus be withstanding the work of the Spirit of God? He did not indicate this was his reason for keeping brethren in the dark.

The baptism of the Spirit (Acts 11:15-18; 2:1-4) came on Cornelius' household before their water baptism in order to reveal and confirm the truth that the Gentiles were to receive the gospel without being bound by the law (Acts 11:15-18; 2:1-4). This case was mentioned later (Acts 11:1-18;; 15:8-12), but it was never repeated. This truth was fully and finally established for all who would accept the will of God in this matter. The author has discussed this case at length in *The Case of Cornelius*.

We benefit from the baptism of the Holy Spirit which came on certain ones in the first century. Through this baptism of the Spirit the gospel was revealed and confirmed so that we now have the faith once for all delivered to the saints. The baptism of the Holy Spirit was designed by God to accomplish this, and this has been accomplished, so that there is now no need for the miraculous baptism in the Spirit. The author has discussed the baptism in the Spirit in greater detail in *The Hub of the Bible, Miracles or Mirages?* and *The Holy Spirit and the Christian*.

Eighth, some may ask whether the following scripture teaches that all receive the miraculous baptism of the Spirit. "For in one Spirit were we all baptized into one body, whether Jew or Greek . . . " (I Cor. 12:13). There is but one baptism which is a part of the unity of the faith which we are to keep (Eph. 4:1-6). If this one baptism is Holy Spirit baptism, why teach that water baptism is for the gospel age? However, the baptism of the great commission, which is bound on all in coming into Christ, is water baptism (Matt. 28:19; Acts 8:37; 10:47-48; 22:16). The new birth which involves the Spirit and water, is not the baptism of the Holy Spirit (John 3:3-5). Water baptism, which is into the name of the Father, the Son, and the Holy Spirit (Matt. 28:19), is into Christ's body or church (Gal. 3:26-27). The baptism mentioned in I Cor. 12:13 was into Christ's body or church (I Cor. 12:13, 27, 28). It is, therefore, water baptism which is the baptism commanded by the Holy Spirit. No one was ever commanded to be baptized in the Holy Spirit. It was a promise to certain ones whom God had in mind. Water baptism is a command which men must obey (Mk. 16:16; Acts 22:16).

This baptism is into the one body. If the baptism of the Holy Spirit is the one baptism binding today, and if it brought one into the body of Christ, why did Cornelius who had received the baptism of the Spirit have to accept water baptism in order to come into Christ and have his sins forgiven? (Acts 2:38). Peter surely taught the same thing about the purpose of baptism to Cornelius that he taught the Jews (Acts 2:38; 10:47-48; compare 22:16; Gal. 3:26-27). One is not in the one body until he has received the baptism of I Cor. 12:13, but one comes into the body through water baptism. This, then, is the baptism of I Cor. 12:13.

Holy Spirit baptism was not performed by men, but was directly from heaven without being done through human agents. The baptism of the great commission involves the hands of men (Acts 8:38). The baptism into Christ which the Corinthians received was administered by men (Acts 18:8; I Cor. 1:14-16).

The baptism in water is unto the remission of sins (Acts 2:38; 10:48; 11:14; Mk. 16:15-16). Holy Spirit baptism was not unto the remission of sins. This is never stated as its purpose, and if it were its purpose, Cornelius would not have needed water baptism.

All who were in the one body had been baptized in or by whatever baptism Paul mentioned in I Cor. 12:13. All in the first century did not receive the miraculous baptism of the Spirit. Pat believes that he was in the body of Christ around twenty-one years before he received Holy Spirit baptism (*Testimony*, 7). How, then, can I Cor. 12:13 be the baptism of the Holy Spirit with miraculous manifestations?

It is not *with* one Spirit, as if the Spirit is the element in which we were baptized, but *in* or *by* one Spirit as the agent in that He has commanded it. Just as Jesus may be said to preach to the Gentiles in preaching to them through others (Eph. 2:17; compare John 4:1-2), just so the Spirit may be said to baptize although He employs men as the agents to do the baptizing. We are baptized in submission to the authority of the Spirit. Men can say Jesus is Lord only "in the Holy Spirit" (I Cor. 12:3). If the Spirit had not revealed to the people on Pentecost, before they became Christians, that they could know that Jesus is both Lord and Christ, they could never have known and acknowledged that Jesus is Lord (Acts 2:36-37). This faith came by hearing the word of God, which is also the word of the Spirit (Rom. 10:8-15, 17). In order that men might be able to say, "in the Holy Spirit," that Jesus is Lord, the Spirit used the agents (apostles) and the instrument (the word) in order to let Israel, and us, know that Jesus is Lord. This is the way the Corinthians learned about Jesus (Acts 18:5-11). Men then had to acknowledge this, or reject the Savior. Through the inspired men, and the word they were inspired to speak, the Holy Spirit has let us know how we are to come into Christ. The Spirit has told us to be baptized into Christ. In or by the authority, and in submission to the instructions, of the one Spirit men were baptized into Christ (Acts 2:36-41). They then received the indwelling of the Spirit and also drank or partook of the word of the Spirit. As J. W. McGarvey pointed out: "Paul here proves the unity of the church by the method of its creation. One Spirit, acting through the apostles and all other evangelists and ministers (I Thess. 1:5; see also I Cor. 4:14-16; Jas. 1:18; I Pet. 1:23, J.D.B.) had begotten people of different races and nationalities and conditions (John 3:5), and had caused them to be baptized into the one church, and had bestowed itself upon them after they had been thus baptized (Acts 2:38). Thus it had made them one organism. Paul speaks of the bestowal of the Spirit under the figure of the living water used by Jesus (John 7:37). As the spirit of a man keeps up the organic unity of the body, so the Spirit of God has vivified and organized the church."

HOLY SPIRIT BAPTISM THE ONE BAPTISM

The unity of the Spirit involves *one* baptism as surely as it involves one faith and one Spirit (Eph. 4:3-6). Several baptisms are mentioned in the New Testament, such as the baptism of suffering, the baptism of John, water baptism, and the baptism of the Holy Spirit. However, there is but one baptism which is for all under the New Covenant and which is a permanent part of the one faith. Is Holy Spirit baptism the one baptism? *First,* if it is, those who have not been baptized in the Spirit are not yet Christians. However, Pat thinks he was a Christian for over two decades before he received baptism in the Spirit. *(Testimony,* No. 30, p. 7). *Second,* if the one baptism is water baptism, Holy Spirit baptism is not that one baptism and, therefore, was not for everyone. It is not involved in keeping the unity of the Spirit in the bond of peace. The author has discussed Holy Spirit baptism in some detail in *Miracles or Mirages?* and *The Holy Spirit and the Christian. Third,* it may be argued that both Holy Spirit baptism and water baptism are included in the new birth (John 3:1-6). If so, those who have not been baptized in the Spirit have not completed the new birth, and those who have not been baptized scripturally in water have not completed the new birth. Yet, some who claim inspiration and baptism in the Holy Spirit oppose what the Spirit teaches in the New Testament concerning baptism. Whatever is involved in the new birth is essential to the new birth, and if both baptisms are required those who do not have both are not yet in the kingdom. Jesus said: "Ye *must* be born anew" (John 3:7). While leaving the final judgment of men to the Judge of all the earth who will do right, we must insist that the last word man has on the subject is that "Ye must be born anew." There is no evidence that the Spirit has repealed this statement of Jesus. *Fourth,* John 3 does not speak of two births—one of water and one of the Spirit—but of one birth which involves water and the Spirit. *Fifth,* the one baptism of Eph. 4:5 is water baptism. To be translated into the kingdom is to be in Christ (Col. 1:13-14). Baptism is into Christ (Gal. 3:26-27). Therefore, baptism is involved in coming into the kingdom. The new birth is into the kingdom, therefore baptism is a part of the new birth. Furthermore, the baptism of the great commission is required of all (Matt. 28:19-20; Mk. 16:16). As the apostles preached under the great commission did they require water baptism? Yes (Acts 2:38; 8:36-39; 10:47-48; 22:16). Samaritans were baptized into Christ before they received, through the laying on of the apostles' hands, the Spirit in a miraculous way (Acts 8:12-13, 14-21). The Spirit of God works through the word of God and brings men to faith and repentance. Also through the word of God He teaches them to

350

be baptized into Christ. The birth of water and the Spirit is the birth ordained by the Spirit, and it is the Spirit who begets us through the word of truth. This new birth is completed when we are baptized into Christ. *Sixth,* are you going to trust the word of the Spirit, which is found in the Bible, or are you going to trust your experience and override the word of God? If you trust the Spirit and His word you must measure all things by the Bible and change your beliefs and experiences when you find they are out of harmony with the Bible. If you have more faith in your experiences, and in your decision that these experiences are from the Spirit, you will override what the Spirit says through the Bible when His word conflicts with your experience. Choose you which will be the authority in your life. Measure all experiences by the word of God, instead of letting your experience decide what God's word must be.

DID TARRYING BRING THE SPIRIT?

Did tarrying help bring the Spirit and tongues, so that today we ought to tarry? No. *First,* the only ones ever told to tarry for the Spirit were the apostles. They were told to tarry in Jerusalem until Christ sent forth the promise of the Father upon them. After the Spirit came, they were to begin in Jerusalem the work of preaching Christ (Lk. 24:47-49, 52). This was to take place in a few days. When it did, they would receive power and begin their work as witnesses of the resurrected Lord (Acts 1:2-3, 5, 8, 22). It happened on Pentecost. The Spirit came, the power came, the preaching started, and the word was confirmed (Acts 2:1-4, 6, 8, 11, 36). Peter said this was the fulfilment of the promise of the Father that the Spirit would be sent (Acts 2:33; Lk. 24:49). The tarrying contributed nothing to the coming of the Spirit. The Lord had told them to wait in Jerusalem until He sent the Spirit. *Second,* nothing is said or implied about the Samaritans tarrying. Nor is it said they prayed for the Spirit. The apostles prayed and then conferred the Spirit through the laying on of their hands (Acts 8:15, 17, 18, 19). *Third,* Cornelius was not praying for the Spirit, nor had Peter told him he would receive the Spirit (Acts 10:44-47). *Fourth,* the disciples in Ephesus were not tarrying or praying for the Spirit, but received the Spirit when Paul laid hands on them (Acts 19:6).

Was witness borne by the Holy Spirit to Pat through the baptism of the Spirit and the gift of tongues? Immediately after claiming these experiences, Pat said, "How can mere human words convey the soul-cleansing thrill of communicating so intimately with Jehovah God, 'His Spirit bearing witness with our spirit, that we are the children of God'!" (Romans 8:16). *First,* it was doubtless an emotionally thrilling experience, but whether it was God's way of cleansing his soul is another matter (Acts 15:9; I Pet. 1:21).

Second, if this was the way the witness was borne, how did Pat know he was a Christian for over twenty years before this? He said during this time he had been a Christian, and there were "times when I was so grateful for the knowledge that I was truly a Christian . . . "

Third, in the author's book on *The Holy Spirit and the Christian* there is a long discussion on "The Witness of the Spirit." Here was briefly mentioned the following: (1) Rom. 8:16 does not say the witness is borne through a still small voice, or through the baptism of the Spirit and the gift of tongues. It does not say *how* it is done. We must learn this from other passages. (2) We can know God's mind on sonship only through what the Spirit has revealed through inspired men (I Cor. 2:10-13; 1:18-21; Acts 18:4-8, 11; Eph. 3:4; I Pet. 1:12; Jude 3). (3) Rom. 8:16 does not say that the witness is borne *to* our spirit, although the Spirit does through the Word bear witness to our spirit. "With" refers to joint witness. When the two witnesses agree we know we are God's children. The Spirit through the Word has borne witness testifying what one must do to become and to remain a child of God. The Spirit knoweth God's mind on this matter (I Cor. 2:11), and whether man has done what God requires. When our spirit witnesses that we have done, and are doing, what God's Spirit says we are to do to become and remain children, the two witnesses agree and we know we are God's children. We know this not by feelings, but by faith in God's word. For us to demand more than His word in order to know that we are accepted by Him, is to doubt the integrity of God by doubting His word. If we say that we do not doubt God's word, but doubt the integrity of our own spirit's witness, we are doubting God's word which clearly says that *the spirit of man can know the things of a man* (I Cor. 2:11). Furthermore, if we cannot trust our own mind and spirit, how could Pat trust his mind and spirit so that he knows he sought sincerely the baptism of the Spirit, that he knows that he got some kind of experience, that he knows the experience was from God, that he knows he was communicating with God, and that he knows this was the witness of the Spirit? He affirmed or implied all these things. He wrote, immediately after quoting Romans 8:16, that: "All *I know* is that I was praising God, loving God, thanking God, and worshipping God, completely free of the restrictions and limitations of my finite mind. I *knew* what I was feeling, and God knew what I was feeling, so what need was there to self-consciously struggle to put my feelings into English words? The Holy Spirit was taking care of the vocal part of it, just as God promised He would! Rom. 8:26."*(Testimony,* No. 30, 10. Italics by J.D.B.) Pat had to use his finite mind to conclude these things were from God, and that he was free from the restrictions of the finite mind. Since Pat did not know what he was saying how did he *know* he was thanking God? If he cannot trust his own mind, how could he know what he was feeling and doing?

Fourth, if Rom. 8:26 applied to Pat's speaking in tongues, why was Pat uttering the unutterable? In what sense could Pat's singing "a thrilling new song" be a case where "the Spirit himself maketh intercession for us with groanings which cannot be uttered." Pat was *not groaning* and he was *uttering.* If Pat had the miraculous guidance of the Spirit, he would not have misapplied this scripture or Rom. 8:16. Romans mentions the creation's groanings, the Christian's groanings, and the Spirit's groanings (Rom. 8:22, 23, 26-27). These three are three different groaners and groanings. Paul did not say that the Spirit's groanings are unutterable groanings which the Spirit utters in and through us. They are the Spirit's groanings as He intercedes for us (Rom. 8:26-28).

Fifth, if speaking in tongues is proof that we are children of God, most of God's children never have witness borne to them that they are God's children. All never did receive the gift of tongues. ". . . to *another* divers kinds of tongues . . . " " . . . do all speak with tongues?" (I Cor 12:10, 30). Since all do not, then on Pat's logic the Spirit fails to bear testimony to most of God's children that they are His children.

Sixth, if George Otis, who persuaded Pat to ask for the baptism and to start speaking and singing in tongues, had the gift of interpretation will he please let us know what Pat said? If he did not have the gift of interpretation, will Pat let us know why he violated the Spirit's instructions and used the gift in the presence of one who was unlearned and did not understand what Pat was saying? If Otis did not know, then so far as Otis was concerned Pat was "speaking into the air," Pat was a barbarian to him, Otis was not edified, Otis was uninstructed and unlearned and could not "say the Amen at thy (Pat's) giving of thanks, seeing he knoweth not what thou sayest" (I Cor. 14:9, 11, 16-17, 19). The "Spirit" which guided Pat in this was quite different, as the above show, from the Spirit who guided Paul. If Pat had the inspiration of the Spirit, and the gift of tongues, as did Paul, Pat would have said: "Howbeit to Otis I had rather speak five words with my understanding, that I might instruct Otis also, than ten thousand words in a tongue." (Compare I Cor. 14:19.)

SPIRIT SAITH

Are the Pentecostals depending on the voice of the Spirit when they follow the supposedly direct, miraculous guidance of the Spirit today? *First,* the Bible is the voice of the Spirit (I Cor. 2:10-13; Rev. 2:1, 7). It is the only word of the Spirit which we have. *Second,* in order to stress this fact, and in an effort to make an impression on Pentecostals, why not reply to their various errors by saying: "But, the Spirit saith . . . " and give what the Bible teaches on the subject. This emphasizes that if we want to do what the Spirit teacheth we must do what He has revealed in the Bible. By emphasizing, in this manner, that the Bible is the voice of the Spirit, we may cause some of them to raise the question as to why their "guidance" was contrary to what the Spirit saith in the Bible.

STRUCK DOWN BY THE SPIRIT?

Shirley Boone saw people fall backward when Kathryn Kuhlman laid hands on them. Shirley thought this was unscriptural until she read John 18:4-6. Later when she met Kathryn Kuhlman she touched Shirley, Shirley fell backward,

Pat caught her, and his arm had a tingling sensation for a time. *First*, if Kuhlman was inspired by the Spirit, or listened to what the Spirit says on the subject in the Bible, she would cease being a woman preacher (I Cor. 14:34-35, 37). If Shirley has gifts of the Spirit, why doesn't she rebuke Kathryn Kuhlman for being a woman preacher? *Second*, Jesus did not lay hands on anyone in John 18:6. *Third*, this did not happen to followers, but to enemies of Christ (John 18:4-6). *Fourth*, a shock which one sometimes gets when shaking hands with another, or the reaction which flows through one in some cases when someone else touches them, is no proof of the supernatural. What scripture teaches that "Spirit-filled" people go around shocking others? *Fifth*, if one is somewhat emotional, and has convinced himself from John 18:6 that the Spirit does such, it is not surprising that Shirley reacted as she did to Kuhlman's touch. *Sixth*, if one suddenly had to catch his wife when she fell backward, it should not be surprising if the unexpected strain on one's arm did not leave one with some sensations.

UNPREDICTABLE?

Is the Spirit Unpredictable? On the basis of John 3:8 Sherrill (111), and Boone maintained that the Spirit does not follow fixed rules. We cannot understand or anticipate on the basis of the word much of the Spirit's leading. Pat thought that "so is every one that is born of the Spirit," means that the Christian is also unpredictable. Pat modified his position by saying the Spirit would not contradict the Bible. If the Spirit and the Christian are unpredictable, what follows? *First*, the working of the Spirit would be lawless, for if they are guided by moral and spiritual laws they would be predictable. Anyone could argue that no "thou shalts" or "thou shalt not" can be bound on a Christian for this would be trying to contain the Spirit with some law. One could not affirm that anything is, or is not, the work of God. One should not expect the wind to blow in the same direction all of the time!!

Second, we could not say that a person must be born again, yet Jesus said it (John 3:7). One could never tell what was involved in the new birth. To show what it involved in the

New Testament would not prove anything, for who can know this is what the unpredictable Spirit, if He is unpredictable, teaches today about the new birth? It could differ from day to day, place to place, and person to person. The brooding Spirit brought order out of chaos in the material creation (Gen. 1:2), but all is chaos in the moral and spiritual realms if the Spirit is unpredictable.

Third, we could not affirm that the narrow way leads to life and the broad way to destruction (Matt. 7:13-14), or what the fruit of the Spirit is (Gal. 5:22-23), or how not to be unfruitful, but to have an abundant entrance into the eternal kingdom (II Pet. 1:5-11), if the Spirit is unpredictable.

Fourth, the author admits Pat was unpredictable—from the author's previous understanding of Pat—in certain matters. (a) The author would never have predicted that Pat would have been so deceived he would think that the course of deception, which he followed in keeping his position from the brethren, was the leading of the Spirit. (b) Who would have predicted that Pat would think that men who teach denominational doctrines and remain in denominational churches are inspired at times, and work miracles by the Spirit? *(Testimony*, 8). (c) Who would have believed that, in spite of his keen mind, Pat would have been so blind as to think he was following the assumed strategy of the Spirit, to keep it from the brethren, while he was telling folks all over the country some of his Pentecostal beliefs? (d) Who would have thought that even without his "guidance system" he would have threatened the author with a lawsuit if the author quoted from his letters. He later repented and with drew the threat. (See p. 375).

Fifth, Pat's argument on the unpredictable Spirit contradicts his argument that we can depend on Jesus to give us the gifts if we obey Matt. 21:22, and his argument on the sameness of Jesus (Heb. 13:8). We have examined these passages elsewhere.

Sixth, we can predict that people who think they are inspired today, and miraculously guided, are often unable to distinguish between their own impulses and the voice of the Spirit.

356

What do you think John 3:8 means? Jesus said: "The wind bloweth where it will, and thou hearest the voice thereof, but knowest now whence it cometh, and whither it goeth: so is every one that is born of the Spirit." *First,* Jesus did not say that we cannot know anything about the wind. However, of any particular gust we can hear the voice, but know neither its ultimate origin nor ultimate destiny. Although the wind obeys its own laws, we do not see the wind, but observe its effects. Just so, we do not see the Spirit, nor do we see the influence which the Spirit has on the heart of man, but we can tell by the effects that he is under the influence of the Spirit.

Second, the word translated "wind" can also be translated "Spirit." Some think John 3:8 means that the "Spirit breatheth where it will . . . " If this is what it means, the lesson is basically the same. We hear the voice of the Spirit which is the word of God, the voice of God (Matt. 22:31), the witness of the Spirit to us (Heb. 10:15), and the Spirit speaking to us (Rev. 2:1, 7). We do not know the source of the Spirit except that He is from God, and we do not know the ultimate destiny except that this, too, is with God. We cannot see the Spirit but even unbelieving husbands can see His influence in the lives of their believing wives (I Pet. 3:1-6).

Third, God is dependable, for His counsel is immutable and in Him there is no variation (Heb. 6:17-18; Jas. 1:17). The Spirit whom God sent is not unpredictable unless God is unpredictable. The unchangeableness of God does not mean that man dictates the laws by which God acts, but God acts in harmony with His revelation of Himself in Scripture. There were various stages in God's revelation of Himself to man, but that revelation, for man on earth, has been completed in Christ and His covenant (Matt. 5:17-18; Heb. 1:1-2; 2:1-4; 10:1; John 14:8-9; Jude 3). His word abides (I Pet. 1:25). The scheme of redemption was not revealed all at once, but it has now been fully revealed (Eph. 1:9-10; 2:13-22; 3:3-21; Jude 3).

Fourth, Jesus, who with the Father sent the Spirit. (John 14:26; 16:7), is dependable and, therefore, predictable. If He had not been predictable, the prophets could not have prophesied His coming, work, death, resurrection, ascension, coronation, and reign. If He is not predictable He is not dependable and we could not depend on Him for salvation.

Fifth, the Spirit works as He willeth and, since He is sent from God He works as God willeth for He has declared to man the things of God and Christ (John 16:12-15). When He maketh intercession for us it is according to God's will (Rom. 8:26-27).

Sixth, the new birth is of God and is, therefore, according to the laws God has laid down. We are begotten of God if we believe (I John 5:1). John does not here say whether repentance and baptism are involved, but other passages show they are. Faith comes through hearing the word of God (Rom. 10:17), therefore the devil wants to snatch the word out of hearts lest they believe and be saved (Lk. 8:12). We are begotten through the word of God (I Pet. 1:22-23, 25). Paul begat the Corinthians through the gospel (I Cor. 4:15). How? Through his preaching of the gospel to them, and their reception of it; thus it was they were brought forth by God's will by the word of truth (Acts 18:8; Jas. 1:18). If a person is not baptized into Christ, he has not completed the birth of water and the Spirit. To be in the kingdom is to be in Christ (Col. 1:13-14). We are born of water and the Spirit into the kingdom (John 3:1-8). To put it another way, we are baptized into Christ when from a heart of faith, trusting in Christ's death for our sins, we are baptized into His death and burial, and are resurrected with Him to walk in newness of life (Gal. 3:26-27; Rom. 6:2-5, 17-18).

Seventh, Christians should strive to be dependable. To the extent that we are determined to live by Christ's teaching, to the extent that we understand His will and how to follow it in a given situation, to that extent we are predictable.

Eighth, from a study of the Bible we are convinced that the Spirit is dependable and, therefore, we can predict that nothing is inspired by the Spirit, or endorsed by the Spirit, which is not taught in the Bible.

Did Pat give examples? Pat cited examples of what he regarded as surprising and unpredictable things which God did in the Bible, and from which he drew the conclusion God may be doing unpredictable (on the basis of what the Bible teaches) things today. As we briefly consider these examples,

358

it should be kept in mind that what may have been surprising in the beginnings of God's revelations to man, would not be in the light of the full revelation which has been made known in the faith once for all delivered to the saints. If something is not a part of that faith, we are not to contend for it, but are to oppose it as it opposes the gospel (Jude 3).

First, why is it surprising that there were non-Jews in Jesus' ancestry? Adam was not a Jew. Because Jesus was to be of the seed of Abraham did not mean that no non-Jew would marry a descendant of Abraham through whom the Christ was to come.

Second, since Christ's mission ultimately embraced the Samaritans, one should not be surprised by his contact with the woman of Samaria. However, Jesus did tell her that the Jews were right, and the Samaritans were wrong, about the place of worship (John 4:20-23).

Third, since Christ had more disciples than the twelve, we should not be surprised that some of these did wonders in His name (Mk. 9:38-40; Lk. 9:49-50). We should rejoice when we hear of any people anywhere who have become members of Christ's church through hearing and obeying the gospel. On the other hand, because some people claim to work miracles does not mean they are acceptable to God (Matt. 7:21-23).

Fourth, the thief on the cross incident should not be surprising. It was under the law, and in line with Jesus' mission of mercy and His willingness to receive the penitent ones who turned to Him.

Fifth, what is surprising about the case of Herod? (Acts 12:2-23). God had visited judgments on people in Old Testament times, and in Acts 5. However, today we could not know that something was a direct judgment of God, for we have no inspired men to reveal this to us.

Sixth, Pat appealed to Rom. 11:33 to show that God's ways are past finding out, and therefore unpredictable to the mind of man. Of course, what God has not revealed, man cannot know. However, Pat contradicts his use of this passage for he believes that he is justified in accepting as the ways of God today some things which are not revealed in the Bible. He thinks that the Holy Spirit is inspiring and giving other

359

gifts to men who are perpetuating denominationalism, and who have not obeyed as the gospel teaches we are to obey in order to come into Christ. How was Pat able to search out God's unsearchable ways and know these things?

Seventh, Jesus did not incur the wrath of Jewish leaders because He did unpredictable things when measured by the word of God. (a) He fulfilled the law and the prophets (Matt. 5:17-18; Acts 26:22-23). (b) They did not have the love or the word of God abiding in them, and did not know the Father nor Christ (John 5:38-47; 16:1-3). (c) Christ violated their human traditions and exposed their sins (Matt. 15:1-20; 23:1-38).

Eighth, did Christ do something unpredictable when He ministered to a Gentile? Although His personal ministry was to the lost sheep of the house of Israel (Matt. 10:5-6), the prophets prophesied that His work ultimately embraced the Gentiles (Gen. 22:17-18; Isa. 49:5-7; Acts 13:47).

Ninth, did Jesus do something unpredictable by violating the sabbath? (a) Did Jesus violate God's law concerning the Sabbath, or just the traditions of the Jews? He said His disciples were guiltless of violating the sabbath (Matt. 12:1-2, 7). (b) God's law made exceptions for those who had to work on the sabbath in order to serve the temple. Christ was greater than the temple, and if His service demanded they do something on the sabbath day it was justified (Matt. 12:5-6). (c) What had been done was justified on the basis of the Old Testament principle in Hosea 6:6 (Matt. 12:7). (d) As Lord of the sabbath, Jesus had the right to declare exceptions (Matt. 12:8). He finally abolished the sabbath (Col. 2:14-17). No one on earth today is "Lord of the Sabbath" so that they can declare exceptions to God's word in order to include the "unpredictable" people. (e) What proof is there that the healing was a violation of the sabbath? (Matt. 12:9-13). The Jews recognized it was rightful to do good even to an animal to relieve its distress on the sabbath day.

Tenth, what surprising and unpredictable things does Pat think God is doing today? He should list them, and then give proof that these are the work of God.

Eleventh, Jesus did not say that John 3:8 meant they would do unpredictable things, therefore, we are not opposing

360

Jesus' statement when we oppose Pat's interpretation and show where it leads.

Twelfth, Pat views Oral Roberts as a man who is baptized in the Spirit. How does he interpret the "wind" reference? He wrote: "Jesus likened the new birth of the soul to the effect of the wind. The Holy Spirit moves within us bringing us to a new birth and into a father-son relationship with God. The Christian's life and nature are shaped by the wind of the Holy Spirit, and as we depend on Him our lives will become more and more like that of Jesus. It will appear to others that we are pointing to someone they must see, as indeed we are. To many people, the Holy Spirit is a vague, indefinable figure of the Godhead who cannot be understood. But the work of the Holy Spirit is very plain to be seen in our lives when our lives are submitted to Him." *(The New Testament With Personal Commentary by Oral Roberts*, 676). *First*, Roberts evidently believes that "wind," not Spirit, is the correct translation. *Second*, there is a comparison between the effect of the wind, and the effect of the Spirit in bringing about the new birth. *Third*, Roberts does not mean that we can actually see the Spirit, but that we see the effect which He works in lives which are submitted to Him. *Fourth*, the work of the Spirit, according to this comment, is very predictable for the Spirit will more and more mould us into the likeness of Jesus. *Fifth*, the author is not saying there is an agreement between himself and Oral Roberts concerning what the new birth is, but it does seem that neither he nor Roberts finds in this passage the idea that the Spirit and the Christian are unpredictable.

VALIDATED BY THE FRUIT OF THE SPIRIT?

If those who claim the gifts also manifest the fruit of the Spirit, are we not obligated to accept their claims? However, the total fruit test includes more than the individuals' manifesting some degree of love, peace, etc., in their lives.

First, to test them by their fruits means that one must include the test of their teaching and practice. If their doctrine contradicts the New Testament, we must repudiate their claims regardless of their fine qualities of personal life.

Second, we must also test them by their so-called miraculous works as well as by their claims. Do they do the wide variety of miracles found in the New Testament and thus do more than healing miracles? Do they do the wide variety of healing miracles which the apostles did? Do their healing miracles have the characteristics of those in the New Testament?

Third, to limit the fruit test to certain moral and spiritual qualities is to ignore other scriptures. It also leads one to place his stamp of approval on some persons whose doctrines grossly contradict the New Testament. One individual wrote: "The only judgment I could render, then, was to judge their fruit. Did they manifest the 'fruit of the Spirit?' In both cases my answer was yes." This seems to refer to the fruit of the Spirit in Gal. 5, in which Paul set forth moral and spiritual qualities such as love, joy, peace, etc. (Gal 5:22-23). Whenever anyone follows a principle which is in the Bible it will bear some fruit in his life even if he does not become a Christian. One cannot use these qualities in his life to prove he is a Christian, or that his doctrine concerning Christ and the Bible is sound. Gandhi, who was not even a professed Christian, had some of these qualities in his life; and some of them to a higher degree than some Christians. There are modernists who deny the inspiration of the Bible, and the divinity of Jesus Christ, who have some of these qualities. Albert Schweitzer did not accept the Christ of the Bible, or the authority of the apostle Paul who penned Gal. 5:22-23 and I Cor. 12:14. However, we must admire the dedication and compassion with which he gave himself in service as a doctor to suffering Africans. (Oskar Kraus, *Albert Schweitzer: His Work and His Philosophy*, London: Adam and Charles Black, 1955). There are Buddhists who have some fine moral and spiritual qualities, but this does not mean we should accept their world view.

Fourth, we must test all things by the word of God. If they do not pass these tests, we must not accept them even if the person in his personal life has some good moral qualities. These moral qualities are the products of principles which he follows, but they are not in themselves the product of his so-called miraculous gifts, nor do they confirm his miraculous gifts.

362

CHAPTER XXII

TONGUES: QUESTIONS AND ANSWERS

The laboring oar is in the hands of the tongues movement. It is not our responsibility to prove that tongues have ceased, since they did cease for centuries. It is their responsibility to prove that they are for us today. This must be done not just through arguments, but through demonstrations which match the revelations and confirmations found in the Bible.

ALL?

Did Paul want everyone to speak in tongues? (I Cor. 14:5). *First,* this statement shows that Paul has no prejudice against tongues. He was willing for everyone to have the gift, although he had rather they had the gift of prophecy. *Second,* Paul knew it was not God's will that everyone have all of the gifts (I Cor. 12:7-11, 18, 28, 29-30). *Third,* since tongues in the congregation were useless when they did not understand, and when no one had the gift of interpretation, surely Paul was just as willing for everyone to have the gift of interpretation so they could profit by the tongues. *Fourth,* Paul's personal desire was that all Israel be saved even at the expense of Paul's salvation (Rom. 9:3; 10:1). However, he knew God would not save Israel in her rebellion and that multitudes were cut off because of their unbelief (Rom. 10:16-21; 11:5, 7-10, 20). Just so, as far as Paul personally was concerned everyone could have the gift of tongues, but he knew this was not God's will.

Did all in Acts who received the Spirit speak in tongues? *First,* all who received the baptism of the Spirit on Pentecost and in the household of Cornelius did speak in tongues (Acts 2:1-4; 10:45-46; 11:16-17). *Second,* those on whom Paul laid hands received the gift of tongues (Acts 19:1-7). *Third,* all baptized believers received the Spirit in a non-miraculous way (Acts 2:38; I Cor. 6:19-20). If this meant they received the gift of tongues, those who do not receive it do not receive remission of sins; for the gift of the Spirit and remission of sins are promised on the same conditions. All Christians did not receive gifts, and all who received gifts did not receive tongues (I Cor. 12:10, 30).

CAN THE SPEAKERS CONTROL THEMSELVES?

Could the one who spoke in tongues control himself, or was the influence of the Spirit such that he could not keep from speaking out? Paul said "the spirits of the prophets are subject to the prophets." (I Cor. 12:32). It may be replied that Paul did not affirm this of the speaker in tongues, but only of those who had the gift of prophecy. To this we reply: *First,* what value would it be to regulate prophesying in a known tongue, in order to keep down confusion which would be caused by more than one person speaking at a time, if the speakers in tongues can speak forth at any time? If they say they cannot contain themselves, it follows that the Spirit would never move them to speak when someone else is speaking, "for God is not a God of confusion, but of peace" (14:33). *Second,* Paul regulated speaking in tongues, as well as prophesying. If the spirit of the tongues speaker was not subject to the tongues speaker it would be impossible for them to conform to this regulation. Paul wrote: "If any man speaketh in a tongue, let it be by two or at the most three and that in turn; and let one interpret" (14:27). *Third,* Paul commanded the speaker in tongues to keep silent if there was no interpreter present. If no one there understood the language, he was not to speak. " . . . if there be no interpreter, let him keep silence in the church; and let him speak to himself, and to God" (14:28). *Fourth,* the purpose of speaking in tongues, and the purpose of prophesying, was to instruct and edify the church. If the speakers in tongues could not control themselves, this lack of control would defeat the purpose of the tongues as surely as the lack of control of a prophet would defeat the purpose of prophesying. Paul said: "For ye all can prophesy one by one, that all may learn, and all may be exhorted; and the spirits of the prophets are subject to the prophets" (14:31-32). It would be as confusing for tongue speakers to be without control as it would be for prophets. The confusion caused by the tongues speakers, speaking in a language no one there understood, would be even greater than that caused by prophets prophesying in the language of the people. Paul said the unbelievers would think they were mad (I Cor. 14:23).

Any tongues speaker who claims that he cannot control his "gift" proves in that very claim that he does not have the gift given by the Spirit, for they were able to control the exercise of the gift. Such a person has also convicted himself of ignorance of the word of God. With the Bible before him, he should know better.

Furthermore, in at least some of the assemblies, of those who speak in tongues, more than one person speaks at a time. If they were guided by the Holy Spirit it seems that at least some of them would know enough—either by a study of I Cor. 14 or by direct revelation—to know that this ought not to be done.

COMPENSATION FOR OUR INADEQUACY IN PRAYER?

Since we are inadequate to express fully unto God our devotion and feelings, Pat thinks that tongues were given to him as a special prayer language to compensate for this inadequacy *(Christian Life,* November 1969, p. 60). *First,* the assumption underlying Pat's position is that any inadequacy on our part will be compensated for by a miraculous gift from God. If this is true, what follows: (a) Do we become inspired teachers because we are inadequate both with reference to what to teach and how to teach? (b) We are inadequate in wisdom, knowledge, and power, so why not get all the gifts? (I Cor. 12:8-11, 18, 24, 27-30). (c) Missionaries are inadequate in foreign languages so why not the gift of languages? (d) All of us are inadequate to some extent in our own language, so why not miraculous powers of speech in English? (e) All of us are inadequate in our understanding of others in that there is always something we do not know about them. Do we have a miraculous gift of complete understanding? (f) All of us are inadequate in understanding foreign languages, so all should have the gift of interpretation. (g) We are inadequate in physical strength and financial means, so why not gifts to compensate for these lacks? (h) All are inadequate in their powers to persuade and to convince, so why not special gifts in these areas?

Second, why is it more adequate to praise God in Latin than in English? Why would one man's native tongue be inadequate for him, but adequate for someone who did not know the language? What proof is there that the communication in the tongue is more adequate? One man was said to have prayed the following in ancient Aramaic: "Dear Lord, I thank you for the years I have been privileged to serve you. Forgive me Lord, for the shortcomings that I have, and please let me serve you even if I am a little man." *(Voice,* January/February 1970, p. 12). This is a good prayer, but surely it is as adequate in English as in Aramaic. "I love you, Jesus," is no more adequate in Latin than in English.

Third, how is one's inadequacy overcome by God giving one a language which one does not understand? God understands us even without our having a gift of tongues.

Fourth, the groanings in Rom. 8:26-27 are not of devotion, nor a gift, nor uttered by man.

DECEPTION EASY

The devil is a deceiver who transforms himself into an angel of light, and his apostles into false apostles of Christ (II Cor. 11:13-15). How easy it is for him to deceive people when once they are convinced that tongues are a series of unintelligible sounds. Anyone can utter unintelligible sounds, and no one would be able to prove that one series of such sounds was genuine and another was a fraud.

DESIRE

Although Paul said to "desire earnestly the greater gifts" (I Cor. 12:31; 14:1), Paul taught that more than desire was involved. *First,* it is doubtful that anyone received any gift if he did not want it. *Second,* if desire were the only condition all Christians could have all the gifts. It is extremely rare that anyone claims all the gifts. Unless a person claims all the gifts he cannot consistently argue that one gets the gifts if he desires them. *Third,* if all could have all the gifts, why did Paul say: "to one . . . wisdom . . . to another faith . . . and to another gifts of healing . . . " (14:8-9). ". . . are all workers of miracles? Have all gifts of healings? Do all speak with tongues? Do all interpret?" (12:29-30). *Fourth,* the body is not just one member, but many, and all the body is not made up of the tongue, etc. The context shows that the illustration of the body and its many members illustrates spiritual gifts although it illustrates other things also (12:18-24). *Fifth,* some few were apostles who had a wide variety of gifts (12:27-28,

29-30). Regardless of how strong the desire, and how pure the life, no one can become an apostle of Jesus Christ today. *Sixth,* "The appeal of Paul is also to the church as a whole. They should desire that the best gifts be manifested in their midst, not that each Christian who has a gift should desire others." (Gromacki, 134). *Seventh,* gifts were given as God willed (12:6, 18, 24; Heb. 2:4), and as the Spirit willed (12:11). "The Spirit worketh, not is worked. He worketh as He will, not as He is bidden." (Chrysostom). Of course, the Spirit worked as God willed (John 16:13-15). See also the discussion on "Prayer and the Gifts."

DISORDER

As Smith observed, tongues in the Bible were *not bestowed during frenzy or followed by exhaustion.* He contrasted this with meetings of Edward Irving, around 1830. "Here, more than in most other cases, were the conditions of long, eager expectation, fixed brooding over one central thought, the mind strained to a preternatural tension. Suddenly, now from one, now from another, chiefly from women, devout, but illiterate, mysterious sounds were heard." *(Comprehensive Dictionary of the Bible* pp. 1133-1134). Although there are those who are far more dignified, as a whole the tongues movement has been characterized by extreme emotionalism, frenzy, and exhaustion in many of their services.

According to some claims, tongues have been accomplished by "wind, fire, perfume, shaking, physical convulsions, electric shocks, lights, perspiration (from the heat of the Holy Spirit), visions, healings, seeing, hearing and touching Christ . . . " (Gromacki, p. 40).

In speaking of what she had seen at "tongues" meetings, Alma White said: "Some had been so long making spectacles of themselves that they showed marked efficiency, and resembled perfectly the dancing dervishes whom I have seen in Egypt. Their quivering bodies, weird song, and tremulous notes were identical with those of the dervishes engaged in religious worship in the caves near the great Pyramid" (105-106).

DO WE FORBID WHAT THE SPIRIT AUTHORIZES?
(I COR. 14:39)

First, Paul never authorized ecstatic utterances, nor any of the tongues speaking advocated today, nor conflicting doctrines which are taught by people in the tongues movement. *Second,* Paul said tongues would cease, and they have (I Cor. 13:8). *Third,* we are heeding Paul's instructions to prove all things, hold fast to the good, and contend for the faith (I Thess. 5:21; Jude 3).

GREEK WIDELY KNOWN?

It has been argued that the gift of languages was unnecessary because Greek was spoken throughout the Roman Empire. *First,* it is a fact the apostles did speak in other languages (Acts 2:4, 6, 8, 11). *Second,* there were many people in the Roman Empire who did not know Greek. The apostles were not to confine themselves to the Greek speaking people. *Third,* the apostles were not to confine their work to the Roman Empire. *Fourth,* the gift of languages served as a sign which helped confirm the truth of the gospel (Mk. 16:17, 20; I Cor. 14:22). *Fifth,* if one's assumption, that the gift of languages was unnecessary, proves that such a gift was not given, it is obvious that a gift of incoherent utterances was unnecessary; for it could not confirm the word, convince the unbelievers, edify the saints, or in any other way contribute to the preaching and confirmation of the gospel.

MAIN PURPOSE?

Ben Franklin thought tongues were given for the individual's edification and praise of God in his private devotions (Mimeographed Letter, December 13, 1966). *First,* he ignored their primary function in revealing and confirming the word (Mk. 16:17, 20; I Cor. 14:1-6; 14:22; Heb. 2:3-4). If he were guided by the Spirit, he would not have made this basic error. *Second,* they could also function for individual edification (I Cor. 14:2, 4, 28).

PAUL HAVE MORE THAN OTHERS?

Why do you think it was important for Paul to have the gift of tongues in greater measure than did anyone in Corinth? (I Cor. 14:18). As the apostle to the Gentiles (Gal. 2:8-9), who took long missionary journeys, it was important that Paul be able to speak to people wherever he went regardless of the language which they spoke.

PENTECOST ONLY?

Is Pentecost the only occasion when tongues were used as a sign to unbelievers? No. *First,* Jesus said tongues were signs (Mk. 16:17). *Second,* the signs mentioned in Mk. 16:17 are the signs which confirmed the word which was preached after Christ's ascension (Mk. 16:19-20). This covers all cases in Acts. *Third,* tongues at Cornelius' household confirmed the truth about the Gentiles, the law, and the gospel. It convinced the Jews who were with Peter (Acts 10:45-47; 11:17), and the brethren in Jerusalem (11:18; 15:7-11). If this was a case of so-called private, ecstatic utterances, it would have been wrong for them to exercise the gift in a group; because no one would have understood (I Cor. 14:2, 27-28). *Fourth,* Acts 19:1-7 is covered by Mk. 16:17, 20. It confirmed the truth that the baptism of John was no longer valid, but that the baptism of the great commission is the valid baptism (Matt. 28:19; Acts 2:38; 19:5). *Fifth,* Paul told the Corinthians that tongues were signs to unbelievers (I Cor. 14:22). When used when people understood them, or when an inspired interpretation was given, they always functioned as signs which accredited the message as being from God. *Sixth,* that Paul spoke in tongues more than others, but that he had rather speak five words which people understood, does not prove that most of his speaking was in private, ecstatic utterance (14:18-19). It simply means that he did not use tongues when no one there understood them. In his extensive travels he had abundant opportunities to speak in languages which were foreign languages to him, but native tongues to those to whom he preached. *Seventh,* Paul did not allow tongues to be used when they could not constitute a sign to unbelievers or edify saints. He did permit, however, the individual to speak to himself and to God (14:2, 27, 28). *Eighth,* why do Pentecostals have millions of cases where tongues—used both publicly and privately—are not used as signs or to edify the audience, and why do they so rarely even claim that a human language was spoken by inspiration?

PRIVATE?

Pat thought that his private devotional experiences should not be a matter of such concern and controversy. *First,* how could it be private when he told others about it, made some public statements, thought that others ought to seek the gifts, and was writing a book on it? *Second,* gifts were to convert unbelievers and edify believers (Mk. 16:20; I Cor. 14:1-22). *Third,* a public affirmation of a position amounts to a public invitation to evaluate the position. *Fourth,* why should Pat be exempt from controversy? *Fifth,* Christians are to give reason for their hope, contend for the faith, oppose publicly when necessary, reprove, rebuke, correct, instruct, charge men not to teach a different doctrine, and war the good warfare (I Pet. 3:15; Jude 3; Gal. 2:4-5, 14; I Tim. 1:3-6, 18-20; II Tim. 3:16; 4:4).

ROMANS 8:26—THE TONGUES OF MEN?

Pat thought this referred to the Spirit speaking in tongues through men *(Testimony,* 10). *First,* Paul spoke of three groaners: (a) The creation (8:19-22). (b) Christians (8:23). (c) The Spirit's intercessions on our behalf (8:26-27). These are not groanings uttered by Christians. *Second,* the tongues were languages which were *understood* by those who knew the language through human learning (Acts 2:4, 6, 8, 11), or by the gift of interpretation (I Cor. 14:27-28). Rom. 8:26-27 were "groanings which cannot be uttered." What men could utter and interpret the unutterable groanings of the Spirit with which *He maketh intercession to God on our behalf? Third,* tongues were signs to unbelievers (Mk. 16:17, 20; I Cor. 14:22), but the unutterable groanings of the Spirit were not heard by men and could not be signs to the unbelievers. *Fourth,* Rom. 8:26-27 does not say these unutterable groanings of the Spirit are uttered through Christians. *Fifth,* a miraculous gift is not necessary for us to have groanings. The creation groaneth, and each Christian groaneth, but this is not a gift of groaning (8:19-22, 23). *Sixth,* all Christians groan (8:23-25), but not all Christians spoke in tongues (I Cor. 12:10, 29-30). We groan in our tribulation while waiting for the translation into the heavenly body (I Cor. 15:35-58; Rom. 8:17-18). *Seventh,* F. L. Godet wrote: "As the apostle had passed from the groaning of universal nature to that of the children of God, he now rises from the latter to that of the Holy Spirit Himself. The gradation is so evident that one is astonished it could have remained unobserved by so many commentators . . . But we must remark the significant difference between this second transition and the former. In passing from the groaning of nature to that of believers, he said: *not only . . . but also*. Now he simply says: *and likewise also*. There is no contrast indicated here; for the groaning of the Spirit is homogeneous with that of believers *(likewise)*, though distinct from it notwithstanding *(also)*, and though there is a gradation from the one to the other . . . " *Eighth*, if Pat had such direct guidance by the Spirit why did he apply this passage to speaking in tongues?

SEPARATE BELIEVERS AND UNBELIEVERS

Were tongues designed to separate believing from unbelieving Christians? Warren Lewis writes: "While glossalalia was certainly a sign for unbelievers, it was as such precisely designed to separate the spiritual sheep from the goats, to single out those whose spirits were attuned to the mysteries of the Spirit from those who were either as yet uninstructd in the Christian experience or who were slow to believe in them. Again citing Barrett, his scholarly words become a prophetic utterance against 'unbelieving' Christians who, in flagrant violation of the apostolic command, are 'forbidding to speak in tongues' " (I Cor. 14:39). *(Mission*, November, 1969, p. 30). *First*, there is a vast difference between rejecting unscriptural tongues and forbidding the genuine gift in the first century. *Second*, if the gift of tongues distinguished the spiritual sheep from the goats why didn't Paul: (a) Blame the spiritual goats for not being attuned, instead of blaming the speakers for exercising the gift before the goats. If they were spiritual, they would have had the gift themselves (I Cor. 14:2-6, 13-19). (b) Instead of forbidding the speakers to speak when no interpreter was present (14:5, 28), Paul should have urged the goats to get the gift so everyone could speak in tongues and each edify himself. (14:4). (c) Why didn't Paul urge all to seek the gift of interpretation so that all could understand and be edified? (14:2, 5, 13-17). *Third*, why did God make so many goats by giving the gift of tongues only to certain ones? (12:10, 11, 30). *Fourth,* since the gift of interpretation was better than tongues, since it enabled the church to be edified, were the interpreters the super-spiritual sheep? (14:5, 19). *Fifth,* isn't it strange that the spiritual sheep were contributing to the confusion in the assembly? (14:4, 26-33, 40). *Sixth,* why did Paul indicate that some of the tongues speakers were conducting themselves as babes? (14:20). *Seventh,* was it a sign of spirituality to talk into the air and treat others as barbarians? (14:9, 11).

SPIRITUALITY?

Were tongues a sign of spirituality? If they were, the church in Corinth, which was behind in no gift, was the most spiritual church (I Cor. 1:4-9). What was their spiritual condition? Contentions (I Cor. 1:11). Carnal (3:1-4). Proud (4:6-13, 18-19). Tolerated a type of fornication which even the Gentiles did not tolerate. Instead of mourning they were puffed up (5:1-2, 6). Some were defrauding brethren (6:8). Knowledge was not being used in love (8:1-12). Conduct at the Lord's supper made it impossible to observe it (11:17-34). Tongues were being exercised in such a way the church was not edified (14:4, 12, 16-19). Confusion in the assembly (14:26-31, 40). Some denied the resurrection (15:12). There were some things to commend (11:2), but on the whole this was not a very spiritual congregation.

What are some of the tests of spirituality? First, whether we feed on, and practice God's word and grow thereby (I Pet. 2:1-2; 1:22; II Pet. 3:18; Heb. 5:12-14). Study, pray, practice, assemble, and teach others. Begin by being a better roommate, child, parent, brother, sister and neighbor. Work as unto the Lord and be considerate of those with whom you come into contact daily as well as otherwise (Col. 3:22-24). *Second,* although we fall far short of perfection, we are known by our fruits; including love (Matt. 7:20; John 13:35; Gal. 5:22-26). *Third,* continue in the apostles' doctrine (Acts 2:42; I Cor. 14:37).

WERE TONGUES THE GREATEST GIFT?

As far as the author can tell, *some* people think that tongues were the greatest gift. They seem to *seek* them more diligently, and to *employ* them more frequently, than any of the other gifts. The tremendous emphasis which some put on tongues reveals that they are neither directly guided by the Spirit, nor have they understood and accepted what Paul said about tongues in comparison with the gift of prophecy. *First,* Paul clearly said that *"greater is he that prophesieth* than he that speaketh with tongues." The only exception was, *"except he interpret,* that the church may receive edifying" (I Cor. 14:5).

Second, what else does Paul say which indicates that tongues were not the greatest gift? (a) Men do not understand the tongues, unless they are interpreted, and what is said is a mystery to them (14:2). The tongues speakers are not speaking to men, but the prophet is (14:3, 28). (b) The tongues edified the speaker, but not the audience, while prophecy edifies the audience (14:3-5, 17). (c) The tongues do not profit the church (14:6). The church does not know what is said, and the tongues speaker utters an uncertain voice (14:7-8). (d) The tongues speaker is merely vibrating the air; he is speaking into the air (14:9). (e) Instead of resulting in communication with one another, and promoting mutual understanding and fellowship, tongues makes them barbarians or foreigners to one another (14:11). (f) The conscious spiritual life of the church is not promoted, for the tongues speaker is not speaking with his understanding so that the audience is instructed (14:14, 15-19). If I Cor. 14:14 means that the individual himself did not understand what he was saying, it teaches that the conscious religious life of the individual was not furthered by his exercise of tongues. He was having an experience which he did not understand, which was mainly emotional in its impact on him, and which bore no fruit in his understanding and, therefore, none in his conscious spiritual life. (g) The listener could not enter into and endorse either the prayer or the song of such a speaker (14:16-17). (h) It is two thousand times inferior to an intelligible message (14:19). (i) Its use without an interpretation was a sign of childishness instead of maturity (14:20). (j) When no one understood it, it could not serve its purpose as a sign to unbelievers (14:22). (k) Instead of serving the purpose of confirming the gospel, and promoting evangelism among unbe-

373

lievers, it served the reverse of this purpose and led unlearned
—unlearned in the tongue—unbelievers to conclude that the
speakers were mad (14:23). In contrast with this, although
prophecy was mainly for the church it could also help evangelize the world through converting unbelievers (14:22-25).

Third, prophecy served to edify the church for in prophecy
one spoke to the church "by way of revelation, or of knowledge, or of prophesying, or of teaching" (I Cor. 14:6). The
gifts of prophecy, of knowledge, etc., were all necessary because the complete truth had not been revealed and confirmed.
However, after it had been revealed, we have what these gifts
brought to earth—the truth of God. The truth, not the gifts
themselves, was that which was of basic importance. The gifts
were valuable only because they were means of revealing and
confirming the truth. We can speak to the church the truth
that was revealed in the first century. Even if someone today
had the gift of a thousand tongues, the one who teaches the
truth from the Bible would still be greater than the tongues
speaker; except he interpret.

WHY DIDN'T PAUL UNDERSTAND
THE LYCAONIANS?

If the apostles knew foreign languages by inspiration, why
did not Paul understand the speech of the Lycaonians? (Acts
14:11-14). *First*, the passage does not say that Paul did not
understand their speech. *Second*, the gift of tongues did not
necessarily include the gift of interpreting foreign tongues
(I Cor. 12:10, 30; 14:26-27). *Third*, there is no evidence that
the gift of tongues meant that one could speak all languages,
or that the gift of interpretation meant one could interpret
all languages.

WHY NOT THE OTHER GIFTS ALSO?

Without interpretation tongues do not edify or instruct
(I Cor. 14:4-5, 18-19), treat others as barbarians (14:11),
and may lead some to think one is mad (14:23). To paraphrase
Paul we say: Since ye are zealous of tongues, "seek that ye
may abound unto the edifying of the church" (14:12). If faith,
prayer, and desire enable one to get gifts, why not get gifts
with which to edify the church?

WHY SPEND TIME OPPOSING THE
TONGUES MOVEMENT?

With the world in need of conversion, Joyce Dennis asked why we spend time opposing the tongues movement. *First,* why do some tongues speakers spend hours exercising tongues in private devotions instead of converting unbelievers in Christ (I Cor. 14:22)? *Second,* why did she and her husband feel that God has called them to work in Hawaii where they are convinced there are opportunities to teach some members of the church and some in denominationalism? *(Testimony,* No. 31, p. 11). Why don't they go to pagans instead? *Third,* she said they were not working to lead the church into these things. This shows that she does not have miraculous gifts or she would know they were to be used to edify the church as well as to convert the world (I Cor. 14:3-6). Why claim gifts and then say that one is not trying to use them for one of their basic purposes? What confusion! *Fourth,* if, as she indicates, many churches are dead because they do not accept these gifts, they should try to raise us from spiritual death through the miraculous gifts. She wrote: "God's Spirit filled me with a supernatural love. I could never of my own strength, declare the love I now feel for that part of Christ's body that worships at the Northside Church of Christ. But Jesus loves them too. I'm sure that Jesus weeps as he looks upon the death taking place in so many churches, just as he wept over Jerusalem because they would not accept Him!" (p. 10). There are dead churches, but not because of a lack of the miraculous gifts. *Fifth,* we oppose the tongues movement because it undermines the sufficiency of the Bible as the standard of faith and practice. It leads to many other errors.

LAWSUIT: AN ADDITIONAL NOTE

After this book was in galley proof, Pat said that when we had talked on the phone in May, he had said that he did not tell his lawyers to threaten me with a lawsuit. He told them to inform me of his legal rights. Either Pat or the author did not remember the conversation rightly, since this was the first time the author had heard this explanation—so far as he could recollect. The author called Pat for the specific purpose of learning whether he had authorized the telegram, he took notes on the conversation, and if Pat mentioned this the author failed to understand the very thing about which he called Pat. He asked Pat if the Spirit had moved him to do this, and Pat said that he, not the Spirit, had done it. When the author read the telegram to Pat, Pat said that was not the way he would have worded it but he did not say that he had not authorized the threat. When Pat mentioned it in a letter, he said he had pangs of regret over having involved the lawyers. The author takes Pat's word for it that the lawyers misunderstood him. However, was there not an implied threat in the very fact that he asked his lawyers to inform me of his legal rights? The incident still illustrates that Pat's "guidance" system was not working well.

A CONCLUDING WORD

The author believes that the attitude which Pat and the author have toward one another demonstrates that it is possible to disagree sharply and deeply and yet to love one another. May we all furnish good and honest hearts so that our study of the word may result in the good seed of the kingdom finding fertile soil. May we keep our hearts open to all that God has for us on all subjects on which He has spoken. "And now I commend you to God, and to the word of His grace, which is able to build you up, and to give you the inheritance among all them that are sanctified." (Acts 20:32).

BIBLIOGRAPHY

Anderson, Sir Robert, *Spirit Manifestations and The Gift of Tongues*, New York: Loizeaux Brothers.

Boise, James Robinson, *Notes, Critical and Explanatory on the Greek Text of Paul's Epistles*, New York: Silver, Burdett and Co., 1896.

Boone, Pat, *A New Song*, Carol Stream, Illinois: Creation House, 1970.

Boyle, Isaac, *The Ecclesiastical History of Eusebius Pamphilus*, Grand Rapids, Michigan: Baker Book House, 1962.

Brooks, R. A., "Instruction About Tongues Speaking," *Charisma Digest*, Los Angeles, California: Full Gospel Business Men's Fellowship International, Number 2, 1969.

Farrell, Frank, "Outburst of Tongues: The New Penetration," *Christianity Today*, September 13, 1963.

Finch, John G., "God-Inspired or Self-Induced?" *Christian Herald*, May, 1964.

Fletcher, William C., *The Moderns*, Grand Rapids, Michigan: Zondervan Publishing House, 1962.

Fraser, Gordon H., "Oral Roberts Visits the Navajos," *The Discerner*, Vol. III, No. 4, 902 Hennepin Ave., Minneapolis, Minn.: Religion Analysis Service, Inc.

Gould, E. P., *Corinthians*, Philadelphia: American Baptist Publications Society, 1887.

Greene, David, "The Gift of Tongues," *Bibliotheca Sacra*, 1865.

Gromacki, Robert Glenn, *The Modern Tongues Movement*, Philadelphia, Pennsylvania: Presbyterian and Reformed Publishing Company, 1967.

Haakonson, R. P., *The Christian News*, January 22, 1968, p. 7.

Hoekema, Anthony A., *What About Tongues Speaking?* Grand Rapids, Michigan: William B. Eerdmans Publishing Company, 1966.

Horton, Wade H., Editor, *The Glossolalia Phenomenon*, Cleveland, Tennessee: Pathway Press, 1966.

Howard, V. E., *Fake Healers Exposed*, Texarkana, Texas 75501, P. O. Box 1717. pp. 39-40.

Hutchins, Robert M., Editor-in-Chief, *Great Books of the Western World, No. 13, Virgil*, Encyclopaedia Britannica,, Inc., Oxford University Press, 1952.

Jennings, George J., "An Ethnological Study of Glossalalia," *Journal of the American Scientific Affiliation*, March, 1968.

Jividen, Jimmy, "Ecstatic Utterances or Languages," *Firm Foundation*, February 18, 1969.

Kittel, Gerhard, Editor, *Theological Dictionary of the New Testament*, Vol. II, Grand Rapids, Michigan: Wm. B. Eerdmans Publishing Co., 1964.

Knox, R. A., *Enthusiasm*, Oxford: At the Clarendon Press, 1950.

Lenski, R. C. H., *First and Second Corinthians*, Columbus, Ohio: Wartburg Press, 1937.

Lewis, Harland G., *Christian Century*, Sept. 5, 1956.

Mann, W. E., *Christian Century*, Sept. 5, 1956.

Martin, G. C., *Ephesians, Colossians, Philemon, and Philippians*, Edinburg: T. C. and C. Jack, Ltd., p. 118.

Pattison, E. Mansell, "Behavior Science Research on the Nature of Glossolalia," *Journal of the American Scientific Affiliation*, September, 1968.

Robertson, A. T., *Word Pictures in the New Testament*, Nashville, Tennessee: Boardman Press, 1931.

Sherrill, John L., *They Speak With Other Tongues*, Old Tappan, N. J.: Fleming H. Revell Company, 1964.

Stagg, Frank; Hinson, E. Glenn; Oats, Wayne E., *Glossolalia, Tongues Speaking in Biblical, Historical, and Psychological Perspective*, Nashville and New York: Abingdon Press, 1967.

Stolee, H. J., *Speaking in Tongues*, Minneapolis, Minnesota: Augsburg Publishing House, 1963.

Tuland, Carl G., "The Confusion About Tongues," *Christianity Today*, December 16, 1968.

Vincent, Marvin R., *Word Studies in the New Testament*, Grand Rapids, Michigan: William B. Eerdmans Publishing Company, 1946.

Warfield, Benjamin B., *Perfectionism*, Philadelphia: The Presbyterian and Reformed Publishing Co., 1958.

White, Alma, *Demons and Tongues*, Zarephath, New Jersey: Pillar of Fire, 1936.

Willis, Lewis J., "Glossolalia in Perspective," in Wade H. Horton, *The Glossolalia Phenomenon*, Cleveland, Tennessee: Pathway Press, 1966.

Womack, Morris M., *Miracles, Fact or Fantasy?* Austin, Texas: Firm Foundation Publishing House, p. 29.

Woodworth-Etter, Mrs. M. B., *Signs and Wonders God Wrought in The Ministry for Forty Years*, Indianapolis, Indiana: Mrs. M. B. W. Etter, 1916, pp. 6, 7, pp. 72-73, 189-191, 439-485.